TRADING PLACES – SMEs IN THE GLOBAL ECONOMY

Trading Places – SMEs in the Global Economy

A Critical Research Handbook

Edited by

Lester Lloyd-Reason

Professor of International Enterprise Strategy and Director, Centre for International Business, Ashcroft International Business School, Anglia Ruskin University, Cambridge, UK

Leigh Sear

Director, Wood Holmes Group, Newcastle upon Tyne, UK

Edward Elgar

Cheltenham, UK • Northampton, MA, USA

Published by
Edward Elgar Publishing Limited
Glensanda House
Montpellier Parade
Cheltenham
Glos GL50 1UA
UK

Edward Elgar Publishing, Inc.
William Pratt House
9 Dewey Court
Northampton
Massachusetts 01060
USA

A catalogue record for this book
is available from the British Library

Library of Congress Cataloguing in Publication Data

Trading places—SMEs in the global economy : a critical research handbook / edited by Lester Lloyd-Reason, Leigh Sear.
p. cm.
Includes bibliographical references and index.
1. Small business. 2. International business enterprises. I. Lloyd-Reason, Lester.
II. Sear, Leigh, 1970-
HD2341.T734 2007
338.6′42–dc22

2006037093

ISBN 978 1 84542 039 0

Printed and bound in Great Britain by MPG Books Ltd, Bodmin, Cornwall

Contents

The editors

Lester Lloyd-Reason is Professor of International Enterprise Strategy and Director of the Centre for International Business Research and Development at the Ashcroft International Business School, Anglia Ruskin University in Cambridge. He is a visiting professor at the University of Paris XIII and serves on the editorial board of a number of journals, including the *International Small Business Journal* (ISBJ). He is a trustee and member of the Board of Directors of the Institute for Small Business and Entrepreneurship. He has been researching and consulting in the area of entrepreneurial management of international SMEs for many years and has considerable experience of managing international research projects in the field of small business support structures, both in central and eastern Europe and in the UK. He has received personal research grants from the British Academy and the Soros Foundation and has acted as strategic adviser to a number of organisations both within the private and public sectors. His current research interests revolve around skills and knowledge development in international small and medium-size enterprises, in particular the transfer of skills and knowledge between SMEs and higher education institutions. Heavily involved in the arts, he serves on the Board of Directors of Menagerie Theatre Company, a production company for new writing based in Cambridge.

Leigh Sear is Director of Research at Wood Holmes Group, a research and consultancy business based in the North East of England. He is a vice-president, trustee and member of the Board of Directors of the Institute of Small Business and Entrepreneurship and an Executive Committee member of the Entrepreneurship, Innovation and Small Business Network of the European Foundation for Management Development. He is also Chair of the Research Advisory Group for the Small Firms Enterprise Development Initiative (SFEDI) in the United Kingdom. Leigh has extensive experience of researching, understanding and supporting small business and enterprise development, and over the last ten years has worked with a range of public and private sector clients at a local, regional, national and international level. His current research interests include: small business support and governance structures, youth enterprise and entrepreneurship, internationalisation of small business and entrepreneurial networks and networking.

Contributors

D. Ray Bagby is the Robert M. and Louise Rogers Chair of Entrepreneurship in the Hankamer School of Business, Baylor University, USA. In addition to his own publications and presentations of papers, he served as executive editor of the *American Journal of Small Business* (AJSB) from 1984 to 1988, and continued in that role when it was converted to *Entrepreneurship Theory and Practice* (ET&P). Ray has been active in the U.S. Association for Small Business and Entrepreneurship, the Entrepreneurship Division of the Academy of Management, the Southern Management Association and the International Council for Small Business.

Telma Barbosa is Lecturer and Researcher of Strategy, Entrepreneurship and SME at the Universidade Federal de Vicosa, one of the leading Brazilian Federal Universities. She is Visiting Research Fellow of Teesside University Business School, where she has developed research work together with Professor Ted Fuller of the Centre for Entrepreneurship and Small Business Development. She achieved her PhD degree at Durham University with a thesis on SME competitive strategy. Her previous research projects have focused on entrepreneurship development and SME start-up factors, and successful SMEs' marketing, competitive strategies and innovation strategies. Her current research interests are SME internationalisation processes and strategies and the role of network and relationship in SME internationalisation and strategic decision making.

Jonathan Calof is an Associate Professor at the School of Management, University of Ottawa, Canada. He focuses his research on international competitive intelligence and international decision making. He is also a co-director of INTRAN (Intelligence Teaching and Research Academic Network) and a board member for CASIS (Canadian Association for Security and Intelligence Studies).

Leo Paul Dana is Senior Advisor to the World Association for Small and Medium Enterprises, and tenured at the University of Canterbury, New Zealand. He also holds the title of Adjunct Professor at the University of Regina, in Canada. He was formerly Deputy Director of the International Business MBA Programme at Singapore's Nanyang Business School. He also served on the faculties of McGill University, Canada and INSEAD, France. He holds BA and MBA degrees from McGill University, and a PhD from the Ecole des Hautes Etudes Commerciales, Canada. He has an extensive research background studying entrepreneurship in different cultures and is the author of a number of books and articles on the subject. He is the founder of the *Journal of International Entrepreneurship*. He has produced 12 books, including the bestseller *Entrepreneurship in Pacific Asia: Past, Present and Future* (World Scientific, 1999), and over 100 journal articles.

Paul Dishman is an Associate Professor of Business Management at the Marriott School of Management at Brigham Young University in Provo, Utah, USA. He holds an MBA in marketing and a PhD in marketing research. He served as president of the Society of Competitive Intelligence Professional (SCIP) Board of Directors in 2003 as well as serving as vice president conferences and education, annual conference chair, and co-chair of the first Academic Conference on Competitive Intelligence.

Hamid Etemad is a Professor of Marketing and International Business at the Desautels Faculty of Management, McGill University, Canada. He received PhD, MSc and MBA degrees from the University of California at Berkeley as well as an M Eng from the University of Tehran. He has published widely: he has edited four book volumes and guest-edited numerous scholarly journal issues, including *Canadian Journal of Administrative Sciences*, *Journal of International Entrepreneurship*, *Global Focus*, *Journal of International Entrepreneurship*, *Journal of International Management*, *Journal of International Marketing*, *Management International Review* and *Small Business Economics*, among others. He is the series editor of the *McGill International Entrepreneurship Series* published by Edward Elgar Publishing. He is the Past President of the Administrative Sciences Association of Canada and current Director of the Business and Management Research Center at McGill University. He is also the Convener of the McGill International Entrepreneurship Conference Series.

Ted Fuller is Professor of Entrepreneurship and Strategic Foresight at Teesside Business School, University of Teesside, UK. His research has included anticipatory management, new technology and enterprise sustainability. He is a member of the international advisory board of *Futures: Journal of Policy, Planning and Future Studies*. He has published extensively on small and medium enterprises and entrepreneurship focusing on the creation of better futures for enterprises. Publications include refereed papers in *International Small Business Journal*, *Journal of Entrepreneurship and Regional Development*, *Futures Journal* and *Emergence*. Ted is also currently vice-president, trustee and member of the Board of Directors of the Institute of Small Business and Entrepreneurship in the UK.

Alan Griffiths is Reader in Economics at the Ashcroft International Business School, Anglia Ruskin University, Cambridge, UK. He is Fellow of the Japan Foundation and previously Research Officer at the Research Institute for the National Economy (Kokumin Keizai Kenkyu Kyokai), Tokyo, as well as Visiting Professor of Economics at Yokohama National University, Japan. Publications include articles on the applied economics of the UK and Japan in the areas of labour, management, trade and SMEs. Books published or edited include those dealing with applied economics, intermediate micro-economics, economic for business and management, and the EU.

Keith Herrmann is Director of Programmes for the Small Enterprise Development team within the Executive Education and Enterprise Department at Durham Business School, UK. He has experience in economic policy research (HM Treasury, Department for Trade and Industry, Department for Education and Skills), the impact of regulation on SMEs, and small business development in South Africa and the United Kingdom, and has been extensively involved in the design, assessment and development of business development programmes in Kenya, Uganda, Tanzania, South Africa and Malawi funded by the UK Department for International Development. He has project experience in developing sector development strategies and researching appropriate business start-up support for university graduates. He has extensive research experience in SME development, and has reviewed business support internationally to develop an evidence base to inform SME policy in the UK (Small Business Service, DTI). Beyond this Keith has experience in business development including designing and delivering 'growth and change' programmes for SME owner-managers, and developing mechanisms to support private sector development. Keith is also currently involved in teaching and mentoring students on the BA in Business degree, the MBA programme and the Biological Sciences and Computer Sciences entrepreneurship electives at the University of Durham.

Ronald Klingebiel is researching in the field of new strategic directions at the Judge Business School, University of Cambridge, UK. He has held lecturing appointments in corporate strategy at the Berlin School of Economics, Germany, and the Ashcroft International Business School, Anglia Ruskin University, Cambridge, UK. Ronald has published in the field of real options planning as a capability for competitive advantage as well as aspects of electronic toll collection. He has engaged in strategic consultancies with Procter and Gamble, DaimlerChrysler and A.T. Kearney. He is academic director of the Centre for Strategic Studies, Anglia Ruskin University, and acts in a strategic advisory capacity for CapGemini.

Tim Mazzarol is Director of the Centre for Entrepreneurial Management and Innovation (CEMI) and an Associate Professor of Entrepreneurship and Strategy at the Graduate School of Management at the University of Western Australia. He has 15 years experience of working with small entrepreneurial firms as well as large corporations and government agencies. This has included strategic management, marketing and support for commercialisation. His research into small business management has been published internationally. He holds a PhD in Management and an MBA with distinction from Curtin University of Technology, and a Bachelor of Arts with Honors from Murdoch University, Western Australia.

Jay Mitra is the Founding Professor of Business Enterprise and Innovation and Director of the Centre for Entrepreneurship Research at the University of Essex, Southend, UK. He is also the Director of the Scientific Committee on Entrepreneurship for the OECD (Organization for Economic Co-operation and Development) and its LEED (Local Economic and Employment) Programme in Paris, France and in Trento, Italy. He has held visiting professorships at the Universities of Bologna and Bari, Italy and Kuopio, Finland and is currently also a visiting research fellow at the Beijing University of Foreign Studies in China. He has published widely on entrepreneurship, innovation, small firm growth and internationalisation, and technology and knowledge transfer between universities and small firms. He has over 20 years of experience in the field, gained while working for a firm of consultants and accountants, in local government, as head of an innovation centre, as an academic, and through two new business ventures of his own in London.

Terry Mughan is Professor of International Management and Director of Consulting and Development at the Centre for International Business, Ashcroft International Business School, Anglia Ruskin University, Cambridge, UK. His research interests have recently focused on business internationalisation strategies, including a study of 1200 companies in the East of England. This project involved data gathering, analysis and recommendations made to the regional authorities and yielded numerous published articles and papers. He has acted as a consultant to UK Trade and Investment and has played a key role in the formulation of the revised International Business Strategy for the region. His is currently Director of the H.I.G.H.E.R. project, a £180 000 study of international mid-scale businesses. Terry has extensive experience as a consultant and trainer to companies of all sizes, in the areas of intercultural management, exporting and strategic transformation. He speaks French and German fluently.

Leslie E. (Les) Palich is Associate Professor of Management and Entrepreneurship and the Ben H. Williams Professor of Entrepreneurship at Baylor University, USA, where he is associate director of the entrepreneurship programme and teaches graduate and undergraduate courses in international management. He holds a PhD and an MBA from Arizona State University and a BA from Manhattan Christian College, USA. With more than three dozen publications to his credit, his research has appeared in *Strategic Management Journal*, *Journal of Business Venturing*, *Journal of Small Business Management*, *Journal of Management*, *Academy of Management Review*, *Journal of International Business* and *Journal of Organizational Behaviour*, among others. His research interests focus on international entrepreneurship, entrepreneurial risk taking behaviour, and the impact of corruption on entrepreneurial activity. He is director of the Baylor in Cuba program and often teaches there and in Europe, as well as directing the Baylor International Technology Entrepreneurship program at the University of Maastricht in the Netherlands.

Stuart Smith is Director of Consultancy at the Wood Holmes Group, Newcastle upon Tyne, United Kingdom. He is an experienced futurist, having carried out a range of projects for FTSE100 and large public sector bodies alike. Having originally trained as an environmental scientist at Imperial College London, he moved into the ICT sector at the height of the dot.com boom and worked for a major telecoms company on futures thinking and the impact of technology on organisational design. He has published widely and has a particular interest in complexity theory, knowledge sharing and social networks.

Stuart Wall is Professor of Business and Economics at the Ashcroft International Business School, Anglia Ruskin University, Cambridge, UK and is a former consultant to the OECD Directorate for Science, Technology and Industry. He has also acted as consultant to British Telecom, and to other telecommunications and media-related multinationals. He has published extensively in a wide range of international business and management areas, including the impacts of information technologies on cross-border flows of both products and foreign direct investment. Together with Alan Griffiths, he has published some of the UK's best-selling undergraduate and postgraduate texts in applied economics.

Richard Wright was the founding Director of International Business Studies in the Faculty of Management at McGill University, Canada. He currently holds the E. Claiborne Robins Distinguished University Chair in the Robins School of Business, University of Richmond, USA. His publications include eleven books and research monographs and numerous journal articles. A co-founder of the annual McGill Conferences on International Entrepreneurship, he is also president of an international management consulting and training firm specialising in Asia and the Pacific. His current research interests focus on the new opportunities and challenges facing small firms in the globalising economy, on which he has edited several books and special journal issues.

Carsten Zimmermann is researching into the interlocking areas of strategy, internationalisation and innovation, in which he has published a series of journal articles and monograph chapters on the resource- and activity-based views of collaboration. Carsten has studied at the Berlin School of Economics, Germany; the Ashcroft International Business School, Anglia Ruskin University, and the Judge Business School, University of Cambridge, UK; and at the Massachusetts Institute of Technology (M.I.T.) in the USA. Carsten has been actively involved in consultancy activities involving the high-technology and telecommunications sectors for KPMG Consulting, Andersen Consulting (Accenture) and A.T. Kearney, amongst others.

Preface

This book is most timely. It arrives at a time when globalisation and new technologies present major opportunities and challenges to the role of the independent small and medium sized business in economies.

Traditionally, in much of the research literature the SME is presented, rather misleadingly, as a form of business organisation which, by its very nature, is essentially parochial in outlook. The sheer scale of the SME sector and its wide diversity of activity, motivational climates, and differentiation in focus and 'ways of organising', have tended to obscure its role in building relationships across national and international boundaries. Much of the previous research has concentrated narrowly upon export performance. However, as this book demonstrates, the concept of internationalization and the facilitation of transactions across a wide range of service and relationship-building activities is a more appropriate template.

In this respect the opportunities provided by the rapidly changing world of information and communication technology and the opening-up of markets world wide, with a corresponding reduction and change in the nature of transactions costs presents a considerable challenge. A range of new management competencies are needed particularly in managing cross-cultural boundary relationships. The book's strength in dealing with many of the emerging issues is underpinned by a truly international range of contributors with a strong mix of practical as well as academic experience.

Allan Gibb
Professor Emeritus, Durham University UK

Acknowledgements

The editors would like to thank all those at Edward Elgar Publishing for their care and professionalism in the publication of this book. We would like to thank Joanne Betteridge for her patience and perseverance and Francine O'Sullivan for getting the ball rolling, for supporting us throughout the project and for bringing the whole thing to fruition.

Numerous people have contributed to the development of this book, not least the authors of the individual chapters. We would like to thank them for their efforts in writing a set of excellent chapters which make this such an exciting and worthwhile text and one which will hopefully challenge and stimulate people to think differently about the global SME.

Finally we would like to mention the generosity, advice and constructive criticism we have received on this book and over the years from our wives, Gill and Viv to whom, together with Leigh's son Robin, this volume is dedicated.

1 Introduction: the role of SMEs in the global economy

Lester Lloyd-Reason and Leigh Sear

Why is this book needed?

The past 20 years have seen an explosion in research into the role of the small and medium enterprises (SMEs) within a global context which has resulted in a considerable body of academic literature and thinking. In part, interest in this area of research has been stimulated by the growing debate on globalisation, its impact on the development of SMEs and the entrepreneurial response required by businesses to deal with increased competition (Ibeh, 2000).

A critical review of this literature however, raises a number of issues in terms of the impact and usefulness of this body of understanding for different stakeholders and groups involved in understanding and supporting SMEs within a global context. For example, both Julien *et al.* (1997) and Sear and Hamilton (2003) question whether this mass of research activity and published material has afforded a clearer view of the key issues surrounding the internationalisation of the SME. The current body of evidence may, in fact, simply serve to increase our lack of understanding in this area and has resulted in the formation of several myths and misconceptions upon which a number of policies and programmes of support for SMEs have been developed and introduced. For example, within the majority of developed market economies, internationalisation is still primarily defined by the policy community as exporting.

In addition, the academic propensity to create problems, models and theories has led to a tendency to conceptualise the experiences of the SME in fragmented, atomised and unrepresentative terms which are poorly suited to the solutions to the problems that businesses actually encounter (Aldrich and Martinez, 2001). Rather than generating a better understanding of the nature and dynamics of the competing tensions in the face of which owner-managers and managers of SMEs need to make decisions, academics and researchers have too often preferred to generalise, hypothesise and model-build across sectors, regions or markets.

In part, this reflects how our understanding of the global SMEs has been generated. There are a number of books on the global SME which collect together various academic contributions without developing a coherent argument as to the role for SMEs in a global trading environment beyond commonly debated issues associated with ICT developments, repositioning of governance structures and so on. There are relatively few contributions which critically review the state of current thinking and challenge existing concepts and theoretical frameworks on how SMEs trade globally. This book seeks to address these shortcomings in the academic treatment of the global SME.

How did the book come about?

The idea for the book emerged from a discussion between the editors and our commissioning editor, Francine O'Sullivan, at a small business and entrepreneurship conference in the UK. A number of papers were presented at the conference which reiterated and reinforced the current state of understanding, as opposed to challenging the boundaries of what we know and how this knowledge was generated, for example papers reinforcing the conflation of internationalisation and exporting, whilst at the same time calling for policy makers to develop more sophisticated approaches to defining internationalisation.

In reflecting on our experiences at the conference, we began to question how best we could try to address this issue. How could we progress the state of current understanding? Perhaps by taking stock of what we know and identifying what we need to know? The germ of an idea began to take shape and we decided to commission a set of authors and commentators to make sense of what we know and to produce a critical assessment and review of current thinking. We would aim to set a coherent research agenda which could bridge the gap between theory and practice, paying particular attention to the needs of policy and practice, to reflect the realities facing smaller businesses as they develop their global activities and relationships.

Out of these discussions, two years later this book has emerged. We have tried to remain true to those late-night arguments in the bar in seeking to present a coherent and relevant research agenda using commentators and researchers who, in their contributions, use their research to provide critical insights into how SMEs are currently experiencing global trading.

Before we look at the structure of the book and consider the key themes emerging from the contributions, we should perhaps define what we mean by global. And why does the text use the term 'global' rather than 'international'? We define global as meaning the process of exporting, importing and the production and distribution of goods and services, including the growth of a firm's engagement and investment in non-domestic markets. But perhaps rather than wrestling with theoretical definitions, the realities of global trading facing SMEs today can best be demonstrated by the experiences of a manufacturing enterprise located in the East of England, UK.

With just 30 employees at a manufacturing plant and an annual turnover of £3.1m, this SME, involved in specialist engineering, also has a manufacturing facility in Sweden and one in China, and has recently bought its suppliers in Romania as part of its supply chain management in order to safeguard its supplies of raw materials. The facility in Sweden manufactures the high-end, high-margin products. The facility in China – set up as part of a strategic alliance with its most aggressive competitor – produces the mass-produced, low-margin, high-volume products.

Its global trading activities are completed by its Romanian acquisition. The firm had sourced many of its raw materials from Romania; however, the supplier was re-acquired by the government and then again offered for sale. Very concerned as to the implications for its supply chain, the firm sent a representative to negotiate with the Romanian privatisation authorities. An entirely separate book could be written on the complexities of the Romanian privatisation process, but after protracted, highly complex negotiations, the Romania firm was finally acquired.

This global operation then allows this firm to sell its products in over 40 countries around the world. This is not atypical of the global SME experience. The traditional view of international trading activity equating to exporting no longer holds. SMEs today are engaging with the global economy through a highly complex set of arrangements, and academics with their antiquated definitions, and policy makers with their export-based policy initiatives are struggling to keep up with the pace of developments. Accordingly, this text boldly embraces the complexities involved in the global trading environment facing SMEs rather then falling back on the rather outdated concept of international trade with its emphasis on the exporting model.

How is the book structured?

The text is divided into three sections which seek to reflect the relationships between SMEs and the global economy. These are:

- Processes and practices of SMEs and global trading.
- Management, leadership and strategy in global SMEs.
- Learning, skills and knowledge in doing global business.

Under each theme, a number of specific issues and questions relating to SMEs in the global economy will be addressed through a range of chapters based on original and critical contributions. The book then concludes with a chapter, written by the editors, on the policy perspectives surrounding SMEs in a global context and the implications this has for the support of SMEs at a local, regional and national level.

Processes and practices of SMEs and global trading

The first section of the book provides a review of a set of questions and issues aimed at developing an understanding of the global trading environment in which SMEs operate, the processes by which they develop those global activities and the types and quality of the relationships between the SMEs and their key stakeholders involved in supporting the development of these activities.

In the opening chapter of this section, Griffiths *et al.* (Chapter 2) explore the nature of global trading with particular reference to SMEs, and has a threefold aim. First, it seeks to investigate the forces of globalisation and sectoral restructuring that have influenced the strategic space in which SMEs must now operate. Second, it assesses some of the strategic initiatives adopted by SMEs in response to these forces, using a practitioner-based focus and case study illustrations where appropriate. Third, it reflects on the implications of the patterns and trends identified for the policy stance of those agencies seeking to increase the share of SMEs in global trading.

The authors note that under a more globalised economic system the internationalisation process for SMEs often involves simultaneous involvement in exporting, importing and other cross-border activities. In other words there is less support for the traditional 'stage or sequential theory', which sees internationalisation as a gradual and progressive process. The increasingly complex nature of global trading for SMEs, they suggest, has serious implications for policy makers and government agencies. They argue that a key global policy stance for increasing SME internationalisation and SME contribution to global trading is the development of a more conducive international entrepreneurial business environment, with the policy focus on 'framework' rather than specific policy instruments.

In their chapter on traditional and emergent forms of global trading, Dana *et al.* (Chapter 3) discuss an alternate approach to globalisation – an approach that involves a multipolar distribution of power and control. Rather than focusing on the internationalisation of a centralised firm with a unipolar distribution of power and control, they suggest that the world is moving toward multipolar networks of firms. As corporations outsource to smaller specialised firms, power and control are becoming increasingly divided among independent SMEs that co-operate voluntarily for increased efficiency and profit. Symbiotic marketing relationships are thus leading to multipolarity. We are hence moving beyond a focus on the firm toward a focus on relationships with multipolar networks. This, they argue, is giving unprecedented opportunities to SMEs in the global economy.

For researchers, this also provides new opportunities, but with new caveats. Rather than focusing on individuals or firms, researchers will benefit from using the multipolar network as a unit of analysis. At the micro-economic level, they argue, we must all stretch our minds beyond a focus on the firm.

The first section is concluded with a profile of SMEs in the United States and Europe provided by Palich and Bagby (Chapter 4). In this chapter, the authors draw upon a number of studies into the global SME to provide insights into the nature and extent of SME internationalisation and the reasons for the expansion of global trading activity. They find that SMEs outnumber large firms in both the United States and Europe, and they tend to outnumber large firms in international trade in almost all industry sectors. Still, they discover that large firms have definite advantages. For example, SMEs in the United States are far more dependent on government initiatives to open foreign markets than are large firms. Almost 90 per cent of US SMEs involved in exporting conduct business from a single location, while the inverse is true for large firms (only about 10 per cent are single-location companies). Also, approximately 17 per cent of SME exports go to affiliates overseas, whereas 40 per cent of large-firm exports go to foreign affiliates. Thus, access to foreign markets tends to be more limited for SMEs.

Nearly 63 per cent of US SMEs had sales in only one foreign market, which tended to be in an English-speaking market, while more than half (54 per cent) of large firms exported to five or more foreign markets. Meanwhile the North American Free Trade Agreement (NAFTA) demonstrates the impact that government policy can have. SMEs exporting to Canada increased 110 per cent from 1992 to 2001, and Mexico became the second highest destination (International Trade Administration, 2003).

Management, leadership and strategy in global SMEs

Based upon these issues raised within the first section, Part 2 of the book focuses on a set of questions related to the management and organisation of global activities by the small business. This section of the book addresses issues related to the influence and role of the owner-manager, the organisational structures required to compete effectively in international and global markets and the impact of uncertainty and unfamiliarity on how activities and operations are managed.

Barbosa and Fuller (Chapter 5) consider how entrepreneurs and their personal and business relations shape global business strategy within the manufacturing sector. Despite a considerable body of literature in this area, the authors contend that a number of critical questions remain unanswered. How and why is international social capital acquired and managed and how does it affect internationalisation? Is there a SME relationship-based strategy of international growth? If so, what are the mechanisms of internationalisation decision making and strategy making? Which are the underlying factors that can be used as a basis for theory development?

The authors argue that entrepreneurs influence their internationalisation process by choosing and managing the relationship networks to which they belong and that the extent of the entrepreneur's network and their networking capabilities are influential in the process of internationalisation. Thus they contend that interventionist policy programmes should focus on the entrepreneurs' networking capability and relationship management skills in order to promote SME internationalisation. It is not only a question of establishing formal networks they argue, but rather providing the conditions for entrepreneurs to expand their own networks and relationship management structures.

The next chapter deals with the issue of how entrepreneurs deal with the current realities of trading globally, particularly the uncertainty and unfamiliarity associated with international activities and markets. Herrmann (in Chapter 6) explores the entrepreneurial abilities and skills that are required by the individual or organisation to trade globally and manage the associated ambiguity, complexity and uncertainty. The chapter seeks to address the lack of clarity in definitions of entrepreneurial skills by proposing a classification of core 'capacities' designed to provide the link between individual behaviour, business organisation development needs, business performance needs and changing societal needs for the global SME.

The chapter highlights that core entrepreneurial abilities and skills demanded by the owner-managers and managers of global SMEs may change over time in response to changes in their environment and hence need to be treated as dynamic and contingent upon the environment. For example, Herrmann considers more informal modes of learning, such as learning by doing, learning by copying and learning by feedback; he highlights that they are equally important, if not critical for coping with and managing the uncertainties and complexities associated with global trading. This is because 'learning by doing' provides information and insights which can be used to respond flexibly and quickly to day-to-day challenges and opportunities and effectively develop trading relationships.

Building on Chapter 6, this section is concluded with a look at the complexities of managing the global operation by Mazzarol (Chapter 7). This chapter argues that SMEs choosing to enter international markets face the same management problems as their larger counterparts, and the same challenges of international market entry. However, unlike their larger counterparts, small firms must operate within overseas markets without specialist management skills and a deep base of financial resources. The chapter draws upon evidence from small high-technology firms in Australia to illustrate examples of how such international operations can be managed. It is a major premise of the chapter that the key success factors in the global operation of the small firm are the quality of its senior management, their commitment to international operations, and their ability to establish close, almost partner-like relationships with leading customers and key suppliers.

The author argues that the success of global operations is contingent on managerial commitment, learning and strategic networking. Most small firms are highly dependent on a few key managers, who must be prepared to make a significant personal commitment to the international market, including very high levels of overseas travel and the capacity to establish close working relationships with customers and suppliers. These managers must be willing to configure their firm's operations to service the needs of overseas customers and adapt their products in response to customer feedback in an ongoing process of continuous quality improvement. Accordingly, policy makers seeking to assist small firms to expand their global operations should focus attention on the development of the management team's international business skills. This should include the area of strategic networking and alliance formation, as well as interpersonal communications.

Learning, skills and knowledge in doing global business

The third section of the book focuses on the skills and knowledge required by a business or organisation to develop and manage global activities. This section assesses and reflects upon the specific skills and knowledge required to scan, plan and resource an increasingly complex set of trading activities, and how this knowledge is acquired through learning, networks and relationships. In addition, the section reviews the learning required to trade globally.

The opening chapter aims to advance our understanding of the internal and external factors which make some small and medium-sized enterprises (SMEs) successful in international markets. Particular attention is paid to global skills and knowledge development that can be made transferable across business sectors via educational and consulting programmes. The ability to learn, argue Mughan and Lloyd-Reason (Chapter 8), is becoming increasingly important in the global economy as SMEs are exposed to greater competition from international rivals in domestic markets and are needing to source materials and clients in overseas markets in order to survive and prosper.

The authors draw upon the findings and issues emerging from an 18-month research project to identify processes, skills and knowledge which characterised the set of companies which emerged from a 1200 sample as successful international businesses. The chapter considers the relevance of these findings to the current and future form and content of support infrastructures which help create and sustain these companies. The chapter concludes with the authors proposing a model of support intervention suited to the global trading and learning environment facing the global SME.

The theme of learning continues in the next chapter, where Calof and Dishman (Chapter 9) examine the role of intelligence in business decision making. They consider intelligence as a decision support system that focuses the entire organisation on scanning its current and future environment. Business intelligence has emerged as a tool for small and large businesses alike. If used properly, the authors argue, it has the potential to assist companies greatly in formulating and implementing better international business decisions. Accordingly, this chapter seeks to describe what competitive intelligence is and how it can be best used by small businesses.

Calof and Dishman argue that competitive intelligence (CI) may be more important for small business than it is for larger ones. Everyone needs to conduct CI to thrive and identify opportunities, but smaller companies cannot absorb market mistakes in the same way that large firms can. Organised properly, good competitive intelligence can level the playing field between small and large businesses, and smaller businesses must take advantage of CI to grow. The chapter suggests that this is increasingly accepted by the business support community and probably explains why governments around the world have been working on programmes and policies designed to support and enhance small business intelligence capabilities.

This section concludes with a discussion of innovative forms of learning and activities of small and medium-sized enterprises in international markets. In this chapter, Mitra (Chapter 10) argues that the successful internationalisation of small and medium-sized firms (SMEs) is a function of their learning process and environments. A mix of theoretical models and empirical evidence are used to identify the modes, forms and methods of learning adopted by SMEs as they enter and grow in an international business environment.

Using the metaphor of the theatre, the author explores different forms of learning at multiple levels of individual, organisational and pan-organisational effort. Consideration of each of these levels of learning yields five sets of propositions. Taken together they offer a framework for analysing how firms internationalise and why they adopt different strategies for engaging in the international market. The chapter identifies complex forms of learning associated with SME internationalisation strategies and actions, and concludes by generating ideas for new communities of creation and innovation across borders.

Policy perspectives

Finally, the book concludes with two chapters, the first of which reviews the impact and influence of future trends and scenarios on how SMEs will need to manage the development of global markets. This is used as the basis for unpacking the implications for policy and practice in supporting SMEs to develop and manage global activities. The author places a particular emphasis on developing strategies which help bridge the gap between theory and practice.

In the penultimate chapter of the book, Smith (Chapter 11) examines the global SME from a 'futures' perspective. The chapter represents a synthesis of data, anecdote, personal experience and theory. As such, the main objective of the chapter is to stimulate thinking in the reader regarding both possible future scenarios for the SME and how 'futures' thinking may contribute to SME development and support.

The author argues that there is much academic discussion about whether globalisation is a real phenomenon or only an analytical artefact ('a myth'). Although the term is widespread, many argue that the characteristics of the phenomenon have already been seen at other moments in history. Some may also conclude that those features that make people believe we are in the process of globalisation, including the increase in international trade and the greater role of multinational corporations, are not as deeply established as they may first appear.

Whether or not globalisation is a genuine phenomenon or what its relative impact will be is possibly still open to question. However, what cannot be denied, is that the world increasingly shares problems and challenges that do not obey nation state borders, notably pollution of the natural environment, economic flows, global disease, international crime and terrorism. The economies of the nations of the world are also more intertwined and this has occurred as a result of several factors. Perhaps the key differentiating factor in this cycle of globalisation is the impact of technology (in all its forms) but in particular information and communication technologies (ICT), and it is these areas that provide the focus for the chapter.

The book then concludes with a review of the major policy implications to emerge from the contributions. Five key policy areas emerge, namely:

1. Internationalisation is more than exporting.
2. Developing an international entrepreneurial environment.
3. Fostering and supporting networks and relationships.
4. Creating a better evidence base on the global SME.
5. Developing skills and knowledge to manage globally.

It is a major contention of this text that policy makers and government agencies are failing to keep up with the pace of change in the global trading environment. SMEs are at the vanguard of these changes and accordingly tend to suffer the most as a consequence of this policy failure. In their conclusion to the text, the editors seek to develop a global policy agenda aimed at creating the circumstances which will release the entrepreneurial talent to be found amongst the stock of global SMEs wherever they may be located around this fast-changing globe of ours.

Bibliography

Aldrich, H. and Martinez, J.E. (2001), 'Many are Called but Few are Chosen: An Evolutionary Perspective for the Study of Entrepreneurship', *Entrepreneurship, Theory and Practice* **25** (4), 41–47.

Ibeh, K. (2000), 'Internationalisation and the Small Firm', in Carter, S. and Jones-Evans, D. (eds) *Enterprise and Small Business*, Financial Times/Prentice Hall, Harlow.

International Trade Administration (2003) *Small and Medium-sized Exporting Companies: A Statistical Handbook*, Office of Trade and Economic Analysis, International Trade Administration, US Department of Commerce, Washington DC, www.ita.doc.gov/TD/Industry/OTEA/sme_handbook/SME_index.htm, accessed 24 November 2006.

Julien, P.A., Joyal, A., Deshaies, L. and Ramangalahy, C. (1997), 'A Typology of Strategic Behaviour Among Small and Medium-sized Exporting Businesses: A Case Study', *International Small Business Journal* **15** (2), 33–50.

Sear, L. and Hamilton, R.T. (2003), 'Matching Supply with Demand: Reflecting on Support for Business Internationalisation in England', in Dana, L.P. (ed.) *Handbook of Research on International Entrepreneurship*, Edward Elgar, Cheltenham, UK and Northampton MA, USA.

PART I

PROCESSES AND PRACTICES OF SMEs AND GLOBAL TRADING

2 Doing business: the nature of global trading

Alan Griffiths, Stuart Wall, Carsten Zimmermann and Ronald Klingebiel

Introduction: context and overview

For the purposes of this chapter, small and medium-sized enterprises (SMEs) are defined as in the EU, namely as consisting of firms employing less than 250 employees, with firms having less than 50 employees being regarded as 'small' and firms having 50–249 employees being regarded as 'medium' in size. The economic environment within which such SMEs operate has been subject to accelerating change over the past half century, including significant sectoral shifts in the composition of national economies combined with the increasing 'openness' of the global economy, sometimes caricatured as 'shrinking space, shrinking time and disappearing borders'. Such changes have had important effects on the strategic behaviour of SMEs as they adjust to a context in which value chains are increasingly reconfigured, not least in terms of geographical location, by multinational enterprises and even by SMEs themselves. Prahalad (1999) paints a vivid picture of a progressively 'discontinuous competitive landscape' under the forces of globalisation, with the established boundaries of industrial and service sectors shifting as technologies converge and new forms of organisational and institutional arrangements emerge.

There is broad agreement on the merits of devising policies to enhance the contribution of SMEs to global trading, since it is widely recognised that SMEs are under-represented in the global economy. For example SMEs typically contribute some 50 per cent of GDP in the developed economies and some 60 per cent of total employment, yet SMEs contribute only around 30 per cent of exports and even less in terms of flows of international investment (OECD 2004).

This chapter explores the nature of global trading with particular reference to SMEs and has a threefold aim. First, it seeks to investigate the forces of globalisation and sectoral restructuring that have influenced the strategic space in which SMEs must now operate. Second, it assesses some of the strategic initiatives adopted by SMEs in response to these forces, using a practitioner-based focus and case study illustrations where appropriate. Third, it reflects on the implications of the patterns and trends identified for the policy stance of those agencies seeking to increase the share of SMEs in global trading.

Globalisation: patterns and trends in global trading

Globalisation is a multidimensional concept, the characteristics of which depend in part on the perspective adopted. Political scientists tend to focus on the emergence of new forms of governance other than the nation state, international relations experts often emphasise the emergence of global conflicts and global institutions and sociologists the rise of global culture and the dominance of the media by global companies. It can be argued that all these perspectives impact on the prospects for SMEs to trade globally. Nevertheless the focus here will mainly be on globalisation from a business and economic perspective, as for example where globalisation is seen as 'a marked increase

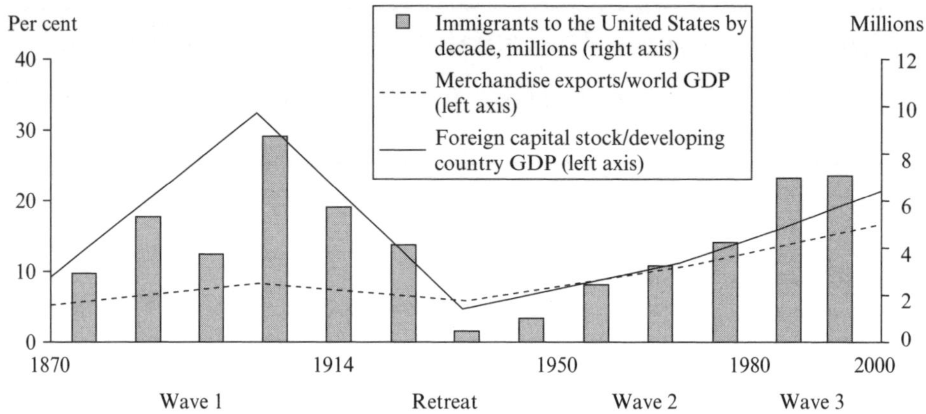

Source: World Bank (2002)

Figure 2.1 The waves of globalisation

in the movement across boundaries of goods, services, investment and people' (DTI 2004). The pace of globalisation from this perspective can be measured in a number of ways, such as the rate of change in the ratio of world exports or world imports to world GDP. Alternatively the rate of change in the ratio of world trade in manufacturers to world manufacturing output may also be used to signify an 'opening up' of world merchandise markets. From an investment point of view, the rate of change in flow of world foreign direct investment (FDI) provides a useful indicator of the increased multinational engagement within the world economy. Finally from a human capital point of view, the increasing rates of movement of people across the globe provide a pointer to a more fluid and responsive global labour market.

Three waves of globalisation

Figure 2.1 provides evidence that the world economy has in fact experienced three waves of globalisation since the 1870s. It uses three measures of globalisation to illustrate the increased pace of global change, that is, the ratio of merchandise exports to world GDP; the ratio of foreign capital stock as a percentage of developing countries' GDP; and the number of immigrants to the US (millions) by decade. The first wave is identified as beginning in the 1870s with rapid advances in transport and communication stimulating trade, investment and migration. After the slump in world economic activity and in these metrics of globalisation during the inter-war years, the pace of globalisation quickened again over the period 1945–1980, with progressive reductions in trade barriers and transport costs during this second wave resulting in a significant expansion of global trade, mainly between the developed economies.

As can be seen from Figure 2.1, all three measures of globalisation have risen substantially in the third wave of globalisation which began in the early 1980s. It may be useful to consider some of the general patterns and trends in global trading which have characterised this third wave before investigating the more specific impacts of globalisation on the SMEs themselves.

Characteristics of the third wave of globalisation

Rapid growth in world trade and investment Between 1980 and 2003 world exports of goods and services more than doubled in real terms, reaching over US$7500 billion in 2003 and accounting for over 23 per cent of world gross domestic product. Put another way, global exports of goods and services have increased at the astonishing rate of almost 5 per cent per year in real terms over the period 1980–2003. Over the same time period flows of world foreign direct investment have quadrupled in real terms, reaching around $700 billion in 2003.

One empirical study of the major 'developed economies' has tried to assess the relative contributions to the recorded rise in the world trade/GDP ratio over the period covered by the third wave of globalisation (Deane 2004). It found that the rise in the world trade/GDP ratio could be attributed to the following factors: fall in the relative prices of tradeable goods (44 per cent); fall in tariffs (21 per cent); increase in country size (13 per cent); rise in real income per head (5 per cent); and reduced exchange rate volatility (3 per cent). These results indicate the positive impacts on international trade of productivity growth (leading to reductions in price levels in the tradeable goods sector), removal of trade restrictions on both goods and services, growth in population size and living standards, and reduced exchange rate uncertainty.

Increased role of developing economies in global trading Global exports of goods and services by the 'developing economies' (GDP per head of $735 or less per annum) has been an important feature of the third wave of globalisation, rising at an above average 6 per cent per year over the period 1981–2002. As a result the exports to GDP ratio in the developing economies has risen from 18 per cent to 33 per cent over this period (Table 2.1), much higher than the 20 per cent to 22 per cent increase recorded for the 'high income economies' (GDP per head of $9026 or more per annum) over the same period.

Increased role of middle-income economies in global trading The 'middle income economies' (GDP per head of $736 to $9205 per annum) such as China, India, Malaysia, Mexico, Philippines and Thailand have also increased their share of world exports and imports at a faster rate than that of the 'high income economies'. These countries have undertaken major reforms during this period, including the liberalisation of trade and investment, improvements in macroeconomic stability and positive developments in 'governance' as in extending the rule of law and the applicability of property rights. Many analysts have attributed such changes in market openness and governance as being causal factors in stimulating rapidly growing national contributions to global trading in

Table 2.1 Exports to GDP ratios (%) 1981–2002

Economy classification	1981	1987	1993	1999	2002
Developing economies	18	19	23	27	33
High income economies	20	21	19	23	22

Source: Adapted from World Bank (2003) UNCTAD (various)

both manufactures and services (Barro 1991, Lipsey 1999, Taylor 2000, Zak 2001, Wallsten 2001). For example, whereas only 25 per cent of the exports of 'middle income economies' were manufactures in 1980, by the early years of the new millennium that figure had risen to 80 per cent. Similarly whilst commercial services comprised 17 per cent of the exports of 'high income economies' but only 9 per cent of the exports of 'middle income economies' in 1980, by the early years of the millennium the gap had narrowed considerably with the figures now being 20 per cent and 17 per cent respectively (World Bank 2002).

Growth of regional and bilateral trading arrangements The third wave of globalisation has been characterised by a degree of 'conflict' between the multilateral trade-based initiatives of international institutions such as the World Trade Organization (WTO) and the more geographically circumscribed initiatives represented by *regional trading arrangements* (RTAs) and *bilateral trade and investment treaties*. There has certainly been a rapid growth in regional trading blocs and associated RTAs in recent times, which give preferential treatment to trade in goods and services between members of those blocs. For example over 100 RTAs were identified by the World Bank in the period 1990–2000, compared to only 14 RTAs in the previous decade (UNCTAD 2003). This has led to the growth of 'insiderisation', whereby multinational enterprises (MNEs) progressively seek to locate productive facilities inside these various regional trading arrangements in order to avoid the protective and discriminatory barriers which would otherwise face their exports to those locations.

Nor is it only within the broad-based regional trading blocs that preferential treatment is available to participating countries and companies. For example there has been a rapid growth in bilateral trade treaties, with around 300 such treaties having been notified to the WTO by the end of 2003. A similar picture can be observed for bilateral investment treaties (BITs), which give preferential treatment to FDI flows between two countries. The number of BITs notified to the WTO more than doubled between the mid-1990s and the end of 2003.

Growth of intra-industry trade Most empirical studies suggest that it is the growth of intra-industry trade flows that has made the greatest contribution to the recorded growth in global trading. 'Inter-industry trade' occurs where countries specialise in the outputs of specific 'industries' in which they are relatively more efficient and the outputs (goods or services) from these different 'industries' are then traded between countries. However 'intra-industry trade' involves the international exchange of goods and services produced within the same 'industry' or 'sector'. This means that countries specialise in producing different products located within the same industry or sector, for example, the US and the UK both produce cars and related components and trade outputs with each other from within this sector.

It is thought that intra-industry trade between OECD countries is some 60 per cent to 70 per cent of total trade for products such as chemicals, machinery and transport equipment, and around 40 per cent for relatively simpler manufactured products such as food products (OECD 2002, p.20). With the growth of such intra-industry trade there is an increasing probability that a single product or service may be the result of combined economic activity in a number of different countries, so that the value chain for a given product increasingly involves operations in more than one country. In this way the old inter-industry specialisation is being increasingly eroded (Bhagwati 2004).

Industrial/sectoral restructuring and reconfigured value chains The growth of intra-industry trade reflects in part the industrial restructuring and reconfigured value chains made possible and stimulated by globalisation, with market liberalisation and increased competitive pressures within a globalised economy both being central to this debate. As regards market liberalisation, whilst only 80 (out of 82) regulatory changes were identified as being 'more favourable to FDI' in 1991, that figure had risen to 194 (out of 206) regulatory changes in 2001 (UNCTAD 2003). By stimulating the quest for cost-competitiveness on a global scale, market liberalisation has in turn played a part in industrial restructuring and value chain reconfiguration. Sakai (2002) identifies economic, technological and governmental forces as the three most important drivers towards global industrial restructuring. From the economic perspective, the increased intensity of global competition has led MNEs to pay still greater attention to Relative Unit Labour Cost (RULC), widely regarded as the most useful single indicator of global competitiveness, where RULC is defined as (relative labour cost/relative labour productivity) multiplied by relative exchange rate. Clearly where globalisation is creating new opportunities for offshoring or outsourcing elements of the value chain, this may permit RULC to fall via a more favourable movement in one or more of its three constituents, thereby enhancing international competitiveness. In practical terms, such a reduction in RULC could be secured by offshoring or outsourcing to geographical locations where relative labour costs were lower, and/or relative labour productivity was higher, and/or relative exchange rates were lower.

Technological forces play both a 'permissive' role and an 'active' role in such value chain reconfigurations. 'Permissive', because new information and communication technologies enable MNEs to coordinate and control geographically dispersed activities better on a global scale, thereby creating new opportunities to shift production and service functions to low-cost centres overseas. 'Active', where technological developments create new products, markets and business opportunities. Governmental forces can also play a key role by further incentivising or impeding relocational opportunities on a global scale, as for example with India creating 17 'special economic zones' (SEZs) in 2003/4 to provide tax and other incentives for inward FDI by multinational companies.

Globalisation: SMEs, internationalisation and global trading

This section examines the contribution of the SMEs to the general patterns and trends identified for global trading in the third wave of globalisation.

SMEs and global industrial restructuring SMEs are involved in global industrial restructuring in at least five main ways (Sakai 2002, p.11): by being partners to strategic alliances; by being participants in mergers and acquisitions; by being specialised suppliers to multinational companies; by being members of global informal networks; and by participating in global electronic networks.

One indicator of the cross-border strategic alliance activities of SMEs can be seen in Figure 2.2, with the total cross-border alliances involving SMEs recorded as 2400 during

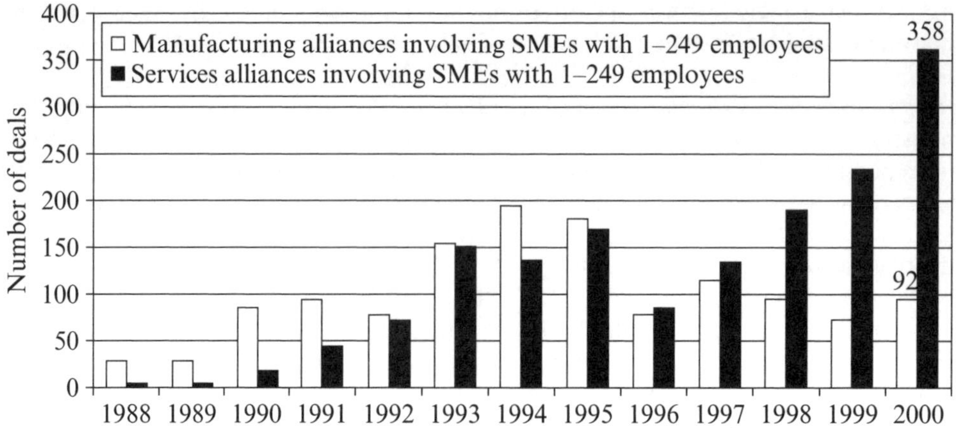

Source: European Commission (2004a)

Figure 2.2 Cross-border alliances involving SMEs, 1998–2000

1988–2000. Alliances in services became increasingly more important during the second half of the 1990s in comparison to the greater importance of manufacturing alliances in the first half of the decade. MNEs have sometimes been able to benefit from 'economies of experience' by forming alliances with local SMEs to exploit their knowledge and experience of the domestic market. SMEs have also become important producers of components and other intermediate inputs for larger firms. Indeed multinationals are increasingly outsourcing some of their non-core activities to smaller SMEs, who often become part of the large company's global supply chain, provided that they are able to meet rigid quality and delivery criteria (UNCTAD 2000). Sometimes SMEs have themselves taken the initiative by 'piggy backing', as in exploiting the distribution networks of large firms to sell their niche products overseas. In addition, SMEs may benefit from cross-border alliances with large firms where these can supply small, technologically advanced firms with the essential funds needed to enhance their research capabilities (Carayannis *et al.* 2000).

In terms of informal networks, SMEs have often formed geographic 'clusters' (OECD 2001) within which small firms can benefit from sharing knowledge and skills and more effectively implementing new product and process innovations and business practices. Electronic networks have also helped SMEs engage in industrial restructuring, as when increased information exchange and market awareness via the internet gives SMEs access to new business opportunities and new business associates.

We have seen that the forces of globalisation and industrial restructuring have had important impacts on both large and small firms. However, it should be noted that globalisation and industrial restructuring affect SMEs and large firms in different ways, a point emphasised by Julien (1996), who identifies four internationally-oriented ways by which SMEs can respond to these forces: by using global linkages with larger firms to supply cheaper imports to the domestic market; by using global linkages with larger firms to be a competitive supplier of direct or indirect exports to overseas markets; by themselves being initiators of geographically dispersed value chains, that is, 'global' SMEs; and by being part of international networks of SMEs.

Source: Numella (2004)

Figure 2.3 SMEs in international networks

The impacts of globalisation will be much weaker for those SMEs in the bottom left-hand quadrant of Figure 2.3, whose activity is mainly local in nature. In contrast, the increased speed of globalisation will have a more significant impact on SMEs which have at least one strong global link, that is, those SMEs which act primarily as importers of goods and services (top left-hand quadrant) or primarily as exporters of goods and services (bottom right-hand quadrant). The impacts of globalisation on SMEs which operate in international networks may not be so dramatic, with these SMEs better able to cope with the dynamics of globalisation through sharing responsibility and knowledge (centre circle). The SMEs most susceptible to the impacts of globalisation are the global SMEs (top right-hand quadrant), where both the inward and outward activities of the (mainly medium-sized) SMEs are set firmly in the international market.

SMEs and the internationalisation processes SMEs often become involved in one or other of indirect exporting, direct exporting or importing as the first stage of a sequential internationalisation process (Johanson and Wiedersheim-Paul 1975). The sequential or stage theory of internationalisation proposes that SMEs typically internationalise by moving progressively from low commitment/risk to high commitment/risk, as in the following chronology:

1. No regular export activity (or perhaps sporadic export activity)
2. Export via independent representatives
3. Establishment of own sales subsidiaries abroad
4. Establishment of production facilities abroad.

SMEs are also seen as beginning their export and internationalisation experience by favouring the less risky markets at a close geographical and psychic distance to the domestic market, before moving on to markets at a greater geographic or psychic distance. However recent studies by Gankema *et al.* (2000) and Havnes and Hauge (2002) have found that SME internationalisation follows a more discontinuous pattern, one that is inconsistent with the sequential or stage theory.

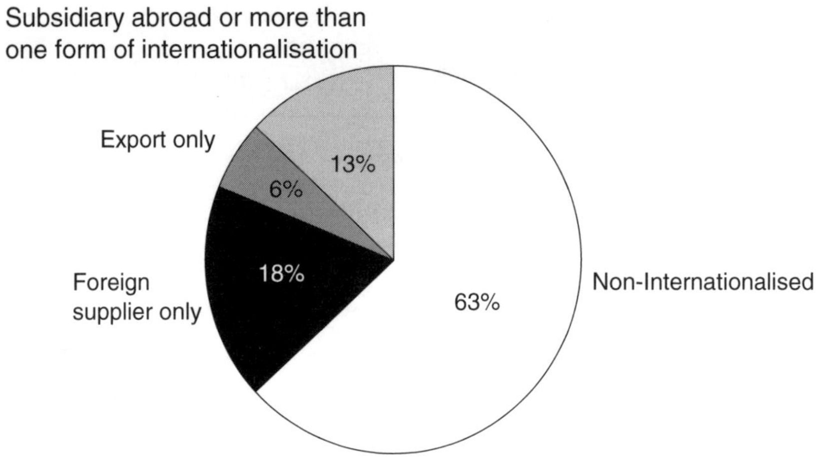

Source: European Commission (2004a)

Figure 2.4 The prevalence of different forms of internationalisation among SMEs

A substantial number of firms which have adopted a global focus from the moment of their conception – the so-called 'born globals' – further challenge the sequential or stage theory. 'Born globals' are defined as 'companies that set up their activity targeting a market that is either global by nature or within a niche field that has a very limited potential on the domestic market' (European Commission 2004a, p.24). Studies have suggested that a significant number of new companies, perhaps as many as one in ten, have begun their existence with a dependence on exports, particularly in the knowledge-intensive industries (Saarenketo and Sundqvist 2002).

However in more recent times evidence suggests that SMEs are increasingly engaged simultaneously in both outward and inward activities (Fletcher 2001). These activities include export and import trade (singly or in combination) together with various forms of foreign partnerships and alliances, foreign direct investment, and overseas production, marketing and R&D functions. In these ways, SMEs are themselves increasingly internationalising their value chain activities from inbound logistics through production, to marketing, sales and after-sales services.

A valuable insight into the role of SMEs within the internationalisation process is provided in a recent report by the *Observatory of European SMEs* (European Commission 2004a) which collected data from interviews with 7837 SMEs across 19 European countries during April–August 2003 (Figure 2.4). The report grouped SMEs into four mutually exclusive categories:

1. Foreign supplier (importing)
2. Exporting
3. Subsidiaries, branches and joint ventures abroad (or a combination of more than one of these forms of internationalisation)
4. Non-internationalised SMEs.

Of all the SMEs interviewed, 18 per cent reported that they were engaged in foreign supplier relationships (importing) only, another 6 per cent were engaged in exporting only, and 13 per cent reported that they had a subsidiary abroad or were engaged in more than one form of internationalisation. In other words 37 per cent of all SMEs were internationally active although the majority (63 per cent) were still non-internationalised. However, it should be noted that the degree of internationalisation may often be underestimated in such studies because indirect exporting (that is, exporting through intermediaries such as wholesale companies) was not recorded. A European Network for SME Research (ENSR) survey in 2002 found that indirect exports were indeed an important contributor to the growth in turnover of SMEs (European Commission 2002).

The data in Figure 2.4 provide some further useful insights. First, while 18 per cent of SMEs import only, another 12 per cent (30 per cent − 18 per cent) are engaged in more complex forms of internationalisation such as importing combined with exporting or with collaboration and/or subsidiaries abroad. Second, while only 6 per cent of total SMEs are exclusively engaged in exports, some 10 per cent of exporters (13 per cent − 3 per cent) combine *both* importing and exporting activity. Such observations lend support to the suggestion that importing may prompt SMEs to export, and vice versa, with 'learning' about trading from an initial foray into the global market (whether exporting or importing) providing transferable knowledge and skills to support a more varied form of international engagement.

This growing tendency for SMEs to be engaged in multiple forms of internationalisation seems to be directly related to SME international competitiveness. For example a recent ENSR survey (European Commission 2004b) found that 69 per cent of SMEs with subsidiaries abroad or more than one form of internationalisation report that 'internationalisation has improved their competitive strength', whereas this was reported to be the case for only 56 per cent and 53 per cent respectively of SMEs involved solely in exporting or solely in importing. The suggestion here is that SMEs involved in more complex forms of internationalisation are exposed to, and develop 'competencies that eventually lead to better overall performance' (European Commission 2004a, p.43). This conclusion is further supported by a number of other recent studies (Majocchi and Zucchella 2003, Werner 2003).

Internationalisation and the size of SMEs There is considerable evidence to suggest that the larger the size of the SME, the greater the degree of international involvement, as indicated in Table 2.2 for SMEs in the European Union. From this table it can be seen that the highest percentage of SMEs involved with overseas subsidiaries or joint ventures is overwhelmingly in the medium-sized category, suggesting that more complicated forms of internationalisation require a higher minimum critical size. As far as exports are concerned, the involvement of SMEs increases directly with size. However it is interesting to note that there is no such relationship between size of enterprise and export intensity. This suggests that the smaller the enterprise, the less likely it is to export, but that once the enterprise does start exporting, then the smaller enterprises tend to export with nearly the same intensity as the larger SMEs. This finding that size of SME and export intensity are not directly related is further supported by a recent German econometric study (Wagner 2002).

Table 2.2 Mode of internationalisation (%) and the size of SME (number of employees)

	0–9	10–49	50–249	Total
Foreign suppliers (importing)	29%	45%	49%	30%
Exports	17%	38%	51%	18%
Subsidiaries/joint ventures	2%	7%	26%	3%
Export intensity[1]				
Less than 10%	49%	45%	39%	49%
11–50%	32%	36%	38%	32%
51–100%	19%	19%	23%	20%

Note:
1. Exports as a percentage of total turnover for export-only SMEs

Source: European Commission (2004b)

Sector of internationalisation and SMEs Figures 2.5 and 2.6 indicate the influence of sector on the propensity by SMEs to internationalise. Figure 2.5 shows that in relation to internationalisation involving SMEs, the category of import-only involvement with a foreign supplier is dominated by the retail and wholesale sectors, whilst the manufacturing, transport and communication, business services and wholesale sectors dominate the export-only category. More varied and committed forms of internationalisation (for example, subsidiaries) are more prevalent in the manufacturing, wholesaling and transport and communication sectors. Figure 2.6 shows export intensity across sectors and indicates clearly that the transport and communication sector has the highest export-only intensity with 35 per cent of SMEs exporting more than 50 per cent of turnover. In contrast, the retail and construction sectors have the lowest export-only intensity.

If Figures 2.5 and 2.6 are compared, one can see that although the share of exporting enterprises varies substantially between the different sectors, once these enterprises become internationalised there is little difference between the export intensity figures in sectors such as manufacturing, business services and personal services. Again, it seems that once SMEs in such sectors enter the competitive environment of a global market, they tend to adapt to the new environment and become just as export orientated as SMEs in the manufacturing sector.

Co-operative international relationships and SMEs From Figure 2.7, it would appear that internationalised SMEs are more heavily involved in both formal and non-formal co-operative activities than non-internationalised SMEs. The extent of co-operative involvement rises progressively as the internationalisation process moves from foreign supplier (import) only, through export only to subsidiaries abroad or more than one form of internationalisation. Among SMEs with subsidiaries abroad or more than one form of internationalisation, 32 per cent engage in formal co-operation and 51 per cent in non-formal co-operation.

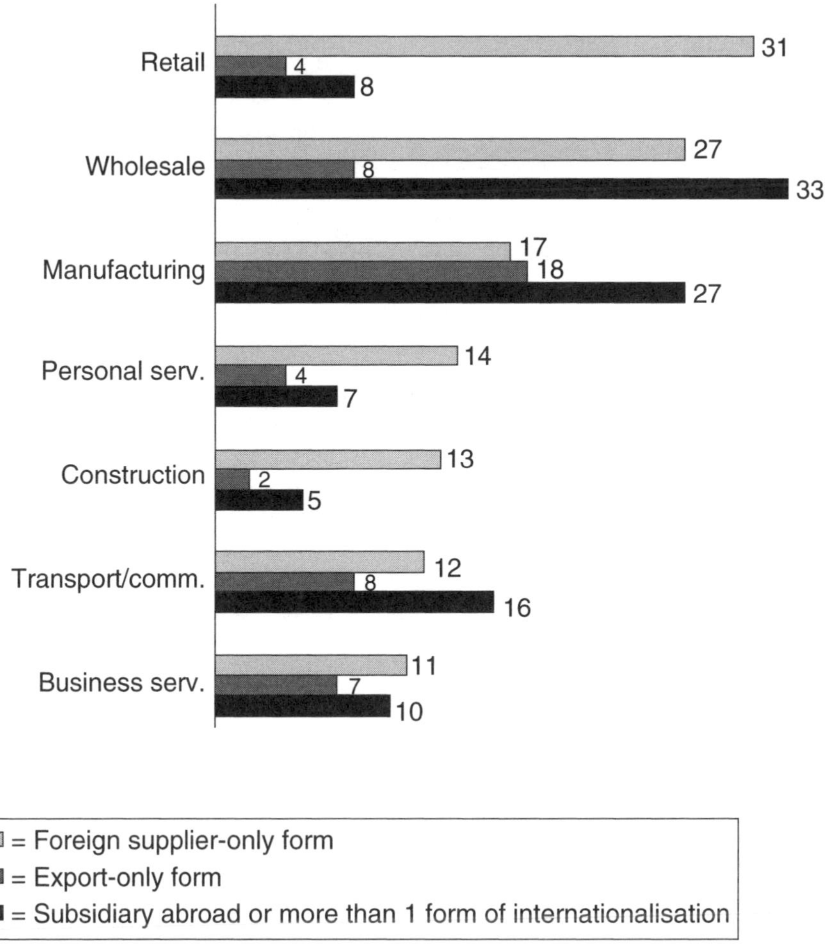

Source: European Commission (2004a)

Figure 2.5 Internationalisation in different sectors

Figure 2.8 suggests that whilst most internationalised SMEs have the majority of their partners from the domestic market, there is a significant number of SMEs in the category 'subsidiary abroad or more than one form of internationalisation' which have foreign SMEs as co-operative partners (22 per cent) or both foreign and national SMEs as co-operative partners (31 per cent). This indicates that SMEs involved in more complex forms of internationalisation tend also to have a higher rate of linkages with foreign and national SMEs. As far as alliances are concerned, we have already seen in Figure 2.2 that this form of internationalising became more prevalent for SMEs during the 1990s as large companies outsourced many of their activities to smaller enterprises, both in the manufacturing sectors and increasingly in the knowledge-based sectors (Contractor and Lorange 2002). Alliances with a more functional purpose, designed to improve marketing, R&D or distribution, also

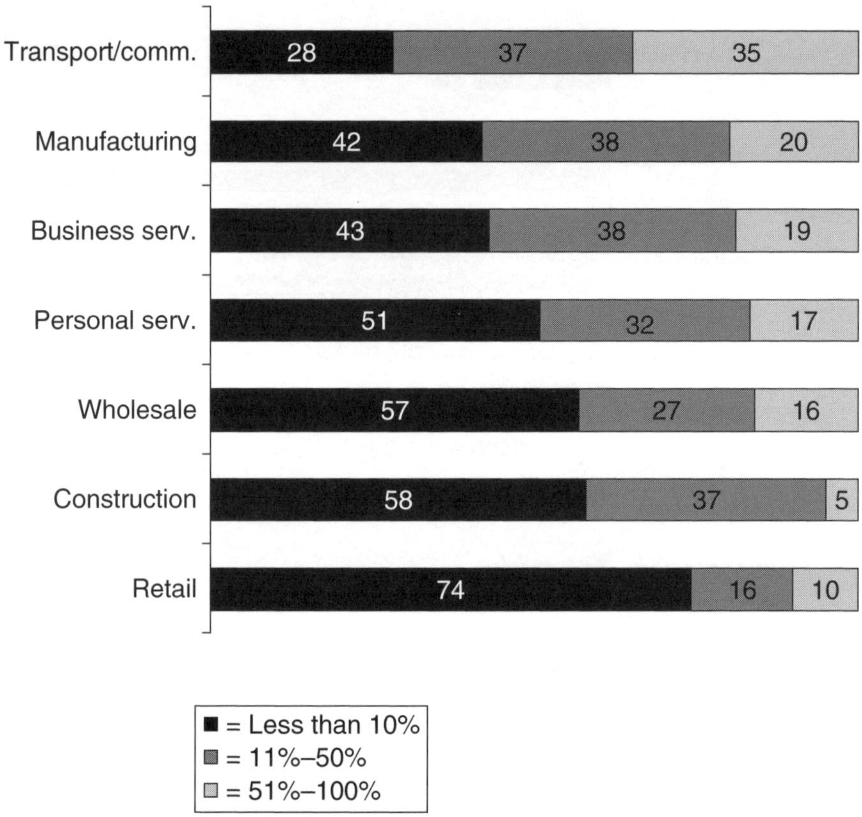

Note: The numbers on the bars are the percentage of SMEs involved in export at the specified intensity.

Source: European Commission (2004a)

Figure 2.6 Export intensity by sector

help SMEs to engage in international networks and to become involved in more complex value chain activities.

Strategic challenges for small and medium-sized enterprises in global trading

We have noted that the pace of globalisation and industrial restructuring has impacted some types of SME more than others. Whilst various studies have been conducted concerning the internationalisation process of SMEs (see, for example, Johanson and Vahlne 1977, Andersen 1993) the research on detailed internationalisation practices and activities that relate to strategic outcomes are still at a developmental stage (Bell, Crick and Young 2004). A methodical analysis of the micro-based activities that shape and direct the internationalisation decisions, especially by medium-sized enterprises, is largely under-researched and it is to this enquiry that the remainder of this section is primarily directed.

The focus in this part of the chapter will be on the resource-based responses to the forces of global trading and industrial restructuring of the telematics sector that is

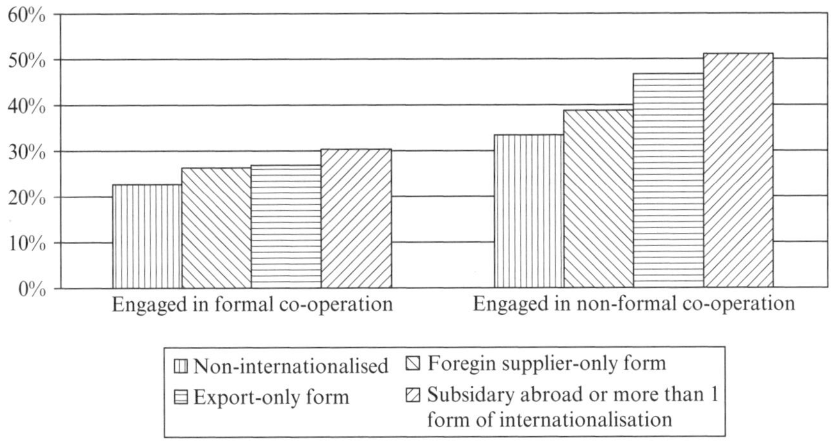

Source: European Commission (2004a)

Figure 2.7 SMEs in formal and non-formal co-operation

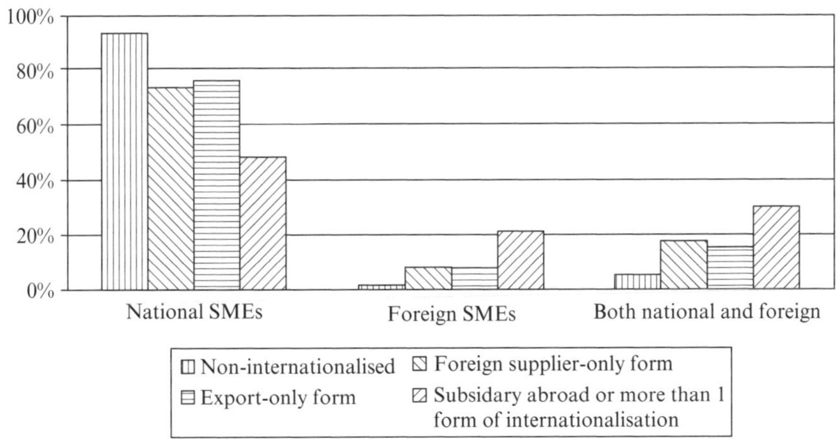

Source: European Commission (2004a)

Figure 2.8 National or foreign SMEs as important partners in co-operation

dominated by a large number of medium-sized enterprises. We seek to address the contention that the strategy debate can be enhanced by a shift away from the more conventional macro-based perspective, with its usual quantitative underpinnings and quest for dependent variables, towards a more micro-based perspective which places greater emphasis on qualitative investigation into the detailed practices of corporate life (Johnson and Huff 1997, Lindell *et al.* 1998, Johnson *et al.* 2003). By drawing upon two research projects, one a broad-based investigation into global trading by SMEs in the East of England and the other a more detailed sector-specific study within the telematics industry, we intend to highlight internationalisation dynamics as well as resource considerations and capability reconfigurations.

Resource-based view of SME internationalisation

The resource-based view (RBV), once stimulated by the groundbreaking papers of Wernerfeld (1984) and Barney (1991), argues that the sustained competitive advantage of a company mainly derives from the capabilities and resources that it is able to develop and control. This set of resources and capabilities can be regarded as a package of tangible and intangible assets that determine the success or failure of a company. In fact as far back as Penrose's (1959) work on the diversification of companies, the analysis of company growth had arguably shifted from a focus on external factors to a more internally oriented perspective of the firm. Since then the emphasis has progressively shifted towards the ability of managers to renew and reconfigure these internal resources in order to create competitive advantages in a context in which intensified global competition and a rapidly changing international environment threaten to diminish their value (Rumelt 1984, De Rond 2003). Internationalisation activities – such as international business planning and resource management, international networking and insourcing/outsourcing decisions – are seen by the RBV as the vehicle by which the firm is able to develop and sustain its competitive advantages (Peng 2001). Developing these competencies is seen as requiring a strong learning commitment in the company and a high receptivity (De Rond 2003), attributes more normally associated with larger companies than with medium-sized enterprises. When taking into account the literature on internationalisation, a key issue is therefore whether the RBV logic can be extended in such a way that it becomes applicable to the internationalisation practices of medium-sized enterprises.

Global trading by SMEs in the East of England

A recent study of global trading by SMEs in the East of England (Lloyd-Reason and Mughan 2003) provides useful insights into practitioner-based influences on SME internationalisation. The study was undertaken on behalf of the East of England Development Agency (EEDA) and it is to this study that we now turn.

The project was split into two phases, in which the initial mapping of international activity throughout the eastern region was achieved through a large-scale telephone survey undertaken between June and August 2002. During the first phase of the project, data on 560 internationalised and 554 non-internationalised SMEs in the eastern region were collected. In phase two of the project, staff at 80 companies were interviewed face-to-face on their own premises between December 2002 and June 2003. The interviews were semi-scripted and recorded. In all cases the person interviewed was the strategic decision maker for international activity (usually the owner-manager in smaller firms). Each interview lasted for about one hour. Building on the findings from the telephone survey, the purpose of the interviews was to obtain deeper insights into company behaviour in international markets, including managerial traits, skills and knowledge needs, problem solving and managerial views of support services.

The qualitative research design was constructed to meet various validity and reliability criteria (King *et al.* 1994, Patton 1987). Thus, further to the extensive phase of semi-structured interviews, techniques of 'triangulation' were used to establish validity by building a series of checks into the research design based on multiple verification, with particular archival and published data of the interviewed companies being used as well as the technique of multiple interviewers. As regards reliability and transparency of the findings, each interview was recorded, summarised and transcribed, generating in excess of 2800 pages of transcript. In addition, three closed questions providing tick box responses using the Lickert scale were included, covering the international mindset of the interviewee, specific problems experienced and support providers used. Finally, the software N6 was used to code the information down to three levels using four key categories:

1. *Motivation*: What are the motivations and drivers for international activity?
2. *Process*: What form does this activity take and how does it impact on the firm?
3. *Problems*: What are the key problems encountered?
4. *Solutions*: Where do they go to find solutions to these problems?

The sample of companies was weighted in favour of those firms with greater levels of experience of international trade since the project sought to identify successful aspects of managerial skills and knowledge development that could be made transferable across business sectors, via training, educational, development and recruitment programmes.

Here we review the results from the qualitative face-to-face interviews, which yielded insights into processes and practices which could not always be discerned from the quantitative analysis alone. This study did not seek to test any particular theory or model of SME behaviour but rather it set out to obtain and present as accurate a picture as possible of the ways in which companies actually behave, based on a qualitative interview process whereby the interviewee was invited to respond to open questions and describe his or her company.

There is an established literature on motivation which seeks to group motivations into different categories. Ibeh (2000) provides a useful overview of this work and identifies four general categories:

- *Internal – proactive* (for example, desire to grow)
- *Internal – reactive* (for example, responding to declining profit margins)
- *External – proactive* (for example, introduction of new legislation)
- *External – reactive* (for example, responding to heightened competition).

The interviewed businesses were allowed to express their own motivations and the drivers underpinning their international activities, as for example in their responses to an open question as to the mechanism by which the business has sought to manage the 'process' of internationalisation.

Three key motivators tended to underpin international trade, accounting for 59 per cent (48 of a total of 81) of the motivations identified.

- Response to an opportunity in the market or an enquiry from a potential customer
- Part of a wider business development strategy
- Operating from the outset in an international market as determined by the nature of the product or service.

The results of the interviews suggest that around 30 per cent of the interviewed businesses started international trading activity in response to an opportunity or an enquiry from a potential customer, with this motivator reflecting some 27 per cent of the total motivators identified.

Approximately 25 per cent of interviewed businesses identified internationalisation activity as part of the process of developing and growing the business, with this motivator reflecting some 17 per cent of the total motivators identified. The decision of whether to engage in international activity was seen here as an integral part of the planning and strategy process within the business.

The international nature of the product or service was identified as the key motivator by just over 20 per cent of the interviewed businesses, reflecting some 15 per cent of the total motivators identified. In the majority of cases, these businesses had been operating internationally since their inception and such businesses are sometimes labelled 'born global', a description appropriate to around one in three of businesses in the Enthusiastic and Successful categories. Details of those categories can be found in Chapter 8. The activities of these businesses included the manufacture of scientific instrumentation, automotive manufacturing, business software development and international recruitment. The nature of such product and service offerings 'forced' the business to operate internationally as the number of customers within the home market fell far short of the 'critical mass' widely regarded as a minimum requirement for such sectors.

These experiences and insights demonstrate the intrinsically proactive nature of the 'born global' motivation and driver, as it 'pulls' the owner-manager into international activity and forces the business to confront key issues such as the type of presence required in overseas markets, how to sell in overseas markets and how to maintain an awareness of developments in international markets.

Telematics and internationalisation

The telematics case study was designed to meet a number of qualitative research criteria (King *et al.* 1994, Yin 1994). We selected an approach that included four key stages of activity, making use of mixed methods and triangulation to provide construct validity. The combination of a small pilot research study in 2003, 45 semi-structured (and subsequently transcribed) interviews with both industry experts and leading academics in the field in 2004/5, and the use of published and archival data, together with consultancy-derived published materials, all provided a useful degree of construct validity. The findings of our approach might therefore be used as a basis to identify best practices within the industry to help better design and target the efforts of the business support agencies seeking to promote internationalisation within the telematics sector.

'Telematics' historically has meant the blending of information, computer and telecommunications technologies in vehicle-related sectors of economic activity, including mobile communication and geographic positioning devices. The telematics sector has encountered difficult times in recent years after a promising beginning so that internationalisation has been seen as a major revenue driver for growth. However, over time, progressively diminishing forecasts for the telematics market have been published, and telematics providers, especially the medium sized, have increasingly felt the painful results of their over-ambitious investments. In this context, providers have become increasingly anxious to identify new potential catalysts, which might push their portfolios into profitability. Whereas telematics solutions in Japan have almost exclusively focused on the need for

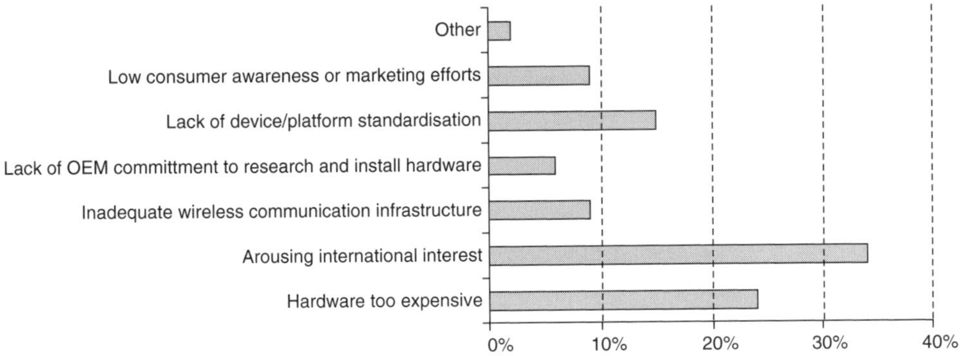

Source: Allied Business Intelligence (2003)

Figure 2.9 Barriers to telematics adoption

an efficient dynamic navigation device, Europe and the US do not seem to have provided a comparable 'critical' application. In these regions companies have scanned the horizon for innovative 'success factors', seeking to replicate the high market penetrations demonstrated in Japan. A recent policy intervention in the EU market, namely the European Union regulations for a transcontinental interoperable electronic toll collection standard, is seen by some market participants as providing new opportunities for companies to reconfigure their internationalisation capabilities. By building on the existing infrastructure and technologies of the electronic toll collection (ETC) systems, medium-sized telematics companies may now be able to penetrate the international market on a larger scale, making telematics more affordable to the European end user.

Underlying internationalisation vertices A recent study by Allied Business Intelligence (2003) indicated the perceived barriers to the large scale international adoption of telematics (see Figure 2.9). In addition to sector-specific impediments – such as the lack of technical standards across product offerings – scale inefficiencies for price competitiveness and missing brand awareness play a major role. In particular, arousing international interest has been seen as one of the key challenges to raising revenues for the medium-sized telematics enterprises, which are facing serious resource restrictions. This lack of international awareness has profound relevance for the managing of internal and external resources across the value chain. As a second step, the medium-sized enterprises in the telematics industry faced the question of selecting between in- and outsourcing activities as a means of strengthening their core competencies and thereby sustaining their competitive advantages. The optimal make or buy models in this industry include strategic versus non-strategic capability categorisations in production processes (see Figure 2.10). As shown, decisions are typically based on resource and time availability to engage in building up crucial internal capability. On the other hand, commodity capabilities, that is, those easily replicated and non-strategic, are only kept in-house as long as the general set-up of the company's production processes allow for cost-competitiveness without substantial investments.

These in- and outsourcing decisions to an extent determine the focus and level of the in-depth capability of telematics firms in the medium-sized segment. Thereby, a high level

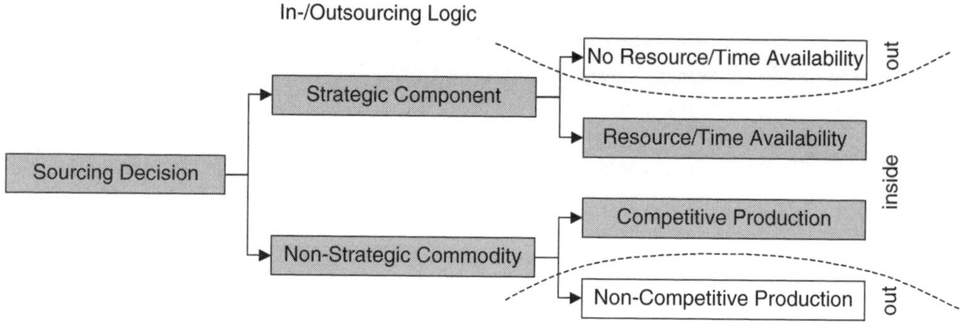

Source: Adapted from Venkatesan (1992)

Figure 2.10 In-/outsourcing decision flow

of speculative specialisation can be witnessed. However, despite the recent history of discouraged market sentiment through innovation flops, a number of market forces are moving in favour of medium-sized firm involvement with the telematics sector. For example, the automotive market is mature, and increasing competition is continually eroding margins, so that large automotive enterprises are increasingly viewing the more flexible medium-sized telematics companies as innovation generators, thereby providing them with new opportunities for product differentiation and ultimately increasing revenues. In addition, telecommunication companies have been suffering from locked-in capital expenditure and also see telematics as an opportunity to leverage billing investments, whilst governmental institutions are pushing for affordable technology to improve traffic management and to fight congestion problems with electronic toll schemes (Stenske 2003).

Key resources and capabilities There are various resources and capabilities that appear essential for medium-sized enterprises to excel in the international telematics sector via the opportunities offered by the ETC system platform. The inability of large automotive enterprises to build up direct customer relationships through vehicle sales, has often been seen as a major reason for constrained telematics penetration rates (Foy 2002). Medium-sized telematics enterprises, however, can act as mediators to provide a solution to this challenge. The interview results found that most automotive companies view participation in telematics – and thereby the interaction with medium-sized companies – as an essential element in generating innovative features to aid the product differentiation seen as vital in securing the large customer base consistent with international mass-market penetration. Thus the receptivity and flexibility of medium-sized enterprises is viewed as one of the key capabilities for internationalisation.

Another crucial issue includes competencies associated with the provision of central services such as billing and customer care. Whereas medium-sized enterprises have adopted innovative approaches regarding international marketing and sales, the survey results suggest that they lack experience and know-how in billing procedures for a large international customer base. However, telecommunications companies usually carry a natural competitive advantage with regard to this capability, one which other companies in the telematics value chain can benefit from. The existing capability configurations of telecommunication enterprises enable them to offer a sophisticated billing service beyond the reach of medium-sized enterprises. A decision as to which billing capabilities to outsource to large telecommunication enterprises is therefore crucial for medium-sized enterprises in the telematics segment. Figure 2.11 indicates how an outsourcing decision as regards the different billing services could be structured.

By unbundling the basic components of the billing part of the company value chain, each activity in a line of processes can be attributed to a certain value set. As indicated in Figure 2.11, this set includes information as to the level of capability relative to competitors as well as its overall value contribution to the business. Whereas 'necessary' in Figure 2.11 signifies that ownership of this part of the value chain is of secondary importance to sustainable development, 'crucial' indicates that significant competitive advantage is derived through unique capabilities for the particular activity.

Further important capabilities include the flexibility of larger companies to deploy technological expertise in order to react rapidly to changing customer preferences and market requirements. This is creating new opportunities for medium-sized companies as the larger, telematics-using companies are required to engage with existing small technological platforms on the market to ensure compatibility. Joint venture and other collaborative arrangements then become more likely within the sector, helping avoid problems such as the need to re-engineer vendor products, problems which might otherwise result in a loss of consumer commitment to the larger companies. ETC system rollout is creating opportunities for extensive value chain co-operation, enabling medium-sized companies to align themselves with common industry standards and thereby more easily access potential economies of scale.

Capability-reconfiguration scenarios Figure 2.12 incorporates a detailed analysis of the two main service clusters within the telematics value chain. Especially as regards fleet management applications, a collaborative arrangement between medium-sized companies within the telematics value chain is seen as increasingly advisable. Whilst this by no means implies less specialisation within the medium-sized telematics enterprises, management does need to be increasingly aware of the imperative to complement their own company's capabilities with those of others across the entire industry value chain. To identify the appropriate partners for effective consortia, firms need to employ the evaluation logic outlined in Figure 2.12 to identify clearly the value-creating activities inherent in their business. All other value-creating activities then need to be leveraged, pooled or outsourced to allow the medium-sized companies to focus on the core activities within their own value chain. The imperative is clear, namely that medium-sized enterprises must abandon merely opportunistic internationalisation approaches if they are to survive within the telematics market. Instead, it is their specialisation and eventually their fit within market openings and alliances that will carry them across borders with a viable, combined value proposition.

Telematic opportunities for medium-sized firms To overcome the dilemma of disproportionate hardware sales and to initiate sustainable revenues to offset the locked-in telematics R&D costs, medium-sized telematics companies need to obtain an international service

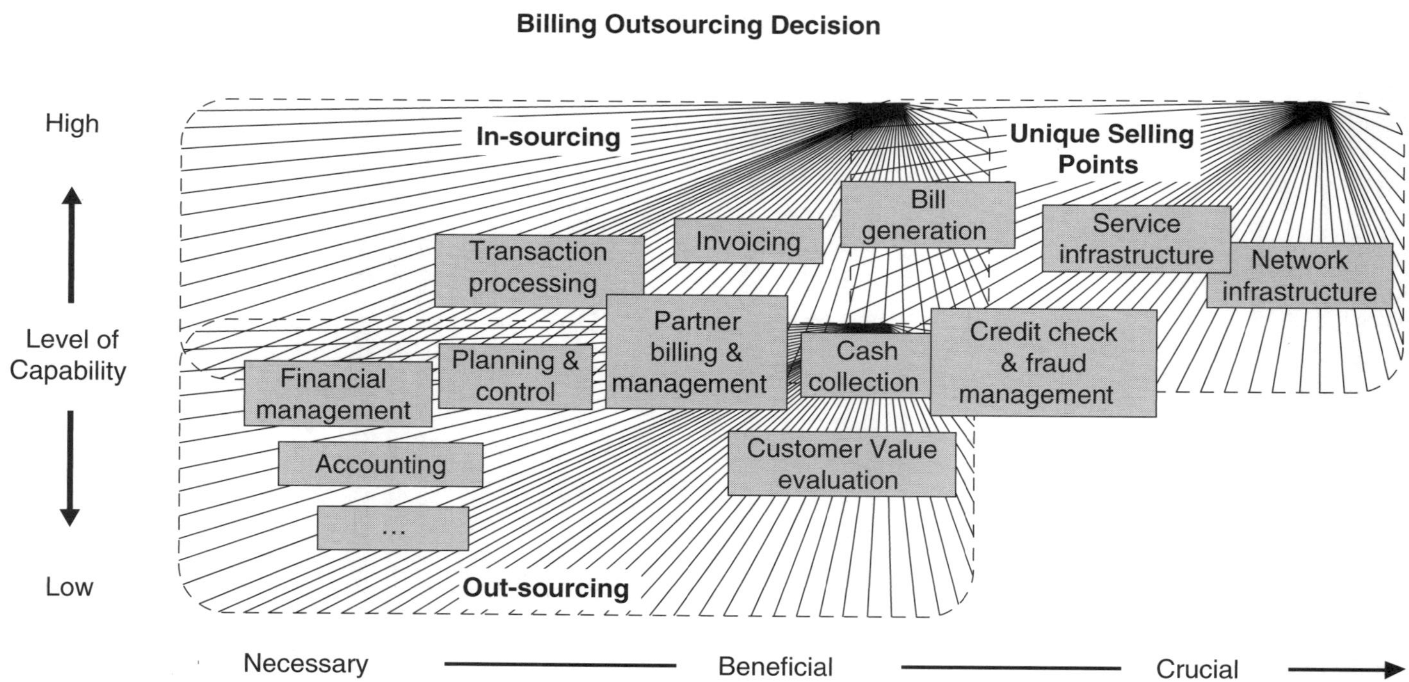

Figure 2.11 Outsourcing the billing function by medium-sized enterprises

Value Chain Tangents for Telematics upon ETC

Importance (Interview)	Value Chain / Affected Services	Hardware	Telecom Infra-structure	Comm. Devices	Appli-cations	Content Devel-oper	System Inte-grators	Vehicle Manu-facturer	Mobile Operator	Tele-matic Portals
64%	Transport Management via ETC	Specialised hardware needed for GPS-enabled ETC-OBUs	Use of existing standards such as GSM or GPRS (future: UMTS)	Use of ETC-OBU transponders via mobile communication devices	High demands for convenient consumer applications & interfaces	Content for transport management mainly through forms of dynamic route guidance features	Integration of telematics application with ETC-OBU and software crucial	Fitment and preparation of vehicle for ETC and telematics requirements	Provisioning of VAS services for enhanced transport management	Customer preference demands convenient features for efficient transport management
	Required Partners									
32%	Traffic Management via ETC	Specialised hardware needed for GPS-enabled ETC-OBUs	Secure mode of data transmission for traffic control essential (data protection)	Use of ETC-OBU transponders via mobile communication devices	Little extra applications as data is not relevant to individual drivers	Little extra content development needed due to central and stationary administration	Moderate integration necessity for floating car data transmission	Fitment and preparation of vehicle for ETC and telematics requirements	Standard provisioning of communication services	Portal services mainly needed on tolling consortia side and for traffic data administrator
	Required Partners									

Notes: OBUs On-Board Units
VAS Value-Added Services

Figure 2.12 Partnering requirements

distribution platform that is affordable. As already noted, the incubator potential of electronic toll collection systems marks the need for a proactive approach by telematics service providers; one route to affordability is for medium-sized telematics companies along the entire value chain to engage proactively in toll tenders across Europe to gain a foothold in the connected business opportunities. A key issue as to the viability of this route will be the extent to which medium-sized companies are able to align their international capabilities and resources accordingly.

Special attention needs also to be devoted to the formation of collaborative arrangements, especially in the billing area. Alliances in telematics-related activity have historically been dominated by short-term agreements creating cross-functional groups to achieve specific tasks, such as the creation of common technological platforms. However, the industry is now about to witness a transformation in the characteristics of medium-sized alliance structures as telematics developments accelerate via electronic toll collection; collaboration along the value chain will take all forms from a loose exchange of ideas to full-sized mergers, as companies seek to position themselves to provide the unique multitude of diverse capabilities required to turn telematics finally into a profitable business space.

Other practitioner-based case materials

Motivations for SME internationalisation Responses by practitioners to questionnaires or in-depth interviews as to the 'why' of SME internationalisation confirm some of the insights of the East of England study and suggest still other motivations. For example, Figure 2.13 summarises the results of an extensive survey of practitioners in 2003 by the

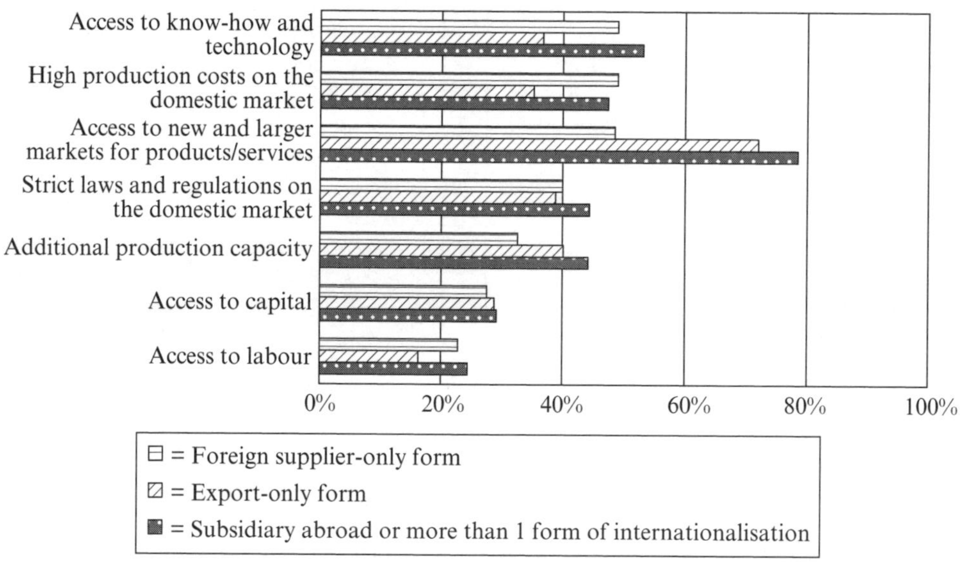

Note: The graph represents the percentage that rated the motive 'important' or 'very important'.

Source: European Commission (2004a)

Figure 2.13 Motives for internationalisation

European Network for SME Research (European Commission 2004a). The suggestions in the East of England study that 'responsiveness to market opportunities' and 'limited/saturated home markets' are key SME motives for internationalisation are also broadly supported in Figure 2.13, with 'access to new and larger markets' being the most frequently cited motive for SMEs that export or have a subsidiary abroad, and is even important to SMEs that only import.

'Access to know-how and technology' is also seen in Figure 2.13 to be an important motive for pure importers as well as for SMEs engaged in more complex forms of internationalisation. This may reflect the suggestion in the East of England study that being 'part of a wider business development strategy' is an important motive, since know-how and technology imply a degree of strategic planning rather than merely an opportunistic response to a market opening for higher sales. Arguably 'access to additional production capacity', also seen as an important motive in Figure 2.13, reflects a more strategic business development motive. The suggestion here is that internationalisation is often initiated to gain access to cheaper sub-suppliers and/or to additional production capacity, reflecting the SME's desire to improve its management of production. However Figure 2.13 provides few further insights into the suggestion from the East of England study that there is an increasing tendency towards 'born global' SMEs, 'pulled' from the outset to adopt a proactive international stance.

Internal competencies and barriers Figure 2.14 shows the results of an investigation into the internal barriers to internationalisation identified by practitioners in the 2003 survey

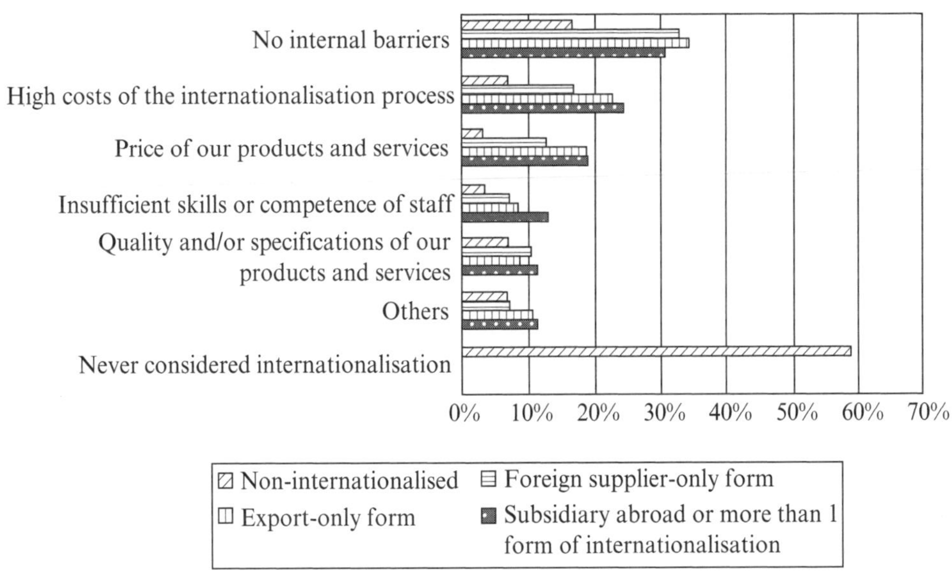

Note: n = 7385

Source: European Commission (2004a)

Figure 2.14 Internal barriers to internationalisation

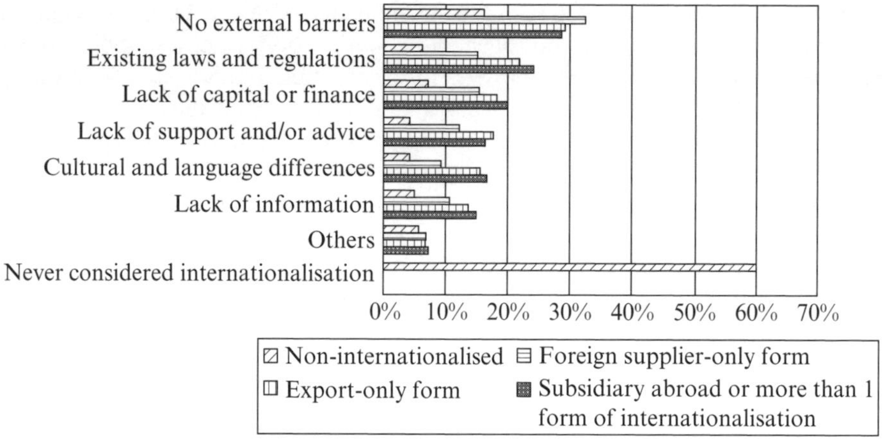

Source: European Commission (2004a)

Figure 2.15 External barriers to internationalisation

by ENSR, the European Network for SME Research (European Commission 2004a). The internal barrier cited most frequently for all three groups of internationalised SMEs in this figure was the 'high costs of the internationalisation process'. These 'costs' might include undertaking market analysis abroad, purchasing legal and/or consulting services, translation of documents, adaptation of products to foreign markets and possibly covering the higher risks involved. Almost one in four (24 per cent) of SMEs involved with a subsidiary abroad or with more than one form of internationalisation find such high 'costs' to be a barrier, with such firms likely to reflect the 'enthusiastic' and 'successful' categories of the East of England study. These SMEs, with their more extensive international involvement, tend also to be the ones which are more aware of other internal barriers such as a skills mismatch, as well as price, quality or specification problems for the products involved in global trade.

The SMEs less engaged in global trade ('curious', 'frustrated' and 'tentative' categories in the East of England study – see Chapter 8) seem less aware of internal barriers and deficiencies than those SMEs more engaged in global trade. As is noted in the ENSR study 'the lack of organisation and planning of strategic efforts may represent a major barrier to internationalisation [but] . . . this type of barrier is, however, only acknowledged once the enterprise has considered or embarked on an internationalisation process' (European Commission 2004a, p.36). The same report goes on to conclude that 'internal competencies of the employees and the managers are thus essential for the internationalisation process' and that for these, often smaller SMEs with limited time and management capacity 'a policy measure should offer to perform some of the practical tasks on behalf of the manager' (op. cit. p.51).

External barriers for internationalisation As can be seen from Figure 2.15, around a third of the internationalised SMEs perceive no external barriers, and the importing-only (foreign supplier) SMEs are the type most likely to see no such barriers. It is again the more internationally engaged SMEs involved in more complex international activities which are likely to perceive the existence of external barriers. In order of importance: problems with existing laws and regulations, lack of capital or finance, lack of support and/or advice, cultural and language differences and lack of information are the external barriers cited the most by internationalised SMEs, especially those with a subsidiary abroad or involved in more than one form of internationalisation.

Interestingly, tariff barriers are not explicitly identified as an external barrier, although it should be remembered that the sample is drawn from EU firms whose global trading is primarily with other EU firms within a protected free trade area. Certainly irregularities and inconsistencies between national and EU technical and legal standards doubtless feature in the 'existing laws and regulations' category, but not tariff barriers themselves.

Conclusions: implications for governmental and agency policies towards SMEs

We noted in the introduction to this chapter that SMEs are under-represented in the global economy. In seeking to redress this situation, a number of policy implications for governments and agencies can be drawn from the analyses presented above. It is to this policy focus that we now turn.

We have seen that SME internationalisation is much more varied and complex than merely exporting. Policy measures should therefore be sufficiently flexible to cover *all* the different SME approaches to internationalisation. In other words policy support should be directed not only to SMEs engaged in exporting, but also to those engaged in activities such as foreign supplier (importing) only, in various collaborative arrangements, in foreign direct investment, and so on. The ENSR Enterprise Survey (European Commission 2004b) suggested that a significant number of SMEs now internationalise to access know-how and/or gain greater access to technology or labour resources. Indeed such types of value chain reconfiguration were shown in the ENSR Enterprise Survey to be the second most important motive for SMEs to internationalise. Policy focus must shift from the traditional stance of 'augmenting overseas sales' of exporters to a more multifaceted approach in support of SMEs entering a broad range of cross-border arrangements and alliances.

The needs of the larger, more internationally engaged SMEs have also been seen to be different from those of the smaller, less internationally engaged SMEs. This suggests a requirement for targeted support which is 'customised' to the requirements of the individual companies involved. An example of targeted support of this kind might be in providing personal support packages for owner-managers of smaller SMEs, including the performance of practical tasks for managers with limited time and management capacity. For larger, more internationalised SMEs, the targeted support might be in helping identify an appropriate foreign business partner for a joint venture or alliance.

Under a more globalised economic system, we have noted that the internationalisation process for SMEs often involves simultaneous involvement in exporting, importing and other cross-border activities. In other words there is less support for the traditional 'stage or sequential theory' which sees internationalisation as a gradual and progressive process. The existence and growth of 'born globals' noted previously is arguably a further challenge to the traditional 'stage theory' and reinforces the need for more proactive and wide-ranging supports for the internationalising SMEs geared to their particular needs, rather than supports based on a false, monolithic presumption of stages through which the internationalising SMEs must inevitably progress.

The larger, more internationally engaged SMEs were also seen to be those most likely to improve their 'competitive strength' via further internationalisation. There is therefore a case for focusing governmental and agency support on these more 'enthusiastic and/or successful' companies, as they are better placed to benefit from such support. This may require a reorientation of conventional policy focus and resource allocation, which has often emphasised the need to help non-internationalised SMEs begin the internationalisation process. The more practitioner-based analyses of problems encountered by SMEs suggest that improving 'planning, manning and scanning' processes for the more committed SMEs would seem to be the policy approach best suited to redressing the internal and external barriers to internationalisation identified by practitioners.

Notwithstanding an increased emphasis on the more committed (and often larger) SMEs, there is certainly scope for further improving the global trading engagement of the non-internationalised SMEs. Almost 60 per cent of these in the ENSR Enterprise Survey (European Commission 2004b) had not even considered internationalising, which may indicate a policy requirement for raising awareness among SMEs as to the benefits that may be obtained from international activities, including improved performance and competitiveness.

Finally, on a global policy level, there is a need for governments themselves to review their own, often unwitting, contributions to inhibiting SME global trading via inappropriate rules and regulations. As noted by the OECD in a recent report,

> the success and growth of international SMEs will be enhanced by a more internationalised infrastructure geared to the smooth growth of firms across borders. This applies to the infrastructure for financial markets, advisory services, information access, telecommunications, intellectual property rights, dispute resolution processes, etc. . . . Governments need to collaborate more to set up monitoring systems to identify these impediments, understand their longer term impact and establish mechanisms for addressing them, at bilateral and multilateral levels. (OECD 2004, p.19)

In other words, a key global policy stance for increasing SME internationalisation and SME contribution to global trading is seen here as the development of a more conducive international entrepreneurial business environment, with the policy focus on 'framework' rather than specific policy instruments.

Questions emerging from the chapter

1. Why are SMEs that are more actively engaged in the internationalisation process seen as being the more internationally competitive SMEs?
2. Examine the case for concentrating government and agency supports on the larger, more successful internationalised SMEs. What types of policy support might be most effective for these SMEs?
3. How relevant is the 'stage/sequential theory' to SME internationalisation? Consider the policy implications of your response to the above question.
4. Examine the case for developing policy supports which are sufficiently flexible to cover *all* the different SME approaches to internationalisation.

5. Why is it increasingly suggested that policies to support SME internationalisation should be 'customised' to the needs of particular SMEs?
6. Consider why *non-internationalised* SMEs are still regarded by many as important for government/agency policy attention. What types of policy support might be most effective for these SMEs?

Bibliography

Allied Business Intelligence (2003), *European Telematics Survey*. London: ABI.

Andersen, O. (1993), 'On the internationalization process of firms: a critical analysis', *Journal of International Business Studies*, 26, 2, 209–31.

Barney, J.B. (1991),'Firm resources and sustained competitive advantage', *Journal of Management*, 17, 99–120.

Barro, R. (1991), 'Economic growth in a cross section of countries', *Quarterly Journal of Economics*, 106, 20, 407–43.

Bell, J., Crick, D. and Young, S. (2004), 'Small firm internationalization and business strategy', *International Small Business Journal*, 22, 23–56.

Bhagwati, J. (2004), *In Defence of Globalization*. Oxford: Oxford University Press.

Carayannis, E.G., Kassicieh, S.K. and Radosevich, R. (2000), 'Strategic alliances as a source of early-stage seed capital in new technology-based firms', *Technovation*, 20, 11, 603–15.

Contractor, F.J. and Lorange, P. (2002), 'The growth of alliances in the knowledge-based economy', *International Business Review*, 11, 4, August, 485–502.

Coviello, N.E. and McAuley, A. (1999), 'Internationalisation and the smaller firm: a review of contemporary empirical research', *Management International Review*, 39, 3, 223–56.

De Rond, M. (2003), *Strategic Alliances as Social Facts: Business, Biotechnology, and Intellectual History*. Cambridge: Cambridge University Press.

Deane, M. (2004), 'Why has world trade grown faster than world output?', *Bank of England Quarterly Bulletin*, Autumn, 310–20.

DTI (2004), *Liberalisation and Globalisation: Maximising the Benefits of International Trade and Investment*, Department of Trade and Industry Economics Paper No. 10, July. London: Department of Trade and Industry.

European Commission (2002), *Highlights from the 2002 Survey*, The Observatory of European SMEs, No. 2002/8. Luxembourg: Office for Official Publications of the European Commission.

European Commission (2004a), *Internationalisation of SMEs*, The Observatory of European SMEs, No. 2003/4. Luxembourg: Office for Official Publications of the European Commission.

European Commission (2004b), *ENSR Enterprise Survey 2003: Internationalisation* (Part A). Luxembourg: EC.

Fletcher, R. (2001), 'A holistic approach to internationalisation', *International Business Review*, 10, 1, 25–49.

Foy, D. (2002), *Automotive Telematics: The One-Stop Guide to In-Vehicle Telematics and Infotainment Technology and Applications*. New York: Red Hat Publishing.

Gankema, H.G.J., Snuif, H.R. and Zwart, P.S. (2000), 'The internationalisation process of small and medium sized enterprises: an evaluation of the stage theory', *Journal of Small Business Management*, 38, 4, 15–47.

Hauge, E. and Havnes, P.-A. (2001), 'The dynamics of SME development: two case studies of the internationalization process', *RENT XV Conference*, Turku 22–23 November.

Havnes, P.-A. and Hauge, E. (2002), Utvikling i Regional Maritim Næring: Internasjonalisering av Leverandørbedrifter (Development of regional maritime sector – internationalisation of suppliers) FoU-rapport No. 1/2002. Kristiansand: Agder Research Foundation.

Ibeh, K. (2000), 'Internationalisation and the small firm' in Carter, S. and Jones-Evans, D. (eds), *Enterprise and Small Business*. Harlow: Financial Times/Prentice Hall.

Johanson, J. and Vahlne, J. (1977), 'The internationalisation process of the firm: a model of knowledge development and increasing market commitment', *Journal of International Business Studies*, 8, 1, 23–32.

Johanson, J. and Wiedersheim-Paul, F. (1975), 'The internationalisation of the firm – four swedish cases', *Journal of Management Studies*, 12, 3, 305–22.

Johnson, G. and Huff, A. (1997), 'Everyday innovation/everyday strategy' in Hamel, G., Prahalad, C.K., Thomas, H. and O'Neill, D. (eds), *Strategic Flexibility*. Chichester: Wiley.

Johnson, G., Melin, L. and Whittington, R. (2003), 'Micro strategy and strategizing: towards an activity-based view', *Journal of Management Studies*, 40, 1, 3–22.

Julien, P.A. (1996), 'Globalisation: different types of small businesses behaviour', *Entrepreneurship and Regional Development*, 8, 1, 57–74.

King, G., Keohane, R.O. and Verba, S. (1994), *Designing Social Inquiry: Scientific Inference in Qualitative Research*. Princeton: Princeton University Press.

Klingebiel, R. (2004), *Deliverance for the Telematics Industry? Profitable Growth through Value-Added Services Allied to Electronic Toll Collection Systems*, Working Paper, Judge Business School, Cambridge: University of Cambridge.
Lindell, P., Melin, L., Gahmberg, H., Hellqvist, A. and Melander, A. (1998), 'stability and change in a strategist's thinking' in Eden, C. and Spencer, J.-C. (eds), *Managerial and Organizational Cognition: Theory, Methods and Research*. London: Sage.
Lipsey, R.E. (1999), *The Location and Characteristics of US Affiliates in Asia*, Working Paper. Cambridge, MA: National Bureau of Economic Research.
Lloyd-Reason, L. and Mughan, T. (2003), *Competing Effectively in International Markets: Identifying Need, Sharing Best Practice and Adding Value to the Eastern Region through Skills and Knowledge Transfer*, Final Report to East of England Development Agency. Cambridge: Anglia Ruskin University.
Majocchi, A. and Zucchella, A. (2003), 'Internationalization and performance', *International Small Business Journal*, 21, 3, 249–68.
Numella, N. (2004), 'Is the globe becoming smaller or is the small becoming global?' in Jones, M.V. and Dimitraos, P. (eds), *Emerging Paradigms in International Entrepreneurship*, Cheltenham UK and Northampton, MA, USA: Edward Elgar.
OECD (2001), *Enhancing SME Competitiveness: The OECD Bologna Ministerial Conference*, Paris: OECD.
OECD (2002), *Economic Outlook*, June, Paris: OECD.
OECD (2004), 'Facilitating SMEs access to international markets', *2nd OECD Conference of Ministers Responsible for SMEs*, Istanbul, 3–5 June.
Patton, M.Q. (1987), *How to use Qualitative Methods in Evaluation*. London: Sage.
Peng, M.W. (2001), 'The resource-based view and international business', *Journal of Management*, 27, 803–29.
Penrose, E. (1959), *The Theory of the Growth of the Firm*, New York: Wiley.
Prahalad, C.K. (1999), 'Changes in the competitive battlefield', *Financial Times*, 4 October.
Rumelt, R.P. (1984), 'Towards a strategic theory of the firm' in Lamb, B. (ed.), *Competitive Strategic Management*. Englewood Cliffs, New York: Prentice-Hall, 556–70.
Saarenketo, S. and Sundqvist, S. (2002), 'Comparison of born global and traditionally internal firms: effects of industry and managerial characteristics' in Saarenketo, S., *Born globals – internationalisation of small and medium- sized knowledge-intensive firms*, Acta Universitas Lappeenrantaensis 145.
Sakai, K. (2002), Global Industrial Restructuring: Implications for Small Firms, Directorate for Science, Technology and Industry STI Working Paper 2002/4 Paris: OECD.
Stenske, T.A. (2003), 'Value added services based on electronic toll collection', paper presented at the *10th World Congress on Intelligent Transportation Systems and Services*, Madrid, 16–20 November.
Taylor, C.T. (2000), 'The impact of host country government policy on US multinational investment decisions', *World Economy*, 23, 635–48.
Tranfield, D. and Starkey, K. (1998), 'The nature, social organization and promotion of management research', *British Journal of Management*, 9, 341–53.
UNCTAD (2000), *Enhancing the Competitiveness of SMEs through Linkages*, TD/B/COM3/EM.11/2 September, Geneva: UNCTAD.
UNCTAD (2003), *World Investment Report 2003*: *FDI Policies for Development: National and International Perspectives*, New York: United Nations.
Varaldo, R. and Pagano, A. (1998), 'Can small and medium enterprises survive in the global economy?' in Kaynak, E., Becker, K. and Kucukemiroglu, O. (eds), *Proceedings of the Seventh IMDA World Business Congress*, Santa Domingo, Dominican Republic, 3–7 June, pp. 1–8.
Venkatesan, R. (1992), 'Strategic sourcing: to make or not to make', *Sloan Management Review*, 70, 6, 98–107.
Wagner, J. (2002), *Unobserved Firm Heterogeneity and the Size-Exports Nexus*: *evidence from German Panel Data*, HWWA Discussion Papers, No 194, Hamburg: Hamburgisches Welt Wirtschafts Archiv.
Wallsten, S. (2001), *Ringing in the 20th Century*, World Bank Research Working Paper, Washington DC: World Bank.
Werner, D. (2003), 'Competitiveness and internationalisation strategies: results of a company survey, IV: Trends', No. 4
Wernerfeld, B. (1984), 'A resource-based view of the firm', *Strategic Management Journal*, 5, 2, 171–80.
World Bank (2001), *Global Economic Prospects and Developing Countries*. Washington DC: World Bank.
World Bank (2002), *Globalisation, Growth and Poverty: Building an Inclusive World Economy*, Washington DC: World Bank/Oxford University Press.
World Bank (2003), *Global Economic Prospects and the Developing Economies.* Washington DC: World Bank.
Yin, R.K. (1994), *Case Study Research, Design and Methods*, 2nd edition, Newbury Park: Sage Publications.
Zak, P. (2001), 'Institutions, Property Rights and Growth', *The Gruter Institute Working Papers*, 2, 1, Article 2, www.bepress.com/giwp/default/vol2/iss1/art2, accessed 24 November 2006.

3 Traditional and emergent forms of global trading

Leo Paul Dana, Hamid Etemad and Richard Wright

Introduction

Traditional approaches to internationalisation focused on a uni-polar and hierarchical distribution of power and control. In this chapter, we discuss an alternate approach to globalisation – an approach that involves a multi-polar distribution of power and control. Rather than focusing on the internationalisation of a centralised firm with a uni-polar distribution of power and control, we suggest that the world is moving toward multi-polar networks of firms. As corporations outsource to smaller specialised firms, power and control are becoming increasingly divided among independent SMEs that co-operate voluntarily for increased efficiency and profit. Symbiotic marketing relationships are thus leading to multipolarity. We are hence moving beyond a focus on the firm toward a focus on relationships with multi-polar networks. This is giving unprecedented opportunities to SMEs in the global economy.

In this chapter, we put emphasis on local and cultural embeddedness. We shall show that this is important when attempting to understand either virtual clusters of the New Economy, or personal clusters of the bazaar. In the words of McMillan, 'On the internet, just as in the bazaar, the methods of exchange are shaped by information and costs of getting it' (2002, p. 47).

Perhaps the future can best be understood by taking a look at the past. In this chapter, we shall examine the multi-polar networks of interdependent SMEs in the traditional bazaar, as well as the emerging relationships and multi-polarity of the New Economy. Similarities prove to be intriguing. Entrepreneurship and internationalisation in the traditional bazaar were conducted around personal relationships and alliances. Technology eventually allowed a shift to the impersonal transactions of the firm-type economy – an economic institution which involves a mode of commercial activity such that industry and trade take place primarily within a set of impersonally defined institutions, grouping people according to organisation and specialisation. In the emerging global scenario, we observe a return to multi-polar networks. The unit of interest is no longer the firm, but the multi-polar network, in which relationships are important.

The objective of this chapter is to provoke readers to think about the nature of SMEs in the global economy. There are some interesting parallels with the traditional bazaar, in terms of information dissemination, pricing, temporal equilibrium, and most significantly, relationships and brand loyalty. Like the structured bazaar, which allowed physical concentration and therefore functioned efficiently, the Web provides concentration and clustering of vendors. Potential buyers and suppliers meet efficiently on-line, and this reduces search costs and minimises disparity caused by geographic fragmentation. With little variation, the style and procedures of Internet searches reflect a certain pattern. A potential buyer finds several web pages, thus learning about supplies and prices from *several* suppliers and alliances – networks of suppliers. Indeed, we are coming full circle to a multi-polar scenario.

We are well aware that an understanding of internationalisation is no longer an option; it is a prerequisite for success in the global marketplace. Indeed, the success of entrepreneurs is a function of their ability to be globally competitive, even if they refrain from competing globally. The question arises, then: 'How can SMEs – lacking economies of scale – compete against large multinationals in the global economy?'

A solution is for small firms to develop relationships with larger firms, creating multipolar networks. We see it happening; entrepreneurs are shedding their desire for independence, as they discover interdependence and relationships to be more profitable. The result is symbiotic marketing, which we define as, 'a marketing effort by multiple parties, each of which benefits from the joint effort, such that added value is created'.

Symbiotic marketing relationships are leading to multi-polarity in the world of business. We are thus moving beyond a focus on the firm toward a focus on relationships with multi-polar networks. A look at the multi-polar networks of interdependent players in the traditional bazaar may enhance our understanding of the emerging relationships and multi-polarity of the New Economy.

This chapter begins with our definitions of three types of economy. We then review related literature. This will be followed by a discussion of the bazaar and the firm-type economy, ideal-types in constant evolution. This will lead us into a discussion of our observations, noting the multi-polar nature of the new global economy. We shall explain that emphasis on relationships and price negotiations are making a comeback. In our discussion, we shall include a variety of elements, including clustering, pricing, competition and the parallel economy.

Definitions

- The **bazaar-type economy** is a social, cultural and economic system in which the physical clustering of vendors facilitates the consumer's comparative information search, by eliminating displacement time. Business is strongly affected by relationships and networks; relationships and preferential treatment are integral to business. Consumers are not treated equally. Different people pay unlike prices. The price paid and the level of service provided is a function of status and relationships. Products and services are personalised, and this leads to customer loyalty. Internationalisation is a function of multi-polar networks involving special relationships.
- The **firm-type economy** is an economic institution in which location is a competitive advantage. In the shopping mall, for instance, an exclusivity clause protects the vendor, limiting competition. The consumer's comparative information search involves displacement time, and an opportunity cost is involved when seeking perfect information. Business takes place primarily within a set of impersonally defined institutions. The flow of commerce is a function of strategy based on optimisation models. The purpose of transactions is to maximise wealth efficiently, and the means to this is rational and unbiased decision making that treats buyers as equals. The price paid and the level of service provided is established by the seller. Products and services are standardised, and this leads to efficiency that in turn allows competitive pricing. Internationalisation is a function of uni-polar strategic decision making centralised at head office.

- The **New Economy** is a cultural and economic system in which the virtual clustering of vendors facilitates the consumer's comparative information search by eliminating displacement time. The flow of commerce is strongly affected by relationships and networks; relationships and preferential treatment are integral to business. Consumers are not treated equally. Different people pay unlike prices. The price paid and the level of service provided is a function of status and relationships. Products and services are customised. Internationalisation is a function of multi-polar networks involving special relationships.

The literature

Traditional approaches to internationalisation focused on a uni-polar and hierarchical distribution of power and control. Internalisation theory (Buckley and Casson, 1976; Morck and Yeung, 1991, 1992; Rugman, 1979, 1981; and Teece, 1985) taught us that, by investing in its own foreign subsidiaries, a firm could expand operations, while maintaining control at head office. Likewise, the eclectic paradigm (Dunning, 1973, 1977, 1980, 1988) focused on ownership-specific and location-specific advantages that a firm can enjoy, while maintaining centralised control. A uni-polar scenario is also implicit in the stage models of incremental internationalisation (Bartlett and Ghoshal, 1989; Bilkey, 1978; Bilkey and Tesar, 1977; Buckley, Newbould and Thurwell, 1988; Cavusgil, 1980, 1984; Cavusgil and Nevin, 1981; Johanson and Vahlne, 1977, 1990; Johanson and Wiedersheim-Paul, 1975; Leonidou and Katsikeas, 1996; and Newbould, Buckley and Thurwell, 1978). Internationalisation can be achieved without giving up power and control; the internationalising firm can maintain its uni-polar distribution of power and control.

An alternate approach to internationalisation assumes a multi-polar distribution of power and control. Rather than focusing on the internationalisation of one centralised firm with a uni-polar distribution of power and control, we can focus on a multi-polar network of firms. Power and control are divided among independent firms that co-operate voluntarily for increased efficiency and profit. Literature pertaining to this networking perspective includes Acs and Dana (2001); Axelsson and Easton (1992); Bodur and Madsen (1993); Coviello and Munro (1997); Dana (2001); Fontes and Coombs (1997); Johanson and Mattsson (1988, 1992); Johanson and Vahlne (1992); Sharma (1992); Sharma and Johanson (1987); Welch (1992); Welch and Luostarinen (1988, 1993); Welch and Welch (1996); and Wilkinson, Mattsson and Easton (2000). Here, the focus is not on the firm, but on a multi-polar system with many smaller firms and networks of their own.

Multi-polar internationalisation is a relatively new phenomenon in the West. Yet the concept is not new at all. We read about it in accounts of the Babylonians, over 2000 years ago. Much later, industrialists of the West developed joint ventures – more structured forms of co-operation, but with the same goal. Joint ventures became a popular means by which multinationals could further internationalise.

While entrepreneurs in the West strove for independence, entrepreneurs of bazaar economies thrived in the long-established networks spanning Indonesia (Geertz, 1963), Indo-China (Dana, 1995b, 1999b), China (Dana, 1998a, 1999a), Central Asia (Dana, 1997, 2000a), and the lands of the former Ottoman Empire and the Mediterranean rim (Dana, 2000b; Sayigh, 1952). The overseas Chinese networks likewise became important instruments for international trade (Shenker, 1994). In Japan, also, symbiotic marketing was reflected in networks of firms (Dana, 1998b; Wright, 1989).

Many Asians brought their networks when they came to the West. Sociology provides us with a rich literature on immigrant entrepreneurs and their ethnic networks (Light, 1972). Loewen (1971) studied the Chinese in Mississippi. Wong (1987) produced a study of self-employment among Han Chinese in New York. Other examples include a report on Han Chinese entrepreneurs in Calgary (Ray, Momijan, McMullan and Ko, 1988); a study of Han Chinese entrepreneurs in Canada (Brenner and Toulouse, 1990); and a description of Han Chinese in Vietnam (Dana, 1994).

There is a considerable interest in minority entrepreneurs and their ethnic networks (Aldrich, Jones and McEvoy, 1984). Blaschke and Ersoz (1986) studied Turkish entrepreneurs in West Berlin; Boissevain and Grotenbreg (1987) reported on Surinamese entrepreneurs in Amsterdam; Dana (1995a, 1996) interviewed minority entrepreneurs in the sub-Arctic; Ladbury (1984) investigated Turkish Cypriots in London; Min and Jaret (1985) analysed Koreans in Atlanta; and Werbner (1984) investigated Pakistanis in Manchester.

Howard E. Aldrich looked beyond ethnic networks and examined social networks. Aldrich and Zimmer (1986) concluded that networking might be an essential requirement for entrepreneurial success. Aldrich, Rosen and Woodward (1987) further demonstrated the impact of network accessibility. Further research includes Aldrich (1989) and Dubini and Aldrich (1991). Members benefit from being involved in a network; it is a symbiotic, interdependent relationship. Acs and Yeung (1999) used the term co-dependence.

While sociologists have focused on networks of entrepreneurs, we also see increasing collaboration between small and large firms. This allows the product of smaller firms to reach global markets more quickly than through independent expansion (Harrison, 1997). Bonaccorsi (1992) and Dana and Etemad (1994, 1995) explained how small businesses can rely on large firms for parts of their internationalisation activities, fusing elements of international business with small business and entrepreneurship. Through this 'scaling up' process, smaller firms can leverage their network resources to shorten the time span and reduce the cost and risk of their internationalisation. Similarly, performing specialised functions for large firms allows small firms to hasten their own learning curve, and to internalise sufficient expertise to become competitive at the global level.

Thus, internationalisation increasingly involves symbiotic relationships among large and small firms. Reynolds (1997) noted that the recent expansion of markets has not been associated with an expanded role for larger firms. Instead, smaller firms are filling niche roles (Buckley, 1997).

Networks of small and large firms can enhance the competitiveness of both types of organisations. By supplying a portion of the high-volume needs of bigger firms, small firms can specialise, achieving their own economies of scale. As these smaller firms become more competitive, capturing scale economies not possible without large-firm linkups, the large firms in turn gain competitiveness by integrating those economies into their own value chains. The large firms also gain flexibility and economies of scope by accessing a number of highly specialised small firms, each producing a small range of components at very substantial scale economies. A further benefit to large firms linking up with smaller ones is the enhanced ability to tailor products or processes to fit local demand or content requirements.

The traditional bazaar

The bazaar is a social and cultural system, a way of life and a general mode of commercial activity which has been in existence for millennia. In the bazaar, economic transactions are *not* the focus of activities; instead, the focus is on relationships and alliances. In this scenario, consumers do not necessarily seek the lowest price or the best quality. An individual buys from a friend, sometimes to help the friend and sometimes to ensure that the friend will reciprocate. The multiplicity of related small-scale transactions results in a fractionalisation of risks. Firms are not perceived as rivals of one another. There is minimal – if any – brand differentiation among merchants. Vendors do not necessarily seek to optimise monetary gain. Economic rationality is not an issue. Segmentation refers to the geographic clustering of producers. Prices are negotiated, as opposed to being specified by the seller.

As noted by Webster (1992), building long-term relationships can be viewed as a social and economic process. Unlike Western relationship marketing, which is customer-centred, whereby a seller seeks long-term business relationships with clients (Evans and Laskin, 1994; Zineldin, 1998), the focus in the bazaar is the relationship itself. In the bazaar, *both* the buyer and the seller seek a relationship.

While the entrepreneur described by Schumpeter (1912, 1928, 1934, 1942, 1947, 1949) is an innovator who causes disequilibrium to profit therefrom, the entrepreneur of the bazaar may simply identify an opportunity for profit (rather than create one). In this way, the entrepreneur of the bazaar corresponds to that of the Austrian school (Kirzner, 1973, 1982).

When examining the bazaar, it is important to understand the relations among the players within it, their organisation and their economic principles. In contrast to the Occident, where segmentation refers to the market, in the bazaar economy, production is segmented, as are retailers. As early as the 1300s, one of the greatest Arab explorers, namely Ibn Battuta, noted the segmentation of producers and retailers. Even today, in the bazaar, shops are still clustered according to the goods offered therein.

While competition in the West is understood to be competition between sellers, in the bazaar economy, competition implies a tension between buyer and seller, rather than between sellers. The lack of information results in an imperfect market, and with few exceptions, such as basic food staples, retail prices are not publicly exhibited, but rather they are determined by negotiations. The customer first tests price levels informally, and only later begins to bargain. Often it is the buyer who proposes a price, which is eventually raised. The establishment of a long-term relationship makes future purchases less costly and even more pleasurable. As transaction-centred costs begin to decline, mainly due to the rise in relationship (or social capital), the overall transaction costs (Williamson, 1985, 1996) begin to approach Williamsonian optimality, whereby buyer and seller feel highly satisfied with the transaction. Geertz (1963) and Dana (2000b) discuss in detail such phenomena of the bazaar.

The firm-type economy

The firm-type sector is an economic institution which involves a mode of commercial activity such that industry and trade take place primarily within a set of impersonally defined institutions, grouping people according to organisation and specialisation. Its underlying assumption is that profit-maximising transactions occur based on rational decision making, rather than the nature of personal relationships. The focus is on impersonal transactions. Weber's (1924) thesis, which focused on asceticism, frugality and thrift, applies.

In this type of economy, the decision space is occupied by product attributes; the buyer and seller are secondary, if not trivial, to the transaction decision. The interaction between the buyer and the product is deemed to be more important than that between the buyer and the seller. Transactions are based on economic rationality and are therefore impersonal in nature. Competition is an activity that takes place between sellers, who engage in segmentation in order to partition the market into like-groups of predictable consumers. Prices are tagged, reflecting market forces. While Western marketing principles (Gronroos, 1989) apply here, market orientation is linked to the maturity of the industrialisation process (Seglin, 1990). Where industrial development is limited, the framework for economic transition may have to rely more on new ventures and on joint initiatives.

The New Economy

Entrepreneurship, during the 20th century, took place within the context of the firm-type economy. In this context, businesses claim to treat clients as equals. It is assumed that profit-maximising transactions occur based on rational decision making, rather than on the nature of personal relationships between entrepreneurs and consumers. The focus is on impersonal transactions. The decision space is occupied by product attributes and by services attached to them, backed by formal warranties. Consequently, the relationship between the buyer and the individual salesman is secondary, if not trivial, to the transaction decision. The interaction between the buyer and the product (and/or service) is deemed to be more important than that between the buyer and the seller. Competition takes place among sellers. Geographic location is often a competitive advantage. Selling prices are dictated by producers or sellers, if not by government regulation.

In the 21st century, we observe a significantly different set of norms. No longer are all people created equal. A frequent traveller on Air Canada can earn 'Super Elite' status, entitling this individual to differential treatment, preferential seating, special promotions, discounts and a personal concierge service. Even more striking, this preferred customer can also benefit from preferential treatment on British Midland, and on the 13 other members of Star Alliance – a global alliance of firms which were formerly competitors. This relationship leads to increased brand awareness, and brand loyalty, although differentiation is less evident than ever before. Airline seats are sold as a commodity, yet brand loyalty prevails. The transaction decision is less concerned with product attributes, and more focused on relationships and preferential treatment. There appears to be less competition among sellers, as formerly rival firms co-operate in global alliances. The unit of interest is no longer the firm but the multi-polar network, in which relationships are important.

Interestingly, this reality is shared with the bazaar-type economy – a social and cultural system, a way of life and a general mode of commercial activity such that most of the flow of commerce is centred on relationships rather than on impersonal transactions. There are infinite opportunities for small-scale speculation. Space, time, production and sales must be well managed, and personal relations must be managed. Together, buyer and seller negotiate prices. A sliding price system results in a price within the prevailing limits. Price can vary greatly, depending on the relationship between buyer and seller. Thus, interaction tends to take place between the buyer and the seller, rather than between the buyer and the product.

Goods and services are being increasingly treated as commodities, with virtually no distinction between the features offered by different producers. The focus has shifted away from the features of the product, to the relationship between buyer and seller. Looking again at the airline industry, we note that not long ago, advertising by Delta Airlines emphasised the use of four-engine aircraft, while United differentiated itself through the use of turbo-props and French-built Caravelles with two aft-mounted engines. Today, the fleets of different airlines vary less than they did in the past. Almost every airline has Airbuses and Boeings, and passengers are less informed about details. Likewise, there is little difference between the mobile phone built by one manufacturer and that built by another.

Another characteristic of the New Economy is that the Web has become a hub for transactions between consumers and suppliers, which are clustered together, reducing the time involved for comparative shopping. Often, it is the buyer who suggests a starting price – as is the case in the bazaar. Even in what was once a very regulated sector, makeusanoffer.com invited customers to state how much they are willing to pay for transportation.

The Web allows entrepreneurs to globalise without the need to have several offices. Internationalisation is decentralised. The Web also allows distributors like amazon.com to avoid high costs of inventory. In Japan, Rakuten launched a very successful concept, allowing vendors to sell produce very rapidly, through its site www.rakuten.co.jp. This operates in a fashion very similar to that of the bazaar.

Indeed, attributes of the New Economy share much in common with the bazaar-type economy. In this economic system, the focus is not on impersonal transactions, but rather on relationships. The multiplicity of related small-scale transactions yields an extensive fractionalisation of risks and of profit margins. Like the bazaar, the New Economy provides infinite short-term opportunities for small-scale speculation. Space, time, production and sales must be well managed, and personal relationships must be managed delicately.

Once again status, relationships and alliances have become important. As was the case in the bazaar, buyers and sellers negotiate prices A sliding price system results in a price within the prevailing limits. Price can vary greatly, depending on the relationship between buyer and seller. Thus, interaction tends to take place between the buyer and the seller, rather than between the buyer and the product. Sounds familiar? Are we heading back to the future? Perhaps we can learn about the future by better understanding the past.

Then and now

Early market places were often seasonal and regional. From this occasional existence arose the structured market – a stable and permanent structure for buyers and sellers to engage in trading. A new paradigm was launched with the creation of the structured bazaar. Entrepreneurs could travel from one country to another and conduct trade at these established trading posts.

Bazaars evolved and thrived in transport-hub cities, many of which were located on ancient trade routes connecting Europe to the Chinese Empire, through the Persian Empire and the Indian subcontinent. The southern Silk Road started from Xian, the capital of the Middle Kingdom (currently in China). With loads of silk and other exotic Chinese products – including gunpowder, the compass, ink, paper and writing instruments – caravans of entrepreneurs headed out to conduct international trade. Indian spices, as well as Chinese commodities, were traded along the journey.

Grand bazaars were vital to the functioning of trading routes, including the Silk Road; bazaars formed an infrastructure resembling the hub-and-spoke system of today's air transportation industry. In some ways, the ancient trading caravans were similar to modern airlines: their working capital was relatively large and they were pressed for time. Grand bazaars served as hubs, connected to each other and supplied by caravans travelling the trade routes. Smaller regional bazaars, in neighbouring towns, absorbed some of the imports brought in by caravans, and supplied some of the goods sold to caravans, or bartered. Bazaars thus functioned as inventory depots for the supply chain of other regional bazaars.

Comparative features

In many ways, caravans resembled trade missions of modern times. The most critical aspect of the ancient caravans was time. The long and arduous voyage between Xian and Rome stretched endurance beyond limits. Although the travellers stopped to resupply along their routes, and rested in organised and strategic locations, the traders could not allow disorganised, inefficient or poor markets to delay their schedule. The ideal bazaars – with a large functional capacity along trade routes – featured the following:

- *Knowledge dissemination*. Up-to-date supply-related information could be disseminated very fast, due to arbitrage aspects of bazaars.
- *Absorptive capacity*. The potential buyers and/or their agents (the intermediaries) collectively had sufficient absorptive capacity to make mutually beneficial spot market transactions with a newly arrived caravan.
- *Supply*. Local entrepreneurs were collectively able to supply international entrepreneurs with food, drink, inventory and even camels for transport.
- *Efficiency*. The ideal bazaar allowed for the efficient performance of market functions – both in terms of time, and barter supplies or gold coins, which were available in sufficient supplies only in grand bazaars.

Functions of the bazaar

The structured bazaar allowed physical concentration, and therefore functioned efficiently, largely thanks to the geographical concentration and clustering of vendors in like occupations. This enabled potential buyers and suppliers to meet efficiently at a predetermined location. This reduced search costs and minimised disparity caused by geographic fragmentation. Thus, the bazaar reduced overall transaction costs, as all parties concerned converged on a central location.

A potential buyer could easily locate the designated part of the bazaar for the goods and services under consideration. Once at that location, it was possible to compare the goods of several dealers within a short span of time. This allowed the shopper to develop a feel for the prevailing market conditions, including the price and supply range. The structured bazaar provided vital market functions including the following:

- *Information search*. Entrepreneurs disseminated their proprietary information regarding new products and emerging trends in supply or demand. At the bazaar, consumers acquired information at an unprecedented speed, allowing for efficient comparative shopping. Likewise, entrepreneurs could learn about the needs of consumers.

- *Updating*. Potential suppliers and buyers quickly updated and upgraded their state of information and incorporated their new knowledge to assume a new position.
- *Temporal equilibrium*. Some potential suppliers and buyers behaved as intermediaries, and they profited from arbitrage.
- *Opportunity for co-operation*. Entrepreneurs of the bazaar engaged in co-operative bargaining and negotiations, forming alliances.

Parallels

With little variation, the style and procedures of trade in the bazaar reflected a certain pattern. A potential buyer enquired about supplies and prices from several suppliers in a concentrated area. This allowed the person to form a reasonably informed opinion about the state of the market at the time. Ongoing arbitrage thus accorded the structured bazaar functional efficiency. Notice how much the structured bazaar resembled the World Wide Web:

- *Knowledge dissemination*. Up-to-date information is disseminated at unprecedented speed.
- *Absorptive capacity*. The potential buyers collectively have sufficient absorptive capacity to make mutually beneficial spot market transactions. Hence, we see the success of auctions on the Web.
- *Supply*. The Web allows small-scale entrepreneurs an opportunity to enter international transactions, formerly less likely to happen.
- *Efficiency*. The Web allows for the efficient performance of market functions.

Like the structured bazaar, which allowed physical concentration and therefore functioned efficiently, the Web provides concentration and clustering of vendors. Potential buyers and suppliers meet efficiently on-line, and this reduces search costs while minimising disparity caused by geographic dispersion. Thus, the Web reduces overall transaction costs, as all parties concerned converge on a central location. Like the bazaar, the Web provides the following:

- *Information search*. International entrepreneurs disseminate their proprietary information regarding new products and emerging trends, and consumers download details with unprecedented speed, facilitating comparative shopping.
- *Updating*. Potential suppliers and buyers quickly update and upgrade their state of information and incorporate their new knowledge to assume a new position.
- *Temporal equilibrium*. Some potential suppliers and buyers behave as intermediaries, and they profit from arbitrage.
- *Opportunity for co-operation*. Again, firms are engaging in co-operative bargaining and negotiations, forming alliances.

With little variation, the style and procedures of Internet searches reflect a pattern. A potential buyer finds several web pages, thus learning about supplies and prices from several suppliers. This allows the individual to form a reasonably informed opinion about the state of the market at the time.

The bazaar was critical to the continued functioning of international entrepreneurship in former times; markets enhanced the efficiency of caravans, by acting as clearing houses. The caravans were thus the predecessors of exporters and export agents, and they manifested many features of modern alliances. In the absence of international law, there was mutual trust and interdependence between entrepreneurs. So too, in the absence of web law, trust is required, as clients rely on the reputation of suppliers and reveal sensitive information to them.

The bazaar agents resembled modern-day importers and import agents, accumulating supplies for normal day-to-day trade, as well as bartering with the caravans. They evidently performed both functions efficiently and reliably, with mutually respect, to the long-term benefit of all parties.

We might add that the bazaar imposed discipline. In the absence of large firms and the current facilities of modern corporations, most agents connected to a bazaar had no choice but to be entrepreneurial. They behaved in ways that we now attribute to creative entrepreneurs, taking and sharing calculated risks, relying on their business network and acting on opportunity, buying or selling as appropriate.

In the bazaar, there was little if any differentiation among clustered sellers. There was considerable co-operation among retailers and among wholesalers. Multi-polar networks were essential for survival, as profitability was a function of personal relationships.

In time, the firm-type economy evolved, shifting the focus from personal relations to impersonal transactions. Everybody was entitled to equal treatment. Rather than haggle over prices, sellers simply posted their firm, non-negotiable, asking prices. Today, once again, we see a focus on status, relationships, price negotiations and multi-polar networks.

On the clustering of producers

In the bazaar, one found the geographical clustering of producers, according to the specialisation of suppliers. This made possible the efficient clearing of products. Transactions ranged from small retail sales to very large and complicated wholesale activities. In time, merchants, intermediaries and even customers found efficiency in specialisation, and this led to geographical clustering.

Typically, a bazaar had an area designated for clothing and another for produce; there was another wing for gold and jewellery, another for carpets, and yet others for spices, fish and so on. Potential buyers and suppliers – of a given good or service – converged on that specific region. Consumers found convenience in the clustering of producers. This facilitated comparative shopping with minimal travel. In medieval towns, streets were often named for the entrepreneurs clustered on them, for example, Bakers Street, Changers' Alley, Fishermen's Wharf, Potato Market, *rue des Bouchers* and so on.

High concentration in a given location is critical to efficiency, as it allows for highly efficient information processing. This includes an information search, a comparative evaluation and decision making. On-line shopping facilitates information search, comparative evaluation and decision making. In the absence of efficient information processing capabilities, geographically scattered markets would tax operational efficiencies. Finding and then accessing geographically scattered suppliers – as compared to having them in a concentrated area – would add to transaction costs; an information search through physical access would become more difficult and limited to one's ability.

Pricing and competition

In the bazaar, the customer first tested price levels informally, and only later began to bargain. Often it was the buyer who proposed a price, which was eventually raised. Once a mutually satisfactory transaction took place, it was desirable to establish a long-term relationship. This made further purchases more pleasurable and efficient. Effective communication was essential, allowing a sale to be equated to pleasure, rather than work.

In the firm-type economy, it is expected of competitors to compete with each other. They often compete on price. One firm asks a lower price than does another, with the hoping of grabbing more market share. Not long ago, British Airways competed with American Airlines in this way.

Nowadays, we see the formation of alliances among former competitors. Consolidators sell tickets at discounted prices, and on the Web potential customers can state the price they wish to pay. As was the case in the bazaar, the buyer proposes the price. Code-sharing blurs product differentiation between airlines. Yet loyalty exists – focused on networks rather than on individual firms. As mentioned earlier, Air Canada, Air New Zealand and British Midland give recognition and special treatment to each other's preferred customers. One fare is valid on any airline of the Star Alliance. Together, acting as a multi-polar network, the members of the Star Alliance compete against members of other alliances. The focus has shifted away from the firm to the multi-polar network.

The parallel economy

Interestingly, multi-polarity applies even to the parallel economy, and this is clearly noticeable in transitional economies. Under central planning, the lack of a legal market economy led to permanent shortages. Survival strategies often involved the emergence of networks in the parallel economy, where inefficient regulations could be circumvented. According to Grossman (1977), this underground activity increased the overall efficiency of resource allocation under central planning. In transitional economies that still lack developed market institutions, it is common to have a high proportion of underground activities. O'Driscoll, Holmes and Kirkpatrick (2001) reported a black market in Laos, larger than the formal economy.

Covert economic activity involves illegal transactions, which often include networks of suppliers, dealers and consumers (Haskell and Yablonsky, 1974; Henry, 1978). Examples include logging in Cambodia and smuggling networks in countries such as the Kyrgyz Republic and Myanmar (O'Driscoll, Holmes and Kirkpatrick, 2001).

Fictitious economic activity (Glinkina, 1999) also involves multi-polar networks. Common in Vietnam, are 'foreign devil companies' involving networks of entrepreneurs inside and outside the republic, in order to benefit from government incentives (Dana, 1999b).

Conclusion

As summarised in Table 3.1, we seem to have come full circle, from the bazaar-type economy (with a focus on relationships and multi-polar networking), to the firm-type economy, and then to the New Economy, in which relationships are important. Multi-polar networking is re-emerging.

Table 3.1 Comparing economies

Bazaar Economy	**Firm-Type Economy**	**Multipolar Network Economy**
Focus on personal relations, alliances and networks	Focus on impersonal transactions	Focus on relationship marketing, alliances and networks
Geographical clustering facilitates information search	Exclusivity clause replaces clustering, complicates comparative shopping	Web allows for easy information search
Flexible prices are negotiated and preferential pricing is based on status and relationships	Prices are indicated by the vendor, and buyers are treated as equals	Flexible prices are negotiated and preferential pricing is based on status and relationships
Would-be competitors co-operate, reinforcing relationship networks	Competition takes place between sellers	Former competitors co-operate for mutual gain, thus reinforcing relationship networks
Brand loyalty is influenced by preferential treatment; brand loyalty – based on relationships – exists even for commodities	Brand loyalty is a function of product differentiation; therefore not applicable to commodities	Brand loyalty is influenced by preferential treatment; brand loyalty – based on relationships – exists even for commodities
Effective unit is the network	Effective unit is the individual firm	Effective unit is the network
Decisions influenced by relationships with members of network; power and control thus decentralised in multipolar networks	Strategic decisions centralised at Head Office; power and control centralised in unipolar fashion, with Head Office central to strategic decision making	Decisions influenced by relationships with members of network; power and control thus decentralised in multipolar networks
Internationalisation takes place along networks of relationships, resulting in a multipolar, decentralised, distribution of power (Dana, 2000b)	Internationalisation takes place under the directives of a centralised Head Office, enabling hierarchic decision making (Buckley & Casson, 1976; Cavusgil, 1980; Dunning, 1973)	Networks facilitate internationalisation, resulting in a multipolar, decentralised distribution of power

The bazaar was rich with personal networks of entrepreneurs. The New Economy, although automated and less personal, also involves clustering. What does this mean for policy makers? Policy will increasingly have to take into account larger geographic regions. In Europe, this has already happened as EU members synchronise their policies. The nation-state is no longer the primary macroeconomic player.

For practitioners the global economy presents countless opportunities; yet it presents also perhaps even more threats. The way to survive is by participating in multi-polar networks. The means to prosper is to be prominent within a network.

For researchers, this also provides new opportunities, but with new caveats. Rather than focus on individuals or firms, researchers will benefit from using the multi-polar network as a unit of analysis. At the microeconomic level, we must all stretch our minds beyond a focus on the firm.

Questions emerging from the chapter

1. What do the bazaar and the New Economy share in common? What are their differences?
2. Explain the concepts of segmentation, as they pertain to different models.
3. What are shortcomings of traditional international business theories?
4. Contrast models of internationalisation.
5. How is the Internet similar to a market?

Bibliography

Acs, Zoltan J. and Leo Paul Dana (2001), 'Contrasting Two Models of Wealth Redistribution', *Small Business Economics* 16 (2), pp. 63–74.

Acs, Zoltan J. and Bernard Yeung (1999), 'Entrepreneurial Discovery and the Global Economy', *Global Focus* 11 (3), pp. 63–71.

Aldrich, Howard E. (1989), 'Networking among Women Entrepreneurs', in Oliver Hagan, Carol Rivchun and Donald L. Sexton, eds, *Women-Owned Businesses*, New York: Praeger, pp. 103–132.

Aldrich, Howard E., Trevor P. Jones and David McEvoy (1984), 'Ethnic Advantage and Minority Business Development', in Robin Ward and Richard Jenkins, eds, *Ethnic Communities in Business: Strategies for Economic Survival*, Cambridge: Cambridge University Press, pp. 189–210.

Aldrich, Howard E., Ben Rosen and William Woodward (1987), 'The Impact of Social Networks on Business Foundings and Profit in a Longitudinal Study', *Frontiers of Entrepreneurship Research*, Wellesley, Massachusetts: Babson College, pp. 154–168.

Aldrich, Howard E. and Catherine Zimmer (1986), 'Entrepreneurship Through Social Networks', in Donald L. Sexton and Raymond W. Smilor, eds, *The Art and Science of Entrepreneurship*, Cambridge, Massachusetts: Ballinger, pp. 3–24.

Axelsson, Bjorn and Geoff Easton, eds (1992), *Industrial Networks: A New View of Reality*, London: Routledge.

Bartlett, Christopher A. and Sumatra Ghoshal (1989), *Managing Across Borders: The Transnational Solution*, Boston, Massachusetts: Harvard Business School Press.

Bilkey, Warren J. (1978), 'An Attempted Integration of the Literature on the Export Behavior of Firms', *Journal of International Business Studies* 9 (1), pp. 33–46.

Bilkey, Warren J. and George Tesar (1977), 'The Export Behavior of Smaller Sized Wisconsin Manufacturing Firms', *Journal of International Business Studies* 8 (1), pp. 93–98.

Blaschke, J. and A. Ersoz (1986), 'The Turkish Economy in West Berlin', *International Small Business Journal* 4 (3), pp. 38–45.

Bodur, Muzaffer and Tage Koed Madsen (1993), 'Danish Foreign Direct Investments in Turkey', *European Business Review* 93 (5), pp. 28–43.

Boissevain, Jeremy and Hanneke Grotenbreg (1987), 'Ethnic Enterprise in the Netherlands: The Surinamese of Amsterdam', in Robert Goffee and Richard Scase, eds, *Entrepreneurship in Europe*, Beckenham, Kent: Croom Helm, pp. 105–130.

Bonaccorsi, Andrea (1992), 'On the Relationship between Firm Size and Export Intensity', *Journal of International Business Studies* 4 (4), pp. 605–635.

Brenner, Gabrielle A. and Jean-Marie Toulouse (1990), 'Business Creation among the Chinese Immigrants in Montreal', *Journal of Small Business and Entrepreneurship* 7 (4), pp. 38–44.

Buckley, Peter J. (1997), 'International Technology Transfer by Small and Medium-Sized Enterprises', *Small Business Economics* 9, pp. 67–78.

Buckley, Peter J. and Mark Casson (1976), *The Future of the Multinational Enterprise*, London: Macmillan.

Buckley, Peter J., Gerald D. Newbould and Jane C. Thurwell (1988), *Foreign Direct Investment by Smaller UK Firms*, London: Macmillan.

Cavusgil, S. Tamer (1980), 'On the Internationalisation Process of Firms', *European Research* 8, pp. 273–281.

Cavusgil, S. Tamer (1984), 'Differences among Exporting Firms Based on Their Degree of Internationalisation', *Journal of Business Research* 12 (2), pp. 195–208.

Cavusgil, S. Tamer and R.J. Nevin (1981), 'International Determinants of Export Marketing Behavior', *Journal of Marketing Research* 28, pp. 114–119.

Coviello, Nicole E. and H.J. Munro (1997), 'Network Relationships and the Internationalisation Process of Small Software Firms', *International Business Review* 6 (2), pp. 1–26.

Dana, Leo Paul (1994), 'A Marxist Mini-Dragon? Entrepreneurship in Today's Vietnam', *Journal of Small Business Management* 32 (2), April, pp. 95–102.
Dana, Leo Paul (1995a), 'Entrepreneurship in a Remote Sub-Arctic Community: Nome, Alaska', *Entrepreneurship: Theory and Practice* 20 (1), pp. 55–72.
Dana, Leo Paul (1995b), 'Small Business in a Non-Entrepreneurial Society: The Case of the Lao People's Democratic Republic (Laos)', *Journal of Small Business Management* 33 (3), July, pp. 95–102.
Dana, Leo Paul (1996), 'Self-Employment in the Canadian Sub-Arctic: An Exploratory Study', *Canadian Journal of Administrative Sciences* 13 (1), March, pp. 65–77.
Dana, Leo Paul (1997), 'Change, Entrepreneurship and Innovation in the Republic of Kazakhstan', *Entrepreneurship, Innovation, and Change* 6 (2), pp. 167–174.
Dana, Leo Paul (1998a), 'Small Business in Xinjiang', *Asian Journal of Business and Information Systems* 3 (1), pp. 123–136.
Dana, Leo Paul (1998b), 'Small But Not Independent: SMEs in Japan', *Journal of Small Business Management* 36 (4), pp. 73–76.
Dana, Leo Paul (1999a), 'Entrepreneurship as a Supplement in the People's Republic of China', *Journal of Small Business Management* 37 (3), pp. 76–80.
Dana, Leo Paul (1999b), *Entrepreneurship in Pacific Asia: Past Present and Future*, Singapore, London and Hong Kong: World Scientific.
Dana, Leo Paul (2000a), 'Change and Circumstance in Kyrgyz Markets', *Qualitative Market Research* 3 (2), pp. 62–73.
Dana, Leo Paul (2000b), *Economies of the Eastern Mediterranean Region: Economic Miracles in the Making*, Singapore, London and Hong Kong: World Scientific.
Dana, Leo Paul (2001), 'Networks, Internationalization and Policy', *Small Business Economics* 16 (2), pp. 57–62.
Dana, Leo Paul and Hamid Etemad (1994), 'A Strategic Response Model for the Internationalisation of Small or Medium-Sized Australian Enterprises', *Bond Management Review* 4 (1), pp. 31–42.
Dana, Leo Paul and Hamid Etemad (1995), 'SMEs – Adapting Strategy for NAFTA: A Model for Small and Medium-Sized Enterprises', *Journal of Small Business and Entrepreneurship* 12 (3), pp. 4–17.
Dubini, Paola and Howard E. Aldrich (1991), 'Personal and Extended Networks are Central to the Entrepreneurship Process', *Journal of Business Venturing* 6 (5), September, pp. 305–313.
Dunning, John H. (1973), 'The Determinants of International Production', *Oxford Economic Papers* 25 (3), pp. 289–336.
Dunning, John H. (1977), 'Trade, Location of Economic Activity and MNE: A Search for an Eclectic Approach', Bertil Ohlin, Per-Ove Hasselborn and Per Magnus Wijkman, eds, *The International Allocation of Economic Activity: Proceedings of A Nobel Symposium Held at Stockholm*, London: Macmillan, pp. 395–418.
Dunning, John H. (1980), 'Toward an Eclectic Theory of International Production: Empirical Tests', *Journal of International Business Studies* 11 (1), pp. 9–31.
Dunning, John H. (1988), 'The Eclectic Paradigm of International Production: A Restatement and Some Possible Extensions', *Journal of International Business Studies* 19, Spring, pp. 1–31.
Evans, Joel R. and Richard L. Laskin (1994), 'The Relationship Marketing Process: A Conceptualization and Application', *Industrial Marketing Management* 23 (5), pp. 432–452.
Fontes, Margarita and Rod Coombs (1997), 'The Coincidence of Technology and Market Objectives in the Internationalisation of New Technology-Based Firms', *International Small Business Journal* 15 (4), pp. 14–35.
Geertz, Clifford (1963), *Peddlers and Princes: Social Development and Economic Change in Two Indonesian Towns*, Chicago, Illinois: University of Chicago Press.
Glinkina, Svetlana (1999), 'Russia's Underground Economy During the Transition', in Edgar L. Feige and Katarina Ott, eds, *Underground Economies in Transition: Unrecorded Activity, Tax, Corruption and Organised Crime*, Aldershot: Ashgate, pp. 101–116.
Gronroos, Christian (1989), 'Defining Marketing: A Market-Oriented Approach', *European Journal of Marketing* 23 (1), pp. 52–60.
Grossman, Gregory (1977), 'The Second Economy of the USSR', *Problems of Communism* 26 (5), pp. 25–40.
Harrison, Bennett (1997), *Lean and Mean*, New York: Gilford.
Haskell, Martin R. and Lewis Yablonsky (1974), *Crime and Delinquency*, Chicago: Rand McNally.
Henry, Stuart (1978), *The Hidden Economy: The Context and Control of Borderline Crime*, London: Martin Robertson.
Johanson, Jan and Lars-Gunnar Mattsson (1988), 'Internationalisation in Industrial Systems – a Network Approach', in N. Hood and Jan-Erik Vahlne, eds, *Strategies in Global Competition*, London: Croom Helm, pp. 287–314.
Johanson, Jan and Lars-Gunnar Mattsson (1992), 'Network Positions and Strategic Action – An Analytical Framework', in Bjorn Axelsson and Geoff Easton, eds, *Industrial Networks: A New View of Reality*, London: Routledge, pp. 205–217.

Johanson, Jan and Jan-Erik Vahlne (1977), 'The Internationalization Process of the Firm – A Model of Knowledge Development and Increasing Foreign Market Commitments', *Journal of International Business Studies* 8 (1), pp. 23–32.
Johanson, Jan and Jan-Erik Vahlne (1990), 'The Mechanism of Internationalisation', *International Marketing Review* 7 (4), pp. 11–24.
Johanson, Jan and Jan-Erik Vahlne (1992), 'Management of Foreign Market Entry', *Scandinavian International Business Review* 1 (3), pp. 9–27.
Johanson, Jan and Finn Wiedersheim-Paul (1975), 'The Internationalisation of the Firm: Four Swedish Cases', *Journal of International Management Studies* 12 (3), October, pp. 305–322.
Kirzner, Israel M. (1973), *Competition and Entrepreneurship*, Chicago: University of Chicago Press.
Kirzner, Israel M. (1982), *Method, Process and Austrian Economics*, Lexington, Massachusetts: Lexington Books.
Ladbury, Sarah (1984), 'Choice, Chance or No Alternative? Turkish Cypriots in Business in London', in Robin Ward and Richard Jenkins, eds, *Ethnic Communities in Business: Strategies for Economic Survival*, Cambridge: Cambridge University Press, pp. 89–124.
Leonidou, Leonidas C. and Constantine S. Katsikeas (1996), 'The Export Development Process', *Journal of International Business Studies* 27 (3), pp. 517–551.
Light, Ivan (1972), *Ethnic Enterprise in America: Business and Welfare Among Chinese, Japanese and Blacks*, Berkeley, California: University of California.
Loewen, James W. (1971), *The Mississippi Chinese: Between Black and White*, Cambridge, Massachusetts: Harvard University Press.
McMillan, John (2002), *Reinventing the Bazaar*, New York: W.W. Norton & Co.
Min, Pyong Gap Min and Charles Jaret (1985), 'Ethnic Business Success: The Case of Korean Small Business in Atlanta', *Sociology and Social Research* 69 (3), pp. 412–435.
Morck, Randal and Bernard Yeung (1991), 'Why Investors Value Multinationality', *Journal of Business* 64 (2), pp. 165–187.
Morck, Randal and Bernard Yeung (1992), 'Internalization: An Event Study Test', *Journal of International Economics* 33, pp. 41–56.
Newbould, Gerald D., Peter J. Buckley and Jane C. Thurwell (1978), *Going International: The Enterprise of Smaller Companies Overseas*, New York: John Wiley and Sons.
O'Driscoll, Gerald P., Kim R. Holmes and Melanie Kirkpatrick (2001), *2001 Index of Economic Freedom*, New York: The Wall Street Journal.
Ray, Denis M., Asley Momijan, W. Ed McMullan and Sylvia Ko (1988), *Comparison of Immigrant Armenian Entrepreneurs in Los Angeles and Immigrant Chinese Entrepreneurs in Calgary*, Faculty of Management Research Papers, Calgary, Canada: University of Calgary.
Reynolds, Paul D. (1997), 'New and Small Firms in Expanding Markets', *Small Business Economics* 9 (1), pp. 79–84.
Rugman, Alan M. (1979), *International Diversification and the Multinational Enterprise*, Lexington, MA: Lexington Books.
Rugman, Alan M. (1981), *Inside the Multinationals: The Economics of Internal Markets*, New York: Columbia University Press.
Sayigh, Yusif A. (1952), *Entrepreneurs of Lebanon*, Cambridge, Massachusetts: Harvard University Press.
Schumpeter, Joseph Allois (1912), *Theorie der wirtschaftlichen Entwicklung*, Munich and Leipzig: Dunker und Humblat.
Schumpeter, Joseph Allois (1928), 'The Instability of Capitalism', *Economic Journal* 38, November, pp. 361–386.
Schumpeter, Joseph Allois (1934), *The Theory of Economic Development*, Cambridge, Massachusetts: Harvard University Press.
Schumpeter, Joseph Allois (1942), *Capitalism, Socialism and Democracy*, New York: Harper and Row.
Schumpeter, Joseph Allois (1947), 'The Creative Response in Economic History', *Journal of Economic History* 7, November, pp. 149–159.
Schumpeter, Joseph Allois (1949), 'Economic Theory and Entrepreneurial History', in *Change and the Entrepreneur*, Cambridge, Massachusetts: Harvard University Press.
Seglin, Jeffrey L. (1990), *The McGraw Hill 36-Hour Marketing Course*, New York: McGraw Hill.
Sharma, D.D. (1992), 'International Business Research: Issues and Trends', *Scandinavian International Business Review* 1 (3), pp. 3–8.
Sharma, D.D. and Jan Johanson (1987), 'Technical Consultancy in Internationalisation', *International Marketing Review* 4 (1), pp. 20–29.
Shenker, Oded (1994), 'The People's Republic of China: Raising the Bamboo Screen Through International Management Research', *International Studies of Management and Organization* 24 (1–2), pp. 9–34.
Teece, David J. (1985), 'Multinational Enterprise, Internal Governance and Economic Organization', *American Economic Review* 75, pp. 233–238.

Weber, Max (1924), *The Theory of Social and Economic Organization*, New York: The Free Press.
Webster, Frederick E. (1992), 'The Changing Role of Marketing in the Corporation', *Journal of Marketing* 53, October, pp. 1–17.
Welch, Denice and Lawrence S. Welch (1996), 'Internationalization Process and Networks: A Strategic Management Perspective', *Journal of International Marketing* 4 (3), pp. 11–28.
Welch, Lawrence S. (1992), 'The Use of Alliances by Small Firms in Achieving Internationalisation', *Scandinavian International Business Review* 1 (2), pp. 21–37.
Welch, Lawrence S. and Reijo K. Luostarinen (1988), 'Internationalisation: Evolution of a Concept', *Journal of General Management* 14 (2), pp. 34–55.
Welch, Lawrence S. and Reijo K. Luostarinen (1993), 'Inward-Outward Connections in Internationalization', *Journal of International Marketing* 1 (1), pp. 44–56.
Werbner, Pnina (1984), 'Business in Trust: Pakistani Entrepreneurship in the Manchester Garment Trade', in Robin Ward and Richard Jenkins, eds, *Ethnic Communities in Business: Strategies for Economic Survival*, Cambridge, Cambridge University Press, pp. 166–188.
Wilkinson, Ian F., Lars-Gunnar Mattsson and Geoff Easton (2000), 'International Competitiveness and Trade Promotion Policy from a Network Perspective', *Journal of World Business* 35 (3), pp. 275–299.
Williamson, Oliver E. (1985), *The Economic Institutions of Capitalism*, New York: Free Press.
Williamson, Oliver E. (1996), *The Mechanisms of Governance*, New York: Oxford University Press.
Wong, Bernard (1987), 'The Role of Ethnicity in Enclave Entrepreneurs: A Study of the Chinese Garment Factory in New York City', *Human Organization* 66 (2), pp. 120–130.
Wright, Richard W. (1989), 'Networking, Japanese Style', *Business Quarterly*, 54 (2), 20–24.
Zineldin, Mosad Amin (1998), 'Towards an Ecological Collaborative Relationship Management', *European Journal of Marketing* 32 (11–12), pp. 1138–1164.

4 Trade trends in Transatlantica: a profile of SMEs in the United States and Europe

Leslie E. Palich and D. Ray Bagby

Introduction

Small and medium-sized enterprises (SMEs) have long found opportunities in the global economy; and as international business has expanded, these opportunities have grown in proportion (Karagozoglu and Lindell, 1998). Today, however, globalization is doing more than creating a new global market that is merely a larger version of yesterday's marketplace. New forces and economic structures are combining to produce global business opportunities that are quantitatively greater and qualitatively different. To operate most effectively in the modern world economy, SMEs need to develop an awareness of its changing nature.

The purpose of this chapter is to provide a profile of the international activities of SMEs in the United States and Europe and to identify and explore a number of changes affecting global potentials for these firms, as reflected in secondary data compiled by the U.S. International Trade Administration and the Observatory of European SMEs. In their contribution to the *Harvard Business Review*, Hermann Simon and Max Otte (2000) referred to the combined region addressed in this study as 'Transatlantica', recognizing that these two major trade blocs have more than an ocean in common. Compared to other nations in the world (including the advanced economies of Asia), 'Transatlantica's countries are much further along in restructuring their trade portfolios around specialized industrial goods' (Simon and Otte, 2000, p. 20). They have many similarities. But despite the parallels, there are also very real differences between the two regions, as our analysis will indicate. Nonetheless, available statistics on SMEs in these two regions are comparable in depth and timeliness and thus offer a reasonable foundation for an assessment of trade trends for these firms. Following a brief description of the source studies upon which we base our research, we report the findings of our analysis of SME trade, which encompasses the nature and extent of firm internationalization and the reasons for this expansion.

A description of source studies

As mentioned above, we lean heavily on data from two major reports in constructing our analysis. Though we cite findings and conclusions from additional sources throughout the chapter, our research is especially indebted to assessments funded by the governments of the United States and the European Union. The first of these is *Small and Medium-sized Exporting Companies: A Statistical Handbook*,[1] which was prepared by staff of the Office of Trade and Economic Analysis at the International Trade Administration (ITA). It is based on statistics generated from the U.S. Commerce Department's Exporter Data Base, which provides a snapshot of American exporting companies – for example, their number, size, industry composition, geographic distribution and other features. We used the 2003 report, a summary based on the latest available data from all firms that could be identified from Shippers' Export Declarations filed in compliance with U.S. regulations, which yielded 238 284 exporting firms[2] and accounted for 85 per cent of all measurable merchandise export value.[3]

Though based on a smaller number of firms, we also used the *2003 Observatory of European SMEs: 2003/4 Internationalisation of SMEs*[4] study to pull together statistics on European SMEs. This report, funded by the European Commission, is extensive and offers uniform data on SMEs from 19 European countries – that is, the then 15 countries of the EU, plus the four member nations of the European Free Trade Area. The report is based on data from 7745 SMEs, a sample that was stratified by industry, enterprise size and country. Overrepresentation of certain countries, sectors and size classes was corrected using appropriate weightings, and all reported percentages refer to weighted findings.

These two reports are similar in that both are government sponsored and are based on data from a large number of firms and from roughly the same time frame (that is, both reports were published in 2003). However, there are obvious differences as well. Of course, the U.S. report focused on firms from a single country, but the EU study included SMEs from 19 nations. Though many refer to the EU as 'The United States of Europe', these nations still represent a wide range of social, technological, economic and political histories and leanings. Beyond this, the Observatory study was designed to analyze a sample of SMEs – albeit an ample and representative subset – whereas the ITA report included data from the entire population of exporting firms and thus is much larger in size and scope. In any case, both studies are of sufficient scale to offer reliable insights into internationalized SMEs in Transatlantica.

It is important to note that the EU report considered internationalization in all its forms, whereas the U.S. report focused on export activity alone, and then only on merchandise rather than services. The U.S. report is also different in that it compares data representing ten years of export activity; the EU report focuses on responses of study participants from a single year. Finally, the two reports use different definitions for SME size categories. The U.S. study defines small companies as those having fewer than 100 employees and medium-sized firms as having 100–499 employees – the groups combined being SMEs. Large firms are those having 500 or more employees, while very small companies have fewer than 20 employees. In the EU study, SMEs includes firms with fewer than 250 employees, which breaks down into micro enterprises (0–9 employees), small companies (10–49 employees) and medium-sized companies (50–249). In our opinion, these definitional differences are not problematic; nonetheless, the reader should keep them in mind while assessing our findings and conclusions.

The expanding global reach of SMEs

Research has shown that even the smallest of businesses are internationalizing at an increasing rate (McDougall and Oviatt, 1999). In fact, start-ups in most of the trading countries of the world are increasingly being launched with cross-border business activities in mind – the 'born-global' trend (Autio, Sapienza and Almeida, 2000; Etemad and Wright, 2003). Entrepreneurs are focusing more on international business as global communications and transportation become more efficient and as trade agreements pry open national markets to foreign competition. Research indicates that size does not necessarily limit a firm's international activity (for example, Verwaal and Donkers, 2002; Wolf and Pett, 2000) and that SMEs often become global competitors to take advantage of their unique resources (Gomez-Casseres, 1997; Pope, 2002).

Blancco Ltd, a Finnish company that specializes in data security and erasure services, exemplifies the 'new breed' of start-up. Launched in 1997 by two university students, the company commercialized its first software application in 1999 and quickly recognized that the real growth potential was in international markets. By 2001, the new business employed 13 people and generated 760 000 euros ($950 000) in annual revenue, 40 per cent of which was from exports. Looking forward, the founders hope to focus first on expanding the business in nations with markets similar to Finland's and then to create strategies tailored to the information protection needs of the individual country markets they have targeted. Internationalization is clearly an important component of the business expansion plans of small companies like Blancco, and the prevailing trend indicates that this approach is likely to become even more common in the future (Nummela, 2002).

Data from the ITA report show that the international business involvement of SMEs is rapidly accelerating. Between 1987 and 2001 the number of SMEs participating in exporting grew by 250 per cent, from 65 871 to 230 736. This latter number accounts for 97 per cent of all U.S. exporters (as indicated in Figure 4.1) and, relative to large firms, the number of SME exporters grew nearly twice as fast between 1992 and 2001. That is, exporting SMEs increased by 113.6 per cent during this period (compared to 56.3 per cent for large firms), and SME export revenues surged from $103 billion to $182 billion.

Most exporting SMEs are surprisingly small. More than two-thirds of all U.S. exporters (69 per cent) have fewer than 20 employees (for a detailed breakdown, see Figure 4.2). This statistic is even more noteworthy when considering that the data are based on merchandise exporters only and do not include services, where smaller firms are likely to participate. Furthermore, this figure does not include importing, an activity in

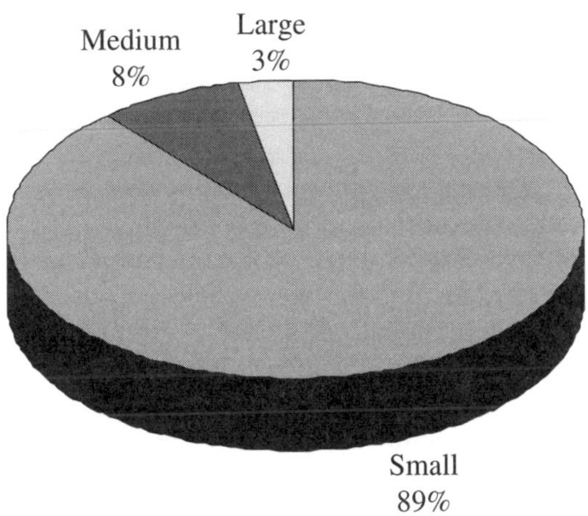

Notes:
1. 238 284 companies exported goods from the U.S. in 2001
2. small = less than 100 employees; medium = 100–499 employees; large = 500 or more employees

Source: U.S. Dept. of Commerce, Exporter Data Base

Figure 4.1 Size composition of U.S. exporting companies, 2001

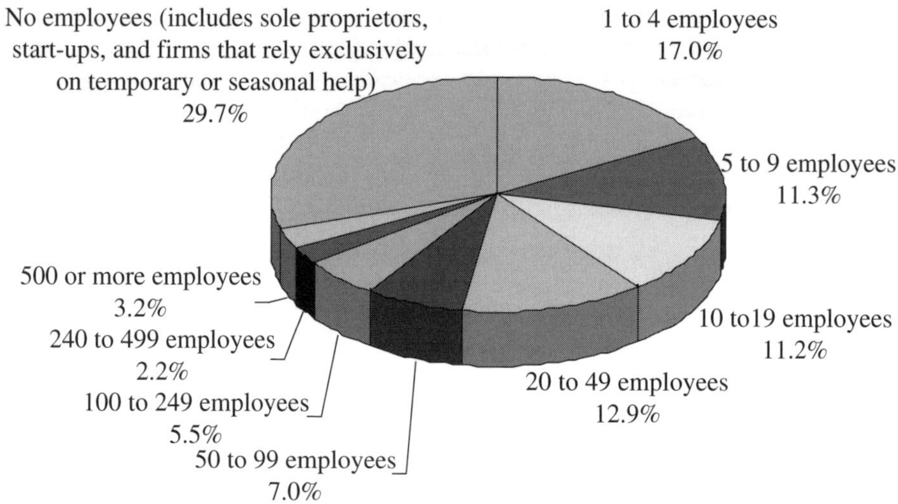

Note: 238 284 companies exported goods from the U.S. in 2001

Source: U.S. Department of Commerce, Exporter Data Base

Figure 4.2 Percentage of U.S. exporting firms in 2001 by number of employees

which Observatory data suggest smaller firms are even more apt to be involved. Thirty per cent of international SMEs in the EU study engaged solely in importing versus 18 per cent in exporting alone; however, export and import activity are more frequently found in combination, which seems to indicate that one promotes the other, an interpretation that is supported by a Dutch study (Elk and Overweel, 1991). This correlation is less than consistent across industry sectors (see Figure 4.3), but these data underscore the main thrust of this section: SMEs in Transatlantica are far more internationalized than common perceptions suggest.

The EU report reveals that only 17 per cent of the micro enterprises (0–9 employees) in their sample had exports or exports in combination with other forms of international business. This number increases to 38 per cent for small companies (10–49 employees) and 51 per cent for medium-sized firms (50–249 employees). Thus, firm size seems to have a significant impact of the internationalization activity of European firms. Furthermore, export intensity (that is, exports as a percentage of total sales) increases with firm size (see Figure 4.4), though these size-related differences are less striking than those related to internationalization. Regarding similarities to American firms, though, we caution the reader that it is difficult to make meaningful comparisons with the ITA data because the US study includes only exporters and uses different firm-size definitions.

SMEs in the United States account for almost 30 per cent of the country's total exports, in dollar terms. Thus, it is worth remembering that although large firms constitute only 3 per cent of all exporters, they produce over 70 per cent of the value in exporting. This is consistent with the global spread of large firm exports. In 2001, 63 per cent of SME exporters traded with only one other country, while 54 per cent of large firms exported goods to five or more foreign markets. Still, SME revenue from exporting rose by 77 per cent

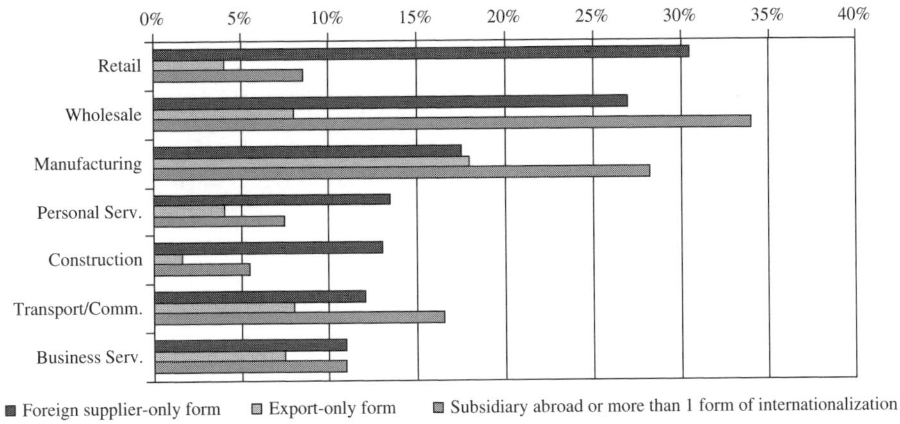

Source: ENSR Enterprise Survey, 2003

Figure 4.3 Internationalization in different sectors

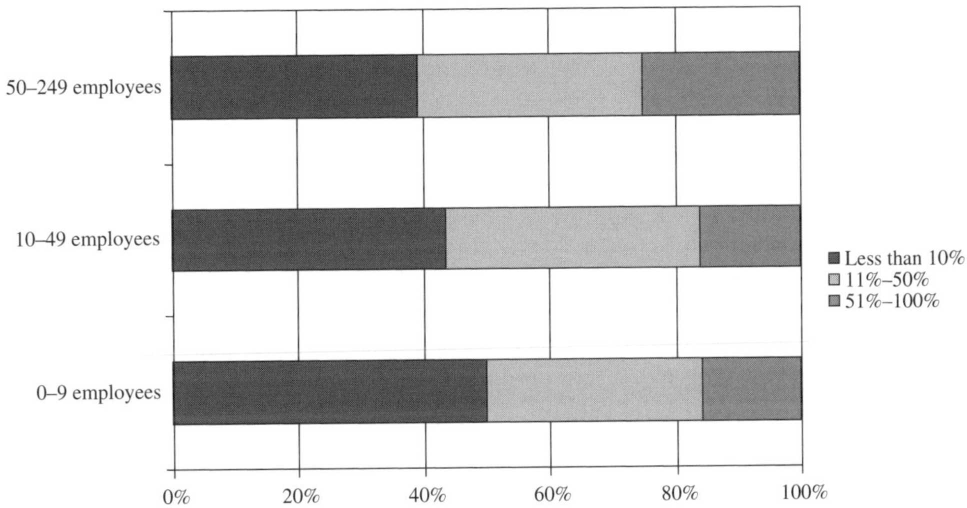

Source: ENSR Enterprise Survey, 2003

Figure 4.4 Export intensity (export in % of total turnover) by size

from 1992 to 2001, and most of these SMEs (90 per cent) achieved these results from a single location as opposed to setting up operations in multiple locations.

In all product groups, the majority of U.S. exporters are SMEs; however, there are some notable differences between categories. For example, SMEs have more than a 90 per cent share in the manufacture of machinery, computers and electronic products, and transportation equipment. They also maintain a dominant share in sectors such as wood products, apparel manufacturing, and printing and related goods. It should also be noted that more than two-thirds of the SMEs are non-manufacturers, and these companies had

60 per cent of total SME exports. And since SMEs constitute 93 per cent of high-tech exporters, it is reasonable to conclude that this category of firms is crucial to the commercialization of cutting-edge products. To provide a broad picture of the industries represented in the ITA study, Figure 4.5 provides a profile of the products exported and the number of SMEs involved with each.

As mentioned above, almost two-thirds of American SME exporters sold to just one foreign market in 2001, and nearly half of all SME merchandise exports that year were directed to four primary markets, to wit: Canada ($37 billion), Mexico ($23 billion), Japan ($16 billion) and the United Kingdom ($9 billion). The European Union accounted for a sizeable 19 per cent of the total market of SMEs, with the preferred location of entry being the UK, followed by the Benelux region, France and Germany, in that order (Prater and Ghosh, 2005); however, NAFTA countries took in about one-third of all SME exports (see Figure 4.6), and these geographically-connected markets accounted for the largest dollar gains during the 1992–2001 period. However, in terms of percentage change in exports, the fastest growing markets for American SMEs during this same time period were Brazil (242 per cent), Switzerland (227 per cent), and Malaysia (220 per cent). One additional observation from the ITA data reveals the important role American SMEs play in a number of small country markets around the world. For example, these companies account for more than 90 per cent of the total exports to Guinea-Bissau, Tajikistan, Somalia and Kyrgyzstan, while dominating 15 other nations (that is, providing 75–90 per cent of the exports to those markets).

The response of SMEs in Transatlantica to the call of business opportunity around the globe has been robust, but the degree of that expansion varies substantially among the European countries. Using import and/or export activity to index internationalization, the Observatory study reveals that this variable is linked to the size of the country in which the SME is domiciled (see Figure 4.7). For example, more than 50 per cent of the SMEs in Luxembourg, Liechtenstein, Ireland and Switzerland do business with foreign suppliers, and of the nine most export-oriented countries (those with 20 per cent or more SMEs that export), only Germany is large. This is consistent with national studies that have suggested that SMEs with specialized production quickly learn that the domestic market provides limited opportunity for expansion, which then forces these companies to look to international countries to support their business ambitions (Braunerhjelm, 2000; O'Malley and O'Gorman, 2001; Elk and Overweel, 1991).

The expanding global strategy options of SMEs

In the past, SMEs typically reached the world via exporting, and this continues to be an important mode of entry; however, during the past decade internationalization has become a much more differentiated business activity. For example, Fletcher (2001) found that the majority of firms in his study were involved with both outward (for example, exporting) and inward (for example, importing or knowledge accessing) activities in their international dealings. Reflecting this trend, the Observatory study sorted SMEs into four groups: (1) importers only, (2) exporters only, (3) SMEs with subsidiaries, branches or joint ventures abroad, or those engaged in multiple forms of internationalization, and (4) non-internationalized SMEs. Obviously, companies falling into group three engaged in more complex forms of internationalization. As indicated in Figure 4.8, the majority of responding SMEs were classified as non-internationalized,

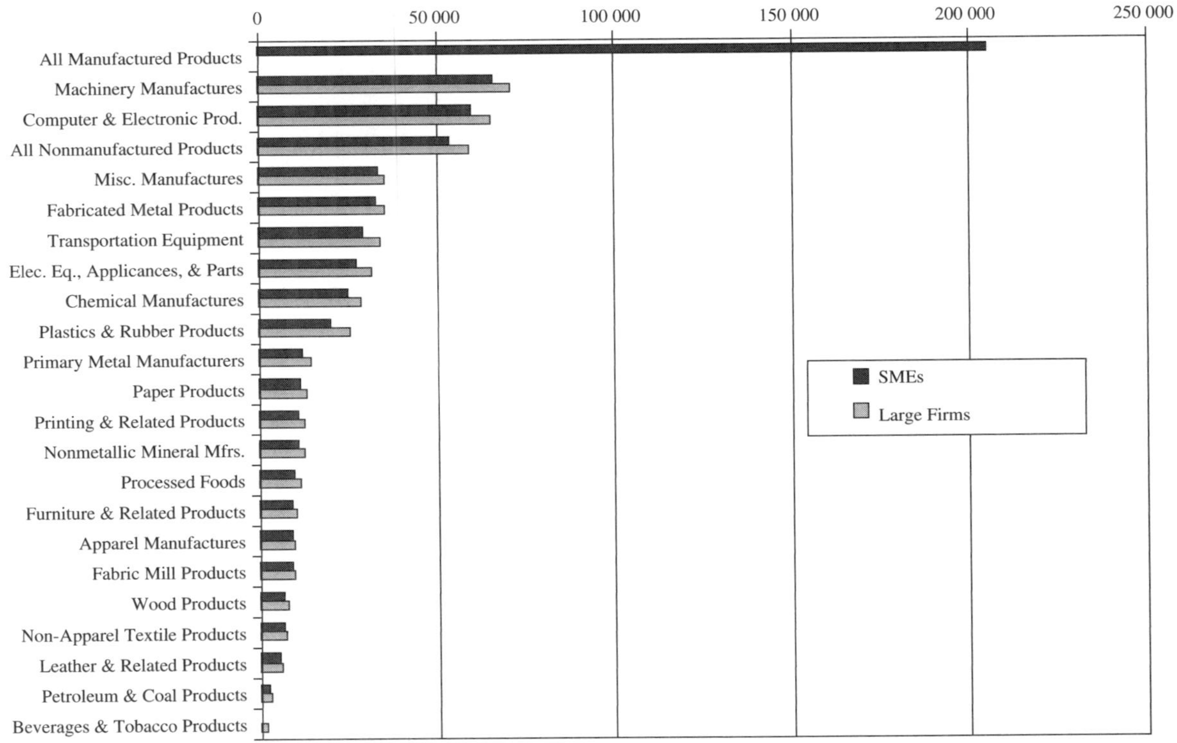

Notes:
1. Definitions: Small and medium-sized enterprises (SMEs) have fewer than 49 employees. Large firms have 50 or more employees.
2. Because firms sometimes export multiple products, exporter count cannot be summed to arrive at a U.S. total.
3. 230 736 SMEs exported goods from the U.S. in 2001

Source: U.S. Department of Commerce, Exporter Data Base

Figure 4.5 Number of exporting firms by manufactured product category, 2001

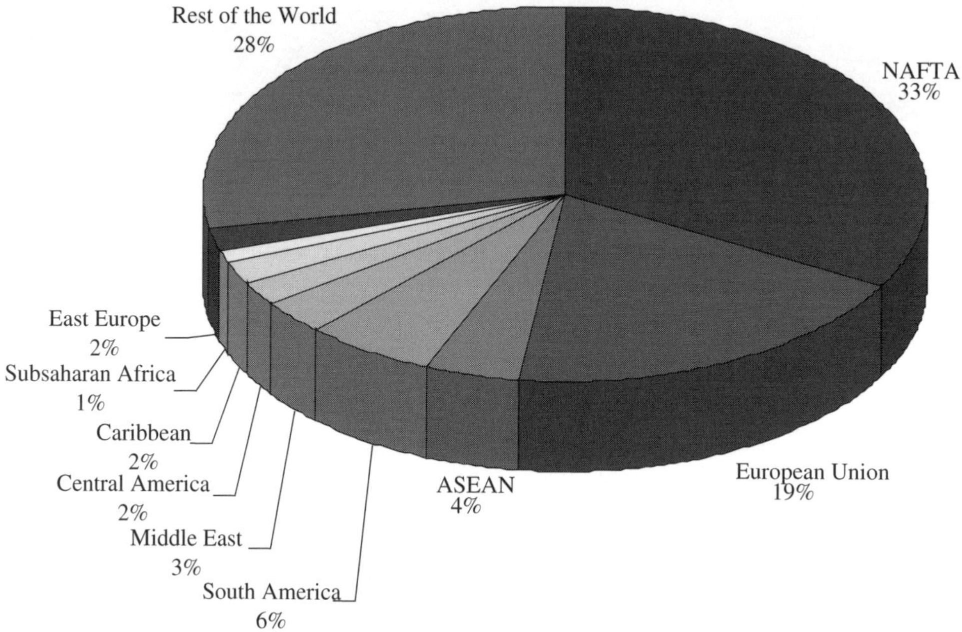

Notes:
1. Definition: Small and medium-sized enterprises (SMEs) have fewer than 500 employees.
2. Figures include only identifiable or 'known' exports – i.e., exports that can be linked to individual firms using information on U.S. declarations.
3. Known value of U.S. merchandise exports from SMEs in 2001 was $182 billion

Source: U.S. Department of Commerce, Exporter Data Base

Figure 4.6 Percentage of total known SME exports sent to world regions, 2001

but it is interesting to note that three times more SMEs import from foreign suppliers compared to the number of exporters, which is often considered the mainstay of SME internationalization.

Outlined below are some of the common strategic options exercised by SMEs that enter the arena of international business. We emphasize, however, that our discussion of these strategies is not exhaustive; rather, these observations simply represent the findings of the two major source studies and other research that informs this discussion.

Export initiatives

In the mid-1960s, international business authority Raymond Vernon observed that American firms introduce new products in the United States and Europe first and later sell them in less-advanced countries as demand in the home market declines (Vernon, 1996). In other words, extending the product life cycle often required global expansion.

The logic of Vernon's framework still applies under some circumstances, but it may no longer provide a sound justification for going global in many of today's international markets. For example, cutting-edge technologies may be as likely to originate in Finland or Singapore as in the United States, indicating market potential in many countries at

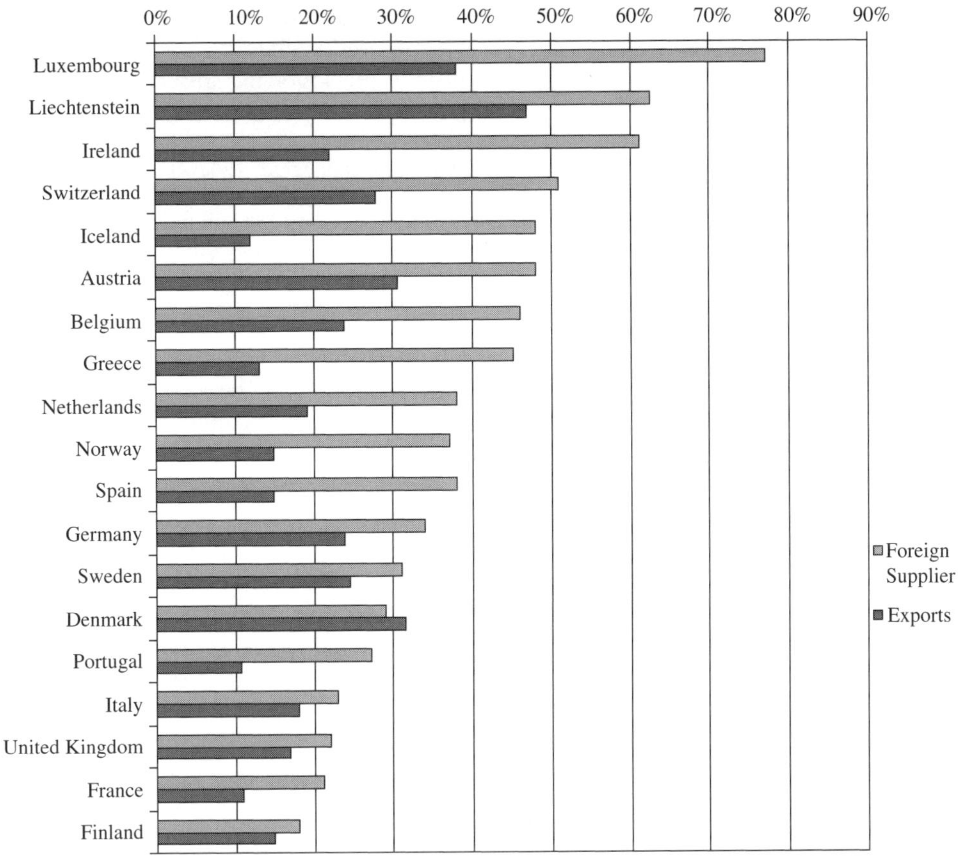

Note: The categories are not mutually exclusive, since one SME may have both export and a foreign supplier.

Source: ENSR Enterprise Survey, 2003

Figure 4.7 Percentage of SMEs with foreign supplier or exports

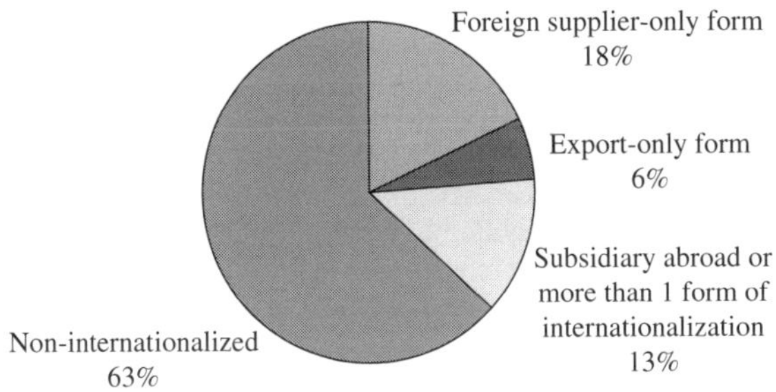

Source: ENSR Enterprise Survey, 2003

Figure 4.8 The prevalence of different forms of internationalization among SMEs

once. And because product life cycles are shrinking, calculated and sequential, market entry planning is more challenging than ever. That is, product life cycle thinking may need to be adjusted to 21st century realities. Consider the following observations of the common scenario today.

> The time lag between U.S. and foreign adoption has . . . disappeared. Today it is essential to roll out new products in several countries simultaneously. . . . No longer does the small company have the luxury of using cash flow from domestic sales to support the building of international marketing a few years later. The ever-shortening product cycle virtually dooms such a strategy. Terrific. Now, in addition to getting the product to work, setting up your new team, getting some U.S. customers, and finding money, you now have to worry about selling in six or eight additional countries, most of whom don't even speak English! (Baty and Blake, 2003, p. 166).

The challenges of operating an SME in a global economy may be great, but these are offset by favorable conditions – for example, the falling costs of communication (Birch, 1999) and increasing government assistance (Foley, 2004).

Increasingly, small firms are entering the realm of international business, especially where customer preferences, income levels and delivery systems are becoming more similar. Television programs, movies and print media shape cultural tastes throughout the world as consumers learn about the lifestyles of others. These influences have spawned globalization by leading the world toward common consumer preferences (Levitt, 1983; Jeannet, 2000), which should ease the way into international opportunities. If markets are globalized, products that sell at home are more likely to sell abroad, with little or no adaptation. This may explain the variation in export intensity reported by European firms according to industry sector (see Figure 4.9). Observatory data show that SMEs in the transport and communication and manufacturing sectors are very engaged in export activity, which is predictable since these products are likely to suit the needs of a global market. In contrast, retail and construction sectors require greater adaptation to local markets and thus exhibit far lower export intensity.

Many SMEs internationalize via exporting, including indirect exporting through intermediaries such as export agents, export merchants, export management firms and export trading firms (Shenkar and Luo, 2004). As mentioned earlier, the decision to sell abroad is often driven by inadequate market potential at home, which translates to greater use of exporting by firms domiciled in small countries. The Observatory report lends support to this conclusion:

> in four relatively small countries, more than 30 per cent of the SMEs export (Liechtenstein, Luxembourg, Denmark, and Austria). Of the nine most export oriented countries (with a share of more than 20 per cent of exporting SMEs), Germany is the only large country. Several national studies (Braunerhjelm [2000], O'Malley and O'Gorman [2001], Elk and Overweel [1991]) stress that the size of the domestic market is a very decisive factor for internationalization. SMEs with a specialized production or some large scale production very soon find that the demand on the domestic market is insufficient for building a sound business. Tendencies towards increasing specialization will probably push an increasing number of SMEs into international business (p. 16).

The ITA study does not offer comparable data because it includes only exporters and thus does not provide the same statistics for American firms. But, again, the report shows that the lion's share of exporters in the United States are SMEs (representing over 97 per cent

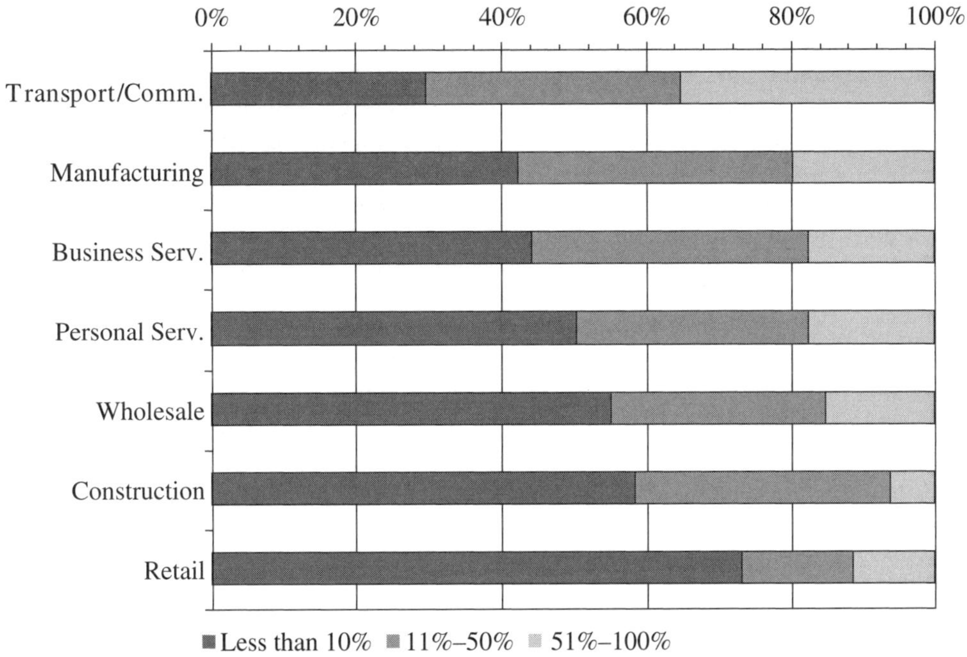

Source: ENSR Enterprise Survey, 2003

Figure 4.9 Export intensity (export as % of total turnover) by sector

of the total), and the number of firms following this strategy is growing rapidly, having increased 113.6 per cent between 1992 and 2001.

Regarding the impact of limited home markets on the decision to internationalize, this dynamic seems to apply to SME foreign direct investment as well as to exporting decisions. For example, Fujita (1998) found that 20.3 per cent of European SMEs identified small markets at home as a factor motivating their investment abroad, compared to 5.8 per cent of SMEs in North America. Given the size disparity between the American market and the individual country markets of Europe, home market limitations seem to play a substantive role in leading SMEs to internationalize.

This trend is illustrated by the experience of Eko-Bio, a natural pharmaceuticals SME in the Netherlands that was founded in 1994 and now has 40 employees. Using a combination of direct and indirect exports (for example, shipping directly to the German market but accessing the Spanish market using one of the top local pharmaceutical distributors there), the company got into the exporting game to enhance its competitiveness. The cost of R&D in the industry is high, but amortizing this expense across a small market like the Netherlands made it impossible to offer products at an acceptable price. The only workable solution was to sell products in multiple markets. Today the company exports its offerings to Germany, France, Spain and South Korea, and it is hoping to break into Scandinavia and elsewhere in Europe. Eko-Bio might not have considered tackling the challenges of exporting its products to other countries if the Netherlands had been able to absorb all that the company could produce.

International sourcing trends

Some SMEs go abroad to obtain resources necessary to operations, like the Oriental rug dealer who scours the markets of Morocco to locate low-cost sources of high-quality Persian carpets. Others are more focused on activities even further upstream, such as gaining access to essential raw materials and other factors of production. For example, in recent years energy-intensive aluminum processors have relocated to Iceland to tap the country's abundant and inexpensive hydroelectric and geothermal power (Bagole, 2001), and a great deal of attention has been paid recently to international outsourcing, especially in low-wage countries such as China and India (Laudicina, 2005). Indeed, the Observatory study found that sourcing abroad was the most common form of internationalization reported by European SMEs.

Beyond raw materials and skilled labor, some of the benefits of location are the result of unique features of a local environment that fit within a distinctive constellation of factors (Porter, 1990). For example, Italian artisans are well known for their design capabilities, Japanese firms have been able to harness optical technologies for application in both cameras and copiers, and Silicon Valley in Northern California provides extremely fertile ground for technology-based innovations. It is not a single factor that presents an advantage; rather, it can be several. Thus, SMEs that depend on these basic strengths may find that location matters.

In any case, the numbers show that sourcing from abroad, in its various forms, is the most common mode of internationalization for European SMEs. Indeed, Observatory data reveal that 49 per cent of internationalized SMEs in Europe are engaged in foreign sourcing alone, which is much higher than the 16 per cent that pursue only exporting; 27 per cent have both foreign suppliers and exports. And as with exporting, the Observatory report indicates that the size of the SME's home is key to the decision to source abroad, with smaller countries demonstrating a greater need to find outside suppliers (see Figure 4.7). Furthermore, the same study reports that firms are looking for overseas sourcing partners with healthy networks of contacts that can link the buyer with improved technology and enhanced market insights (p. 10).

As mentioned earlier, the Observatory study shows that international sourcing is often found in combination with exporting. This dynamic is illustrated in the experience of Apple Boxer S.A., a Greek undergarment maker that was started in the late 1980s and today employs more than 75 people. Within a few years of its founding the company was exporting products to the Netherlands, Germany, Belgium, the Czech Republic and Cyprus, but recently the company has had to make some adjustments to its export program. Because of its high production costs and in response to intensified competition from abroad, Apple Boxer was forced to discontinue its direct exports to all markets but Cyprus and to explore options for sourcing from countries with low-cost manufacturing – specifically, China, where production costs are 65 per cent lower. The road to cheap sourcing has created its own unique set of headaches, including transportation delays and bureaucratic impediments, and these have forced the company to keep its core production line at home – but the advantages far outweigh the drawbacks. Today, with its reduced cost structure and strengthened competitive position, the company has been able to negotiate more favorable terms with Greek sub-suppliers, expand its domestic sales and reorganize its distribution system in Cyprus Observatory study – see note 1. The future is full of opportunities, the result of a new international sourcing system that complements the firm's evolving export program.

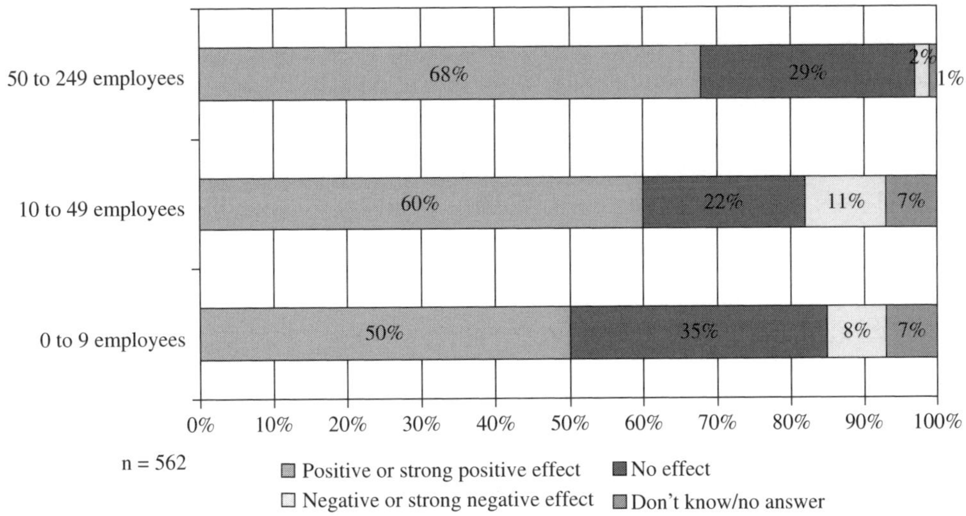

Source: ENSR Enterprise Survey, 2003

Figure 4.10 Effect of foreign subsidiaries on sales, by enterprise size

Cost-cutting initiatives

Sometimes firms internationalize to reduce their cost of doing business, such as those related to raw materials, labor and manufacturing overheads. David Kirkham owns Kirkham Motor Sports Inc. This small company's ten employees complete the final assembly of high-performance Cobra automobiles at its Utah-based facility. To be cost-competitive, however, the firm established an overseas subsidiary to relocate the labor-intensive production of aluminum car bodies and frames to a MiG (Russian fighter jet) factory in Mulec, Poland, where 40 workers apply their advanced metal-fabrication skills to turn out these automotive works of art (Birch, 1999).

Proportionately few SMEs actually set up subsidiaries abroad. In most European countries, only 1–4 per cent of SMEs have taken this bold step, leaving larger SMEs to reap the greatest economic benefits from direct investment (see Figure 4.10). The proportion of SMEs with overseas subsidiaries exceeds 6 per cent in only three countries in Europe – 7 per cent in Switzerland, 9 per cent in Denmark and 11 per cent in Iceland – each of which are small countries with very open economies (Observatory report, 2004, p. 17). But a closer look at the data offers some insight into the purpose of these subsidiaries abroad:

> It is worth noticing that . . . more than one third of the SMEs with subsidiaries abroad . . . have no exports. This demonstrates that the creation of subsidiaries abroad is not merely a question of getting a sales platform for the company's products. Foreign subsidiaries can just as well be a platform for access to cheap labour (e.g., via sub-suppliers) or to access knowledge and technology (p. 15).

This highlights the importance of cost management for SMEs, an increasingly important factor for competitiveness (Laudicina, 2005).

Kirkham Motor Sports went global to control costs by locating labor-intensive operations in low-wage countries, but the critical factor is not always labor. For example, transportation costs would probably be the controlling factor for an SME that sells cement products used in construction (for example, concrete columns, bridge girders and formed statuary), goods that are extremely heavy but do not command a premium price. Since the cost of overseas transportation could exceed the price of the product, international sales may make sense only if the firm locates production in-country and near customers.

The emerging foci of international SMEs

Competition in the 21st century requires competencies that once were of little interest to SMEs. And going beyond the traditional drivers detailed above to emphasize emerging motivations for international business can certainly make going global more interesting. One international entrepreneurship expert describes the motivations to internationalize as follows:

> Certainly the overall motivation is increased sales, but that is the simple answer. A more complex analysis opens the door to the real fun – the larger game. Ultimately the goal of global trade is to expand the scope and reach of your company so that the tools and resources available to fight your competition give your company an unbeatable edge – an edge that renews and transforms itself faster than the competition can keep up (Foley, 2004, p. 5).

To put it differently, SMEs get involved in international business to do more than expand profitable markets. It is also becoming important to consider the new dynamics of the competitive environment. These businesses are no longer insulated from global challengers, especially in the age of the Internet. Therefore, it is important to adjust to emerging realities by recognizing dynamic markets around the world that are beginning to open and then locating near those business opportunities (Karagozoglu and Lindell, 1998). And since new technologies, competencies and experiences are essential to performance and can be costly to obtain, it becomes important to develop these competitive potentials and recover the investment over a larger market (Qian, 2002). These changes in the world of business are further promoting an interest in going global.

Changing market configurations

To develop market opportunities outside the home country, SMEs typically search for those countries with the greatest commercial potential. In the past this involved expanding into developed countries (those with high levels of widely distributed wealth), but companies are now paying greater attention to emerging markets where income and buying power are growing rapidly (Luo, 2000). The U.S. Department of Commerce has labelled the largest of these countries as Big Emerging Markets (see Table 4.1).

Due to their immense populations and potential market demand, countries such as China and India have attracted the greatest attention. Combined, these two nations account for nearly 40 per cent of the world's 6 billion inhabitants, fertile ground for international expansion. SMEs are among the competitors battling for position in these emerging markets. Indeed, the ITA report reveals that of the 15 most important export markets for SMEs in the U.S., four of these – Brazil, China, Mexico and South Korea – are Big Emerging Markets. This trend is illustrated by Dahlgren & Co., a medium-sized

Table 4.1 Big emerging markets

Country	2002 Population (in millions)	2002 Wealth (GNI per capita)	2001–2002 Economic Growth (GDP Growth, %)
Argentina	36.5	4220	−10.9
Brazil	174.5	2830	1.5
China	1300	960	8.0
India	1000	470	4.6
Indonesia	211.7	710	3.7
Mexico	100.8	5920	0.9
Poland	38.6	4570	3.0
South Africa	45.3	2500	3.0
South Korea	47.6	9930	6.3
Turkey	69.6	2400	7.8
World	**6200**	**5120**	**1.9**

Source: Adapted from The World Bank Group, *World Development Indicators*, 2003, http://www.worldbank.org/data/countrydata/glossary.html, 4 June 2004.

company of 170 employees in Crookston, Minnesota that specializes in custom processing, roasting, flavoring and packaging of sunflower seed products. But as an international business, 50 per cent of the firm's $50 million in sales comes from exports sold in more than 30 countries around the world. Dahlgren & Co. has specifically targeted the market in China because of its potential, which may explain why its web site features Chinese, as well as English languages (Klein, 2000).

Leveraging competitive advantage

SMEs are usually niche players that pursue opportunities passed over by large firms due to neglect, inadequate expertise or high cost structures (Shenkar and Luo, 2004). Many SMEs offer highly differentiated products with underlying technological advantages (Pope, 2002); in fact, recall that the ITA study confirms that over 93 per cent of all high-tech exporters in the U.S. are SMEs, and these account for 19 per cent of total high-tech export revenue (ITA report, pp. 2, 18).

An SME possesses a competitive advantage when its products or services are superior to those of competitors. However, the firm's strength in the home market may translate well to international markets that are uniquely suited to the product offered. The cost of developing a competitive advantage is rising, reflecting the increasing cost of technology and demand for sophisticated products. These markets also desire differentiated products that satisfy their unique needs and interests (Verwaal and Donkers, 2002). Because fewer consumers in the home market would be interested in a highly-differentiated (and often more expensive) product, it may become necessary to search for international markets with the same unique demand to increase sales and recover product development costs (Qian, 2002). Therefore, some SMEs find that international expansion is now essential to good performance. Because they follow more focused business strategies (with limited domestic market potential) and often aspire to grow rapidly, efforts to exploit competitive advantage across international markets may be even more important to SMEs than to their large counterparts (Shrader, Oviatt and McDougall, 2000; Zacharakis, 1997).

This is especially true when the domestic market is small to begin with, which is suggested by the data in Figure 4.7.

Martin Goodwin and Bob Henry, founders of MSS Global, understand the potential of a global niche. Their U.S.-based company sells *Retail*, a software program they created in 1993 to help retailers efficiently track inventory, calculate pricing, gather customer data and measure cashier productivity. The market interest for this focused product in the U.S. was healthy, but nonetheless limited, leaving MSS Global with scant opportunity to recover development costs. To overcome this constraint, Goodwin and Henry decided to go global. Using strategic partnerships, MSS Global managed to sell nearly 25 000 licenses in 20 countries before the close of the year 2000, and the growth continues. Because half of its annual revenue comes from international markets, MSS Global can attest to the importance of going global to exploit unique competencies abroad (Doggett, 2000).

A growing emphasis on learning

As a firm produces a product or offers a service over time, it can usually find ways to work more smartly or generate experience-based efficiencies by expanding volume. Most credit these outcomes to learning effects and economies of scale. Learning effects exist when an employee gains insight from experience that leads to improved work performance. Learning can also take place at the level of the firm if the experiences of individual employees are shared, leading to improved practices and production routines across the organization (Hitt, Dacin, Levitas, Arregle and Borza, 2000).

The importance of learning for SMEs is clear, and the Observatory report indicates that establishing international business relationships through shared R&D and/or innovation activities can help firms achieve that objective. Helpful SME learning relationships often result from successful strategic alliances with complementary partners from the host country (or elsewhere) or through the establishment of foreign subsidiaries (Shenkar and Luo, 2004). Indeed, Observatory report writers provide evidence to support this conclusion: 'The findings so far suggest that internationalization, though risky, has a positive effect on competitiveness. However, international collaboration seems to have a greater impact than international sales on SMEs' competitiveness' (p. 45). The report offers data showing that both strategic alliances and foreign subsidiaries (but especially the former) have a marked and positive impact on the competitiveness of SMEs.

Though Prater and Ghosh (2005) did not find evidence of American SMEs using strategic alliances to establish a position in Europe, this strategy is popular with SMEs doing business in other country contexts, including China (Worldsources, 2000) and elsewhere. As a case in point, the Observatory study found that of the SMEs in their sample that implemented more complex strategies (that is, having overseas subsidiaries or branches or using combination approaches), 32 per cent engaged in formal cooperation with other firms and 51 per cent used informal cooperation (as indicated in Figure 4.11). And as competition intensifies and companies are forced to focus on their core competencies, it becomes increasingly important to outsource non-core activities, which often requires the formation of strategic alliances. These alliances can be used to obtain new technologies or market insights, among other objectives. It follows that international alliances will be all the more important in the future as the global economy becomes even increasingly knowledge-based (Contractor and Lorange, 2002).

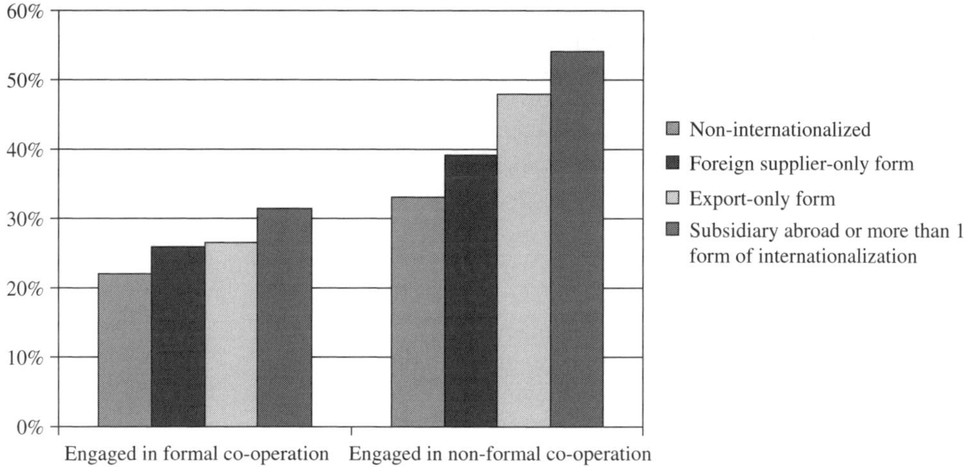

Source: ENSR Enterprise Survey, 2003

Figure 4.11 SMEs in formal and non-formal co-operation

Powex is a Finnish company that knows well the great potential of strategic alliances in the new global economy. As a manufacturer of monitors and control equipment for the energy industry, the company conceived of a new device that would use ultrasound ranging technology to measure directly the power flowing through overhead power lines. However, it needed a partner that could help it learn about the technology and assist it in bringing the new instrument to market. It found an alliance partner in Superule Systems, an Irish firm with a firm grasp of the technology, as well as an established international marketing network. Together the two companies formed Supapow, a joint venture located in Ireland, to manufacture the new product and sell it internationally. As a result of their combined contributions, an otherwise infeasible new commercial venture is now viable (IRC Network, 2005a).

The importance of learning is clearly revealed by the Observatory report. For example, this study points out that as many as 38 per cent of European SMEs establish overseas subsidiaries but do not have any exports; this suggests that these subsidiaries are used for purposes beyond merely establishing a sales platform, and accessing knowledge and technology is a likely explanation. Indeed, the survey found that access to know-how and technology was the second most cited internationalization motive for SMEs that employ complex strategies (such as setting up overseas subsidiaries), and 48 per cent of exporters sell abroad specifically to gain knowledge, at least in part. These findings provide further evidence of the growing importance of learning to SMEs with international ambitions.

The value of learning through internationalization is illustrated in the experience of an Irish SME called Dromkeen Food Ingredients (DFI), which uses spent yeast acquired from the brewing industry to make various food additives. DFI's managing director believed the company could make many different products from yeast if it had the necessary technology, so it established a working alliance with Tas Consult of Antwerp, Belgium to develop processing technology that would lead to new products. The Belgian firm has also helped DFI to market its new high value-added yeast products throughout Europe. This international partnership has been extremely successful. Today the two companies are working together to find new niche markets for the products they develop (IRC Network, 2005b).

Gains from learning are greatest during the start-up period, but efficiencies from economies of scale continue to rise as the business grows and volume increases (Pope, 2002). This allows the company to spread its investment across more units of output and to acquire more specialized (and thus more efficient) plants, equipment and employees (Makadok, 1999). A study by Verwaal and Donkers (2002) demonstrated that smaller firms can also realize economies of scale by specializing in exports with a view toward developing export relationships of significant size.

The benefits of learning effects and economies of scale are clear, but these efficiencies are even more apparent in SMEs deploying complex technologies (Qian, 2002). As indicated earlier, 93 per cent of all U.S. exporters of advanced technology products in 2001 were classified as SMEs, and these companies generated 19 per cent of high-tech export revenue that same year (ITA, 2003, p. 2). Firms such as these can accelerate the gains from experience curve efficiencies by emphasizing business expansion (assuming this growth is manageable). One way to accomplish this is by paying close attention to international business opportunities. Before the early 1990s, start-ups were encouraged to consider international expansion only after establishing a solid position in their domestic market (Brush, 1997). Times have changed. Recent studies have shown that starting with a global presence or internationalizing early on leads to increased performance, especially sales growth. For high-potential ventures, sales growth is usually considered the most important dimension of performance (Wolf and Pett, 2000). In part, experience curve efficiencies justify this emphasis, and thus an interest in global expansion. The emerging technologies that enable accelerated globalization are likely to stimulate the interest of start-ups and SMEs in international business (McDougall, Shrader and Oviatt, 2000).

The advantage of location

As noted earlier, SMEs sometimes go global to obtain needed inputs, locating near natural resources. Or they may venture abroad to reduce costs, locating labor-intensive production in low-wage countries, manufacturing heavy items near customers to reduce transportation costs, or taking other measures. These advantages have long been recognized (Hill, 2006). However, the emerging global economy emphasizes other factors related to location.

In recent years, a number of regional free trade areas (most notably, the North American Free Trade Agreement and the European Union) have formed to facilitate commerce by reducing tariffs, simplifying commercial regulations, or even adopting a common currency. To understand how trade agreements can motivate SMEs to go global, consider how the formation of the EU persuaded many entrepreneurs to expand into international markets. As these countries talked about coming together, many non-European executives feared that a 'Fortress Europe' mentality would result (Hill, 2006). That is, they assumed that increased trade between European countries would discourage trade with other nations. In response, many businesses outside the region – large and small – located physical facilities within Europe to guarantee future access to that market.

In hindsight, many have concluded that the EU has not seriously hindered trade with firms outside Europe; nonetheless, firms have taken similar measures to ensure market access in other trade areas. For example, after the creation of NAFTA, a number of Japanese firms located manufacturing facilities in Mexico to guarantee access to the North American market. In any case, locating within a trade bloc offers the advantage of reduced tariffs on trade within that region. Indeed, NAFTA officials accelerated the schedule of tariff reductions, thus providing advantages earlier than expected to firms located within the region (Gardner, 1998).

Regarding intraregional expansion, economic integration can have an even more immediate and substantial impact on the international trade of SMEs by lowering barriers to exports. For example, the ITA study found that the formation of NAFTA led to a disproportionate increase in the share of total exports of American SMEs to Canada and Mexico, from 24 per cent in 1992 to 33 per cent in 2001. The exports of these companies to Canada rose 110 per cent over the same period, and Mexico was the second most popular destination for this trade. As a parallel suggesting that economic integrations can have a noticeable impact on the pattern of SME trade, the Observatory study reports that the largest markets for European SMEs are Germany, France, Italy and Spain. This makes sense, given the logic of trade bloc formation – historical ties, cultural and linguistic similarities, business practice compatibilities and geographic proximity tend to make trade between nations possible, even probable (Prater and Ghosh, 2005).

Finally, a new location trend is emerging for SMEs: following large client firms. As major corporations locate operations abroad, their suppliers may find it necessary to go global along with the client firm to ensure the continuation of important sourcing contracts, and a firm's dependence on a major customer relocating abroad may leave it with no alternative. Thus, SMEs may have far less control over their international location plans than do large multinationals (Prater and Ghosh, 2005). For example, Ford Motor Co. is convinced that taking its suppliers overseas ensures quality, reduces start-up costs and helps meet local content restrictions. So when the auto giant decided to open a new plant in Europe, it offered a multi-year contract to Loranger Manufacturing Corp., a medium-size automobile parts manufacturer based in Warren, Pennsylvania. But there was a catch: the contract required Loranger to locate near the new plant. Since Ford was its primary customer, the small supplier accepted the offer, and today Loranger owns a plant in Hungary where it employs 150 people and generates nearly $10 million in sales. Loranger's experience suggests that entrepreneurs do not always initiate their own adventures abroad (Cullen, 1999).

Implications for policy, practice and research

Available data indicate that SMEs outnumber large firms in both the United States and Europe, and they tend to outnumber large firms in international trade in almost all industry sectors. Still, large firms have definite advantages. For example, SMEs in the United States are far more dependent on government initiatives to open foreign markets than are large firms. Almost 90 per cent of U.S. SMEs involved in exporting conduct business from a single location, while the inverse is true for large firms (only about 10 per cent are single-location companies). Also, approximately 17 per cent of SME exports go to affiliates overseas, whereas 40 per cent of large-firm exports go to foreign affiliates. Thus, access to foreign markets tends to be more limited for SMEs. Nearly 63 per cent of U.S. SMEs had sales in only one foreign market, which tended to be English-speaking, while more than half (54 per cent) of large firms exported to five or more foreign markets. The North American Free Trade Agreement (NAFTA) demonstrates the impact that government policy can have. As mentioned earlier, SMEs exporting to Canada increased 110 per cent from 1992 to 2001, and Mexico became the second highest destination (ITA, 2003).

Additionally, SMEs in the United States report the following, at least perceived, barriers or obstacles to international trade:

- Difficulty locating prospects
- Identifying reliable foreign representatives
- Lack of management expertise in international business
- Inability to deal with up-front costs to develop foreign markets
- Tariff and non-tariff barriers such as regulations and red tape
- Shifting currency values
- A general lack of information
- Language difficulties and integration with the other country's culture
- Finding qualified employees to conduct international business.

These problems are cited in NFIB (2004) and/or Shenkar and Luo (2004).

The European Observatory reported finding a plethora of basic policy measures to promote SME internationalization, but most of these were aimed at exporting only. Their document goes on to recommend a more holistic approach based upon four elements, specifically:

> Firstly, managers of SMEs typically have limited time and management capacity. A policy measure should offer to perform some of the practical tasks on behalf of the manager, especially in the case of SMEs with no international experience. Secondly, studies indicate that SMEs often need specific, targeted support. The services provided should be 'customized' i.e. be tailored to the problems of the individual company. Such targeted support might for instance be assistance in identifying an appropriate foreign business partner. Thirdly, one of the key findings of this report is that internationalization is more than just exporting. Policy measures, whether general or company-specific, should therefore comprise all the different approaches to internationalization and the support should include, not just exporting and FDI, but also other activities, e.g. collaboration, foreign sub-suppliers, etc. Finally, the fact that SMEs with only foreign suppliers perceive external barriers to internationalization to almost the same extent as exporting SMEs also suggest the need for policy measures to address internationalization in a broad manner (EC, 2003, p. 51).

These same points would appear to be valid for the United States as well, based upon the perceived barriers.

Research in the area of SME internationalization could be aided by adopting standard classifications of SME size. This would permit better comparison of the data and enable researchers to see any similarities or differences across countries. Such comparisons could only strengthen the ability to prescribe policy that could be helpful to SMEs seeking to internationalize, regardless of country of location. The easiest way to achieve this standardization might be through a consortium of journal editors publishing SME research, who could requiring the use and reporting of prescribed classifications as a prerequisite to publication. Governments could assist in the process by collecting and reporting data on all forms of internationalization in accordance with these same classifications. The provision of such data would remove the obstacles to survey methods of obtaining information and facilitate the ability of the researcher to study relevant questions and to determine better the extent of SME involvement in international markets.

Clearly the problems confronting SMEs have some similarity the world over. Joint research efforts could assist in better identifying the primary problems and recommending policies that could enhance SME participation in the global arena. We have to believe that this would be a good thing for all concerned.

Questions emerging from the chapter

1. What forms of internationalization do SMEs undertake? Which seem to be most prevalent? Do these make sense?
2. Does firm size present significant obstacles for competing internationally? Can you cite any examples to support your contention?
3. Does the size of the country in which the SME is located influence its likelihood of internationalization? Why?
4. What factors or trends in the general environment have made it easier for SMEs to compete globally? Can you think of anything in the future that might enhance or degrade their capability to compete?
5. Do most SMEs involved in international trade establish multiple locations to facilitate international operations? Do you believe this is a good strategy?
6. Is there any correlation between the size of the firm and the amount of international activity in which the firm engages? Do you think industry affects this phenomenon?

Notes

1. See http://www.ita.doc.gov/td/industry/otea/docs/SMEstat-hbk2002.pdf. We accessed the report on 8 December 2004.
2. These were *mostly* U.S.-domiciled firms, but the study also includes data from U.S. affiliates of foreign firms that export goods from the United States.
3. The study could not link export documents to the remaining 15 per cent of export value for a variety of reasons (for example, misreporting by firms, errors in collection and processing and coverage problems), but we see no reason to assume that this small percentage of unreported data would have substantially distorted the findings.
4. See http://europa.eu.int/comm/enterprise/enterprise_policy/analysis/doc/smes_observatory_2003_report4_en.pdf. We accessed the report on 8 December 2004.

Bibliography

Autio, E., Sapienza, H.J. and Almeida, H.J. (2000), Effects of age at entry, knowledge intensity, and imitability on international growth. *Academy of Management Journal*, 43, 909.

Bagole, J. (2001), Iceland transforms itself into a hotbed of new industries. *Wall Street Journal*, 13 March, p. A21.

Baty, G.B. and Blake, M.S. (2003), *Entrepreneurship: Back to Basics*. Washington, DC: Beard Books.

Birch, D. (1999), Thinking about tomorrow. *Wall Street Journal*, 24 May, p. R30.

Braunerhjelm, P. (2000), *Knowledge Capital and the 'New Economy'*. Berlin: Springer.

Brush, C.G. (1997), Export entry in small companies: Effects of timing on strategy and performance. *Journal of Small Business Strategy*, 7, 53–67.

Cheng, J.L.C. (1995), *Global managerial effectiveness*. Paper presented at the national meeting of the Academy of Management, Vancouver, British Columbia, Canada.

Contractor, F.J. and Lorange, P. (2002), The growth of alliances in the knowledge-based economy. *International Business Review*, 11, 485–502.
Cullen, J.B. (1999), *Multinational Management: A Strategic Approach*. Cincinnati: South-Western.
Doggett, S. (2000), Your company. *Los Angeles Times*, 11 October, p. C6.
Elk, E. and Overweel, M.J. (1991), *SME: Full Speed Ahead*. Amsterdam: ABN-AMRO Bank.
Etemad, H. and Wright, R. (2003), Internationalization of SMEs: Toward a new paradigm. *Small Business Economics*, 20, 1–4.
Fletcher, R. (2001), A holistic approach to internationalization. *International Business Review*, 10, 25–49.
Foley, J.F. (2004), *The Global Entrepreneur: Taking Your Business International*. Chicago: Jarmic Press International.
Fujita, M. (1998), *The Transnational Activities of Small and Medium-Sized Enterprises*. Boston: Kluwer Academic Publishers.
Gardner, H.S. (1998), *Comparative Economic Systems*. Fort Worth: Harcourt College Publishing.
Gomez-Casseres, B. (1997), Alliance strategies of small firms. *Small Business Economics*, 9, 33–44.
Grant, R.M. (1987), Multinationality and performance among British manufacturing companies. *Journal of International Business Studies*, 18, 79–89.
Hill, C.W. (2006), *Global Business Today*. Boston: McGraw-Hill Irwin.
Hitt, M.A., Dacin, T., Levitas, E., Arregle, J. and Borza, A. (2000), Partner selection in emerging and developed market contexts: Resource-based and organizational learning perspectives. *Academy of Management Journal*, 43, 449–467.
IRC Network (2005a), *Joint Venture Company to Manufacture Electrical Monitoring Equipment*. http://irc.cordis.lu/success/completesuccess.cfm?SUCCESS_ID=1, accessed 24 May 2005.
IRC Network (2005b), *New Yeast Processes Makes Sales Rise*. http://irc.cordis.lu/success/completesuccess.cfm?SUCCESS_ID=115, accessed 24 May 2005.
Jeannet, J.-P. (2000), *Managing with a Global Mindset*. London: Financial Times Prentice Hall.
Karagozoglu, N. and Lindell, M. (1998), Internationalization of small and medium-sized technology-based firms: An exploratory study. *Journal of Small Business Management*, 36, 44–59.
Kim, W.C., Hwang, P. and Burgers, W.P. (1993), Multinationals' diversification and the risk-return trade-off. *Strategic Management Journal*, 14, 275–286.
Klein, K.E. (2000), The bumpy road to global trade. *Business Week*, 9 October, p. 32.
Laudicina, P. (2005), *World Out of Balance: Negotiating Global Risks to Seize Competitive Advantage*. New York: McGraw-Hill Ryerson.
Levitt, T. (1983), The globalization of markets. *Harvard Business Review*, 61(3), 92–102.
Luo, Y. (2000), Entering China today: What choices do we have? *Journal of Global Marketing*, 14, 57–82.
Makadok, R. (1999), Interfirm differences in scale economies and the evolution of market share. *Strategic Management Journal*, 20, 935–952.
McDougall, P.P. and Oviatt, B.M. (1999), A framework for understanding accelerated international entrepreneurship, in A.M. Rugman and R.W. Wright (eds), *Research in Global Strategic Management*, vol. 7, Stamford, CT: JAI Press, pp. 23–40.
McDougall, P.P., Shrader, R.C. and Oviatt, B.M. (2000), International entrepreneurs: Risk takers or risk managers? in Sue Birley and Daniel F. Muzyka (eds), *Mastering Entrepreneurship*, London: Financial Times Prentice Hall, pp. 246–250.
Mitchell, W., Roehl, T. and Slattery, R.J. (1995), Influences on R&D growth among Japanese pharmaceutical firms, 1975–1990. *The Journal of High Technology Management Research*, 6, 17–32.
NFIB (2004), *International Trade*. Volume 4, issue 1, prepared by Lara Chamberlain, NFIB National Small Business Poll series, William J. Dennis Jr (series editor). Washington DC: NFIB Research Foundation.
Nummela, N. (2002), Controlling the growth of a Born Global. *International Journal of Entrepreneurship and Innovation*, **3**, 2, 221–6.
O'Malley, E. and O'Gorman, C. (2001), Competitive advantage in the Irish indigenous software industry and the role of inward foreign direct investment. *European Planning Studies*, 9, 311–322.
Palich, L.E. and Gomez-Mejia, L.R. (1999), A theory of global strategy and firm efficiencies: Considering the effects of cultural diversity. *Journal of Management*, 25, 587–606.
Pope, R.A. (2002), Why small firms export: Another look. *Journal of Small Business Management*, 40, 17–26.
Porter, M.E. (1990), *The Competitive Advantage of Nations*. New York: Free Press.
Prater, E. and Ghosh, S. (2005), Current operational practices of U.S. small and medium-sized enterprises in Europe. *Journal of Small Business Management*, 43, 155–169.
Qian, G. (2002), Multinationality, product diversification, and profitability of emerging US small- and medium-sized enterprises. *Journal of Business Venturing*, 17, 611–633.
Shenkar, O. and Luo, Y. (2004), *International Business*. Hoboken, NJ: John Wiley and Sons.
Shrader, R.C., Oviatt, B.M. and McDougall, P.P. (2000), How new ventures exploit trade-offs among international risk factors: Lessons for the accelerated internationalization of the 21st century. *Academy of Management Journal*, 43, 1226–1247.

Simon, H. and Otte, M. (2000), The new Atlantic century. *Harvard Business Review*, 78(1), 17–20.
Vernon, R. (1996), International investment and international trade in the product cycle. *Quarterly Journal of Economics*, 80, 190–207.
Verwaal, E. and Donkers, B. (2002), Firm size and export intensity: Solving an empirical puzzle. *Journal of International Business Studies*, 33, 603–613.
Wolf, J.A. and Pett, T.L. (2000), Internationalization of small firms: An examination of export competitive patterns, firm size, and export performance. *Journal of Small Business Management*, 38, 34–47.
Worldsources (2000), Survey on SMEs gives thumbs up to joint ventures. *Hong Kong Mail*, 22 September.
Zacharakis, A.L. (1997), Foreign markets: A transaction cost perspective. *Entrepreneurship Theory and Practice*, 21, 23–39.

PART II

MANAGEMENT, LEADERSHIP AND STRATEGY IN GLOBAL SMEs

5 Entrepreneurs and their personal and business relations: shaping manufacturing SMEs' global strategy

Telma Barbosa and Ted Fuller

Introduction

Research on SME internationalisation has focused on a number of issues including export decision associated factors (for instance, Ford *et al.* 1980; Cavusgil 1984; Aaby and Salter 1989); export behaviour and performance determining factors (Denis and Depelteau 1985; Beamish and Munro 1987; Reid and Rosson 1987; Dichtl *et al.* 1990; Gemunden 1991; Holzmuller and Kasper 1991) and successful export strategies (Namiki 1988; Baird, Lyles and Orris 1994; Cavusgil and Zou 1994; Dhanaraj and Beamish 2003). However, an impeding criticism has been put forward: SME internationalisation research lacks theoretical foundation (Gemunden 1991; Mendenhall, Beaty and Oddou 1993; Ellis 2000; Dhanaraj and Beamish 2003).

Internationalisation theories (the economic-based theories, the process, behavioural-based theory and the network approach) are concerned with large companies and their subsidiaries, and their application to SMEs is not said to be entirely supported by empirical findings (Rao and Naidu 1992; Bell 1995; Crick 1995; Reuber and Fischer 1997; Zafarullah, Ali and Young 1998), given their determinism and disregard for the role of the decision makers in making strategic choices (Andersson 2000). The network theory concerns companies which benefit from a priori highly internationalised networks (Blankenburg 1995) and so would not apply to the case of SMEs 'whose network horizon is limited to the local market' (Ellis 2000).

But what is the rationale of SMEs' internationalisation process, decision making and strategy? It is reasonably well established that SMEs operate through their relationships and their networks, relying on social capital rather than market forms of power and governance (Larson 1992). The literature on networks as resources for SMEs is extensive (Birley 1985), as is the institutional sense of social embeddedness of firms in their environments (Granovetter 1973; Uzzi 1997). From a strategic perspective SMEs adopt network relationship strategies in the everyday business activities (Holm *et al.* 1999) and such strategies are a significant explanation of the choices and decisions that they make (Fuller and Lewis 2003).

Thus, it seems a reasonable proposition that a strategic orientation to relationships will also be manifest in the choices made with respect to internationalisation. In fact, Fletcher (2004) found that the internationalisation process among 'late starter' SMEs was resonant with their everyday understandings and practices that had been socially constructed in relation to the local and regional context. Moreover, the resource-constrained internationalising SMEs are found to interact with external environment agents and network actors to leverage their resources (Zacharakis 1997) and to have access to market opportunities, knowledge and experience (Chetty and Holm 2000; Ellis 2000; Eriksson and

Chetty 2003). In that, entrepreneurs play an influential role and their motivation, wish, action and human capital are the triggers of SMEs internationalisation (for example, Cavusgil 1984; Manolova *et al.* 2002).

However, a number of questions still remain unanswered:

- How and why is international social capital acquired and managed and how does it affect internationalisation?
- Is there an SME relationship-based strategy of international growth?
- What are the mechanisms of internationalisation decision making and strategy making?
- What are the underlying factors that can be used as a basis for theory development?

The purpose of the chapter is to demonstrate the mechanisms of the internationalisation process for manufacturing SMEs from a relationship network. In particular, it is intended to demonstrate the foundations of entrepreneurs' internationalisation decision making strategy. The chapter is derived from a qualitative and interpretative research work whose method is described in Appendix 5.1. The study focused on SMEs of business-to-business sectors which were involved with international businesses for a number of years and which considered international business an important and substantial part of their operations.

In order to investigate the implications of networking and relationship to the manufacturing SMEs' internationalisation process, this was looked at from two perspectives, based on the work of Johanson and Mattsson (1988):

- The company's foreign market extension, that is, the entrance into a new foreign market
- The company's foreign market advancements.

Foreign market extension comprises the classical decisions on market, partner and entry mode. Foreign market advancements comprise the developments after market entry, whether increasing market presence in the same markets (penetration) or entering new, different market segments (diversification). The market entries of each case are described in Appendix 5.2.

International extension (foreign market entry) strategy

Foreign market extension is the company's entrance into a new foreign market. The normative literature states that international market entry decisions encompass an orderly and linear string of other decisions, which are market selection, exchange partner selection and entry mode decision. Moreover, these are amongst the most critical decisions in the internationalisation process of a firm, since they influence the firm's commitment of resources, strategy, planning, operations and development (Reid and Rosson 1987).

SMEs are believed rarely to adopt the market-research based, systematic approach to international markets and identification and selection of clients (Papadopoulos 1987), relying on ad hoc, non-rational decisions (Liang and Stump 1996; Liang and Parkhe 1997) or on unplanned and unsolicited orders.

Our study found a different situation. The SMEs' foreign market entry is caused by networking activities and the strategy adopted does not always follow a normative, orderly string of decisions. We found two concomitant patterns of internationalisation, one that follows a more traditional perspective and another one that is less conventional. We also found that decisions are not generally made on an ad hoc basis, but on the basis of perceptive, personal criteria of risk reducing factors. The more traditional internationalisation pattern consists of a deliberate, intentional foreign extension strategy. The less conventional pattern comprises an unintentional, evolving foreign extension strategy. These strategies are shown in Box 5.1 and Figure 5.1.

BOX 5.1 THE PATTERNS OF SME INTERNATIONALISATION

Intentional pattern

1. SME entrepreneur takes the decision to internationalise
2. SME entrepreneur chooses market
3. SME entrepreneur searches for a partner/connection to facilitate entry
4. SME entrepreneur takes partner decision based on perception criteria
5. Market entry follows

Unintentional pattern

1. Network member (or an outsider) proposes SME internationalisation
2. SME entrepreneur takes partner decision on the basis of perception criteria
3. SME entrepreneur takes the decision to internationalise based on partner decision
4. Market definition follows
5. Market entry follows

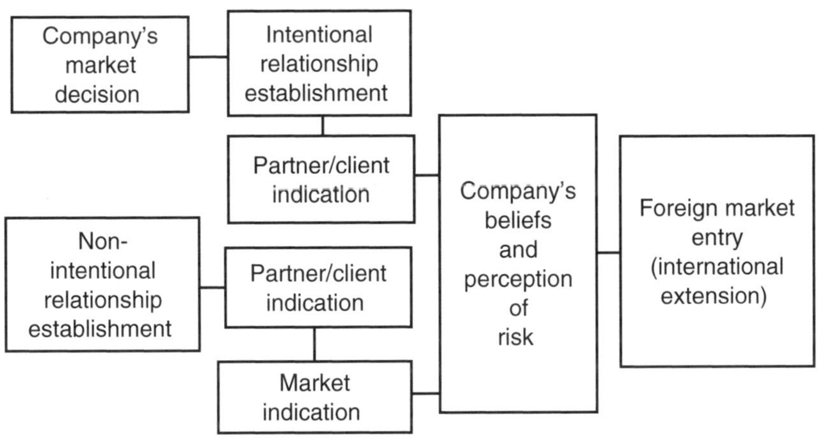

Figure 5.1 SME international extension (entry) strategy

The intentional dimension of SME foreign market extension strategy

Internationalisation is seen as a means to an end. In certain cases, the entrepreneur takes the decision to internationalise in order to escape local market instability, to 'spread the risk of being in business', or to grow out of national market problems. Internationalisation is also seen as a strategy for firm growth:

> We realised, however, that engineering and manufacturing in England, even in the 1960s and early '70s was quite typical and that caused two problems, one the supply problem not being able to find good used machinery and the other one was when there was a down turn in England there was no market to sell it on. So we had to look further afield (Case study SME).

After entrepreneurs decide to internationalise, they then select a foreign market. In our study, out of 24 entries, only on four occasions were markets selected by the company. These markets were in the EU (mainly Italy), North America, India and Spain. In those cases, the criteria were the supposed or expected sales potential of the market in the first place, and then handiness. By this SMEs meant language similarity, knowledge of the culture and geographic proximity. These selection criteria are not in disagreement with what is generally expected in the literature.

What is interesting from the study is the mechanism through which entrepreneurs implement their strategy. After deciding about the market, whatever the criteria may be, they then look for a network connection to facilitate entry. On these occasions, intentional relationships are established:

> I think what we also realised in the mid-70s that there was a much bigger market and that was in the Americas, North America, principally and also in Mexico . . . So we realised to get some contacts we would have to go to America. So I went to the United States . . . and the reason I went was to submit an application to join the American [specified industry] Trade Association which covered . . . (Case study SME).

The intentional dimension comprises networking activities that are intentionally established with the purpose of entering into foreign markets, after the owner-manager takes the decision to internationalise. These activities can be represented by participation in trade missions, exhibitions or fairs; participation in seminars; becoming a member of trade associations; contacting international trade promotion agencies and embassies; or initiating associations or alliances with potential partners.

Entrepreneurs embark intentionally on networking activities in order to facilitate foreign extension. Entrepreneurs regard these events and institutions as promoters of a pro-business environment. For instance, trade associations and trade promotion agencies are regarded as sources of new contacts and of clients' information, and hence, new business. By providing directories, Internet sites and cross-references of members, and by organising meetings and exhibitions, they also reduce the risk of engaging with international operations as perceived by the owner-managers. Finally, they help entrepreneurs overcome certain barriers to internationalisation such as foreign language and culture. The following entrepreneurs' commentaries illustrate the role and importance of trade associations and trade missions:

> the reason we joined was really, not because we wanted to be in the association but because it opened up other markets to us which would take our goods maybe when our market was depressed (Case study SME).

> [If they were not members of the Association] it would be more difficult to sell, particularly in Europe (Case study SME).

> We became members [of the American Trade Association] in 1975 and that opened up those markets to us to such an extent we used to exhibit in trade shows [in the US, Canada and Mexico] . . . and we got some good business there (Case study SME).

> The opportunity there is the commercial attachés in the embassy were actually finding up these people for you. They contacted who we needed to speak to. Whereas in the past I had to do that myself – which is a little bit difficult in countries where English is not their first language. Doing this way, the contacts were given to me. And it is up to me to see if I can arrange a meeting with them, which I was able to do. I think that is probably one way of going forward (Case study SME).

The non-intentional dimension of SME foreign market extension strategy

An opportunity to enter into a new foreign market may come unexpectedly, such as orders by an importer. The literature has approached that as an unimportant issue, or as a demonstration that SME internationalisation lacks formality. However, importers usually initiate negotiation motivated by knowledge of the company's reputation that they have gathered from all sorts of sources, and that can be considered networking. It is well known that a company can enter an international network as a result of 'interaction initiatives taken by other firms which are insiders in the network in the specific country' which have become motivated to engage in interaction (Johanson and Vahlne 1990). That motivation might be derived from 'foreknowledge of potential partners' reputation and/or personal experience and relations', which can reduce the exchange risk (Larson 1992).

Most frequently, an opportunity to internationalise or to enter into a new foreign market comes from invitations or proposals by someone whom the entrepreneur knows. They are people such as owner-managers' business and personal contacts, their friends, foreign clients, local clients that get internationalised, members of trade associations, people met at seminars and trade missions, and employees' contacts. These people construct the SME international network.

The following entrepreneur's statement illustrates the role of personal contacts, who totally influenced the company's decision to establish in the US. This firm was recommended to a US company by the son of an English businessman who was a lifelong friend of the entrepreneur and had done business with the firm for 25 years:

> We had to do it. And I have to say, if I had had proper resources and the technical ability to have looked into it properly we wouldn't have done it. It was ignorance totally that led us through . . . Yes Michel [owner-manager's business and personal contact fictitious name] did influence us in the respect that if he hadn't approached someone that we knew, we probably had never exported to them in the first place. Secondly with regard to us moving over there, he had the influence that we had to find that position of trust – and that is all it comes. As I said earlier above everything else I believe it is people – We liked him and he liked us (Case study SME).

The SME international network starts most frequently from home, initiated by acquaintances, relations and contacts whom the entrepreneur met previously, and not necessarily with the purpose of internationalisation. They include old friends and personal contacts of the owner-managers and managing directors, old owner-manager business contacts, old clients and employees.

This is another example of how an SME network starts from home. A nine-year-long relationship with a local client that became internationalised caused the company's entrance into Tunisia as a supplier of the local client's Tunisian subsidiary. In turn, that relationship led to entrance into Russia, by means of a recommendation by a Tunisian client engineer worker who was sent to work in Russia:

> What happened was, it was actually for [the British company named] who were in Tunisia . . . they couldn't get hold of some items, they actually rang [the British company named] in England spoke to someone who bought things from our company and asked for recommendation for a supplier, we were recommended by them, we were then contacted directly by [the Tunisian subsidiary] by British buyers who were not happy with their indigenous suppliers (Case study SME).

> . . . we had an engineer who worked in [the Tunisian subsidiary] then moved to work in Russia; he's British and he then got us into . . . Russia (Case study SME).

Owner-managers' personal friends and business contacts may act together and create an SME international network. In our study, a British personal friend of an entrepreneur who worked as an engineer of a steel company in Holland managed to get them a two-year contract. Later, that same person visited Nigeria and recommended his friend's company to a Nigerian subsidiary of a Lebanese company. Later still, this company was recommended to the company's headquarter in Lebanon by that same friend and by the Nigerian subsidiary managers:

> At the same time we'd been previously dealing with the Netherlands with a local man who knew us and he went into Nigeria . . . he recommended a company that should deal with us because they were looking for someone to support them in Nigeria. They contacted us and we started dealing with this company based in Lebanon, which had a warehouse and office in Nigeria (Case study SME).

> Someone, a friend of my father's and mine got a job for this British company in Turkmenistan. . . . They couldn't find any where to get the goods, so they rang us up and . . . we ended up dealing out there, massively (Case study SME).

The entrepreneurs' social and business relations play an important role in the process of SME internationalisation. They recommend the SME to prospective clients, provide information on a company's reputation, bring in knowledge of market and potential clients, and in certain cases, provide resources and infrastructure to the internationalising firm. In so doing, they reduce uncertainty and minimise the risk of the international operation, as perceived by owner-managers. As a consequence, owner-managers perceive the international operation and route as safer. These are the embedded criteria of entrepreneurs' internationalisation decision making. The proposal to internationalise will be accepted by the entrepreneur if he or she judges it worthwhile. We will return to this subject in a later section.

Foreign market selection

SMEs do not usually choose their own foreign markets. These are generally determined by the network member who provides the internationalisation opportunity and facilitates entry. It is up to entrepreneurs to decide about the business proposition. To take that decision, the entrepreneur takes into consideration the potential partner profile and the possible outcomes of the relationship. If the partner is approved, then the business proposal

Table 5.1 Market decisions made by network members and type of network connection

Company	Market	Entry connection
BMO	China	MD's personal contacts led to a visit in China, where a Chinese businessman was met
JMT	Sri Lanka	Order by an importer
	Thailand	Order by an importer
	US	Manager of a UK supplier's subsidiary in the US, whom the MD knew personally, proposed to import product
	Finland	Company chooses client and then contacts UK trade agency and local embassy for further information. References from the American new customer eases entry
MEB	US	Trade fair that led to a contact with a prospective client
	S. Ireland	Seminar, where prospective client was met
PNPS	Tunisia	Domestic client that was internationalised made a recommendation to its Tunisian subsidiary
	Libya	A newly hired sales manager brought in new contacts
	Russia	Tunisian client's engineer went to work with UK company's subsidiary in Russia and recommended them
	Turkmenistan	Owner manager's personal friend who worked for a British company in Turkmenistan, recommended them
	Malaysia and Australia	Malaysian businessmen, friend of the MD, placed direct orders and also introduced them to new clients
	Holland	MD's personal friend who worked for a Dutch company which had connection with a British client, recommended them for a two-year project
	Nigeria	Order by a Nigerian agent, based on internet information
	Lebanon	MD's Dutch personal friend recommended them to a Lebanese subsidiary in Nigeria and from there to Headquarters
HPCL	Germany	Company chooses distributor amongst established business contacts and contacts them directly
	Holland	Company chooses distributor amongst established business contacts and contacts them directly
	France	Major German client introduced them to its French subsidiary
	Greece	A long-time friend, owner of a firm in a complementary sector, with whom they work together informally
	S. Ireland	A long-time friend, owner of a firm in a complementary sector, with whom they work together informally

is accepted. This means that SMEs' foreign markets are predominantly determined by the established network of relationships and connections (see Table 5.1). Moreover, on all these occasions the market decision follows the client/partner decision, thus inverting the normative ordering of the classical decisions of market choice-client/partner selection. This also implies that SMEs enter foreign markets that are known to their partners/clients and benefit from their market knowledge.

In this way, relationship and networking are important dimensions of SME international extension strategy. The way they influence international extension is by causing foreign market entry. Moreover, their causal effects are mediated by the entrepreneurs' beliefs and perception of risk (see Figure 5.1).

In summary, SMEs' international extension strategy is composed of two dimensions: an intentional dimension and an evolving, non-intentional dimension. The intentional dimension takes place when the entrepreneur takes the decision to internationalise and chooses foreign markets. In order to enter the foreign market, the entrepreneur intentionally makes efforts to establish relationships with network actors that can help and facilitate entry. This choice is mediated by the beliefs and perceptions of the entrepreneur of the network actor's capability to provide the expected help and to reduce uncertainty and risks related to foreign entry.

The evolving, non-intentional dimension takes place when the companies get internationalised in an unexpected manner. This arises when previous contacts and relationships present the opportunity to internationalise, suggesting foreign partners and/or clients and also foreign markets. The entrepreneurs' final decision to carry out the international extension is mediated by their perception of the risks and uncertainty involved. These, in turn, are influenced by the amount of trust and confidence embedded in the established relationships.

Foreign market penetration (expansion) strategy

Foreign market expansion comprises the developments that take place after market entry, whether increasing market presence in the same market segments (penetration) or entering new, different segments (diversification). In our study, expansions were identified in 14 foreign markets and all of them were triggered or facilitated by networking activities and relationships. The development of the personal relationships and of the business appear inextricably linked. Previously established business and personal contacts of the owner-managers and/or managing director are a source of opportunities for increased foreign sales, foreign market penetration, and even market diversification. In the same way, the newly established foreign partner promotes relationship development with other partners, and, in turn, brings new business opportunities to the established relationship. The following experiences of the case study SMEs exemplify the causal influence of networking activities on the international penetration of the companies:

> And that worked very well for about six months and I got a telephone call and he said 'have you ever thought about setting up in the USA?' . . . Michel had a big site and he said 'we could develop a building here' – which we did at his site. . . . Seven years ago we found a company in the USA. It is in New Hampshire, 70 miles north of Boston (Case study SME).

> At the same time we'd been previously dealing with the Netherlands with a local man who knew us and he went into Nigeria. He wasn't in a position to do any buying but he recommended a company that should deal with us because they were looking for someone to support them in Nigeria. They contacted us and we started dealing with this company based in Lebanon, which had a warehouse and office in Nigeria (Case study SME).

Foreign market expansion strategy is far from being formally planned. Excluding unexpected contacts from foreign clients, it is observed that foreign market growth is dependent on prior, established relationships of owner-managers and managing directors and/or on the development of the newly established relationships that caused foreign market entry (see Table 5.2). This is to say that, as with the international extension strategy, the foreign market penetration or expansion strategy of SMEs involves two dimensions: an intentional dimension and a non-intentional dimension.

The non-intentional dimension is represented by previously established relationships, both personal and business, that eventually turn into the source of international growth. The intentional dimension is comprised of two other aspects: the intentional development of the newly established relationship in the foreign country and the deliberate search for new contacts to initiate new expansion (such as through trade fairs, trade missions and trade agencies). In this way, as the relationship becomes closer, business is developed and the market expanded.

In the context of the SME, although entrepreneurs do not plan their foreign market growth, in the sense that they do not establish formal targets and formal action plans, they do work on the mechanisms that promote international growth. These mechanisms involve relationship building, and comprise maintenance of previous personal and business relationships and contacts, the development of relationships with newly established partners and actively searching for sources of new relationships. Figure 5.2 presents the SME strategy for international penetration.

The rationale of SMEs' internationalisation strategy development

SME internationalisation strategy involves relationship building and development. Why do SMEs rely on relationship building in order to grow internationally? We again found that the beliefs and perceptions of owner-managers and managing directors play a relevant role. They do so, first of all, because they believe foreign relationships and relationship building is the way of doing business and increasing exports. In their words, doing business depends on relationships. Without the dialogue, the trust and confidence embedded in the relationship, there is no way of succeeding in business:

> We started by meeting people. It is the way really that . . . I still feel meeting people is one of the better ways of doing business. And it is the same with foreign business . . . I think that as time goes along, we will endeavour to meet people and export more due to meeting people (Case study SME).

> and I think that is the only way because if you don't have the trust and if you don't have the dialogue and you don't feel confident then how can it possibly succeed? (Case study SME).

Secondly, entrepreneurs believe in relationship building because they expect some outcomes. They expect these to be market opportunity, market intelligence, knowledge and information, communication capability, competitive advantage and differentiation regarding foreign markets. They reason that these outcomes will facilitate the job of doing international business and will help them manage their international business. The following comments from the case studies illustrate this issue:

> It is important to have a quality product, but doing business depends on the relationship you maintain with your client really. In our case, we can't just sell the product; it's the other part that comes with it that matters most. It's the only thing we can differentiate ourselves anyway (Case study SME).

Table 5.2 Relationship and network connections that caused foreign market penetration

Company	Market	Networking/relationship	Role of the network members
JMT	US	Old business and personal contacts	Established JMT as its distributor in the UK and later became JMT's distributor in the US market
		Participation in a trade mission	Business contact which later led to an important new client
		Development of the relationship with new client – planning to establish direct sales operations	New orders
MEB	US	Old business and personal contact (the son of a long-term supplier and friend)	Recommends MEB to the importer he works with
		Development of the relationship with American partner	Encourages the establishment of a company; provides market knowledge and physical resources; helps running the business
		New client	Direct contact with the company based on information available on the internet
	Southern Ireland	Development of the relationship with first client and visits by representative	Recommends other prospective clients. Word of mouth about MEB. Visits to old and prospective clients
HPCL	Germany	Development of the initially established relationship (old pump distributor)	Continue running the business, although not as successfully as expected due to lack of resources
	Holland	Development of the initially established relationship (old pump distributor)	Finds new clients to replace their old pump with the new one
		Old MD personal friend and business contacts are established as new distributor	Source of knowledge about market, specific technology product and similar product
	Southern Ireland	Development of the relationship with first client and visiting the market place	Word of mouth, confidence in company's ability to solve their problem
		Old UK clients	Recommend HPCL to their subsidiaries in S. Ireland – new orders
		Local distributor that establishes in SI	Help with selling to established clients and finding new ones
	Greece	New distributors met at trade fair	Knowledge of the former product and its markets

PNPS	Tunisia	Establishing and developing relationship with new owners of Tunisian business and meeting new clients	Word of mouth; recommendation to other companies
	Turkmen-istan	Establishing and developing relationship with new owners of Turkmenistan business and meeting new clients	Word of mouth; recommendation to other companies
	Nigeria	A businessman, old friend of the owner-manager	Recommendations to a Lebanese subsidiary in Nigeria
BMO	Europe – Italy	Development of relationship with European Trade Association members	Guidance on doing business, code of ethics and business site; new contacts/helping each other to doing business
	US	Development of relationship with American Trade Association and members	Market information and specific market opportunities
	India	Development of personal relationship with clients	Market knowledge, new clients, new business
	China	Development of personal relationship with client	A follow-up visit that led to a new client
		Owner-manager personal contact, an old friend who established a business in China	Facilitator of market development; new clients. Distributor of information to prospective clients

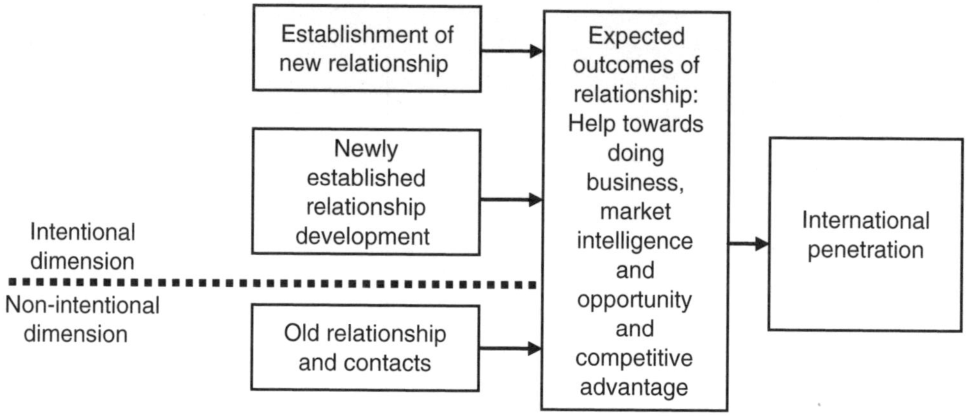

Figure 5.2 Traditional model of SME international expansion strategy

> We had tried previously to get in – tried various methods not that we had visits from the USA, we'd been on trade visits, toured the USA, we travelled up and down the country. We believed that doing business as a group would be better than any other ways (Case study SME).

> From a business point of view they are another set of eyes and ears in that particular marketplace and they can be very useful although I won't want to maintain a friendship just to exploit that situation but they can be very useful, they are very good for instance . . . they are a good source of information but I think it is always better to work with people that you respect and trust (Case study SME).

These expectations are an element of control: entrepreneurs in SMEs take a newly established relationship further, establish a new one and/or rely on an old relationship in order to achieve international market penetration as long as they believe these relationships will provide the expected outcomes: helping to do business, accessing market intelligence, identifying market opportunities and providing competitive advantage. If the expected outcomes are interrupted for any reason, then the relationship is terminated. The following experiences of the interviewed owner-managers illustrate this underpinning rationale of relationship building:

> So it's a little bit, if one has a small business, you're making things and selling them on a worldwide basis, the most important thing of all is market intelligence. To try to go into China, I wouldn't now attempt it but I have a good agent who could speak the language and we work on certain terms (Case study SME).

> After all these years of trading with our American representatives, both the current one and the original one, we now know how things work there. We have also done a bit of research ourselves . . . We now have enough knowledge about the market. The US is the largest single market in the world for pharmaceutical equipments and we have been doing pharmaceutical equipment for 15 to 20 years (Case study SME).

International relationship management strategy

Before we discuss how SMEs manage their relationships within an international context, it is important to understand the concept of international relationships as perceived by the case study businesses.

Entrepreneurs indicate that there are relationships based on trust that the business terms are going to be met, without necessarily involving personal knowledge of the partners, and there are relationships based on more intimate and personal knowledge and contacts. Different cultures call for different types of relationships. The following comments illustrate this issue:

> Sometimes when [we] don't have relationships, I mean I guess the guys in Turkmenistan, I don't know anything about the people there, but we have got a relationship because . . . they just buy from us because they know they can trust us, if they get the stuff they get it at the right price so that's one sort of relationship (Case study SME).

> The people in Tunisia call us up and we talk about things and when I go over there I can take them out. We'll go out for a drink if I go over there and we can talk about business as well. Also, they rely on us heavily, so there are different terms of business relationships but also there are elements of personal relationship in all of this as well, or lack of personal relationship in regard to the Russian ones (Case study SME).

The management of international business is embedded in the concept of relationship development, which, in turn, aims at taking the relationship beyond the commercial purpose to the point of personal and close knowledge of the partner. This has more to do with friendship, and becomes the aim or philosophy of relationship building. As the relationship between partners evolves to the point of friendship, business is developed. Business becomes exchange between companies. People involved in the business transaction become colleagues or friends that know each other by their names, like each other and find they have many things in common. That knowledge is shared by all the entrepreneurs in the study and was a key element of their narrative during the interviews:

> [The business we do] that it's an exchange between companies. So we all work as colleagues not as competitors. . . . Although I don't remember when I met the guy we now know the name of each other and this makes it very easy for us (Case study SME).

> I have become a personal friend of the owner and it's a big business, it employs about 12 000 people and like what happens in business, we have become friends, he is the same age as I am, and when I go he will not allow me to stay in a hotel. I stay in his home. When he came here he stayed in my home (Case study SME).

> I would consider the people in Germany to be good friends . . . I consider them to be friends as well as friends through business and I think it is very important, very important that you have that relationship (Case study SME).

As with all sorts of relationship, international relationship also implies trust and a sense of fairness attributed to a balance between mutual effort and mutual benefits, which in turn, promotes fair advantages for both partners. One of the key insights which is revealed by this study is that, if there is an imbalance in that respect, the relationship is not considered a good one and partners will look for a way to finish it:

> But I have to say it has not worked that well. In fact, we have done very well for this American company over here and they have really done nothing for us at all over there . . . I do not see them putting much effort into it . . . They have not expanded [our business there] in five years, whereas, we have almost doubled their business in the UK. It has fallen well below their original estimates anyway. And it is absolutely known they are going nowhere (Case study SME).

> It may be that when you find a distributor someone who you think you can work with you would work with them for a year and you would then give them the support that they require from sales and marketing and technical and when it is required but the times come when if they don't have any success then you have to move on and try and find somebody else so the whole issue is under constant review basically (Case study SME).

The presence of trust and sense of fairness makes formal organisation or formal contracts between partners unnecessary. Formalisation only occurs when it is seen as source of advantage for both partners:

> We did not have any official arrangements with this initial company – there was no written agreements – it was just 'we sell to you and you can sell to anyone' – based on our friendship and mutual trust (Case study SME).

> Initially, we did not have any formal contract. We had trust; we met and liked each other (Case study SME).

> We were doing a bit ad hoc, we were putting money into it, and he was putting money into it. We hadn't formed a company, officially. The goods were being sold through his company name (Case study SME).

> No it's a partnership, a gentleman's agreement basically. We need them and they need us so we work together (Case study SME).

In this study it was concluded that relationship is seen as a multidimensional concept which evolves from a commercial perspective to a friendlier and more personal one. This is consciously managed by the SME as a way of managing the business itself. The perception of trust and sense of fairness (mutual benefits and effort) must accompany the process.

Relationship development strategies

The critical or key practices of international relationship building are:

- *Approaching a foreign client with an open mind.* To build international relationships and business, it is necessary to approach the target market with a positive attitude towards it and the ability to accept the perspectives of businesses in that market and the associated culture. This includes speaking their language, understanding their traditions and appreciating their food and drink:

  > Obviously you will not go with a closed mind to any market place because you have to accept the way that they are, you're in their country. We try and speak a bit of the language when we're there but I'm dreadful with language. I can never remember any words but I always try and say hello and goodbye in what the native language is, I always try and drink the local beers and eat the local foods. I've had food poisoning a couple of times but they respect that obviously. I made a mistake with the coffee one time but if you keep trying and enjoy their company they'll enjoy yours and hopefully you'll get more work (Case study SME).

- *Compliance with the relationship rules and expected roles.* In a relationship, partners have their own individual rules and roles, implicitly or not. For the relationship to be developed, and consequently to be maintained, partners must comply with those rules and roles. Breaking the rules and/or not fulfilling the roles are potential causes for dissatisfaction and disappointment that will lead eventually to the cessation of the relationship.

- *Being cooperative and supportive*. This means not only helping partners and other stakeholders to sort all their problems, but being cooperative in a broader sense. A partner needs to be there for whatever is needed, in order to make sure that the aims are achieved. This involves being able to act for the benefit of both partners because:

  > We need them and they need us so we work together (Case study SME).
  >
  > they are now our distributor and that means we will work along with them to give them the support that they require (Case study SME).

- *Joint effort*. That is, to build a relationship, it is necessary that both parts put effort into the development of the relationship. The effort required to build relationships can be of various types and will include meetings and visits, helping solving clients' difficulties, meeting the promises, complying with the expected roles and rules of the relationship, demonstrating trust in the partner, and ensuring fair treatment of the different parties in the relationship.

Summary and implications

This chapter has suggested that the internationalisation process within manufacturing SMEs is driven and made possible by the social and business networks of the entrepreneurs. Their international network starts most frequently from home. Alternatively, internationalisation can also be prompted by an international network insider who is motivated to interact with that particular SME on the basis of the company's public reputation or on the experiential knowledge in respect of that company. SME internationalisation is a pattern that emerges and is shaped by an array of formal and informal relationships.

Entrepreneurs are able to choose and manage the relationship network to which they belong. Their decision making is based on perceptual, individual criteria. Entrepreneurs choose to enter a new foreign market or to expand their business into an existing foreign market so long as they:

- trust the partner who proposes or facilitates the internationalisation opportunity or international growth
- trust that the relationship will bring the expected outcomes.

SME internationalisation strategy encompasses two coexisting dimensions: one that is intended and deliberate and another that is unintended and evolving. This difference implies that entrepreneurs influence their internationalisation process by choosing and managing the relationship network to which they belong. It also suggests that the extent of the networks of the entrepreneurs and their networking capabilities are influential in the process of internationalisation. Thus, interventionist policy programmes should support the development of the networking capabilities and relational abilities of the entrepreneur, in order to promote SME internationalisation. It is not only a question of establishing formal networks, but providing the conditions for entrepreneurs to expand their own networks of relationships and assisting in the development of skills to underpin relationship management. Other commentators have suggested that increased competitive pressures demand increased cooperation among firms (Barringer 1997). Thus, efforts to encourage entrepreneurs' networking capability will be beneficial for the whole economy.

Finally, this chapter is based on the experiences of the SMEs of the business-to-business sector and, as is known, businesses within this sector are more dependent on relational capabilities. Therefore, in terms of moving on the state of current thinking, the proposals made in this chapter should be extended to be verified in different industries and geographic settings.

Questions emerging from this chapter

Five key questions emerge from the consideration of the influence of the networks of the entrepreneur on the development of international activities and markets. These are:

1. How does networking and relationship management support the development of international activities and markets?
2. What are the differences between the intentional and non-intentional dimensions of networks?
3. What key information sources underpin the intentional dimension of networking?
4. Who typically constitutes the network of the international SME?
5. What is the role of trust in the building of international networks and relationships?

Bibliography

Aaby, N.E. and Salter, S.F. (1989), 'Management Influences on Export Performance: A Review of the Empirical Literature 1978–1988', *International Marketing Review*, **6** (4), 7–26.

Andersen, O. (1993), 'On the Internationalization Process of Firms: A Critical Analysis', *Journal of International Business Studies*, **24** (2), 209–31.

Anderson, J.C., Hakansson, H. and Johanson, J. (1994), 'Dyadic Business Relationships within a Business Network Context', *Journal of Marketing*, **47** (Fall), 55–67.

Andersson, S. (2000), 'Internationalization of the Firm from an Entrepreneurial Perspective', *International Studies of Management Organizations*, **30** (1), 63–92.

Baird, I., Lyles, M.J. and Orris, J.B. (1994), 'The Choice of International Strategies by Small Businesses', *Journal of Small Business Management*, **32** (1), 48–59.

Barringer, B. (1997), 'The Effects of Relational Channel Exchange on the Small Firm: A Conceptual Framework', *Journal of Small Business Management*, April, 65–79.

Beamish, P.W. and Munro, H. (1987), 'The Export Performance of Small and Medium-Sized Canadian Manufacturers', *Canadian Journal of Administrative Sciences*, **3** (1), 29–40.

Bell, J. (1995), 'The Internationalization of Small Computer Software Firms: A Further Challenge to Stage Theories', *European Journal of Marketing*, **29** (8), 60–75.

Bilkey, W.J. and Tesar, G. (1977), 'The Export Behaviour of Smaller-Sized Wisconsin Manufacturing Firms', *Journal of International Business Studies*, **8** (1), 93–8.

Birley, S. (1985), 'The Role of Networks in the Entrepreneurial Process', *Journal of Business Venturing*, **1**, 107–17.

Blankenburg, D. (1995), 'A Network Approach to Foreign Market Entry' in Moller, K. (ed.), *Business Marketing: An Interaction and Network Perspective*, Kluwer, Boston MA.

Cavusgil, S.T. (1984), 'Differences Among Exporting Firms Based on their Degree of Internationalization', *Journal of Business Research*, **12**, 195 208.

Cavusgil, S.T. and Zou, S. (1994), 'Marketing Strategy-Performance Relationship: An Investigation on the Empirical Link on Export Market Ventures', *Journal of Marketing*, **58** (January), 1–21.

Chetty, S. and Holm, D.B. (2000), 'Internationalisation of Small to Medium-Sized Manufacturing Firms: A Network Approach', *International Business Review*, **9** (1), 77–93.

Crick, D. (1995), 'An Investigation into the Targeting of UK Export Assistance', *European Journal of Marketing*, **29** (8), 76–94.

Denis, J.E. and Depelteau, D. (1985), 'Market Knowledge, Diversification and Export Expansion', *Journal of International Business Studies*, **16** (4), 77–89.

Dhanaraj, C. and Beamish, P.W. (2003), 'A Resource-Based Approach to the Study of Export Performance', *Journal of Small Business Management*, **41** (3), 242–61.
Dichtl, E., Leibold, M., Koglmayr, H.G. and Mueller, S. (1990), 'International Orientation as a Pre-Condition for Export Success', *Journal of International Business Studies*, **21** (1), 23–41.
Eisenhardt, K.M. (1989), 'Building Theories from Case Study Research', *Academy of Management Review*, **14** (4), 532–50.
Ellis, P. (2000), 'Social Ties and Foreign Market Entry', *Journal of International Business Studies*, **31** (3), 443–69.
Eriksson, K. and Chetty, S. (2003), 'The Effect of Experience and Absorptive Capacity on Foreign Market Knowledge', *International Business Review*, **12**, 673–95.
Fletcher, D. (2004), 'International Entrepreneurship and the Small Business', *Entrepreneurship and Regional Development*, **16** (4), 289–305.
Ford, D. (1980), 'The Developments of Buyer-Seller Relationship in Industrial Markets', *European Journal of Marketing*, **14**, 339–53.
Fuller, T. and Lewis, J. (2003), 'Relationships Mean Everything', *British Journal of Management*, **13** (4), 317–36.
Gemunden, H.G. (1991), 'Success Factors of Export Marketing: A Meta-analytic Critique in the Empirical Studies' in Paliwoda, S.J. (ed.), *New Perspectives on International Marketing*, Routledge, London.
Granovetter, M. (1973), 'The Strength of Weak Ties', *American Journal of Sociology*, **78** (6), 1360–80.
Holm, D.B., Eriksson, K. and Johanson, J. (1999), 'Creating Value through Mutual Commitment to Business Network Relationships', *Strategic Management Journal*, **20** (5), 467–86.
Holzmuller, H.H. and Kasper, H. (1991), 'On a Theory of Export Performance: Personal and Organizational Determinants of Export Trade Activities Observed in Small and Medium-Sized Firms', *Management International Review*, **31**, 45–70.
Johanson, J. and Mattsson, L. (1988), 'Internationalisation in Industrial Systems – A Network Approach' in Hood, N. and Vahlne, J.E. (eds), *Strategies in Global Competition*, Croom Helm, London.
Johanson, J. and Vahlne, J. (1990), 'The Mechanism of Internationalisation', *International Marketing Review*, **4** (7), 11–24.
Larson, A. (1992), 'Network Dyads in Entrepreneurial Settings: A Study of the Governance of Exchange Relationships', *Administrative Science Quarterly*, **27**, 76–104.
Liang, N. and Parkhe, A. (1997), 'Importer Behavior: The Neglected Counterpart of International Exchange', *Journal of International Business Studies*, **38** (3), 495–530.
Liang, N. and Stump, R.L. (1996), 'Cognitive Heuristics in Overseas Vendor Search and Evaluation: A Proposed Model of Importer Buying Behavior', *International Executive*, **38** (6), 779–806.
Manolova, T.S., Brush, C.G., Edelman, L.F. and Greene, P.C. (2002), 'Internationalization of Small Firms: Personal Factors Revisited', *International Small Business Journal*, **20** (1), 9–31.
Mason, J. (1996), *Qualitative Researching*, Sage Publications, London.
Mendenhall, M., Beaty, D. and Oddu, G. (1993), 'Where Have all the Theorists Gone? An Archival Review of the International Management Literature', *International Journal of Management*, **10** (2), 146–53.
Namiki, N. (1988), 'Export Strategy for Small Business', *Journal of Small Business Management*, **26** (2), 33–7.
Papadopolous, N. (1987), 'Approaches to International Market Selection for Small and Medium-Sized Enterprises' in Rosson, P.J. and Reid, S.D. (eds), *Managing Export Entry and Expansion: Concepts and Practice*, Praeger, New York.
Rao, T.R. and Naidu, G.M. (1992), 'Are the Stages of Internationalization Empirically Supportable?' *Journal of Global Marketing*, **6** (1–2), 147–70.
Reid, S.D. and Rosson, P.J. (1987), 'Managing Export Entry and Expansion: An Overview' in Rosson, P.J. and Reid, S.D. (eds), *Managing Export Entry and Expansion: Concepts and Practice*, Praeger, New York.
Reuber, A.R. and Fischer, E. (1997), 'The Influence of the Management Team's International Experience on the Internationalization Behaviours of SMEs', *Journal of International Business Studies*, **4**, 807–25.
Uzzi, B. (1997), 'Social Structure and Competition in Interfirm Networks: The Paradox of Embeddedness', *Administrative Science Quarterly*, **42** (1), 35–67.
Yin, R. (1984), *Case Study Research*, Sage Publications, Thousand Oaks, CA.
Zacharakis, A.L. (1997), 'Entrepreneurial Entry into Foreign Markets: A Transaction Cost Perspective', *Entrepreneurship Theory and Practice*, **21** (3), 23–39.
Zafarullah, M., Ali, M. and Young, S. (1998), 'The Internationalization of the Small Firm in Developing Countries: Exploratory Research from Pakistan', *Journal of Global Marketing*, **11** (3), 21–40.

Appendix 5.1: The research method and approach

The present chapter is derived from a qualitative and interpretative research work aimed at understanding the mechanisms of the internationalisation process in manufacturing SMEs from a relationship network perspective. The exploratory nature of the research and the wish to contribute to theory elaboration led to the choice of a case study approach (Yin 1984; Eisenhardt 1989).

We set out to study SMEs involved with international businesses for a number of years, which considered international business an important and substantial part of their operations and not something done on a casual and infrequent basis. Moreover, they needed to belong to business-to-business sectors, since relationship management is a concept most often related to industrial, institutional and services markets rather than consumer markets (Anderson *et al.* 1994). Due to these definitional restrictions, it was imperative to use listings provided by institutions and agencies which could provide detailed information on the companies, for the selection of the cases.

Out of 14 interviewed companies, 5 were considered adequate for the study purpose. Eisenhardt (1989) recommends that the number of cases be kept between 4 and 10 because with less than 4, it will be difficult to build theory. With more than 10, the volume of data will be difficult to deal with and review. Thus 5 cases were considered an adequate sample size for the purpose of the present study.

In each company, data was generated in respect of every separate foreign market or, at least, from the entries in the company's most important markets according to the interviewee's own criteria. This means that each foreign market entry is approached as a discrete unit of the study. That approach is in compliance with other similar research projects as undertaken by Cavusgil and Zou (1994) and Ellis (2000). Data were generated in a narrative way undertaken by the respondent in a historical perspective. The aim was to develop rich, in-depth and detailed descriptions of each individual market entry and of the developments that followed.

In order to investigate the implications of networking and relationship to the SMEs' internationalisation process, two critical incidents were used, based on the work of Johanson and Mattsson (1988):

- The company's foreign market extension, that is, the entrance into a new foreign market
- The company's foreign market advancements.

Foreign market extension comprises the classical decisions on market, partner and entry mode. Foreign market advancements include the developments after market entry, whether increasing market presence in the same markets (penetration) or entering new, different market segments (diversification). To this end, a qualitative analysis technique was adopted.

The descriptions given by the interviewees were analysed by means of cross-sectional and categorical indexing of categories that were devised straightforwardly from the interview schedule (Mason 1996). A complete analysis was carried out in each case followed by a cross-case comparative analysis based on comparing and connecting categories across the five transcripts. To this end, a set of analytical charts were constructed. The analysis consisted of looking for pattern of similarities.

Appendix 5.2: Description of market entries of each case

Case 01: BMO

BMO was established in 1969 as a small rebuilder of secondhand machines and tools. Its job entailed finding and solving the fault, rebuilding and coating the machines to bring them back into good serviceable conditions and then resell. Most often innovations were made so as to add value to the machines. In the early 1970s BMO turned to the international market. Its major motivations for internationalisation were to find alternative ways to cope with the UK markets' downturns and sort out supply problems. Internationalisation brought a tremendous growth to the company. Presently, BMO offers a large range of conventional metal cutting equipment to a wide range of industries and it has become a worldwide business with international reputation. Its major foreign markets are: Italy (1972), North America (1975), India (1980) and China (1987).

BMO's internationalisation process

1970s: Home market (membership of a European Trade Association) → Entrance into **EU** (Relationship development with Trade Association's members) → **EU** market expansion/penetration – mainly into **Italy**

1975: Home market (membership of North America Trade Association) → Entrance into **North America and Mexico** (relationship development with North America Trade Association's members) → North America Markets expansion/penetration

1980: Home market (contacts with Engineering Federation and English institutions in India) (direct contacts to Indian companies) → entrance into **India** (relationship development with Indian companies + development of personal relationship) → India market expansion/penetration

1987: Home market (personal friend visits China + meeting a Chinese businessman) → Entrance into **China** (follow-up visit by company's engineers + contact with British Institutions of Commerce) → new business in China (MD personal relations + establishment of an agent) → China market expansion/penetration.

Case 02: JMT

JMT was established in 1982 as a general manufacturer supplying products for industries such as the pharmaceutical, health care and hospital, petrochemical and food industries. Since 1996 it has concentrated on sterilisation products aimed at the pharmaceutical industry in particular, and also health care and hospitals. Its internationalisation started in 1990 as a means of 'spreading the risk of being in business'. Presently, the attitude of the company's directors towards internationalisation is that this is a strategy for firm growth. The major foreign markets are Sri Lanka (1990), Thailand (1992); USA (1994); Finland (2000). Other markets are Australia, Italy, Iran and the Middle East, and India, but these are not recurrent and represent very small percentages of sales. JMT has been attempting for many years to enter into the EU (France and Germany) but has encountered a number of difficulties.

JMT's internationalisation process

1990: Home market (contacted by importer) → entrance into **Sri Lanka**
1992: Home market (contacted by importer) → entrance into **Thailand**
1994: Home market (contacted by the manager of a UK supplier's subsidiary in the US who was a friend of the owner-manager → entrance into **US** (contact leaves the company) → business reduced.
1998: (European market manager of an American Company + US distributor) → expansion into the US (trade mission contact) → new client-direct sales operations being planned
2002: Home market (trade agency + foreign client) → Entrance into **Finland**.

Case 03: MEB

MEB is a family business, manufacturer and repairer of an extensive range of traditional, industrial and high-precision saws and accessories. Established in 1964, the company has always aimed at innovation and quality, having the most up-to-date equipment and technology, including robotics. MEB has had a continuous, steady but slow growth. Today, MEB has become an international company with a joint venture in the USA.

According to the company's MD, internationalisation 'started by meeting people', which 'is one of the better ways of doing business'. The company's international debut was in the early 1980s, to France, following a German trade fair. That business lasted only for two years. Presently, the most important foreign markets are the USA and Southern Ireland. The company also exports to other countries but in a very small, not recurring scale.

MEB's internationalisation process

Early 1980: Home market (seminar talk + met potential clients) → **Republic of Ireland** (visits, personal contacts and clients recommendations) → market extension
1996: Home market (the son of a previously long-term friend and supplier + US importer) → entrance into **US** market (relationship with US importer) → establishment of partnership (further developments of the relationship) → joint venture
2001: Home market: (contacted by another **US** company) – direct sales.

Case 04: PNPS

PNPS was established as a family business in 1984 supplying pipes, fittings and associated items to the gas and oil industry, both offshore and onshore. In 1997 it turned into a limited company but remained a small company employing eight people. Exports started in 1995 unexpectedly, and became the company's major business (export sales represented 95 per cent of the total turnover in 2003). The company has been actively exporting for about eight to nine years now. In 2003, the company was sold to a foreign group. Before that, the major overseas markets were Tunisia, Turkmenistan, Lebanon and Nigeria. The company also had business in Russia, Libya, Holland, Malaysia and Australia.

PNPS's internationalisation process

1995: Home market (UK client recommendation) → Entrance into **Tunisia** (relationship with Tunisian directors + visits) → Tunisia market expansion

1995: Home market (new employee's contact) → Entrance into **Libya** (employee leaves) → business ceased

1996–1997: Home market (Tunisian client's employee) → **Russia** → (subsidiary taken over) → business ceased

1997–1998: Home market (owner-manager's personal friend) → entrance into **Turkmenistan** (relationship development) → Turkmenistan market expansion

1998: Home market (MD's business and personal contact) → entrance into **Malaysia** and **Australia** → business ceased because the market became too competitive

1999: Home market (MD's personal friend who worked for a Dutch company) → **Holland** – (contract ends and Dutch friend leaves) → business ceased in 2001

1999: Home market (contacted by Nigerian agent via internet) → **Nigeria** market entrance

1999: Home market (Dutch friend's recommendation) → contacted by a Nigerian subsidiary of a Lebanon-based company → **Nigeria** market – 2001 (friend's recommendation + Nigerian subsidiary recommendation) → **Lebanon**.

Case 05: HPCL

Established in 1919, HPCL is a family business in the field of manufacturing, repairing and distributing a whole range of pumps and transmission systems with applications in various industries. Their international activities started in 1985 when a new export sales director joined the company with a plan to import and distribute in the UK an innovative, versatile type of pump he had experience with from his previous employment as an international manager. In 1992 when the original manufacturer ceased operations and the product's patent expired, HPCL decided to manufacture a similar pump range. It had substantial experience with the product and knowledge of the market. Moreover, due to a long-term relationship between the export sales director and the former pump manufacturer, HPCL had access to its client's dataset.

Export started in 1995 by contacting the former distributors and buyers of the product. At present, the most important markets are Germany, Holland, France, Ireland, Greece and Spain. The firm also does or have done a little business with other countries such as Denmark, Switzerland, Sweden, Canada, the Oman, Taiwan, the Caribbean, Grenada and Australia.

HPCL's internationalisation process

1995: Home market (contacting old product distributor) → entrance into **Germany** (development of friendship) → German market expansion (1999) (German client) → **France** (trade fair + new distributors) → French market expansion

1996: Home market (contacting old product distributor and buyers) → **Holland** (contacting friend, ex-employee of a competitor and making him a distributor) → Dutch market expansion

2001: Home market (a friend, owner of a complementary business) → entrance into **Greece** (participation in exhibition + new distributors) → new business in Greece → market expansion

2002: Home market (a friend, owner of a complementary business) → entrance into **Southern Ireland** (development of personal relation with a client) (UK market distributor starts working in SI) (UK clients' SI subsidiaries become clients) → SI market expansion

2003: Home market (contacts with British commercial embassy trade department) → (find a distributor in Spain) → entrance into **Spain**.

6 Managing with complexity, uncertainty and ambiguity

Keith Herrmann

It is well known that change is the signifier of the contemporary world. During the last twenty years a multitude of factors have combined to revolutionise the landscape of the global economy, resulting in a 'new economy' highly reliant on the exploitation of science, technology and knowledge. This globally interconnected economy has also seen the rise of emerging economies, e.g. the BRIC's (Brazil, Russia, India and China), competing directly with the established economic order. The impact of globalisation is forcing many established economies to become increasingly dependent on the creativity and innovative energy of its entrepreneurs and is spawning a new form of industrial revolution (Leadbetter 1999; Kusum *et al.* 1999). These features of global change have exerted pressure on commercial organisations (businesses) to cope with the pervasive influence of lower-cost competitors, the increased provision of high-quality goods and services by emerging economies, and the accelerated obsolescence of current technologies.

At an organisational level businesses have also had to deal with demands for change emerging from the processes of international deregulation, persistent advances in technology, and increased global competition emanating from a customer-driven market place. The impact of globalisation and the high rates of change in the market place have created conditions of trade which are unprecedented. Many small firms trading globally are having to cope constantly with the uncertainties and pressures of a globalised world in which the competitive advantage of firms is no longer dominated by lowest price, but are influenced by a whole variety of factors related to added value, exploiting the core competence of the firm and delivering to customer demand under increasingly pressurised timescales (Etemad and Wright 2003). Change has been imposed on many organisations, both in the private and public sectors, and driven by conditions of ambiguity, uncertainty and complexity, demands increasingly creative responses, often underpinned by management approaches located in the domain of entrepreneurship (Hannon and Atherton 1998; Gibb 1999).

For many small businesses trading in global markets, the challenge of managing is severe, akin to dealing with ever-changing weather conditions on an Artic expedition. Never sure of the conditions, never sure of whether or not they have all the gear to cope, firms like these only survive and grow through developing an entrepreneurial response and a sensitive approach to managing their stakeholders.

One of the major challenges facing small firms trading in global markets is that of managing and coping with the significant levels of risk arising from the uncertainty and complexity that comes with trading globally. This chapter will explore some of these uncertainties and complexities and consider how the ambiguities of trading in foreign markets require small firms to develop an entrepreneurial response as a way of managing and/or coping. In considering some of the external factors in the broader task environment of the small firm and how they engage in trading globally, the chapter will also argue that this entrepreneurial response is grounded in the 'life world' of the small firm entrepreneur (Gibb 2002).

The chapter reflects on the experiences of two case study businesses which each have to cope with a range of very different types of uncertainty and complexity in their trading environment. It will highlight a number of the strategies and coping mechanisms adopted by these firms and demonstrate how the external environment and the associated complexity has a significant impact on the ability of the small firm to engage in global trade.

Global pressures

The chapter first considers the task environment of the typical small firm operating in the global market place. Figure 6.1 outlines some of the global pressures facing small firms and how these pressures are changing the relationships between individuals, their organisations and the wider society. The key drivers within this model are the phenomena of globalisation and the resultant forces of competitiveness and innovation. Gibb's (1999) model of the entrepreneurial paradigm shows how globalisation has an impact on the state, on the organisation of business activity, on public services and on individuals, and has generated significant uncertainty and complexity in the task environment of the small firm. It will be argued that the characteristics of the global

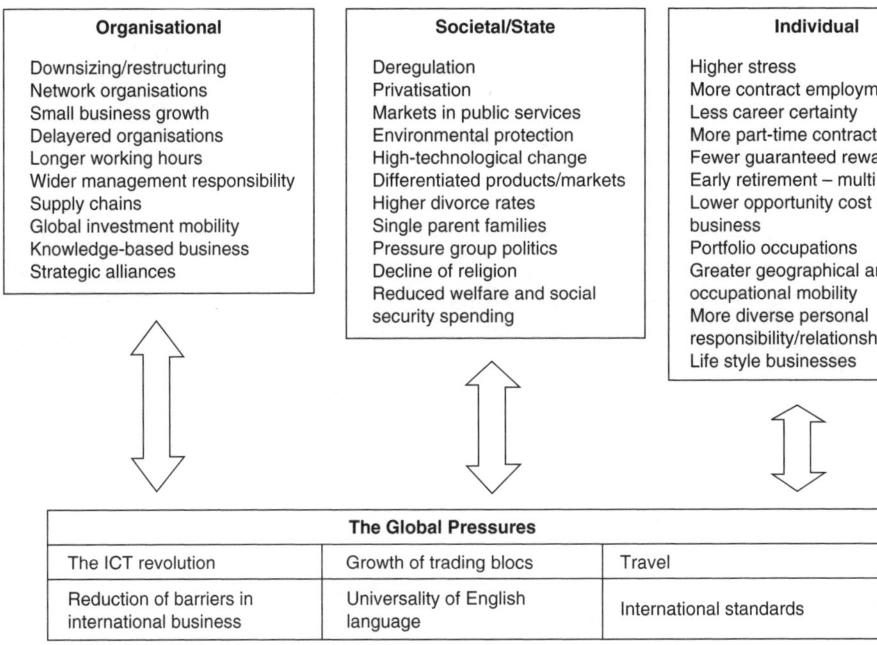

Source: Adapted from Gibb (1999)

Figure 6.1 Gibb's model of the entrepreneurial paradigm

market place outlined herein and the consequent uncertainty and complexity arising from this task environment requires an entrepreneurial response from small firms trading globally.

The literature on SMEs in the global economy shows that large firms have a variety of strategies for managing and responding to many of the aforementioned global pressures identified by Gibb (Freel 1997; Vinnell and Hamilton 1999; Klofsten and Jones-Evans 2000; Ensley *et al.* 2000; Minkes and Foxall 2000; Smallbone and Wyer 2000; O'Gorman 2001). Large firms engage in market repositioning strategies, develop alliances, engage in mergers and acquisitions and develop strategies for achieving greater control of international markets (Murtha *et al.* 2001). By contrast, many small firms involved in trading globally do not have the resources nor do they have the capability to adopt these kinds of strategies. As the case study in Chapter 1 shows, small firms adopt a different strategic posture when building global alliances. This often involves a configuration of loose global networks and personal associations rather than formal arrangements bounded by contractual alliances and mergers and acquisitions. As with large firms though, this brings with it the challenge of managing more dispersed and complex stakeholder relationships at local and international levels with greater degrees of associated complexity and uncertainty (Bernasconi *et al.* 2006).

Given that trust is one of the key principles of trade, small firms have to manage relationships where in some cases they have not even met their trading partners on the other side of the world as a result of internet-based trading platforms. This raises a number of questions, primarily related to what proxies exist for establishing, gauging and maintaining levels of trust. Small firms develop a variety of different coping mechanisms for managing global supply chains. The engineering business profiled in Chapter 9 took the option to buy out one of its principal suppliers in Eastern Europe as a way of managing the complexity contained within its supply chain and establishing direct control over its trading arrangements – an illustration of managing global pressures through formal integration as opposed to managing via the strength of 'weak ties' (Granovetter 1983).

As the case studies in this chapter will reveal, small firms trading in global markets face an inordinate number of hurdles and challenges. They are often faced with substantial risk by working with trading partners with whom they have had no working relationship. They have to respond quickly to international trade opportunities and be flexible in order to meet quick turnarounds on enquiries from customers. They have to be creative and innovative in solving problems in global supply chains to ensure that orders are completed as required. They have to be persuasive and committed to seeing things through. The case studies will show how dogged persistence in the face of the many challenges and hurdles that make trading globally so difficult for many small businesses is a key requirement for success. Many of these characteristics are identified by Gibb (1993) as entrepreneurial characteristics (see Table 6.1).

The entrepreneurial 'life-world'

As explained, the 'life-world' of the small business entrepreneur as espoused by Gibb (1999) is a useful metaphor for the 'life-world' of the global trading small firm – it involves managing uncertainties, complexities and ambiguities on a day-to-day basis. In assessing the global operations of small firms we can identify a number of characteristics which shape

Table 6.1 Behaviours, skills and attributes of enterprising people

Skills	⇐ Behaviours ⇒	Attributes
• Problem solving • Creativity • Persuasiveness • Planning • Negotiating • Decision making	• Acting independently • Actively achieving goals • Flexibly responding to challenges • Coping with and enjoying uncertainty • Taking risky actions in uncertain environments • Persuading others • Commitments to make things happen • Opportunity seeking • Solving problems/conflicts	• Self-confident • Autonomous • Achievement-orientated • Versatile • Dynamic • Resourceful

Source: Gibb (1993)

this 'life-world' and influence the way in which these firms respond to the direct influence of their customers (or key stakeholders) and to the more indirect influence of their external task environment. These characteristics include:

- Higher degrees of uncertainty and complexity to manage – with the factors of production relying on global supply chains, customers in geographically dispersed locations and product orders subject to currency fluctuations, unreliability in the freighting system and the risk of non-payments for goods delivered and services rendered.
- Wider span of control – the global trading small firm has to contend with managing suppliers and customers all over the world in a value chain that is geographically dispersed and thus requiring a global system of control.
- Greater customer dependency – with a global customer base where cash flows are stretched by time as it takes even longer to deliver to customer needs, small firms are highly dependent on their customers to secure the sustainability of the business. It is often very difficult to replace an export client with another as the effort required to secure global business is resource and time intensive.
- Highly decentralised networks – with global supply chains on the demand and supply side, small firms have to manage relationships based on informal links and alliances. Given that their key stakeholders are removed from their control and thus on the periphery of their physical task environment, they have to rely on the strength of 'weak ties' to manage relationships. Small firms seldom have the resources to deploy their employees to represent their interests and thus have to use third-party agents. Aside from the practical challenges and costs of building reliability and trust in these relationships, their remoteness creates more complexity in the supply chain.
- A sense of total responsibility for the success and failure of the business – given the exposure to risks, many of which are often out of the immediate control of the small firm owner-manager, global trade highlights the sensitivity of the business

> to success and failure. The Thorncroft case study outlined below demonstrates that the success and failure of trading globally is contingent upon variables which are very often beyond the control of the firm, but can nonetheless have a significant impact on the continued survival of the business. Unanticipated events (for example, their goods being impounded by the US Food and Drug Administration) can seriously disrupt the relationship between buyer and seller. On the other hand, poorly developed export strategies can also result in less optimal outcomes (for example, closure of routes to market due to lack of anticipated sales).

Within this entrepreneurial 'life-world' there are many lessons for the global trading small firm. As this chapter will outline, it is imperative that small firms become more entrepreneurial to cope with the global pressures and uncertainties arising from trading globally. Small firms can also develop these entrepreneurial traits by designing their businesses to be entrepreneurial. This is based on adopting the same learning models used by entrepreneurs. Gibb (1999) argues that entrepreneurs learn by doing, by making mistakes, by copying, by experiment, by problem solving and opportunity seeking, and from more explicit formal sources. The entrepreneurial small firm learns from its stakeholder environment – from its suppliers, its customers, its bank, accountant and solicitor and even its competitors. Embedding these modes of learning into the modalities for trading globally is critical for helping the small firm to cope with the uncertainty and complexity that surrounds it. The case studies in this chapter highlight how small firms respond to and cope with uncertainty through developing responses couched in a way of learning that accurately reflects the 'life-world' of the entrepreneur.

Despite the call for an entrepreneurial response to the complexities of global trade, little is known about the actual skills required of managers of global SMEs. Much of today's management literature is grounded in a functionalist response – providing managers with management and strategy development tools, for example, Porter's five forces model or the more traditional SWOT or PEST analysis and corporate strategy models which do not reflect the 'life-world' of the globally trading small firm (Lyles *et al.* 1993; Hannon and Atherton 1998). Although many of these strategy models provide powerful diagnostic tools, they often only offer time-bound insights into global trends and seldom equip managers to deal with rapid change, uncertainty and shifts in global markets. By contrast, Gibb (1993) argues that coping with uncertainty and complexity requires enterprising behaviours underpinned by enterprising skills and attributes to ensure speed of responsiveness, anticipation of market change and coping with the challenges of operating in the global market place. Table 6.1 outlines some typical examples of the behaviours, skills and attributes required of enterprising people.

These behaviours, skills and attributes are crucial to igniting the creativity and innovation which is central to achieving and sustaining success in the global market place. They can be strongly associated with the requirements of trading globally; they are associated with managing a dynamic growing business, with coping with the risks of potential failure, with the need to exhibit high rates of innovation and with adopting a holistic approach to management beyond the functionalist skills of marketing, financial management, production and HR management. To summarise, catalysing entrepreneurial action is required as the standard response.

Managing complexity in the global trading small firm

Having established that many of the external pressures facing small firms require an entrepreneurial response, the next section outlines two case studies to highlight how firms respond to these pressures in practice. The case studies show that firms encounter a complex trading environment fraught with complexity and uncertainty. The following section also explores the coping mechanisms small firms adopt for dealing with these high levels of uncertainty in the trading environment, and will outline a number of responses which are formulated around taking entrepreneurial action as a first principle.

Aside from introducing and discussing the case studies, this section will also explore the following aspects regarding how small firms manage their external task environment and the stakeholders which have a bearing on their trading activities:

- Stakeholder management – this is fundamental to how small firms build global networks and alliances, make sense of the emergent trends in their industries and cope with the increasingly complex relationships that are required for trading globally. Having the capacity to nurture 'know who' networks of external stakeholders is crucial to the future survival of the firm.
- Networks and relationship management – there is a need to build strong relationships with key stakeholders given the wider span of control involved in trading globally. Managing networks and relationships is important for penetrating new markets and developing new business with existing clients and customers (that is, managing stakeholders). Having the capacity to manage decentralised and autonomous units and loosely connected networks is critical to managing in the global environment in which many small firms compete.
- Developing the entrepreneurial organisation – the culture of an organisation has a direct bearing on its competitiveness and its ability to respond to external pressures. Hence the design of entrepreneurial organisations is another requirement for helping firms respond to global complexity and manage their interface with key stakeholders. Having the internal capacity to configure entrepreneurial organisations is also important to ensure that they are able to cope with the challenges of greater turbulence in the environment.
- Flexible strategic orientation – this involves continually scanning the task environment of the small firm for opportunities and threats which may have an impact on its continued survival and growth. Being strategically aware of future opportunities is also achieved by 'bringing the future forward' for key customers by demonstrating how newly configured products, technologies and strategic added value are incorporated into the future strategy of the firm.

Many small firms recognise the need to respond to the changing needs and demands of an increasingly competitive environment. As outlined above, it is suggested that global competition requires small firms to adopt an entrepreneurial response. The increasing internationalisation of the market place and the related need to cope flexibly with the 'global' aspects of greater complexity and uncertainty in managing the small firm are well illustrated by the case studies outlined in this section. The remainder of this chapter explores how small firms respond to uncertainty and complexity. The stories of these two businesses are stark in their contrast – they describe businesses involved in international trade in different countries, and have been chosen because they provide unique insights into how different the challenges of trading globally are and how the external trading environment is (a) very different for each firm, (b) has significantly different impacts on the competitiveness of each firm and (c) provides useful lessons about the challenges of managing in the global environment. Notwithstanding these differences the two case studies have a number of similarities. Both firms face the vagaries of making sense of the global trading environment, for example, dealing with international trade quotas, import tariffs and the regulatory aspects of importing and exporting. The experiences of both firms demonstrate that the challenges of trading internationally are significant. Appendices 6.1 and 6.2 outline the experiences of the case study businesses with the import and export process, and even though Thorncroft's experiences were not of the same scale as SUCOMA's, the costs and challenges of managing the trading process were significant for both firms.

Thorncroft – bottling success in new markets

Thorncroft produces a range of cordials and sparkling drinks that are made from original recipes, a number of which have been passed down through the family of the two owners, Guy and Sheila Woodall, for generations. The cordials and drinks have a national reputation, having being used in recipes featured on television, and are sold through high street outlets, supermarkets, health stores and delicatessens.

Thorncroft is based in Stockton near Middlesbrough, one of the large industrial cities in North East England well known for being the location of Europe's largest chemicals plants (see Figure 6.2). Thorncroft is fortunate to be located near a major sea port, and therefore benefits from ease of access to the logistics and transport infrastructure. The current level of turnover is approximately £1.5 million, although profitability has increased over the last five years. The firm currently employs six people in the North East of England, with bottling and production subcontracted to a contract bottler nearby. Thorncroft currently exports to 16 countries. The business exports directly to the USA, Canada, South Africa, Ireland, Belgium, Germany, France, Norway, Australia and Japan. Other customers, especially in the health food trade, export products on behalf of Thorncroft to Sweden, Denmark, Dubai, Hong Kong, Malaysia and Thailand. The business has encountered a number of problems in terms of developing new markets such as the United States over the last ten years.

SUCOMA – international sweeteners for trade

The sugar industry in Malawi is centred on the Sugar Corporation of Malawi (SUCOMA). It has invested heavily in the milling and estate operations and supported the development of local businesses through a programme of outsourcing its production and service operations. SUCOMA has agricultural and milling assets at Nchalo in the south east of the country and Dwangwa in the mid-central region. SUCOMA estates grow around 1.9 million metric tons (mT) of sugar cane each season, and combined with the cane grown by independent farmers, process about 2.1 million metric tonnes of cane into 240 000 mT of sugar.

International trade for SUCOMA and many of its smallholder suppliers is crucial for growing the business, but also for the alleviation of poverty in poor rural communities across Malawi. Foreign exchange earnings not only help stabilise the economy of one of

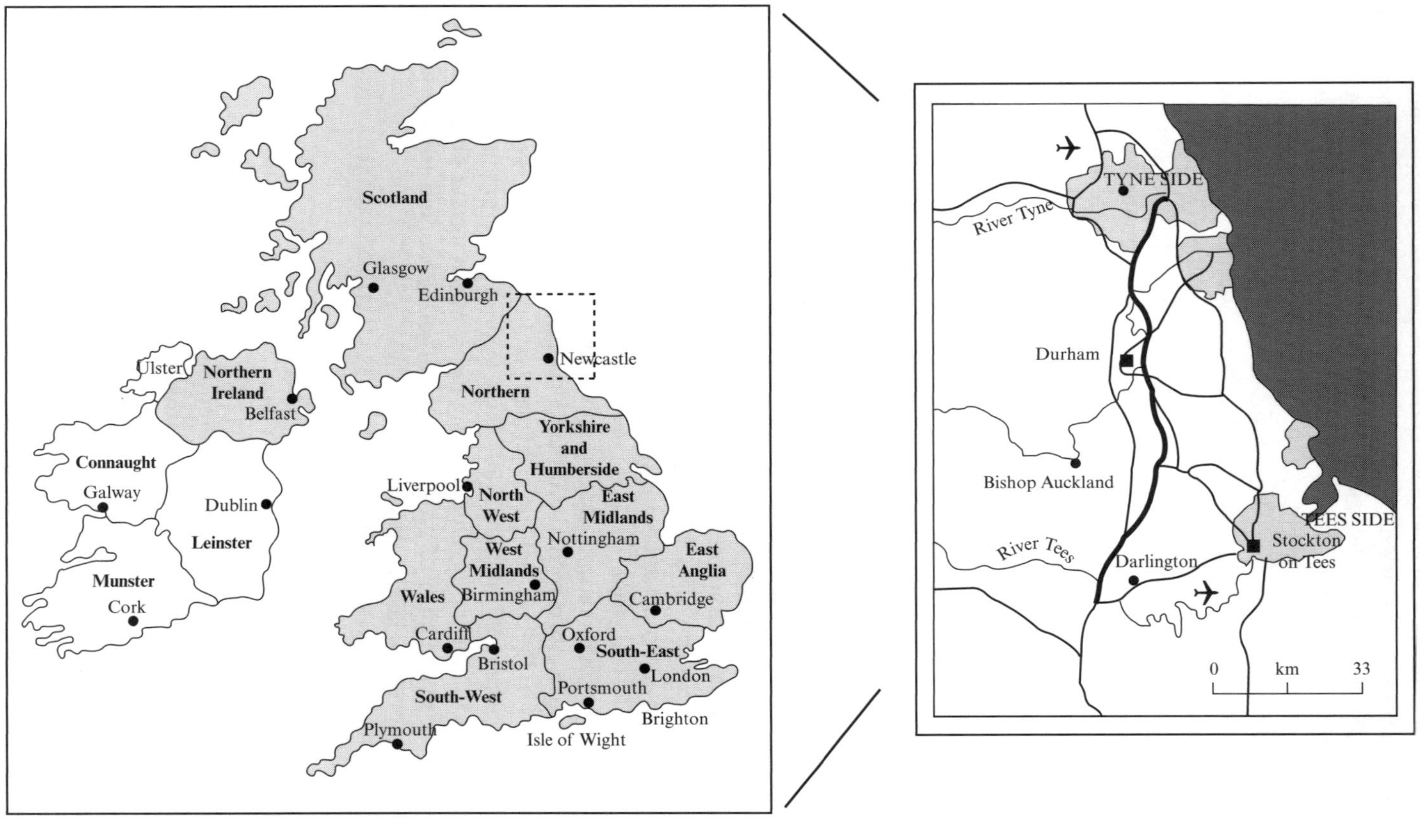

Figure 6.2 Thorncroft's location in the United Kingdom

the world's poorest nations, but have a very direct effect on local communities and the viability of rural smallholder farmers. SUCOMA exports sugar to the EU and neighbouring countries in Southern Africa. The EU preferential sales are the most lucrative, with the highest contribution per mT for Malawi sugar producers, and it benefits from having a preferential market for annually committed volumes. By contrast, regional market sales are more volatile and sensitive to world market prices.

Unlike Thorncroft, SUCOMA in Malawi is constrained by operating in a landlocked country. Aside from this, the transport infrastructure in that part of Southern Africa is a significantly limiting factor, not only in terms of cost but also in terms of how long it takes for goods to be transported. Figure 6.3 illustrates the location of the SUCOMA plantations and operations within Malawi.

The next section explores in greater detail the four themes highlighted in the introduction to this section, and, using the case studies, provides a commentary on how firms cope with the everyday complexities of global trade.

Stakeholder management

In the global trading environment in which small firms operate, whether exporting or importing, there is a need for managing a wide range of tasks and interdependencies with a complex and dispersed network of stakeholders. This is a prerequisite for trading globally, and includes managing customers, suppliers, bankers, accountants, solicitors, regulatory authorities, freight intermediaries, customs control agencies and foreign exchange authorities (Gibb 1999, 2002). Managing these 'know who' networks is the small firm's primary vehicle for influencing its immediate task environment. Understanding and responding to stakeholders' needs, and building close relationships based on trust, are fundamental ingredients for success in global trade (Hannon and Atherton 1998). Given that many of the aforementioned stakeholders may reside in other countries and have different cultural traditions and ways of doing business, sensitive stakeholder management may well be the operating imperative that ensures successful trade (Etamad and Wright 2003).

The engineering business highlighted in Chapter 1 was encumbered with a very sensitive situation with one of its suppliers in Eastern Europe when the government in that country wanted to outlaw the private ownership of businesses. Only through careful and sensitive stakeholder management was it able to ensure a continuous supply of components and negotiate a settlement with the government which allowed it to buy out its supplier in order to secure the supply of components.

Building trust – finding the right proxies

As an imperative for successful global trade, trust is fundamental to maintaining the complex web of relationships that facilitates the transacting of business between parties. Given the global nature of the trading environment it can be very difficult for small resource-constrained firms to develop appropriate 'codes of conduct' (proxies for establishing trust) for trading globally. Small firms do not have the abundance of resources that large firms have at their disposal to utilise local employees on the ground to supervise and manage the transfer of goods across continents and borders. In addition to this there are the cultural aspects of trading in other countries to contend with and manage. There are the complexities of language, different legal systems, international banking requirements,

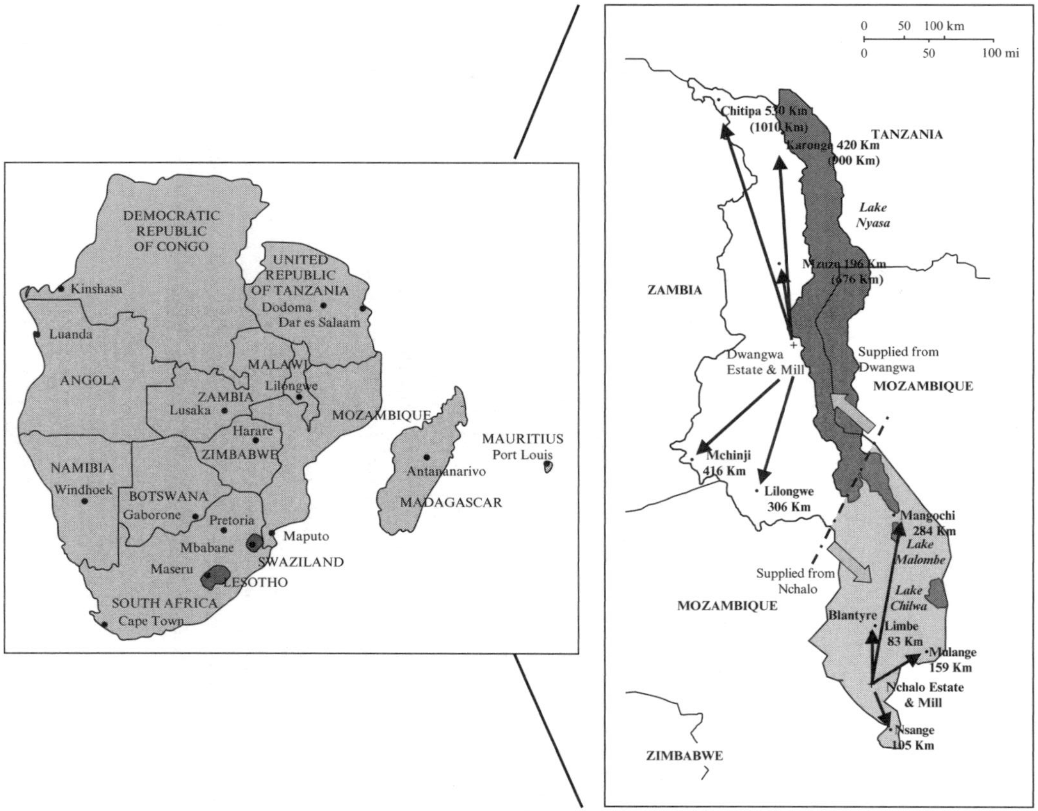

Source: SADC Country Profiles

Figure 6.3 SUCOMA operations in Malawi

customs regulations and global trade quotas to negotiate and make sense of. These are often no easy matter for the small firm operating in such an environment. Outlined below are some of the principal 'codes of conduct' which firms use to establish binding obligations with their trading partners. Many of these comply with international norms and are recognised internationally:

- The standard codes of conduct which govern international trade often involve intermediaries that facilitate exchange between the buyer and the seller. Banks are involved through issuing letters of credit, a bank-to-bank commitment of payment in favour of an exporter (seller), guaranteeing that payment will be made against certain documents that, on presentation, are found to be in compliance with terms set by the buyer. Many of these exchanges (for example, letters of credit) are governed by a set of rules published by the International Chamber of Commerce (ICC) called 'Uniform Customs and Practice' (UCP500).
- Where goods are shipped by sea freight and covered by a full set of bills of lading, title is retained by the exporter until these documents are properly released to the buyer. Unfortunately, for airfreight items, unless the goods are consigned to the buyer's bank no such control is available under an air waybill or air consignment note, as these documents are merely 'movement certificates' rather than 'documents of title'.
- In relation to online trading, firms use a variety of intermediary agencies to establish the required levels of trust to conclude the transaction. Trusted couriers are used to transfer goods and services. Online intermediaries use encryption technologies to stand as guarantor for the transaction by managing the electronic transfer of funds. These organisations are self-regulated and achieve legitimacy through endorsement from internet service providers and the financial services sector (banks).

As with the majority of other smaller businesses, Thorncroft started to export through informal channels and in response to requests from other business contacts and networks. The business was attracted to exporting because the owners liked to travel, and developing overseas markets presented them both with an opportunity to travel and see different countries. Thorncroft used their network of informal contacts and friends to access the US market. A friend offered to import the product into America on its behalf. This coincided with the business exhibiting its products in America. The owners attended food fairs and found they only received a small number of orders. Despite the attempt to access the US market using their networks, the level of sales was not encouraging and not as successful as they had anticipated.

Small firms have to contend with change in the legislative and regulatory environment that governs international trade. They also have to monitor and be aware of the 'natural laws' (for example, cultural norms and codes of conduct) related to doing business internationally. Notwithstanding the use of informal networks and stakeholder management by small firms, the rules of global trade are now also dominated by international trade agreements and repositioning in the power of trading blocs (for example, trade quotas and import tariffs). This brings additional complexity to managing what is conceptually a simple transaction between a buyer and a seller.

Managing relations with government

In some countries there is a marked lack of compliance with international protocols and 'codes of conduct'. Very often this is not due to the lack of regulatory frameworks but the fraying of the fabric of civil society – where there is little regard for the rule of law, where civil society and its elected representatives in government are not able to use the force of respect for the law as a device for creating an enabling framework for international trade, there is little chance for certainty and stability (Gibb 1999). The lack of compliance with these codes of behaviour reduces the economic efficiencies of transactions and increases the costs of doing business.

Living with day-to-day uncertainty like this requires an entrepreneurial response. In Malawi for example, SUCOMA used its contacts with key government ministries to establish a dialogue about the difficulties with the import process, which was hugely complex and created opportunities for intermediaries to extract additional rents out of the system. Notwithstanding the significant revenues generated from foreign sales SUCOMA found that within the processing environment a disproportionate amount of time and money was invested in managing the importing process for materials required for the production of sugar. Some of these challenges are highlighted below:

- Imported goods, such as specialist irrigation and factory parts, materials and transportation equipment were not only costly in terms of finance but also in terms of timescale – it took on average 3–4 months to import an item from South Africa from the date the order was placed to receipt.
- SUCOMA had approximately US$2 million of imported goods delayed due to paperwork losses, preventing payment to suppliers.
- Delayed payments had an impact on operational issues but also increased financial exposure as the rate of interest ran at 2 per cent per month.
- The cost to finance the importing of materials was estimated at US$750 000 for the interest and duty charges alone.
- The process of importing was hugely complex with far too many steps in the process, involving far too many individuals and agencies of government.

Outlined in Figure 6.4 is the current importing process. The areas highlighted have been identified as areas where immediate action could be taken to shorten the process. The proposed removal of certain redundant processes was also highlighted (white perforated boxes).

As a result of the informal personal 'know who' relationships that SUCOMA officials had established with key stakeholders in the Malawi government they were able to leverage their influence to establish a dialogue between leading industry players. This led to some progress being made with the regulatory framework:

- The National Reserve Bank reviewed all their procedures for importation.
- The requirement for Exchange Control Allocation was removed. Prior to this an application for foreign currency had to be made to the Commercial Bank with a pro-forma invoice for the allocation of funds to confirm that payment could be made for the goods.
- The duplication of handling and consequent delays to the payment and processing of invoices in foreign currency would be eliminated by a single payment process for

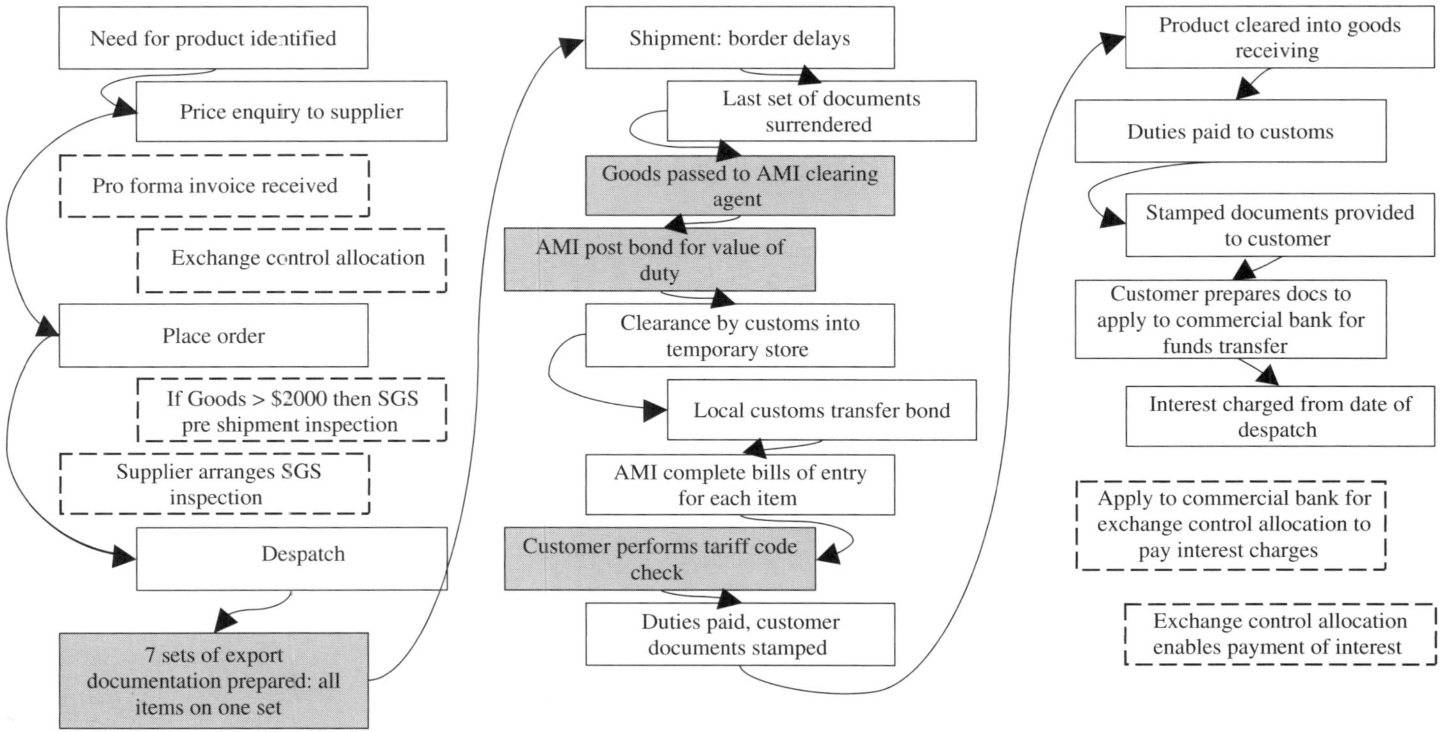

Source: Agar, McGrath and Herrmann (2002)

Figure 6.4 Proposed import process for Malawi

invoices, thereby reducing overall interest payments. It was projected that the savings from this action alone totalled about US$625 000.

- Changing the pre-payments system for imported goods meant a saving of about two weeks on the process, thus saving on administrative costs and financing charges. The Nchalo Estate calculated that if it could make pre-payments for its imported products and therefore avoid the interest charges associated with the lengthy importation process, SUCOMA would benefit from a saving of US$1.6 million.

Although the Malawi example is perhaps one of extremes – most small firms do not have contacts with government ministers – it is a useful illustration of how 'know who' can stimulate connections and networks and establish the trust to deal with significant regulatory challenges in order to improve the efficiencies of government processes.

A key challenge for the future is how the pervasiveness of the internet and communication by email rather than face-to-face or personally over the phone will influence the stakeholder management strategies firms adopt. These new forms of global communication do not necessarily provide the trust that creates and stimulates the relationships required for trading globally. This is a significant issue for many small firms as they often do not have the resources to develop personal networks or to ensure that they are able to develop the proxies for trust needed for electronic trade and thus find themselves under severe pressure to go with the trend of online trade rather than using their personal stakeholder networks. If one considers the resource base of our two case study businesses in the context of their geographic closeness to market and access to ICT technologies, one can extrapolate a line of thinking that involves Thorncroft finding it easier than SUCOMA to access international markets through e-commerce. On the other hand, it could well be argued that electronic commerce may well be of greater benefit to SUCOMA, and as outlined below could assist such firms to create the entrepreneurial space within which their employees and their smallholder farmers could increase efficiencies in the supply chain to improve their global competitiveness through being 'closer' to the market.

Relationship management

Gibb (1999) argues that managing relationships with the stakeholder environment is vital to a firm's ability to engage in trading globally. Gibb further develops this argument by classifying business management as 'managing the interdependency with a network of stakeholder relationships under conditions of uncertainty with limited resources'. Paradoxically, as small firms seek to design new products, develop new markets and find new ways of serving customers through increasing their global reach, they become even more dependent on a more complex network of stakeholders. Many small firms manage these interdependencies by developing personal trust networks within which transactions are framed to reduce the uncertainty in the trading environment. Thorncroft has used this strategy to expand its business globally. New markets have been developed in an ad hoc way, based on informal ties with networks of people who the owners meet informally through holiday travel and attending trade shows rather than any strategy based on a strategic assessment of the global market place. These trust networks have underpinned the success of Thorncroft's approach to trading globally and ensure that it is able to manage the high levels of uncertainty in its trading environment.

Developing close personal relationships based on trust is crucial to helping firms reduce uncertainty in business dealings. This relationship management process requires constant attention and commitment to building and maintaining personal contact. It also involves the firm engaging in a two-way knowledge transfer process with its key stakeholders (customers) to capture their requirements and anticipate their future needs. This is crucial for sustaining competitive advantage in a trading environment where competitors are global, where knowledge is easily obtained and where very often loyalty between customer and provider is not guaranteed (Hall and Bennett 2002).

The next section on organisational design focuses specifically on creating the freedom within firms for employees to build and nurture close personal ties with their stakeholders, for example, customers and suppliers. However, it is also important that small firms make these personal 'know who' networks more explicit and allow employees to engage in activities beyond the confines of their job roles. This boundary-spanning activity encourages the diffusion of knowledge across the organisation and also ensures that personal trust networks are converted into organisational knowledge (Hartshorn 1998). Such activity could also be enhanced through the enabling use of ICT technologies that are sensitive to people's individual needs for ownership of knowledge and 'know who', but also recognises the need to build institutional memory (Cunningham 2001). ICT technologies and knowledge management systems need to act as a porous membrane between the firm and its customers rather than a customer relationship management exercise that is reduced via technology to a contacts database.

Designing entrepreneurial organisations

In order to respond to the high levels of uncertainty and ambiguity in the trading environment and the complexity of managing a vast and dispersed array of stakeholders, small firms operating in global markets need to consider how their organisations are designed and configured. The experiences of the two case studies highlight a number of strategies related to achieving fit between the organisational structure and the external environment. These include:

- Developing holistic management approaches rather than functional forms of management which compartmentalise ways of responding to the challenges of trading globally (Senge 1993). In Thorncroft, the management team worked in partnership with external associates and partners to take advantage of global market opportunities. This involved having a loose management and partnership arrangement that allowed the team the freedom to experiment and try things out, learn by making mistakes, take initiative and develop innovative responses to customer needs.
- Developing a leadership style that encourages managers and staff to build strong relationships with stakeholders, based on trust as the primary principle of management decisions, that is, allowing decision-making prerogative to be dispersed throughout the organisation rather than centralised at the top (Schein 1985; Burkinshaw 1997; Deakins and Freel 1998). SUCOMA has, after some years of neglect, worked hard at engaging the smallholder schemes at Kasinthula and the Nchalo Estate. This has involved recognising that leadership exists in other parts of the organisation that helps it develop alternative sources of sugar cane at competitive prices. Aside from the poverty alleviation achieved through integrating smallholder suppliers into the

value chain, it has also helped SUCOMA negotiate better terms of trade through the EU Preferential Trade Agreement. This was only achieved by engaging stakeholders and empowering the management of the supply chain at its lowest levels.

- Accepting an open-ended approach to the configuration of organisational structure which tolerates ambiguity and overlap in the assignment of tasks within the firm and allows people to take ownership of tasks and build personal networks in order to build credibility with customers (Hartshorn 1998). This also involves rewarding employees based on their ability to deliver to customer needs rather than in line with prescribed job descriptions and roles. After experimenting unsuccessfully with co-opting the landlord of the property where the business was located to allow it to focus on other areas of the business, Thorncroft offices are now located within the premises of the contract filler in Stockton-on-Tees. This has allowed the owners the space and time to focus on the growth of the business in new international markets.
- Creating flexibility within organisations to cope with and anticipate change. This means creating the organisational space (openness) for individuals within the firm to have the freedom to exercise their enterprising capacities for opportunity seeking, creativity and innovation, taking independent initiative, and having the responsibility for managing the risks they take (Katz and Gartner 1988; Hamel and Prahalad 1994; Gibb 1999). SUCOMA has a flexible contractual arrangement with its smallholder farmers that allows them the freedom to widen the variety of crops grown beyond sugar to ensure that their families have sufficient food supplies to survive the summer months when there is little rain.
- Ensuring that the management team are imbued with the following characteristics – seeing things through despite complexities and challenges, tolerating mistakes and encouraging learning and sharing of knowledge (Senge 1993; Gibb 1997; O'Gorman 2001). These characteristics are crucial for coping with the challenges of international trade. The lessons learnt by Thorncroft when the FDA impounded its shipment were quickly incorporated into the export planning and management systems back at the office in North East England while they dealt with the immediate and urgent matter of getting their goods released and delivered to customers.

The case studies demonstrate that it is important to provide an organisational structure to support and harness a positive attitude to enterprise within organisations. Beyond having the technical competencies of managing the exporting and importing process, it is one of the ways of coping with uncertainty and complexity inherent in the activity of trading globally. Designing organisations so that they allow the employees to take initiative and to make decisions and respond in the ways outlined above is crucial to the very survival of the small firm in the global arena (Gibb 1999).

Flexible strategic orientation

Managing in the global environment requires that firms have the requisite 'know how' and 'know who' to compete. However, relying on technical knowledge and networks alone to meet current customer needs only ensures survival for today. It does not ensure future success. Hence anticipating future complexity in the processes of global trade is also critical to the survival of the business. Knowing how to cope with cash flow shortages, avoiding over-reliance on a limited number of customers and over-trading, and having systems in place to develop trust with key stakeholders (customers and trade intermediaries) are taken for granted as key requirements for success. In the global market place, however, scanning the task environment of the small firm for opportunities and threats which may have an impact on its continued survival and growth is also necessary.

Anticipating customer needs by 'bringing the future forward' based on understanding market trends is also crucial for managing in the global environment. Given the highly competitive nature of the global economy and the realities of competing against large multinationals with global reach and scale of operations, and infinite resources, it is crucial that small firms are able to anticipate global trends in order to remain competitive. This ability to 'bring the future forward' for their customers by anticipating global trends and responding proactively to meet customer demand is fundamental to the global trading small firm. Rather than corporate approaches to strategy development, research shows that small firms in comparison to large firms use their stakeholder network to keep in touch with trends and future demand for their products or services (Hannon and Atherton 1998). As with Thorncroft, it is argued that small firms use their ability to be more strategically aware, to engage directly with their stakeholder networks, and to spot opportunities and respond rapidly instead of engaging in formal planning processes as is often the case with large firms (Gibb and Scott 1985; Carpenter 1986; Brytting 1991).

The Thorncroft case study highlights how myopia, inertia about market trends and the need to 'educate' the customer by 'bringing their future forward' meant that exporting to the USA was not as successful as anticipated. Thorncroft was very bullish at the time of entry into the American market, partly because it had received feedback and information from brokers that people liked the product and would be willing to buy it. However, reflecting on its experiences, Thorncroft concluded that exporting involved a far greater level of resource and effort than had been envisaged and that there were a number of issues surrounding the acceptance of the product in overseas markets. Two key issues were:

- Outside the UK, there was no real substantive market for cordials and dilutables. This compounded the issue of how to market the product. In the US, the technique of explaining the advantages of the product (cordials) to potential customers, on a one-to-one basis, was much more difficult to achieve through importers and wholesalers.
- Countries outside the UK did not understand what elderflower was and why people should drink it.

The experience of exporting to America also highlighted that the American market was highly formalised and structured and that the barriers to entry were somewhat high. Thorncroft was required to 'jump through regulatory hoops' it had not anticipated. The lack of strategic planning for entering the US market was exacerbated by a number of mistakes made by Thorncroft that resulted in products being retained at dockside and not being allowed entry into the market. The firm found that it was particularly difficult dealing with and satisfying the requirements of the Food and Drug Administration (FDA). Being more strategically aware of the intricacies of international trading opportunities would have resulted in greater success. Thorncroft could have undertaken more detailed market research before exporting goods to the US. Its reliance on 'strong' ties by using its own contacts and networks could have been supplemented by contact with government agencies responsible for promoting international trade ('weak' ties) or staff could

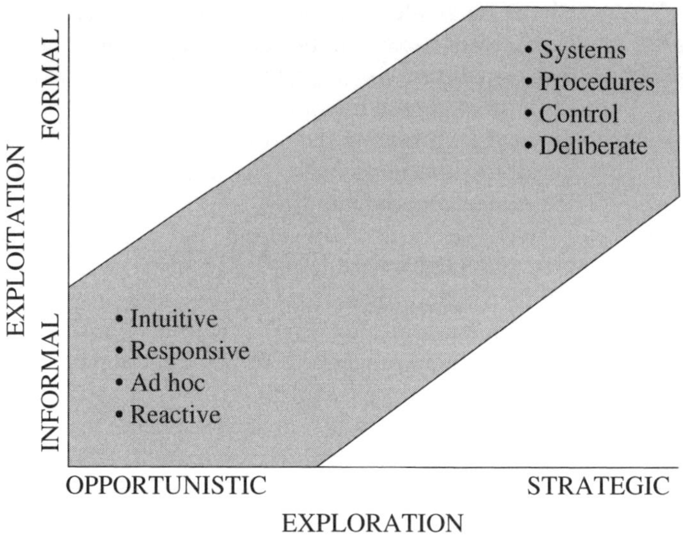

Source: Herrmann and Wright (2003)

Figure 6.5 Approaches for exploring and exploiting opportunities

have participated in a trade mission to acquire the required knowledge about export procedures for the United States (Granovetter 1983).

Despite the problems associated with breaking into the US market, Thorncroft developed a number of specific geographical markets by using a similar approach – by responding to informal leads or one-off requests. For six years, Thorncroft exported to France, which it found easier as it was able to find people to work with who liked the product, but these relatively high levels of interest and positive feedback did not translate into commensurate levels of export activity.

The ad hoc approach of the Thorncroft experience mirrors the findings about a cluster of high-value engineering firms in the North East of England. Herrmann and Wright (2003) found that firms had a variety of approaches. Figure 6.5 shows that the type of approach and the formality of the process varied in how firms explored and exploited new business opportunities. Those businesses with more experience of the export process and a stronger orientation to how new business opportunities were generated internationally, adopted a strategic approach that filtered new business ideas through a step-by-step process from the start. At the other end of the continuum, firms with fewer systems used more informal approaches in which they were more flexible and opportunistic about the way in which they generated new business opportunities.

Opportunistic approaches

The research by Herrmann and Wright op. cit., found that firms which used opportunistic approaches were customer-driven, reactive and responsive to customer needs and requirements. As a result, they tended to be 'close' to their customers, but in the majority of cases the analysis also indicated that this meant they had haphazard ways of responding to customer needs. Often these firms had no framework or system for analysing the feasibility of a potential business opportunity. Despite this, responsiveness to customer need helped firms build strong relationships with their customers. On the other hand, these entrepreneurial actions sometimes led to a dilution of the core business, or an overextension of the resources available in the business.

> We often feel like we have 'small builder syndrome' – we get too busy and don't have any time to do anything. We also find it difficult to do forward planning – we should have a schedule of projects lined up but we don't (Herrmann and Wright 2003).

These firms were highly responsive to their customers' needs, but in a reactive rather than in a 'strategic' way. Their dialogues with customers were generally about price, quality and speed of delivery, rather than a discussion about how new business opportunities with their customers was going to lead to the growth of their relationship in a mutually beneficial way. In most cases they were prompted to explore a new area of business by a customer specifying a particular need.

The approaches used by these firms mirrors that of Thorncroft. Its export strategy involved relying on contact with ad hoc networks to explore new business opportunities. Although highly responsive, this evolutionary approach resulted in the company exporting to 16 different markets in the world without reference to a coherent internationalisation strategy. It could be that this somewhat 'carefree' approach created unnecessary complexity in the production and client management processes as each client/customer was bound by different standards for product safety and packaging and procedures for managing the export–import process.

Strategic approaches

Adopting a 'strategic' approach involved having systems in place to manage new business opportunities as they arose, for example by having cross-functional project teams, and having procedures and management processes to regulate the process of commercialising a business opportunity. Businesses with strategic approaches were also quite deliberate and to some degree deterministic in their approach to seeking out new business opportunities (Sear and Atherton 1998). In structural terms, these firms used a range of formal and informal mechanisms for operationalising new business opportunities. Exploring new business ideas was often compartmentalised within internal research and development departments or formal joint venture arrangements.

The research of Herrmann and Wright also found that these two approaches were not mutually exclusive methodologies for exploring and exploiting new business opportunities. A number of the strategically-oriented firms allowed and/or encouraged innovation and opportunism in their businesses.

> Selling an application of our product to the Ministry of Defence happened accidentally rather than strategically – they approached us. The risk to us was minimised as this was additional work, a new market outside of our core business (Herrmann and Wright 2003).

SUCOMA used both formal and informal strategies for exploring and exploiting new business opportunities. It was extensively and formally involved in supporting government negotiations on 'Everything But Arms trade deal and the EU Preferential Trade Agreement'. Outside of these formal trading arrangements it also sold opportunistically in regional and local markets where prices were more volatile, volumes not guaranteed and it had to compete with traders from other countries who operated outside of the formal Southern African Free Trade Agreements monitored by the Southern African Development Community trading bloc (SADC).

Summary

In summary, the case studies highlight the importance of adopting an entrepreneurial approach in relation to how small firms engage with external stakeholders, manage their network of contacts to expand their field of influence, develop an entrepreneurial culture within their organisations and adopt strategies and day-to-day practices that enable them to be more strategically aware of their external environment. These mechanisms for coping with the complexities and uncertainties of trading globally also require firms to adopt a strategic posture which encourages the development of the following core competencies:

- The ability constantly to ask 'what if' questions about the current state of the business and its anticipated growth trajectory.
- A constant search for new opportunities by adopting both opportunistic and strategic approaches.
- The effective monitoring of the external environment – not as a part of a strategic planning exercise, but as a day-to-day practice. This involves being aware of market trends, being intuitively attuned to the market place and taking a position on future change and being aware of customer needs.
- The ability to 'bring the future forward' for customers by not only responding to their needs but also 'informing' them about the future and developments in the product and service range to accommodate future requirements.

Hence the operating context of any small firm trading globally should be as one that learns how to deal with high levels of uncertainty and complexity on a daily basis, and how to cope with and respond to global competition, high rates of product innovation and excessive product and technological obsolescence. Fluctuation and uncertainty in market trading conditions are therefore no longer obstacles to be overcome but opportunities to be explored and exploited.

Questions emerging from this chapter

1. Given the trading experiences of businesses such as those highlighted in this chapter, what can we learn from the similarities and differences between businesses trading globally?
2. What implications for trade policy are there from businesses located in different parts of the world, operating in different sectors, and faced with benign versus intrusive public policy regimes which either enable or disenable a firms' ability to engage in global trade?
3. How do we engage in a process of mutual experience exchange which helps businesses in different parts of the world learn from each other about the key lessons of success of making global trade an achievable reality?

4. What skills and competencies are required by small businesses trading globally to help them cope with and manage the uncertainty and complexity that is implicit in trading in global markets?

Bibliography

Agar, J., McGrath, J. and Herrmann, K. (2002), *Malawi Private Sector Partnerships: Briefing Note 1 – Sugar Sector Value Chain*, DFID, London and Malawi.

Bernasconi, M., Harris, S. and Moensted, M. (2006), *High-tech Entrepreneurship: Managing Innovation, Variety and Uncertainty*, Routledge, London.

Brytting, T. (1991), 'Spontaneity and Systematic Planning in Small Firms – A Grounded Theory Approach', *International Small Business Journal*, **9** (1), 45–63.

Burkinshaw, J. (1997), 'Entrepreneurship in Multinational Corporations: The Characteristics of Subsidiary Initiatives', *Strategic Management Journal*, **18** (3), 207–229.

Carpenter, M.A. (1986), 'Planning vs. Strategy – Which Will Win?', *Long Range Planning*, **19**, 50–53.

Cunningham, M. (2001), *B2B – How to Build a Profitable E-commerce Strategy*, Pearson, London.

Deakins, D. and Freel, M. (1998), 'Entrepreneurial Learning and the Growth Process in SMEs', *The Learning Organization*, **5** (3), 144–155.

Ensley, M.D., Carland, J.W. and Carland, J.C. (2000), 'Investigating the Existence of the Lead Entrepreneur', *Journal of Small Business Management*, **38** (4), 59–79.

Etemad, H. and Wright, R. (ed.) (2003), *Globalisation and Entrepreneurship: Policy and Strategy Perspectives*, Edward Elgar Publishing, Cheltenham UK and Northampton, MA, USA.

Freel, M.S. (1997), 'Towards an Evolutionary Theory of Small Firm Growth'. Paper presented to the 20th ISBA National Conference, Belfast, November.

Gibb, A.A. (1993), 'The Enterprise Culture and Education: Understanding Enterprise Education and its Links with Small Businesses', *International Small Business Journal*, **11** (3), 11–34.

Gibb, A.A. (1997), 'Small Firms Training and Competitiveness: Building upon the Small Business as a Learning Organisation', *International Small Business Journal*, **15** (3), 13–29.

Gibb, A.A. (1999), 'Can We Build "Effective" Entrepreneurship Through Management Development?' *Journal of General Management*, **24** (4), 1–22.

Gibb, A.A. (2000a), 'Corporate Restructuring and Entrepreneurship: What can Large Organisations Learn from Small?' *Enterprise and Innovation Management Studies*, **1** (1), 19–35.

Gibb, A.A. (2000b), 'SME Policy, Academic Research and the Growth of Ignorance, Mythical Concepts, Myths, Assumptions, Rituals and Confusions', *International Small Business Journal*, **18** (3), 13–35.

Gibb, A.A. (2002), 'In Pursuit of a New "Enterprise" and "Entrepreneurship" Paradigm for Learning: Creative Destruction, New Values, New Ways of Doing Things and New Combinations of Knowledge', *International Journal of Management Reviews*, **4** (3), 233–269.

Gibb, A.A. and Scott, M. (1985), 'Strategic Awareness, Personal Commitment and the Process of Planning in the Small Business', *Journal of Management Studies*, **22** (6), 597–631.

Granovetter, M. (1983), 'The Strength of Weak Ties: A Network Theory Revisited', *Sociological Theory*, **1**, 201–233.

Hall, D. and Bennett, D. (2002), *Hallmarks for Successful Business*, Management Books, London.

Hamel, G. and Prahalad, C.K. (1994), *Competing for the Future*, Harvard Business School Press, Boston MA.

Hannon, P. and Atherton, A. (1998), 'Small Firm Success and the Art of Orienteering: The Value of Plans, Planning and Strategic Awareness in the Competitive Small Firm', *Small Business and Enterprise Development*, **5** (2), 102–119.

Hartshorn, C. (1998), 'Innovation in SME Management Learning: The Role of the "Boundary Spanner"'. Paper presented to the XII RENT Conference: Research in Entrepreneurship and Small Business, Lyon, 25–27 November.

Herrmann, K. and Wright, J. (2003), 'New Venture Development in Value-added Engineering and Technology'. Paper presented to the 2003 International Entrepreneurship and New Venture Creation Conference: Theory, Concepts and Practice, Durham, September.

Katz, J. and Gartner, W.N. (1988), 'Properties of Emerging Organizations', *Academy of Management Review*, **13** (3), 429.

Klofsten, M. and Jones-Evans, D. (2000), 'Comparing Academic Entrepreneurship in Europe: The Case of Sweden and Ireland', *Small Business Economics*, **14**, 299–309.

Kusum, S. and Vinnicombe, S. (1998), *Downsizing and Survivor Syndrome: A Case Study of HR's Perception of Survivors' Responses*, Cranfield School of Management, Cranfield, UK.

Kusum, S. Vinnicombe, S. and Tyson, S. (1999), 'Downsizing and the Changing Role of HR', *International Journal of Human Resource Management*, **10** (2), 906–923.

Leadbetter, C. (1999), *Europe's New Economy*, Centre for European Reform, London.
Lyles, M.A., Baird, I.S., Orris, J.B. and Kuratko, D.F. (1993), 'Formalised Planning in Small Business: Increased Strategic Choices', *Journal of Small Business Management*, **31** (2), 38–50.
Minkes, A.L. and Foxall, G.R. (2000), 'Entrepreneurship and Organisation: Thoughts on an Old Theme', *International Journal of Enterprise and Innovation*, **1** (2), 85–89.
Murtha, T.P., Lenway, S.A. and Hart, J.A. (2001), *Managing New Industry Creation: Global Knowledge Formation and Entrepreneurship in High Technology*, Stanford University Press, Stanford CA.
O'Gorman, C. (2001), 'The Sustainability of Growth in Small and Medium-sized Enterprises', *International Journal of Entrepreneurial Behaviour and Research*, **7** (2), 60–75.
Porter, M.E. (1985), *Competitive Advantage*, Free Press, Boston MA.
Porter, M.E. (1996), 'What is Strategy', *Harvard Business Review*, Nov–Dec.
Prahalad, C.K. and Hamel, G. (1990), *The Core Competence of the Corporation, Harvard Business Review*, May–June.
Schein, E.H. (1985), *Organisational Culture and Leadership*, Jossey-Bass, San Francisco.
Sear, L. and Atherton, A. (1998), 'How Small Businesses Generate Orders: Developing Process Understanding'. Paper presented to the ICSB World Conference, Naples, June.
Senge, P. (1993), *The Fifth Discipline: Art and Practice of the Learning Organization*, Century Business, London.
Smallbone, D. and Wyer, P. (2000), 'Growth and Development in the Small Firm', in Carter, S. and Jones-Evans, D. (eds) *Enterprise and Small Business: Principles, Practice and Policy*, Financial Times Prentice Hall, London.
Vinnell, R. and Hamilton, R.T. (1999), 'A Historical Perspective on Small Firm Development', *Entrepreneurship, Theory and Practice*, **23** (4), 5–18.

Appendix 6.1: Thorncroft – bottling success in new markets

Thorncroft produces a range of cordials and sparkling drinks that are made from original recipes, a number of which have been passed down through the family of the two owners, Guy and Sheila Woodall, for generations. The cordials and drinks use fresh natural ingredients, many of which are gathered directly from the wild. They have a national reputation in the UK, having being used in recipes featured on television, and are sold through high street outlets, supermarkets, health stores and delicatessens.

The key customers of Thorncroft include large UK supermarkets, health stores and independent stores and off-licences. In total, Thorncroft has about 30 customers. The three key competitors in the cordials market are Rock, Belvoir and Bottle Green. However, there is a slight differentiation in the market. Belvoir has focused heavily on organic cordials, whilst Thorncroft has established a brand related to health, well-being and the use of quality ingredients. Thorncroft has experimented with sparkling drinks based on the cordials but this raises a question over what is the company and what is its key source of advantage. At the moment, the focus of the business is on cordial concentrates.

The current level of turnover is approximately £1.5 million, although profitability has increased over the 1990s. The firm currently employs six people in the North East of England, with bottling and production subcontracted to a contract bottler in Stockton-on-Tees. The production line produces 245 000 bottles every 24 hours seven days a week. This equates to approximately eight container loads a day. Thorncroft currently exports to 16 countries. The business exports directly to the USA, Canada, South Africa, Ireland, Belgium, Germany, France, Norway, Australia and Japan. Other customers, especially in the health food trade, export products on behalf of Thorncroft to Sweden, Denmark, Dubai, Hong Kong, Malaysia and Thailand.

However, it has encountered a number of problems in terms of developing new markets such as the United States over the last ten years.

Getting drunk with success – developing the business

Thorncroft used its strong and personal relations with one of the buyers from a leading supermarket to build sales volumes, using the consequent growth to access other supermarket chains. However, this informality in the relationship created a number of relatively unrealistic perceptions and expectations in terms of dealing with other supermarkets, especially in terms of how to develop relationships with buyers and develop awareness of the product, in comparison to its more established competitor brands.

On the back of increasing sales, Thorncroft developed two new cordials (nettle and pink ginger) in 1994 which, like the elderflower cordial, were also produced as sparkling drinks. Despite the rapid growth of the business, the owners recognised that they understood relatively little about how to manage and run a small business effectively and felt that the business was surviving through chance and success rather than effective management and planning.

It was in the mid-1990s, against this context of growing sales and success, that they first explored the notion of exporting and developing new markets outside the United Kingdom. They felt that with the business growing so successfully in the UK, there must be opportunities to sell the product overseas.

Drinking abroad – developing new markets
As with a majority of other smaller businesses, Thorncroft started to export through informal channels and in response to requests from other business contacts and networks. One of the main drivers and motivations to exporting was that the business was starting to grow and the owners could perceive a huge market for their products which had the potential to be exploited and contribute to existing sales growth. In a way though, Thorncroft had become 'drunk' on the potential of the product as it was not aware of the problems and challenges associated with exporting it to overseas markets. The business was attracted to exporting because the owners liked to travel, and developing overseas markets presented them both with an opportunity to travel and see different countries. Therefore, there was a feeling that exporting would be a good idea, fun, and provide an opportunity to travel and this convinced them that they should commit resources to developing new overseas markets.

Breaking into America Thorncroft once again used the owners' network of informal contacts and friends to access the US market. A friend offered to import the product into America on their behalf. This coincided with the business exhibiting its products in America. They attended food fairs and found that although they received a small number of orders from the fairs, it was not as successful as they had anticipated. Despite the attempt to access the US market using their networks, the level of sales was not encouraging and nothing happened on a substantial scale.

At the time, they were confident that they would be able to sell in the American market, partly because they had received feedback and information from brokers that people liked the product and would be willing to buy it. Reflecting on these experiences, Thorncroft concluded that exporting involved a far greater level of resource and effort than had been envisaged and that there were a number of issues surrounding the acceptance of the product in overseas markets. Two key issues were:

- Outside the US, there was no real substantive market for cordials and dilutables. This compounded the issue of how to market the product. In the UK, the technique of explaining the advantages of their product (cordials) to potential customers, on a one-to-one basis, was much more difficult to achieve through importers and wholesalers.
- Countries outside the UK did not understand what elderflower was and why people should drink it.

The experience of exporting to America also highlighted that the American market was highly formalised and structured and that the barriers to entry were somewhat high. Thorncroft was required to 'jump through hoops' that were felt unnecessary. This was compounded by a number of mistakes by Thorncroft that resulted in products being retained at dockside and not being allowed entry into the market. The firm found that is was particularly difficult dealing with and satisfying the requirements of the US Food and Drug Administration (FDA).

Exporting elsewhere Despite the problems associated with breaking into the US market, Thorncroft has developed a number of specific geographical markets in response to informal leads or one-off requests. For six years, it has exported to France. This was easier as it was possible to find people to work with and who liked the product, but these relatively high levels of interest and positive feedback did not translate into commensurate levels of export activity.

In addition to France, Thorncroft has exported products to South Africa, Japan and Norway. The South African market was initially developed via a contact made at a trade show in Paris in 1994, after which it was approached by this contact about the possibility of selling to Woolworths, the equivalent to Marks and Spencer in South Africa. Thorncroft spent time with the contact explaining of the nature of the product and the contact went away and developed a label for the product. Thorncroft printed the label and kept up stock levels to be able to respond to ten-week lead times. Based on such an approach, Thorncroft successfully sold to Woolworths for a period of four years until the strength of the pound against the South African rand reduced the attractiveness of importing the product for the contact.

The business also sold a reasonable amount of cordial each year to Norway. A chance meeting created an opportunity to sell in a market which knew about elderflower. As a result, there was no need to undertake a sales and marketing exercise to raise awareness of the need to drink elderflower, as well as encouraging people to drink cordial. In all, Thorncroft sold a reasonable amount of the product to Norway over a four-year period. However, the level of sales started to decline after the importer of the product lost interest in the business to focus on other activities during his retirement.

The process of exporting to Japan started when the sister-in-law of a small regional wholesaler approached Thorncroft at a trade show. Due to the nature of regulations and legislation in Japan, it was extremely difficult to export food and drink products there. However, Thorncroft overcame this difficulty by using its Japanese contact as an intermediary. The Japanese wholesaler mediated between Thorncroft and the Japanese Customs and Excise, which meant that a great deal of the associated paperwork and regulations were dealt with by the importing wholesaler. This drastically reduced the barriers to entry for Thorncroft.

Going to Australia In 2002 Thorncroft visited Australia to do a trade show and found that a former employee wanted to import the product into the Australian market. The advantages of using someone known to the firm were significant – this agent knew the business as a former employee, understood the import processes for Australia as she worked for a company importing French wine, and was keen to be directly involved in marketing the product on a one-to-one basis, doing things like tastings to convince people to buy it.

Therefore, whilst using the same formula as with previous attempts in developing new markets, that is, through friends, this time the friend had a business background, had knowledge of routes into the market and access to sources of key information which were useful to Thorncroft.

Drinking to overseas success – the way forward for Thorncroft

The business never developed a 'formula' by which to export its core elderflower cordial product successfully to other markets. Thorncroft has accumulated testimonials and evidence to deal with the challenges of trading globally, but there remains a feeling within the business that although there are opportunities for trading globally, there is a question over how to make sure that these overseas markets are successfully developed.

Appendix 6.2: Malawi sugar exporting

Durham University Business School (DUBS), along with its Malawian partners, Kadale Consultants and Imani Development, facilitated the development of private sector partnership processes as part of an initiative supported by the United Kingdom's Department for International Development (DFID) for stimulating economic growth in Malawi through private sector development. The DUBS project team worked in five key industrial sectors in Malawi: tourism, tea, cotton, textiles and garments and the sugar industry. The case study outlined below explores in detail the challenge faced by smallholder sugar producers and their value chain partners in accessing and trading in the global market place.

Globally, sugar is one of the most highly-protected agricultural commodities. Of global sugar production, about 72 per cent is sold within the country of origin at protected prices. Of the balance, most is traded in the preferential markets and the remaining volumes on the world free market. Few countries in the world can produce sugar at the low price levels dictated by the world market; however Malawi, as one of the most cost-efficient producers of sugar, is able to do so. Therefore in order to protect the local producers from exposure to world market prices, all countries, except Australia, protect their domestic trade through sets of tariffs. These tariffs are key to the protection of the domestic markets.

The sugar industry in Malawi is centred on the Sugar Corporation of Malawi (SUCOMA). It has invested heavily in the milling and estate operations and supported the development of local businesses through a programme of outsourcing the service operations. SUCOMA has agricultural and milling assets at Nchalo in the south east of the country and Dwangwa in the mid-central region. SUCOMA estates grow around 1 900 000 mT of sugar cane each season and combined with the cane grown by independent farmers, process about 2 100 000 mT of cane into 240 000 mT of sugar. The sugar value chain consists of three core stages – growing, processing and marketing.

International trade for SUCOMA and many of its smallholder suppliers is crucial for growing the business, but also for the alleviation of poverty in poor rural communities across Malawi. Foreign exchange earnings not only help stabilise one the world's poorest nations, but also have a very direct effect on local communities and the viability of rural smallholder farmers. Table 6.2 outlines the components of the sugar value chain and highlights some of the key challenges producers have in trading globally in a commodity in which global competition is substantial and import tariffs provide artificial protection, especially to farmers in the developed economies of the West.

Smallholders and exporting impacts

The Kasinthula Smallholders Scheme (KCGL) benefits around 1100 households. It is operating efficiently, with cane yields above those of its competitors. Sugar cane sales per smallholder were in excess of MK400 000 ($5000) per smallholder for the year 2001/02. However after including costs of production and most significantly, the cost of finance, the scheme made a loss of some MK140 000 ($1900) per smallholder in 2001/2. The original financing for the scheme in the form of hard currency loans and bank overdrafts are the main factors behind these costs. Two macroeconomic effects outside the control of KCGL have had a significant adverse effect on the financing of the scheme. Firstly, a series of major currency devaluations of the Malawi Kwacha, dropping from MK15 to MK76

Table 6.2 Barriers to growing, processing and marketing

Growing	Processing	Marketing
Encompasses the supply of sugar cane. Involves both estate-driven and smallholder schemes.	Involves the conversion process from the receipt of the sugar cane at the factory through to the point at which it is sold into the distribution network	The three key market routes are domestic sales, preferential market sales to Europe and the USA and regional market sales.
Main barriers	**Main barriers**	**Main barriers**
• Skills relating to cash-flow and financial management are particularly lacking. • Poor roads and lack of appropriate transportation make it difficult for sugar cane haulage in the wet weather. • Smallholder and estate growers pay large haulage costs, accounting for approximately 13% of the cost base of the estates. • Cost of security to combat the theft of irrigation pipes has a significant impact both financially and operationally upon the Estate. US$2.25 million cost of lost cane due to loss of irrigation. • Irrigation methods in the Shire Valley are energy intensive. For the Nchalo Estate 11% of its cost base is energy.	• Cutting and processing in the 30-week season absorbs 80% of the annual cash flow in 60% of the year. The cost of borrowings to manage cash flow during these peak times is very high given the high rates of interest in Malawi. • The costs of imported goods, such as specialist irrigation and factory parts, materials, transportation equipment are not only financial but also timescale-related – it takes on average 3–4 months to import an item from South Africa from the date the order is placed to receipt. • SUCOMA had approximately US$2 million of imported goods in delay due to paperwork losses preventing payment to the suppliers. • Delayed payments impact operational issues but also increase financial exposure as the interest runs at 2% per month. • Cost to finance the importing of materials is estimated at US$750 000 for the interest and duty charges alone. • Social responsibility programmes to meet gaps in public provision, e.g. housing, medical facilities and schooling, absorb approximately 12% of the cost base at each location.	• SUCOMA distributes sugar throughout Malawi and covers all distribution and management costs of its depots, therefore the sugar price is the same across the whole country. • Opportunities to develop regional sales out of the depots are limited as regional currencies cannot be accepted for payments. • The transport infrastructure within Malawi creates a barrier to ensuring comprehensive product availability. This is expensive due to haulage costs and transportation surtaxes, and is labour-intensive, insecure and unreliable. • Access to the ports for exporting sugar is a major problem with the Ncala and Beira routes relatively expensive. • It has taken 4 years to replace a bridge following collapse during the wet season. During this time the transportation costs were US$2.5 million, of which the impact of the bridge being out of commission on SUCOMA was US$1.2 million. Transportation costs should have been US$1.3 million.

to the US dollar have had a direct effect on KCGL's cost base. Secondly, the persistently high interest rates at around 50 per cent for commercial borrowers have made capital investment near impossible and the cost of borrowings to cover global trading activity has significantly raised the firm's cost base.

The combination of the above factors has resulted in a build-up in the debt, despite interest payments of MK20 million per year by KCGL to reach the level of MK530 million by March 2002. Overall, the scheme has demonstrated that were it not for the impact of these financing costs there would be potential for smallholder farmers to increase their income significantly compared to the previous returns they obtained from subsistence farming.

Quota restrictions

Worldwide, 121 countries produce sugar from either sugar beet (mainly Europe and the US) or sugar cane (supplying over two-thirds of the world's sugar supply). Sugar is one of the most traded of commodities, with exports accounting for over a quarter of global production. However due to heavy subsidies and protectionism it also suffers from one of the most distorted global markets. It costs well over 50 per cent more to produce sugar from beet than from sugar cane, but heavy subsidies lead to excessive production in the EU and the US, damaging the stability of international markets and production. The EU has among the highest sugar production costs – around $660 to produce one tonne of white sugar, yet Europe exports more white sugar than any other block of countries. This has two effects:

- Firstly, selling sugar in Europe is impossible due to the protection upon the markets, and only countries with preferential trade agreements can sell to EU customers.
- Secondly, the availability of Europe's excess sugar exported at subsidised prices captures potential developing markets and depresses the world prices.

The EU preferential sales are the most lucrative sales with the highest contribution per mT for Malawi sugar producers. The EU sugar quota also benefits Malawi in that it provides a preferential market with annually committed volumes. By contrast, regional market sales are more volatile and sensitive to world market prices.

The Everything But Arms (EBA) agreement has been proposed by the EU to remove all restrictions on imports from the 48 Least Developed Countries (LDCs) on all imports other than those classified as arms. This came into effect on 1 January 2001 for all commodities except for sugar, bananas and rice, for which the removal of restrictions will be staged, leading in principle to full elimination by 2009. There is still some uncertainty as to whether this process will be completed as proposed and the effects on sugar prices are unclear. Displaced European volumes may just end up depressing world prices further, which will harm certain elements of Malawi's global trade.

The EBA agreement should deliver a favourable impact to Malawi, but it is anticipated that the revenues generated under the EBA agreement will be considerably less than the current preferential sales level. The current Sugar Protocol provides that the beneficiaries receive prices related to those applying within the EU. Under EBA the price received by producers would be subject to negotiation with importers. Therefore EBA allows countries such as Malawi to export unlimited quantities of sugar to the EU, but at lower prices, probably much lower than those which apply to the quota-restricted preferences of the Sugar Protocol. In addition the EBA will increase the level of European exports and further deflate the regional market prices, making regional sales more competitive.

Malawi has trade quota agreements with the EU, the USA and South Africa. The Everything But Arms (EBA) agreement has meant that Malawi qualifies for the removal of the quota system on imports and full duty relief provided for all commodities except arms. This is being introduced under a phased approach with full liberalisation on import volumes and duty being achieved by 2009.

The preferential market quotas have been stable for the last five years. With the introduction of the EU EBA agreement there is an expectation that the volumes will increase in line with product availability from qualifying countries such as Malawi.

Initially the EBA volumes will replace the EU Special Preferential Sugar (SPS) quota with the benefit of the phasing in of duty relief. However with the EBA quota rising from 75 000 mT in 2001–2002 to a projected 198 000 mT in 2009 when full duty relief is available, Malawi should experience considerable increases to the quota volumes if fully implemented. Post-2009 LDC sugar exporters will receive unlimited duty-free access to the EU for LDC sugar. The mechanism for enabling this growth and managing the volumes from other sources is still to be confirmed.

7 Managing the global operation

Tim Mazzarol

Small firms that choose to enter international markets face the same management problems of their larger counterparts, and the same challenges of international market entry. However, unlike their larger counterparts, small firms must operate within overseas markets without specialist management skills and a deep base of financial resources. This chapter examines the key aspects of how small firms can manage their international operations, specifically their export marketing and foreign joint venture activities. The term 'globalisation' is used to refer to the process of exporting and the production and distribution of goods and services, including the growth of a firm's engagement and investment in overseas markets (Graham 1999).

The role and importance of small firms to the global economy is illustrated by their relative contribution to the business activity within most countries. An example is that of the 18 countries that comprise the Asia Pacific Economic Cooperation (APEC) region, where small firms comprise over 98 per cent of all enterprises, 60 per cent of all private sector employment and 30 per cent of all direct export activity (APEC 2002). Within the United States small firms (that is, businesses with less than 500 employees) comprise in excess of 70 per cent of all firms, whilst in Europe small firms, of which 20 per cent are engaged in exporting, account for around two-thirds of all employment (European Commission 2003; US Census 2004). Whilst small firms typically account for around 95 per cent of all business activity in most economies and around half of value-added production, they contribute less than one-third of manufactured exports and below 10 per cent of foreign direct investment (OECD 2004b). Small firms continue to be under-represented within the global economy despite the opportunities that can be derived from international trade (O'Byrne 2002).

For the purposes of analysis, the definition of a small firm adopted in this chapter is that used by the European Commission, which defines small to medium-sized enterprises as having fewer than 250 employees and less than 50 million euro in annual turnover (OECD 2004b). It should be noted that small businesses are those with less than 50 employees and below 10 million euro annual turnover, and micro-enterprises have less than 10 employees and 2 million euro in annual turnover (OECD 2004b). This is similar to definitions used by APEC, where small businesses have below 100 employees, or in Australia, where a business is small if it has below 20 employees and medium with less than 200 employees (ABS 2002; APEC 2003).

This chapter begins with an overview of the role of small firms in the global economy drawing upon OECD and APEC studies, and then reviews the literature relating to the management of international markets as it relates to small firms. It then draws upon evidence from small high-technology firms in Australia to illustrate examples of how such international operations can be managed. It is a major premise of this chapter that the key success factors in the global operation of the small firm are the quality of its senior management, their commitment to international operations and their ability to establish close, almost partner-like relationships with leading customers and key suppliers.

The internationalisation of small firms

A useful starting point in understanding the managerial issues associated with the globalisation of small firms is the work of the so-called 'Uppsala school' of internationalisation (Johanson and Vahlne 1977). Their study of Swedish firms from the 1970s found that internationalisation is a process of managerial learning. Incremental in nature, internationalisation frequently commences with the firm entering foreign markets where cultural similarities are highest, thereby reducing the level of 'psychic distance'. Market experience and knowledge builds the confidence of the firm's management team, leading to greater commitment to the export market, which in turn leads to enhanced knowledge and further commitment to the overseas market. This self-reinforcing cycle sees managerial learning as the key driver for future globalisation.

A contemporary study undertaken in the United States into the exporting behaviour of small firms identified a six-stage process of internationalisation. The first stage in this process was no interest in exporting. During the second stage the firm was likely to respond to unsolicited export orders, but frequently did not follow up and commence regular exporting. In stage three the firm's management typically begins to explore export opportunities actively; and by stage four will have experimented with exporting to 'psychically proximate' markets in keeping with the internationalisation pattern noted by the Uppsala School. Having committed to an overseas market, the firm's management will begin to learn and adapt to the market's conditions during the fifth stage. As the international experience of the firm's management team grows, the sixth stage is likely to see them seeking export opportunities in psychically distant markets. Future internationalisation is likely to proceed in stages with the capacity of the firm's management to learn and adapt to overseas markets being a key factor in the pace of globalisation (Bilkey and Tesar 1977).

The importance of management

Research has suggested that the size of the firm is less important than the quality and dynamism of the management team. For managers within small firms their willingness to respond to unsolicited export orders is likely to be important as this can help to shorten the export development cycle. Managers may wish to target psychically proximate markets and gradually formulate an export development policy and plan designed to explore new markets (Bilkey and Tesar 1977).

Management attitudes towards exporting and international trade have been found to be highly important in determining the success of globalisation within small firms (Czinkota and Johnston 1983). As the experience of managers within international markets grows they are likely to switch from indirect to direct methods of exporting. This is important because greater control over the product or service within the export channel will provide the firm with greater control and enhanced levels of market information. Selling costs can also be reduced by removal of intermediaries and the firm will strengthen its relationship with the customers through direct contact. While the direct export process involves more compliance costs, this is likely to be viewed as acceptable given the other benefits already outlined (Brady and O'Bearden 1979).

Research into the pattern of international activity and trading within small firms suggests that exporting is typically initiated by a key senior manager, who is influenced by such factors as family background, foreign birth or overseas education and experiences.

Younger managers are more likely to engage in exporting than their older counterparts. It is also likely that the firm's management will have decided that it has some form of competitive advantage to allow it to compete overseas, or it may be under pressure from within its domestic market. Export motivations are often opportunistic and driven by customers (Bilkey 1978).

The internationalisation process followed by these firms is consistent with the Uppsala School's theory showing that early target markets are psychically proximate and that export development is incremental in nature following defined stages. Small firms seeking to expand overseas are advised to target markets where their management feels comfortable doing business, and to develop each market in-depth before moving on to new ones. Attention should be given to long-term growth rather than short-term profit. It is also important for the firm's management to seek to match its capabilities to those of successful exporters. Language skills, experienced sales and marketing staff should be part of this. The quality of the management team is probably the single greatest determinant of success in exporting (Bilkey 1982).

The export behaviour of a firm is therefore less likely to be influenced by its size than its management team and the managerial attitudes and experience of the firm's senior managers. In this sense the firm's organisational culture is likely to be a significant determinant in the internationalisation process. Culture can serve as a trigger or barrier to the firm's export behaviour and global ambitions. There seems to be some similarity between medium-sized firms and large firms over such issues, with managers from these types of companies sharing similar attitudes and values than is the case with their smaller counterparts. Managerial attitudes and experience are therefore viewed as the key factors in the globalisation of small firms (Abbas and Swiercz 1991).

Does size matter?

Although the role of management has been viewed as being more important than the sheer size of the business, research has sought to examine the impact of size on internationalisation (Cavusgil and Nevin 1981). Empirical analysis has produced mixed results, suggesting that size may have an impact on export intensity (for example, the level of export sales as a percentage of total sales) (Burton and Schlegelmilch 1981). This may also be related to the firm's performance in international markets, which is likely to be influenced by the managerial competencies and experience of the management team (Moini 1995).

The size of a firm's workforce – frequently used to distinguish small firms from large – has not been found to be a significant influence over export behaviour. However, some evidence has been found to suggest that size does matter, at least in some instances (Bonaccorsi 1992). Further, as the firm develops its international operations it is likely to move from indirect export (for example, using export agents) to forward integration into the export marketing channel with a shift toward direct control and the building of overseas production or sales facilities (Cavusgil 1984).

A firm's propensity to export may be related to the size of its sales turnover, the number of markets that it is serving or able to serve, specific markets served and such factors as the stage of its internationalisation and strategic intent. As a business grows in scale its capacity to service multiple overseas markets will increase and it is likely that very small firms will find it difficult to engage in exporting due to resource constraints. In this regard the smaller firm may possess a more negative attitude toward internationalisation (Calof 1994).

The process of a firm's internationalisation appears incremental in nature, following a pathway in which the management's propensity for exporting is contingent on a combination of internal and external factors. Rational economic decisions about which foreign markets are likely to return the best results from investment are balanced with the evidence that managerial learning sees internationalisation follow an incremental, staged approach. Managerial learning and the capacity for the management to form and use international networks also appears significant (Coviello and McAuley 1999).

The importance of managerial learning

For the majority of small firms the key element in determining their success is the managerial skills and capacity of their senior managers, who are typically both owners and managers, and who need to balance any future growth against their own personal commitments and managerial competencies (Gibb and Scott 1985). Within international markets the types of competencies that are likely to be valuable include:

- Proficiency in multiple languages
- Experience of having travelled or worked abroad
- Willingness to move with confidence from one country to the next
- Cultural sensitivity and understanding of cultural differences
- Global or international vision.

It is also considered to be desirable for managers to have the capacity to work in multinational and multi-cultural teams (Eyre and Smallman 1998).

Within many small firms the level of formal management education is limited (Hankinson, Bartlett and Duchenaut 1997). Although small business owner-managers are generally experienced in their industries, their relative lack of formal management skills can be an impediment to their business performance (Hankinson 2000). Research into the learning behaviour of small firms suggests that there are at least three forces at work that need to be considered. The first of these is the individual learning process that the manager might undertake. This may be either formal or informal in nature and is typically motivated by the need to solve specific problems associated with the business. The generation of tacit knowledge through learning by doing is a common outcome. The second force at work is that of the firm's internal context including the organisational culture and communications flows. An important influence within the internal context is the previous experience of key managers within the firm. Finally, the third force at work is the environment external to the organisation. Here a major source of knowledge and learning is derived from both formal and informal business networks, which the firm's management will access for advice, ideas and knowledge (see Chapter 5; also Anderson and Boocock 2002).

Evidence from studies of small exporting firms suggests that the key factors motivating internationalisation are less associated with money and more with the opportunity to acquire new knowledge and skills while simultaneously broadening the firm's capacity. For most small firms the decision to export is fraught with risk and uncertainty, and the costs associated with the establishment of an export market may make any profits marginal in the early years. Under circumstances such as these the management of a small firm is likely to look for other things to motivate its continued involvement in overseas markets. This additional factor appears to be the opportunity for new learning, and this may be more important to the continued engagement in international markets than profits (Burpitt and Rondinelli 2000).

The importance of market-seeking behaviour

Previous research into the internationalisation of firms has highlighted the importance of managerial attitudes and the ability of managers within small firms to respond to unsolicited approaches from foreign customers, find psychically proximate markets and gradually expand their international operations through a process of learning by doing. However, there is evidence that many small firms, particularly those engaged in high-technology areas, are 'born global' (Knight and Cavusgil 1996). Such firms are found in most industries but are characterised by management that sees the world as their natural marketplace. Of importance to such firms is the skill of marketing, with strong emphasis on state of the art communications technologies to assist them to keep in contact with overseas customers. Such firms tend to adopt product differentiation strategies to secure competitive advantages (Knight et al. 2000).

The emergence of 'born global' firms was recognised during the 1990s with the advent of the Internet and the opening up of markets previously closed in the Cold War era to many service firms (Moen 2002). Since 2001 there has been recognition that the most appropriate way to view the globalisation of small firms is through a blending of entrepreneurship and marketing theory (Fillis 2001). Such firms are challenging the original Uppsala model of internationalisation by aggressively targeting overseas markets without waiting for the incremental learning and preference for psychically proximate markets. However, such firms are typically found within the high-technology sector where products are more naturally plugged into global supply chains, and international market-seeking behaviour becomes an essential element in securing venture capital financing and market growth. Without access to global supply chains and international financial markets such firms would struggle to commercialise their technologies (Gurau 2002).

From a strategic perspective the most common behaviour found among small firms is that of an opportunistic or emergent strategy (Mintzberg and Waters 1984). The high-technology, 'born global' small firm can be likened to that of a 'prospector' that seeks to gain competitive advantage through innovation and new product development, as compared to other firms that are more content simply to defend market share and react to market changes (Miles *et al.* 1978). Analysis of the relationship between the strategic orientation of small firms and their internal resources suggests that technology-focused 'prospector' firms are likely to be as successful as managerial 'analyser' firms that make use of marketing strategies to gain an enhanced competitive position (Borch and Huse 1993).

Research into the strategies followed by small firms seeking pathways to globalisation indicates that attention might be given by management to one of two avenues. The first focuses on global market opportunities while the second is more regional in nature. Global firms tend to sell the majority of their products overseas and follow a highly focused product strategy with a few specialised items being the core of their export activity in a wide range of overseas markets. By contrast the more regionally oriented firms remain heavily engaged in their local or domestic market and tend to offer a wide range of products in only a few overseas countries. The regional firm is more likely than the global firm to seek direct control over its marketing channel, even moving to establish its own manufacturing operations offshore. Small firms seeking to globalise successfully need to follow emergent focused strategies supported by a management style that is entrepreneurial and able to learn and adapt within overseas markets (Chetty and Campbell-Hunt 2003).

It is important for small firms seeking to secure a competitive advantage in international markets to possess entrepreneurial and internationally focused management teams. Their commitment to global competitiveness and to viewing the world as an opportunity for growth is critical to success (Ibeh 2003). Research evidence suggests that enhanced export performance is associated with the development of a competitive export strategy. This competitive strategy is likely to be influenced by the export competencies of the firm's management, their capacity to seek out information about overseas markets, and the quality of these sources of market intelligence (Julien and Ramangalahy 2003).

For small firms seeking to expand into international markets, the most important relationship is with the customer, particularly leading customers who assist the firm to develop its market access and enhance its products and services. Such close relationships with customers allow these firms to gain access to high-quality information on market conditions which is crucial to the process of new product development and innovation (Mazzarol 2003b).

The importance of networks and alliances

Networks and alliances give small firms an opportunity to build strategic market positions that offer enhanced competitive advantage (Ostgaard and Birley 1994). Most small firms lack the resources to implement all their desired strategies. However, as explored within Chapter 5, through the formation of networks and alliances, a small firm can create new market value, widening its range of customers or the reach of its products. It can also build up its capability by acquiring access to resources that it does not possess, and it can defend its market position by collaborating against new market entrants or substitution threats (Jarrett 1998).

For small firms seeking to secure competitive advantage within foreign markets, the creation of a joint venture with a local partner can prove a successful strategy. Such alliances offer the small firm access to local market knowledge and information, as well as the resources and networks of the partner firm. However, the selection of an appropriate joint venture partner is a crucial decision that can prove highly challenging (Kirby and Kaiser 2003). A problem for the managers of many small firms is their lack of experience in dealing with foreign partners and the associated language and cultural skills required for international business. Yet a successful alliance strategy can assist the firm to increase sales channels, access new market intelligence and accelerate the return to investments in marketing (Chen and Huang 2004).

Overseas customers can be an important element in the strategic network of the small firm. Analysis of the strategic networks of businesses suggests that they operate on three levels. The first is the 'production network' layer, which comprises the supply chain relationships, including customers and suppliers with whom the firm is closely engaged. The second level is the 'resource network' layer, which comprises horizontal relationships such as with banks or venture capital suppliers, research centres, government agencies and chambers of commerce. Finally, the third level is the 'social network' layer, which includes the interpersonal relationships that develop between the management team of the firm and other actors within the first two levels (Holmlund and Tornroos 1997).

Customers in overseas markets are generally highly important to small firms because they generate the cash flow to make the international business activity worthwhile. They also assist the firm in determining how it will configure its products or services and adapt them to meet the needs of the foreign market. An important aspect of dealing with overseas customers is how they might exert influence over the supply chain relationship and the nature of such influence strategies. The influence strategies followed by customers can vary from one geographic area to another, and are likely to change over time. Research suggests that customer influence strategies will change the intensity and nature of the relationship between the firm and its customers.

A categorisation of four generic types of relationship has been identified, determined by whether the relationship has low or high levels of mediation (for example, use of legal controls, financial rewards or penalties or coercive actions such as threats to take the business elsewhere) or high or low levels of non-mediation (for example, expertise, knowledge or reputation). The four types of relationship are:

- *Inert complacent* where the two partners are generally satisfied with the relationship, but there are low levels of mediation or even non-mediated influences. Such relationships are characterised by loose cooperation and coordination.
- *Collaborative strugglers* with low mediated but high non-mediated influence. This type of relationship is characterised by high levels of trust, understanding and satisfaction.
- *Problematic satisfiers* who have high mediated but low non-mediated influence. In this type of relationship the power lies mainly with the customers, who use contractual agreements but who elicit little trust and understanding.
- *Hazardous agitators*, where levels of both mediated and non-mediated influence are high. In this group there are uncertainty, distance and mistrust, often resulting in a doomed or stagnating relationship (Leonidou and Katsikeas 2003).

Learning how to manage international relationships with customers or joint venture partners is therefore an important skill that managers within small firms must develop to ensure sustainable success in international operations. The formation of international joint ventures is likely to be a major element in the long-term success of a small firm's globalisation strategy. However, the ability to keep a joint venture from collapsing appears contingent on the capacity for both partners to learn at broadly similar rates. Knowledge exchange is a critical element of the operation of an international joint venture. Partners must learn about each other and develop congruity in relation to their mutual goals and vision. Where one partner becomes too dependent on the other because their rate of learning is slower, it is likely that conflict will arise. The level of manager interaction within the social network layer can also be important, with personal relationships bounded by trust and mutual respect being highly important. Most international joint ventures follow a four-stage development process. This starts with formation of the partnership and moves to development of the joint venture that includes selection and appointment of the management team. In the third or implementation stage, a set of activities occur, including the development of vision, associated strategies and plans and identification of staffing needs. Finally in the advancement stage, the mutual learning and knowledge transfer between partners is the key feature of continued success (Schuler 2001).

While customers offer the most important relationship for small firms, there is also a significant role for key suppliers. Such suppliers are essential to the firm's ability to undertake its business and influence its international competitiveness by offering quality components, speed of delivery, flexibility or price advantages. As a small firm grows it will expand its relationships with key suppliers. Firms tend to rely more heavily upon suppliers during periods of growth, and need to ensure that they maintain effective relationships with key suppliers. It is important for the management of a small firm to select its suppliers carefully to ensure that they remain effective over the long term and can offer the firm continued support throughout the growth cycle. Small firms that succeed in following growth strategies tend to rely upon a few key suppliers, with whom they form strategic partnerships. They are also likely to concentrate on making these relationships work to their advantage. The successful small firm engaged in a growth process within international markets is unlikely to have an open market approach to securing its suppliers. Rather than relying on competitive bidding by suppliers, it is more likely that they will build upon key suppliers with whom they have close alliances built on trust and mutual learning (Beekman and Robinson 2004).

The importance of other factors

A review of current thinking on internationalisation over the past thirty years suggests that the majority of small firms are likely to follow an evolutionary path to internationalisation in which the attitudes and experience of the firm's senior management are likely to be critical to the decision to export and expand overseas operations. Small firms that are engaged in high-technology areas or that have products or services that are best sold into global markets may break this paradigm and follow a 'born global' strategy (Gurau 2002). Managerial learning plays an important role in the successful globalisation of the small firm, with the management team's experience of living or working within a foreign market helping to determine international market selection decisions. For most small firms the ability to form strong networks and alliances with leading customers, key suppliers and joint venture partners is likely to determine success. Cooperative strategies involving partnerships within the supply chain are likely to be a strong preference among small firms engaged in international markets. Personal social networks of the senior management of the firm and the influences of leading customers and key suppliers are also likely to play a role in ensuring export success (Gemser, Brand and Sorge 2004).

Successful exporting behaviour is also likely to be linked to the firm's ability to invest in staff training, process innovation, outsourcing and the use of export support and promotion programmes (Alvarez 2004). Small firms seeking to engage in global operations are likely to face a variety of internal and external barriers. Major internal barriers are the lack of information about overseas markets, or a lack of skills and competencies in exporting. Many small firms also suffer from poor international marketing competencies with inadequacies in relation to product, pricing, promotion, distribution and logistics within overseas markets. Major external barriers are heavy compliance costs associated with regulatory burdens, and a lack of government support to exporters. Other factors such as tariff and non-tariff barriers, unfavourable currency exchange rates and language or cultural barriers might also play a role.

Whilst small firms can address internal barriers, they can usually do little about external factors, particularly those relating to the economic or regulatory environments (see Chapter 2). This suggests that managers from small firms seeking to engage in international operations need to acknowledge any potential barriers to their export development and seek to enhance their knowledge about foreign markets by making use of internal databases, market intelligence from customer and supplier networks, and market research services. In addition, there may be a need to set priorities for dealing with such problems, and to devote time to analysing the causes of each while estimating their ability to resolve them. Using such information as can be obtained, they should seek to take corrective action and monitor progress using feedback from customers, agents or other sources of information (Leonidou 2004).

The best source of information on market performance for small firms is likely to be their customers, or at least their overseas agents. This is particularly the case for those firms engaged in the development of new products or those involving high technologies. While the benefits of partnering with key suppliers is likely to be viewed as valuable by small firms engaged in international markets, the most beneficial from a financial perspective is likely to be with their leading customers. The benefits accruing to the small firm across its production network layer are likely to overwhelm those found within the resource network layer. In other words working with leading customers and key suppliers to enhance existing products and services is likely to generate more immediate financial benefits to the small firm than working with third parties on R&D or new product development, or engaging with government agencies to secure export support assistance (Mazzarol 2004b). The value placed upon professional market research agencies, government export development services, business advisers and banks is likely to be substantially less than for customers, agents and their own market research efforts (Chaudhry and Crick 1998).

Evidence from small high-technology firms

To illustrate the operational behaviour of small firms within global markets and the relevance of current thinking to the practices adopted by small firms, the remainder of the chapter draws on evidence from a series of studies undertaken within the Australian high-technology sector. During the period 2002–2004, a series of research studies were undertaken into the networking and strategic alliance behaviour of small firms engaged in the Australian information communications technologies (ICT), defence technologies, marine engineering, shipbuilding and digital content sectors (Mazzarol 2003a; Mazzarol 2004a; Mazzarol *et al.* 2004). A feature of these industries was their high level of 'born global' firms and the need for these firms to engage actively in international operations with respect to both their production and resource networks. These industries were all located in Western Australia, which is one of the most geographically isolated regions in the world. The location of the region imposes significant logistical hurdles on managers seeking to maintain global operations.

A survey was undertaken of 114 firms within high-technology industries in Western Australia, involving a postal questionnaire which was sent to the chief executive officer (CEO) of each firm. Ninety-five per cent of these firms had less than 200 employees.

Table 7.1 Importance of communication types with leading customers

Question item	Important
The importance when working with customers:	
Face-to-face contact between senior managers	86%
Face-to-face contact by technical staff	71%
Face-to-face contact by sales & marketing staff	65%
The importance when working with customers:	
Customer contact via email	75%
Customer contact via telephone/fax	48%
Customer contact via trade shows	27%

Note: Results based on a survey of 114 small businesses

Sixty-three per cent were engaged in exporting with at least one leading customer being located overseas. The average length of time firms had been involved in exporting was 11 years, with some firms having been engaged in overseas markets for over 33 years.

At a general level, a key outcome from the survey was that 56 per cent of the exporting firms reported that their overseas customers were either important or critically important to their overall business performance, with 76 per cent reporting that these leading customers acted as market opinion leaders who helped to gain credibility for their products. For the majority of these firms, leading customers were viewed as playing an important role in driving performance by demanding high quality and service. Almost half the firms considered their leading customers as acting as developmental partners for ideas that the firm had originated, or major sources of new ideas or new need identification. Eighty-two per cent of the exporting firms reported having worked with their leading customers to improve products. These findings highlight the use of customer feedback to enhance organisational learning as well as product and market development.

In terms of managing the relationship with leading customers, the most important form of communication was that of face-to-face contact between senior managers of both firms. Table 7.1 shows the proportion of respondents who felt that different types of communication were important in working successfully with leading customers. The table suggests that direct contact between technical staff and customers is considered important by more respondents than direct contact with the firm's marketing and sales staff. This is due to the need for such face-to-face visits to involve discussions over the technical development of the products. By comparison with marketing or sales managers, technical or production managers are more likely to identify opportunities for further product improvement when they talk to the customers. Also worthy of note from Table 7.1 is the relatively high importance placed on email by the firms. The ability to communicate with leading customers located overseas using the Internet is a major bonus to small firms seeking to develop global markets. The frequency of such contact is also worthy of consideration. Among the firms engaged in international markets, 57 per cent reported face-to-face meetings taking place between leading customers and senior managers at least monthly. Similar meetings between sales and marketing staff and leading customers were

Table 7.2 Importance of overseas sources of technology

Question item	Important
The importance of source for new technology:	
Other companies in your industry	31%
Companies in other industries overseas	19%
Overseas universities and research institutes	9%
The importance of source for new technology:	
Overseas key suppliers	46%
Overseas leading customers	24%
Parent or sister company	20%

Note: Results based on a survey of 114 small businesses

taking place on at least a monthly basis by 65 per cent of firms. Seventy-three per cent of firms reported meetings taking place between their technical staff and leading customers on a frequency of at least once a month. Eighty-four per cent of companies reported being in daily or weekly email contact with their leading customers.

In terms of key suppliers, significantly fewer firms had formal contracts or agreements with overseas firms, with over half the respondent firms claiming that suppliers located overseas had little real impact on their performance. Only 24 per cent of firms considered suppliers within their overseas markets to be a key source of innovation. Compared with customers, the role of suppliers as a source of new ideas or as an important partner in the firm's performance was generally viewed as being of less relevance.

With respect to alliances and networking, 13 per cent of the 114 firms surveyed reported having export distribution agreements with locally based partners. Thirty-two per cent of firms reported that some product development was being undertaken with overseas partners and 16 per cent some form of process innovation. A further 17 per cent had commenced joint production activities with overseas partners, while 31 per cent were involved with joint marketing and distribution links with overseas partners. Only 10 per cent of firms were engaged with overseas partners for the raising of venture capital.

The use of strategic alliances to secure access to new technology was also examined within the survey. Thirty-six per cent of the technologies used by these small firms were reportedly sourced from overseas. As shown in Table 7.2, the most important overseas source of new technology was key suppliers, followed by other companies in the same industry. Overseas leading customers were also an important source of new technology for about a quarter of the firms. These findings highlight the importance of using overseas networks to small firms in accessing new technologies that can be applied to their production. Small firms have been found to make use of strategic networks and alliances to secure access either to new market opportunities, additional resources or the protection of existing market share (Jarrett 1998).

Therefore, the outcomes from the survey highlight the importance not only of customers and suppliers as sources of market information and advice on new product development and technology, but also the need for senior managers to maintain close personal contacts within these networks. This is a key theme within Chapter 5. Managerial learning through this continuous communication with customers and suppliers would appear as the key outcome with benefits to the firm's operations and innovation.

Managing global operations: case studies

The following sections of the chapter help to illustrate further the nature of how small firms manage their global operations, by drawing upon case studies from three selected industry sectors: shipbuilding, boatbuilding and wireless communications.

Cases from the shipbuilding sector

The commercial shipbuilding sector may be defined as those firms engaged in the design and construction of vessels greater than 8–10 metres in length. Since the 1980s, Australian shipbuilders have invested substantially in innovation, research and development, and workforce skills training and development. Despite having only a modest industry by world standards, Australian shipbuilders, particularly those engaged in the construction of lightweight aluminium multi-hulled vessels, have positioned themselves as significant actors within the global market (ASA 2003). Sixty-five per cent of the industry's turnover is generated from defence-related activities, with commercial shipbuilding, repair and maintenance making up the remainder (IBIS 2003). Three case studies are selected to illustrate the pattern of activity in this sector. For purposes of confidentiality these firms have not been identified. They are referred to merely as Shipbuilders 1, 2 and 3. All were well-established firms based in Western Australia and specialising in the design and construction of aluminium vessels from 10 to 100 metres for a range of civil, police and military purposes. The three firms all undertook their own design work, but outsourced varying amounts of the production operations, usually in areas of specialist engineering. At the time of the project, all three firms had grown to a size where they were able to establish divisional structures and develop greater in-house capacity. Between 50 and 80 per cent of their production was sold to overseas customers.

These customers were located throughout the world, with Europe, North America, Asia and the Middle East all being targeted for market development. All three shipbuilders maintained close and highly cooperative relationships with their leading customers. The nature of these relationships was generally close and based on fairly high levels of trust. Communication intensity between the shipbuilders and their leading customers was high. In all cases the main point of contact between the firm and the customer was the CEO, who was responsible for initial establishment of the relationship and also ensuring that it continued smoothly. The CEOs of the firms were found to be highly networked individuals who used their personal and professional links to secure new contracts and reinforce existing ones. These CEOs were also major shareholders in the firms and were the individuals that had founded the businesses.

As highlighted in the survey results, it was common for the CEOs of these three firms to be travelling overseas regularly to meet with customers and ensure that a personal touch was put on the company's products. There was a trend in one of the shipbuilders (Shipbuilder 3) to encourage contact between customers and lower-level management from the company. It was felt that this assisted in keeping the entire firm in touch with the needs of customers.

The three shipbuilder firms worked closely with their customers over the design, development and manufacture of each vessel. As explained by the CEO of Shipbuilder 1 the company had a policy to 'be honest to customers . . . have their trust . . . know what they want and deliver exactly as requested'. These close customer relations had led to the generation of new sales as well as enhancing the product performance and securing customer referrals to new potential customers. However, despite these close customer relationships, all shipbuilders viewed their ability to retain their customers as dependent on their ability to offer: (i) high-quality, on-time and on-cost delivery; and (ii) products tailored specifically to the needs of the customer.

Customers were viewed by the shipbuilders as being sensitive to price, but also attracted by their ability to deliver tailored products. Shipbuilder 3 gave an example of a contract to build a new vessel for a buyer who was known to be price sensitive. Three local firms tendered for the work including Shipbuilder 3, who was surprised to find the contract let to a competitor for a final bid price that was AUD$100 000 more than the next highest bid. According to Shipbuilder 3, this was attributed to the ability of the successful tender to know exactly the style of vessel required by the customer and tailor its offer to these needs.

All three shipbuilders exported the majority of their products. For example, 80 per cent of the vessels produced by Shipbuilder 1 were sold to overseas customers, with most new business coming from marketing activities and referrals from existing customers. The firm's management team used their leading customers to provide market intelligence over competitor activities. The main focus of attention for Shipbuilder 1 was not on the customer firm, but on key personnel within these firms. They targeted people within their customer organisations who served as 'gatekeepers', able to open the door to more networks and new customers.

The three shipbuilders also maintained joint ventures with other firms both within Australia and overseas. For example, Shipbuilder 1 supplied some vessels in a kit form to a joint venture partner in Asia which undertook the final assembly. This was frequently necessary in defence-related contracts where the foreign government required some local offset production to help boost its own defence industry capability. Within the local defence industry sector, collaborative alliances were normal for large contracts, in which shipbuilders joined with defence specialists in armaments, electronics and other naval systems to complete the final product. Such alliances were viewed as an opportunity to enhance capabilities and transfer new knowledge and technologies. The larger shipbuilders were also establishing spinout ventures with a focus on the design and manufacture of specialist components. The creation of these new ventures was designed to enable the sale of these new technologies and services to other rival shipbuilders.

Cases from the boatbuilding sector

The boatbuilding sector is characterised by a relatively large number of small firms producing vessels of less than 8–10 metres in length. It is difficult to estimate accurately the precise number of firms within the Australian boatbuilding sector, their size and annual turnover. Within Western Australia it has been estimated that there are around 200 firms engaged in boatbuilding of which most are very small (Sensis 2003). The sector can be broadly divided into luxury and mainstream boatbuilding. Luxury boat builders need to invest larger sums of private capital to acquire land, tooling and skilled labour for the production of craft that can take up to 1 or 2 years to complete. For the lower-end leisure craft sector, capital investments are typically smaller at start-up, but increase as the business grows and expands.

Within the luxury boat segment of the market, buyers are located throughout the world with no specific concentrations geographically. Such customers can also be difficult to reach for new entrants to the market. Each luxury craft is custom made and may take an average of one and a half years to complete. Buyers initiate purchase and initially have considerable bargaining leverage. The potential for repeat purchase adds to their power. In the lower-cost small leisure craft sector, the buyers consist mainly of dealerships and business-to-business interactions. Dealerships are located both within Australia and overseas. Many dealerships are difficult to reach for new market entrants due to pre-existing relationships with competitors. Each boat is standardised with minor custom-made alterations, and takes an average of four weeks to six months to build. The dealerships usually initiate the purchase and have considerable bargaining leverage. Boatbuilding demands the development and delivery of products that fit tight price–quality–performance ratios, plus the ability to deliver on time to such specifications. Prices can vary substantially depending on fit-out and features, as well as basic construction materials. It is relatively easy for customers to switch from one builder to another, although in practice a high degree of customer loyalty is to be found. In general the customers' propensity to change boat builders is linked to their financial resources and personal preferences.

Four case study firms were identified and selected for analysis – boat builders A, B, C and D. Boat Builder A was a specialist manufacturer of sports, fishing and pleasure craft, motor yachts and luxury 'marine limousines' that serve as tender boats for super-luxury motor yachts (the parent vessel is usually in excess of 75 metres in length). These limousine tenders are valued at AUD$1 million to AUD$2 million each and service the very high premium end of the market. Such craft can take up to one and a half years to complete and require the use of both advanced composite fibreglass materials, and expert craftsmanship in the design, finish and fit-out. Boat Builder B was an award-winning manufacturer of luxury yachts in excess of 50 metres in length, each of which sell for over AUD$50 million. Such vessels typically take up to two years to complete. Boat Builder C manufactured fibreglass catamarans and employs innovative hull designs to achieve reduced noise and enhance stability. Boat Builder D was a manufacturer of aluminium vessels for the leisure craft sector. It manufactures in volume. All four of these boat builders were locally owned and had well-established track records within the industry.

Customers for Boat Builder A were primarily multi-millionaires comprising a global market of little more than 1000 people. Also included in the customer list were brokers, who contracted to supply luxury leisure craft of the kind produced by Boat Builder A, captains of luxury yachts, and boat designers who served as sources of referral. All the firm's customers were located overseas in all parts of the world. There was an equal mix of new and repeat customers. Customers were generally sourced via word of mouth referral, or when viewing the products. Sales contracts were on a boat/project basis and were different every time. It could take up to 18 months to get a contract signed and the building started. A contract could last for approximately one and a half to two years and would generally stipulate price, timing and specifications. Boat Builder A worked closely with its customers to improve its end products and service. The nature of the relationship with customers was very personal and friendly, but a long-lasting relationship with such customers was not usually possible. Demand was usually cyclical as the purchase of luxury goods was sensitive to changes in global economic cycles.

Customers played an essential role for Boat Builder A in enhancing credibility and increasing sales, sourcing new ideas through their personal requirements, providing access to new customers and maintaining high quality standards. Direct contact with customers was important so the CEO travelled overseas for an initial contact and to negotiate the contract. Afterwards communication was mainly via email and phone on a weekly or daily basis. The firm's location did not seem to be an impediment to doing business on a global scale. The customers of Boat Builder B were also largely multi-millionaires mostly located overseas. As with Boat Builder A, it was important for the CEO and senior management of the firm to maintain close personal relationships with customers during the contracting and production process. All boats were sold prior to the firm commencing production and most customers become closely involved in the design stage to ensure that their individual requirements were met.

By comparison, Boat Builder C was only exporting 60 per cent of its product, with domestic sales having previously played a much stronger part in the business. However, competition within the local domestic market had increased in recent years, with falling sales forcing the firm to seek greater exports. The lead customers for Boat Builder C were retail, foreign governments, businesses and overseas dealerships. Overseas government contracts were seen as a good source of repeat business. As a result, Boat Builder C had sought to establish strong formal business relationships with its foreign government customers, although this was not easy to maintain. The firm's civil export markets were different again, with the key point of contact being overseas dealerships. These agents were a good source of market intelligence on the standards required for finish and fittings in these foreign markets. Boat Builder C had established fairly close personal contact with its key international distributors and sought to keep such dealerships 'comfortable' with the firm as a 'reliable supplier'. The management team at Boat Builder C was willing to listen to any suggestions made by such foreign distributors.

Boat Builder D was the smallest of the case study firms and sold most of its product within the domestic market via intermediary retailers which also provided after-sales service and support to customers. The lead customers for Boat Builder D were domestic and overseas dealerships located throughout Australia, New Zealand, the Pacific and Europe. The firm recognised these dealerships as vital to its success and maintained regular contact. However, many of these dealers had well-established relationships with rival boat builders and were frequently reluctant to harm such existing relationships by favouring one manufacturer over another. The company had made a decision to own and operate its own retail operation in the Perth market with a view to using this business to get a stronger feel for the market and end-user customer. As with the other boat builders, Boat Builder D made significant adjustments to its products when exporting in order to ensure that finishes and fittings were tailored to international standards and tastes. The company sought to partner with its foreign distributors to secure enhanced market penetration and intelligence of local market conditions. Over time a series of strong, formal relationships had emerged between Boat Builder D and some of its overseas dealers.

While key suppliers were mainly located within Australia, the majority of the leading customers of the case study firms were overseas. These customers played a significant role in driving product innovation and quality, particularly at the luxury end of the market. New ideas for product development and improvements were commonly sourced to customers or overseas-based distributors. Regular contact, usually face-to-face, was frequent and supported by emails and telephone calls on a continual basis.

Cases from the wireless technologies sector
The wireless technologies sector is complex, involving a variety of different actors engaged in software applications development, content developers and enablers, infrastructure providers, network operators, device and equipment manufacturers and retailers. Since the first wireless telephony communications were commercialised in 1983, the wireless technologies industry has seen rapid and complex changes in the scope of its services, user growth, technological configurations and supply strategies.

The industry is characterised by rapid rates of technological innovation and high intellectual barriers to entry. It has been estimated that the take-up rates of wireless technologies triples every 16 months, outpacing even computer power, which doubles every 18 months. From 1983 to 2001 the number of components in mobile phones increased from 250 to 900 while at the same time mobile phone sizes reduced significantly. In 2001 it was estimated that there were around 640 million users of wireless products and services globally (Constance and Gower 2001).

In analysing this industry sector, eight case studies were undertaken with organisations engaged within different parts of the production network layer. These were operating principally as application developers, infrastructure providers, device manufacturers and retailers. For reasons of confidentiality, the eight case study firms examined in this study cannot be identified, but their general profiles can be outlined. All but two were successful commercial enterprises that had experienced good growth and were well-recognised within their respective areas of activity. The other two were non-commercial organisations with a predominately R&D function. One of the firms (Wireless Case Study Firm 7–WCSF 7) was headquartered overseas.

Within their production network, the majority of the case study firms had formal agreements with suppliers and customers, mostly overseas. These firms were involved in design and testing (alpha and beta) of applications, devices or equipment. Two of the firms were application developers and four were device or equipment manufacturers. Hardware component design and manufacture has become something of a commodity process and is undertaken increasingly in low-cost countries, outside Australia. For the majority of these eight firms their major markets were overseas. The firms understood that the Australian market was too small and the domestic wireless technologies industry too limited for them not be actively engaged globally. Only by developing international linkages could these firms remain competitive and credible within their sector. The major activities or functions within the production network layer of the wireless technologies sector were hardware R&D, components manufacture, software R&D, alpha and beta testing, marketing, distribution and after-sales service. None of the case study firms undertook all these activities, focusing instead of areas of specialisation.

The production network layers found among the application developers were similar in structure. For example, Wireless Case Study Firm 1 (WCSF 1) had a production network composed of a number of key R&D hardware and component suppliers, R&D software development partners, alpha and beta test sites and a global distribution and integration firm. This firm obtained hardware components from its key suppliers to provide the physical part of its products while it supplied the software component in collaboration with software partners. The testing of the entire system was undertaken using alpha and beta test sites in conjunction with its lead customers. Once the testing phase was completed, the firm distributed its product through a global distributor with which it had a close association. Most of these linkages were formal agreements and were with overseas organisations. By comparison WCSF 2 also had a production network composed of a number of R&D hardware and component suppliers, R&D software partners, alpha and beta test sites and a global distribution and integration firm. As with WCSF 1, the majority of these relationships were formal alliances with overseas organisations. WCSF 2 recognised that the Australian market was too small and that it must develop strong linkages to international partners.

Of the four firms engaged in the manufacture of devices and equipment, only one firm (WCSF 7) sought to capture a wide spectrum of the activities along the production network. WCSF 4 was a niche player providing component design and testing services. Its customers were mainly located overseas, predominately in North America and Asia, and were generally large firms engaged in the manufacture of components. It was the function of WCSF 4 to provide the design services for future components that are then manufactured in Singapore and China. WCSF 5 had a production network composed of specialised suppliers, and a small number of lead customers in established and emerging markets overseas. Each of these relationships was formal in nature. Because all the key suppliers and lead customers were located abroad, the senior managers of WCSF 5 spent much of their year travelling. They saw the Australian market as of significantly less importance than the international markets.

WCSF 6 was primarily a research organisation focusing on hardware and software R&D that it sold or licensed out to other firms. Although headquartered in Australia, the firm did not view the local market as particularly important and saw its main collaborative links as being with lead customers overseas. WCSF 6 was focused on research and new product design and development. The management of the firm viewed their relationships with lead customers as arms length in nature.

WCSF 7 was a Singapore-based subsidiary of a larger Asian-owned corporation headquartered in Hong Kong. It was included in this study as a comparison to the Australian companies. This firm undertook a wide range of activities in the design and development of wireless electronic devices. Its business network comprised key suppliers, lead customers and venture capital providers. This financial partnering was considered a major part of the firm's network. WCSF 7 had a production network composed of several hardware and component suppliers and operators, dealers and retailers. It operated as a vertically integrated organisation undertaking most activities within the production network. Most of its alliances were formal in nature.

One case study (WCSF 1) highlights the operation of the resource network layer for firms within the wireless technologies sector. The resource network of WCSF 1 was quite large in both scale and scope. Access to technology and knowledge was secured via software partners, trade shows, industry groups, Bluetooth groups, beta test sites, telecommunications network operators and even competitor firms. WCSF 1 was engaged in establishing a users group involving some of its competitors so that they could learn from each other and cooperate for a win-win scenario. There were no linkages with any of the local Australian universities. However, informal links did exist with local and international universities to secure both technical specialists and management expertise. Such links were based on the experience of the senior managers of WCSF 1, who tended to return to the European universities where they had obtained their qualifications to seek future graduate employees. WCSF 1 viewed its links to venture financing as critical to its continued growth. Several venture capital firms had invested in the company and held positions on its board. The firm had secured its financing from the United Kingdom and the United States, and had established offices in London and New York to ensure that it could maintain adequate communication with its partners.

Most of the case study firms had comprehensive social networks, usually based around their senior executives and key technical staff. It was widely felt among these firms that the social network layer was the most critical because everyone in the company was involved in social networks. Such interpersonal contacts were recognised as valuable channels of information and knowledge flow, as well as sources of technology transfer and innovation. Many of the engineers and managers within these firms maintained contact with their social networks via email and telephone, as well as face-to-face contact at social occasions and trade shows. It was estimated that around 60 to 70 per cent of managers' time was taken up maintaining their social networks. Engineers in the same process spent a slightly less but still significant amount of time on network maintenance and development. Many managers travelled widely to maintain such contacts, particularly overseas. Engineering and technical staff were also frequently involved in such visits, or with the installation of products. Such direct contact with customers was viewed as beneficial to the firm's ability to service its contracts properly and understand the needs of the market. An important observation of the social networking within these firms is that most of these linkages were with people located overseas rather than in Australia.

For example, the social network maintained by WCSF 2 was quite complex. The CEO of the company considered this a critical network for enhancing the flow of ideas and information. All managers and engineers maintained contact with individuals within their social network using a combination of email, telephone and face-to-face visits. The CEO also wrote personal letters to customers, suppliers and other important network partners to facilitate and strengthen these relationships. Frequent overseas travel by managers within the business allowed personal contact to be maintained with important actors in the network, as well as identifying new alliances, especially with new customers. Because WCSF 2 had a worldwide market, such international travel was essential despite the time and cost involved. While the senior managers and sales staff were regularly visiting customers, the firm maintained a policy of having engineering staff personally involved in the installation of products and communicating directly with customers.

Conclusions

The overall pattern emerging from this analysis of the experiences of the case study firms is that the success of global operations is contingent on managerial commitment, learning and strategic networking. This is reflected in the review of the literature outlined earlier in this chapter, and reinforced by the findings from the survey and case studies of small high-technology firms operating in the international market place. Most small firms are highly dependent on a few key managers who must be prepared to make a significant personal commitment to the international market, including very high levels of overseas travel and the capacity to establish close working relationships with customers and suppliers.

Whilst the majority of firms may follow an incremental process in their export development, the innovative, technology-intensive firms are more likely to be market seeking or 'born global' in nature. Success within global markets requires high-quality and innovative products or services. This must be backed up by a total commitment to working with the customer to find ways to improve the existing products. Continuous product development is linked to the firm's capacity to work in close, partnership-like relationships with leading customers. The entire senior management team from the firm, including the technical and R&D staff, need to have regular face-to-face contact with customers to facilitate organisational learning and enhance product development and quality. It is not likely that such export intensity can be undertaken on a casual or part-time basis.

Strategic networking with customers, suppliers and third party resource network actors such as research centres or venture capital providers, is also an essential element in the maintenance of global operations. The formation and maintenance of these strategic networks is the primary responsibility of the firm's senior management, often the CEO or MD, and is part of their social networking. Personal contact with customers, suppliers or other network actors on both a social and professional level is essential if the firm is to retain and strengthen its networks. This requires senior managers to possess highly developed interpersonal skills and the ability to operate comfortably in foreign business environments and deal with different cultures.

These findings suggest that managers from small firms seeking to engage in exporting or international business activities must be prepared for a total commitment to the development of international activities. They must be willing to configure their firm's operations to service the needs of overseas customers and adapt their products in response to customer feedback in an ongoing process of continuous quality improvement. These same managers must seek to build strong, partnership-like relations with their leading customers and key suppliers, and to build systematically a strategic support network to assist the business with its market and product development.

Policy makers seeking to assist small firms in expanding their global operations should focus attention on the development of the management team's international business skills. This should include the area of strategic networking and alliance formation, as well as interpersonal communications. Assisting small firms to invest in innovation and new product development is also a key area for policy support. Without ongoing investment in new technologies and product development, it is unlikely that small firms will retain any sustainable competitive advantage. Finally, small firms would benefit from assistance in lowering the cost of travel and communications.

A key potential bottleneck for many small firms, particularly those with high-technology products, is reliable access to low-cost broadband Internet and telecommunications services. It can be seen from the results of the survey of Australian firms that managers from small firms are in almost daily contact with customers using such ICT services. Firms located in some remote or regional areas away from major telecommunications hubs are restricted in their ability to deal with long-distance customers due to poor quality ICT services (Papandrea and Wade 2000). A similar case can be made for access to low-cost and flexible air and freight services. The cost of doing business for small firms located in distant geographic areas is likely to be high. If managers cannot readily access low-cost air travel or communications services their firms will be effectively restricted from participating in the global market. This will in turn have flow-on consequences not only for the productivity of the firm but also for the local economy.

Future research should focus on the distinction between market-seeking 'born global' firms, particularly those engaged in high-technology, innovation-intensive sectors, and the more mainstream industries. It is questionable whether there remains any industry that could compete within a global market and be low technology. Researchers might examine the continued relevance of the 'Uppsala School's' model of incremental internationalisation to see how the growth of ICT and low-cost air travel over the past 30 years has changed these assumptions from the 1970s. Finally, future research should focus on the role of strategic networks and their use by small firms in the development of competitive advantage. The need for such evidence and insights is echoed within Chapter 5. There remains much work to do in defining the nature of strategic networking by small firms, understanding how such networks form, how they are sustained, their role in the adoption and diffusion of innovation, and how they are managed.

Questions emerging from the chapter

In closing this chapter, we can pose six critical questions that need further analysis and exploration:

1. What are the key qualities required of managers from small firms who are seeking to engage in global markets?
2. What is 'managerial learning' within the context of a small firm's global business operations and why is this so important?
3. Is there an optimal size for a small firm to reach before it can effectively engage in overseas markets or can a firm be 'born global'?
4. What are the distinctions between 'born global' firms and the more traditional mode of internationalisation, and are these distinctions relevant today?
5. What is the nature of strategic networks and alliances for small firms within international markets and what is their importance to business development?
6. What are the roles of leading customers and key suppliers in the global operations of small firms with reference to the case studies?

Bibliography

Abbas, A. and Swiercz, P.M. (1991). 'Firm Size and Export Behavior: Lessons from the Midwest', *Journal of Small Business Management*, **29** (2), 71–78.

ABS (2002), *Small Business in Australia 2001*, Cat. 1321.0, Australian Bureau of Statistics, Canberra, Commonwealth of Australia.

Alvarez, E.R. (2004), 'Sources of Export Success in Small and Medium-sized Enterprises: The Impact of Public Programs', *International Business Review*, **13** (3), 383–400.

Anderson, V. and Boocock, G. (2002), 'Small Firms and Internationalisation: Learning to Manage and Managing to Learn', *Human Resource Management Journal*, **12** (3), 5–24.

APEC (2002), *Profile of SMEs and SME Issues in APEC 1990–2000*, APEC Secretariat, World Scientific Publishing, Singapore.

APEC (2003), *Small Business and Trade in APEC: A Report Highlighting the Contribution of Medium, Small and Micro Enterprises to the Asia Pacific Region*, Asia Pacific Economic Cooperation (APEC), Singapore.

ASA (2003), *WA Shipbuilding*, Australian Shipbuilders Association, Available from: www.washipbuilders.com.au/ [September, 2003].

Beekman, A.V. and Robinson, R.B. (2004), 'Supplier Partnerships and the Small, High-Growth Firm: Selecting for Success', *Journal of Small Business Management*, **42** (1), 59–77.

Bilkey, W.J. (1978), 'An Attempted Integration of the Literature on the Export Behavior of Firms', *Journal of International Business Studies*, **9** (1), 33–46.

Bilkey, W.J. (1982), 'Variables Associated with Export Profitability', *Journal of International Business Studies*, **13** (2), 39–55.

Bilkey, W.J. and Tesar, G. (1977), 'The Export Behavior of Smaller-Sized Wisconsin Manufacturing Firms', *Journal of International Business Studies*, **8** (1), 93–98.

Bonaccorsi, A. (1992), 'On the Relationship between Firm Size and Export Intensity', *Journal of International Business Studies*, **23** (4), 605–636.

Borch, O.J. and Huse, M. (1993), 'Informal Strategic Networks and the Board of Directors', *Entrepreneurship Theory and Practice*, **18** (1), 23–37.

Brady, D.L. and O'Bearden, W. (1979), 'The Effect of Managerial Attitudes on Alternative Exporting Methods', *Journal of International Business Studies*, **10** (3), 79–84.

Burpitt, W.J. and Rondinelli, D.A. (2000), 'Small Firms' Motivations for Exporting: To Earn and Learn?' *Journal of Small Business Management*, **38** (4), 1–15.

Burton, F.N. and Schlegelmilch, B.B. (1981), 'Profile Analysis of Non-Exporters versus Exporters Grouped by Export Involvement', *Management International Review*, **27** (1), 38–49.

Calof, J.L. (1994), 'The Relationship between Firm Size and Export Behavior Revisited', *Journal of International Business Studies*, **25** (2), 367–387.

Cavusgil, S.T. (1984), 'Differences among Exporting Firms based on their Degree of Internationalization', *Journal of Business Research*, **12** (2), 195–208.

Cavusgil, S.T. and Nevin, J.R. (1981), 'Internal Determinants of Export Marketing Behavior: An Empirical Investigation', *Journal of Marketing Research*, **18**, 114–119.

Chaudhry, S. and Crick, D. (1998), 'Export Information Providers: Are they Meeting the Needs of SMEs?' *Marketing Intelligence & Planning*, **16** (3), 141–149.

Chen, H.-L. and Huang, Y. (2004), 'The Establishment of Global Marketing Strategic Alliances by Small and Medium Enterprises', *Small Business Economics*, **22** (5), 365–377.

Chetty, S. and Campbell-Hunt, C. (2003), 'Paths to Internationalisation among Small to Medium Sized Firms: A Global versus Regional Approach', *European Journal of Marketing*, **37** (5/6), 796–820.

Constance, S.C. and Gower, J.R. (2001), *A Value Chain Perspective on the Economic Drivers of Competition in the Wireless Telecommunications Industry*, Massachusetts Institute of Technology, Cambridge, MA.

Coviello, N.E. and McAuley, A. (1999), 'Internationalisation and the Smaller Firm: A Review of Contemporary Empirical Research', *Management International Review*, **39** (3), 223–256.

Czinkota, M.R. and Johnston, W.J. (1983), 'Exporting: Does Sales Volume Make a Difference?' *Journal of International Business* Studies, **14** (1), 147–153.

European Commission (2003), 'European Observatory for Small and Medium Sized Enterprises', *Europa: Activities of the European Union*, http://bookshop.europa.eu/eGetRecords

Eyre, P. and Smallman, C. (1998), 'Euromanagement Competences in Small and Medium-sized Enterprises: A Development Path for the New Millennium', *Management Decision*, **36** (1), 34–42.

Fillis, I. (2001), 'Small Firm Internationalisation: An Investigative Survey and Future Research Directions', *Management Decision*, **39** (9), 767–783.

Gemser, G., Brand, M.J. and Sorge, A. (2004), 'Exploring the Internationalisation Process of Small Businesses: A Study of Dutch Old and New Economy Firms 1', *Management International Review*, **44** (2), 127–150.

Gibb, A.A. and Scott, M. (1985). 'Strategic Awareness, Personal Commitment and the Process of Planning in the Small Business', *The Journal of Management Studies*, **22** (6), 597–632.

Graham, P.G. (1999), 'Small Business Participation in the Global Economy', *European Journal of Marketing*, **33** (1/2), 88–97.

Gurau, C. (2002), 'The Internationalisation Process of UK Biopharmaceutical SMEs', *Journal of American Academy of Business*, **2** (1), 241–248.

Hankinson, A. (2000), 'The Key Factors in the Profiles of Small Firm Owner-Managers that Influence Business Performance: The South Coast Small Firms Survey, 1997–2000', *Industrial and Commercial Training*, **32** (3), 94–98.

Hankinson, A., Bartlett, D. and Duchenaut, B. (1997), 'The Key Factors in the Small Profiles of Small-Medium Enterprise Owner-Managers that Influence Business Performance', *International Journal of Entrepreneurial Behaviour and Research*, **3** (4), 168–175.

Holmlund, M. and Tornroos, J-A. (1997), 'What are Relationships in Business Networks?' *Management Decision*, **35** (4), 304–309.

Ibeh, K.I.N. (2003), 'Toward a Contingency Framework of Export Entrepreneurship: Conceptualisations and Empirical Evidence', *Small Business Economics*, **20** (1), 49–68.

IBIS (2003), *IBIS World Database*, www.ibisworld.com.au.

Jarrett, D. (1998), 'A Strategic Classification of Business Alliances: A Qualitative Perspective Built from a Study of Small and Medium-sized Enterprises', *Qualitative Market Research*, **1** (1), 39–49.

Johanson, J. and Vahlne, J.E. (1977), 'The Internationalization Process of the Firm: A Model of Knowledge Development and Increasing Foreign Market Commitments', *Journal of International Business Studies*, **8** (1), 23–32.

Julien, P.A. and Ramangalahy, C. (2003), 'Competitive Strategy and Performance of Exporting SMEs: An Empirical Investigation of the Impact of their Export Information Search and Competencies', *Entrepreneurship: Theory and Practice*, **27** (3), 227–245.

Kirby, D.A. and Kaiser, S. (2003), 'Joint Ventures as an Internationalisation Strategy for SMEs', *Small Business Economics*, **21** (3), 229–309.

Knight, G.A. and Cavusgil, S.T. (1996), 'The Born Global Firm: A Challenge to Traditional Internationalisation Theory', *Advances in International Marketing*, **8** (1), 11–26.

Knight, G.A., Masden, T.K., Servais, P. and Rasmussen, E. (2000), 'The Born Global Firm: Description and Empirical Investigation in Europe and the United States', *American Marketing Association Conference Proceedings* (1999), **11**, 104–26.

Leonidou, L.C. (2004), 'An Analysis of the Barriers Hindering Small Business Export Development', *Journal of Small Business Management*, **42** (3), 279–302.

Leonidou, L. and Katsikeas, C. (2003), 'The Role of Foreign Customer Influences in Building Relationships with US Exporting SMEs', *Long Range Planning*, **36** (3), 227–252.

Mazzarol, T.W. (2003a), *Innovation Linkages: Strategic Networks and Alliances within the Western Australian ICT Sector*, Centre for Entrepreneurial Management and Innovation, Graduate School of Management, University of Western Australia, Perth.

Mazzarol, T.W. (2003b), *Strategic Networking among High Technology Firms: Evidence from the Western Australian ICT Sector*, ANZAM 2003 Conference, 2–5 December, Fremantle, Western Australia.

Mazzarol, T.W. (2004a), *Industry Networks in the Australian Marine Complex: Strategic Networking within the Western Australian Maritime Engineering Sector*, Centre for Entrepreneurial Management and Innovation, Graduate School of Management, University of Western Australia, Perth.

Mazzarol, T.W. (2004b), *Small Firms, their Customers and the Value of Strategic Alliances and Networks to Innovation*, ANZAM Conference 2004, 8–11 December, Dunedin, New Zealand.

Mazzarol, T., Patmore, R., van Heemst, N., Wong, J. and Adam, D. (2004), *Digital Communities: A Study to Determine the Feasibility of Creating a Digital Content Industry Cluster in Western Australia*, Centre for Entrepreneurial Management and Innovation, Graduate School of Management, University of Western Australia, Perth.

Miles, R.E., Snow, C.C., Meyer, A.D. and Coleman, H.J. (1978), 'Organisational Strategy Structure and Process', *Academy of Management Review*, **3** (3), 546–562.

Mintzberg, H. and Waters, J. (1984), 'Of Strategies, Deliberate and Emergent', in *Readings in Strategic Management*, Open University Press, Milton Keynes.

Moen, O. (2002), 'The Born Globals: A New Generation of Small European Exporters', *International Marketing Review*, **19** (2/3), 156–175.

Moini, A.H. (1995), 'An Inquiry into Successful Exporting: An Empirical Investigation Using a Three-Stage Model', *Journal of Small Business Management*, **33** (3), 9–25.

O'Byrne, P. (2002), 'Australia: Doubling SME Exporters', *International Trade Forum*, **2**, 12–13.

OECD (2004a), 'Facilitating SMEs Access to International Markets', *Promoting Entrepreneurship and Innovative SMEs in a Global Economy*, Organization for Economic Cooperation and Development, Istanbul, Turkey 3–5 June.

OECD (2004b), 'SME Statistics: Towards a More Systematic Statistical Measurement of SME Behaviour', *Promoting Entrepreneurship and Innovative SMEs in a Global Economy*, Organization for Economic Cooperation and Development, Istanbul, Turkey 3–5 June.

Ostgaard, T. and Birley, S. (1994), 'Personal Networks and Firm Competitive Strategy: A Strategic or Coincidental Match?' *Journal of Business Venturing*, **9** (4), 281–306.

Papandrea, F. and Wade, M. (2000), *E-Commerce in Rural Areas: Case Studies*, Rural Industries Research and Development Corporation, Canberra ACT.

Sensis (2003), *Yellow Pages Business Directory*, Telstra Sensis Pty Ltd.

Schuler, R.S. (2001), 'Human Resource Issues and Activities in International Joint Ventures', *International Journal of Human Resource Management*, **12** (1), 1–52.

US Census Bureau (2004), 'Number of Small Businesses Continues to Grow: Nevada and Georgia Lead the Way', *U.S. Census Bureau News*, 30 November, www.census.gov/Press-Release/www/releases/archives/economic_surveys/003102.html, accessed 24 November 2006.

PART III

LEARNING, SKILLS AND KNOWLEDGE IN DOING GLOBAL BUSINESS

8 Skills and knowledge needs of the global SME

Terry Mughan and Lester Lloyd-Reason

Introduction

The aim of the chapter is to advance understanding of the internal and external factors which make some small and medium-sized enterprises (SMEs) successful in international markets. Particular attention is paid to global skills and knowledge development that can be made transferable across business sectors via educational and consulting programmes. The ability to learn is becoming increasingly important in the global economy as SMEs are exposed to greater competition from international rivals in domestic markets and are needing to source materials and clients in overseas markets in order to survive and prosper. This imperative is however a difficult one to respond to for organisations with limited financial and human resources. The classical model whereby governments provide a range of services to help offset these disadvantages is an important element of the SME landscape and has to be considered when assessing company behaviour and options and market conditions. We will propose a model of support intervention which we believe is suited to the global trading and learning environment.

In this chapter we will build upon the resource-based view (RBV) as well as the process theory in international business (IB) to provide valuable insights into the company experience of internationalised SMEs and propose the conceptual model of 'planning, manning and scanning' as the key to performance building. We will draw upon the key findings and issues emerging from an 18-month research project to identify the processes, skills and knowledge which characterised the set of companies which emerged from a 1200 sample as successful international businesses. We will consider the relevance of these findings to the current and future form and content of support infrastructures which help create and sustain these companies.

Theoretical review

The review draws upon two major theoretical frameworks: the process literature of international business (IB) and the resource-based view (RBV). These two fields have become increasingly overlapping since the 1990s as the literature on international business moved away gradually from a macro-economic perspective, invoking theories of strategic management. We contribute to this more micro perspective of internationalising strategy in order to take forward existing questions about the international business planning, resource management, international networking and market intelligence gathering of small and medium-sized enterprises.

The process theory on small internationalising enterprises

Various studies have been conducted concerning the internationalising process of SMEs (see, for example, Johanson and Vahlne 1977; Andersen 1993) but the research on detailed practices and activities that relate to strategic outcomes are still at a development phase. This view is supported by the literature review of Coviello and McAuley

(1999) that identifies only 16 journal articles on the specific topic of the process of export within the 10-year period preceding the year 1999, the majority of which focuses on macro activities. Also, most of these studies concentrate solely on manufacturing firms on a macro level and only two studies compare service firms and manufacturing organisations.

When further analysing the literature on exporting processes, different stages of export activity can be identified, ranging from non-exporters to those with a high international marketing engagement. A gradual and phased development in distinct stages is described in some of the export process literature (see Melin 1992; Gankema, Snuif and Zwart 2000). Usually these models differentiate between four and eight categories. Andersen (1993) argues that in general terms these models can be categorised into two major clusters: U-Model and I-Model.

The U-Model, named after a study organised by the Uppsala School, describes the process of export as 'a gradual acquisition, integration and use of knowledge about foreign markets and operations and a successively increasing commitment to foreign markets' (Johanson and Vahlne 1977). The organisation of the U-Model takes into account strategic choices and organisational forms, with organisational learning and experience also depicted (Nordstrom 1991). However outside factors, such as cultural distance, foreign market selection and entry, organisational forms, expansion, marketing strategies and access to information, also influence the process of exporting and internationalising (Morgan and Katsikeas 1995). Thus, the possibility of testing the U-Model is very limited.

A number of further criticisms of the U-Model of internationalisation have been expressed in the literature. Thus, for example, Newbould, Buckley and Thurwell (1978) argue that firms do not necessarily adopt persistent organisational approaches towards exporting. Further criticism points towards the formulation of boundaries between stages as well as the applicability of 'stage' theories (Bell, Crick and Young 2004; Knight 2000).

The second model, the so-called I-Model, is an innovation-related model. The term is obtained from the studies carried out by Cavusgil (1980), where the decision to internationalise is regarded as an innovation to the company. Based on Vernon's (1966) product life cycle, the various stages of internationalisation are distinguished along the ratio of export sales to total sales, representing the extent to which a firm is involved in export activities. Stage one represents a firm that is solely interested in the domestic market and not interested or willing to experiment with exporting, whereas stage five represents a firm where the export sales to total sales ratio is 40 per cent or more with the firm being heavily dependent on foreign markets (Gankema 2000). A detailed analysis of the activities that constitute the everyday internationalisation decisions and activities, however, is largely under-researched.

The resource-based view

Ignited by the groundbreaking papers of Wernerfeld (1984) and Barney (1991), the resource-based view (RBV) has become one of the predominant foundations in the literature of strategic management. Hereby Barney (1991) argues that sustained competitive advantage of a company mainly derives from the capabilities and resources an enterprise is able to develop and control. This set of resources and capabilities can be regarded as packages of tangible and intangible assets that determine the success and failure of a company. Ranging back to Penrose's (1959) work on the diversification of companies, the argument of company growth moved from an outside perspective towards an inside respective of the firm. In practice that means a greater focus away from the traditional product-based competitive advantage towards less tangible resources (Lopez 2002).

Research on the RBV was further developed when Grant (1991) introduced a practical framework that visualized the dependency of resources, capabilities and competitive advantage on the formulation of strategy and the identification of resource gaps. He thereby classifies resources into 'strategic' and 'not strategic' (Lopez 2002). Barney (1991) is among the first to specify the criteria used to make this classification. These criteria include the resource value as well as the extent to which it is rare and difficult to imitate and substitute.

When taking into account the literature on international entrepreneurship, it becomes apparent that a distinctive new sub-field is emerging that incorporates the RBV logic into the internationalization of small enterprises. However, this sub-field still seems in its infancy when measured by the number of articles in top-tier journals. It is therefore our aim to contribute to this new research field through the use of a large cross-industry empirical study that incorporates both theories.

Empirical basis

The aim of this chapter is to advance understanding of the internal and external factors which make some small and medium-sized enterprises (SMEs) successful in international markets. Taking the IB and RBV theories into account, this study set out to explore the need and support for small and medium-sized enterprises in the Eastern region of the United Kingdom using a multi-methodological framework. Since a number of studies into related areas have recently been completed both within the region and nationally, we have drawn upon these reports to help inform our findings. Our approach included four key stages of activity:

- A large-scale telephone survey of 1200 firms throughout the eastern region to provide a map of international activity within the region. The survey involved a stratified sample across sectors and geographical location to reflect the characteristics of the six counties of the eastern region of the United Kingdom.
- Face-to-face interviews on the premises of 80 firms, lasting between one and two hours, with either the owner-manager or the individual responsible for international action. The aim was to gain insights into why and how firms become involved in international activity, and of course, why they sometimes do not, how they manage their international activity, what problems they encounter and where they go to find solutions.
- Face-to-face interviews with many of the key players within the business support community within the region.
- Analysis and review of the quantitative and qualitative data generated by these activities to identify policy implications and recommended action programmes aimed to help better design and target the efforts of the business support agencies and educational institutions in the East of England and build economic growth through international excellence.

The quantitative study

The mapping of international activity throughout the eastern region was achieved through a large-scale telephone survey undertaken between June and August 2002. During this period 560 internationalised and 554 non-internationalised SMEs were interviewed. A further sample of 101 larger companies in the region were also interviewed as a control group.

The telephone interviewing technique was used to collect data because of the rapidity of data gathering, accuracy and efficiency. The questionnaire was designed to determine the extent and nature of international activity within the region. While this activity was explored in terms of penetration of international activity and so on, this chapter focuses on the barriers and obstacles reported by executives. The questionnaire was fully structured, with response categories defined prior to the study, informed by literature relevant to internationalisation. The questionnaire was pilot tested on a small number of respondents to ensure understandability prior to the main survey.

The sample frame used was obtained from Business Link and listed known exporters and non-exporters stratified by county and broad business area (primary, secondary and tertiary). The listings were a random sample of organisations but in the final event nearly all organisations recorded as exporters were approached during the survey. A target was set of an achieved sample of 550 organisations in each of the two categories of internationalised and non-internationalised. Samples of this size typically yield results accurate to within four to five percentage points according to statistical theory. A further sample of 101 larger internationalised organisations was also included in the study for comparison (250+ employees). The final sample turned out to be 554 non-internationalised, 560 internationalised and 101 larger companies.

The qualitative study

In phase two of the project, 80 companies were interviewed face-to-face on their own premises between December 2002 and June 2003. The interviews, which were undertaken by senior academics within the Ashcroft International Business School (Cambridge), were semi-scripted and were recorded. In all cases the person interviewed was the strategic decision maker for international activity (usually the owner-manager). Each interview lasted for about one hour.

Building on the findings from the telephone survey, the purpose of the interviews was to obtain deeper data about company behaviour in international markets, including managerial traits, skills and knowledge needs, problem solving and their views of support services. The interview schedule included a mix of open questions where the interviewees were encouraged to talk about their motivations and experiences in their international activities, and closed questions concerning specific problem areas, where they looked to for support and their opinion on the effectiveness of the support provided.

The sample of companies to be interviewed was selected from the larger sample on the basis of experience of international trade, skills and knowledge and the application of these to their international activities. The key consideration was not the volume of international activity, but rather how effective the application of their experiential learning had been in contributing to turnover generated from international activities. In this respect, mode of activity, geographical location and sector were regarded as secondary considerations.

For the purposes of analysis, as indicated above, each interview was recorded and transcribed, generating in excess of 2500 pages of transcript. In addition, following the completion of each interview, a two-page summary of the key points emerging from the interview was produced, providing a further 160 pages of text. Finally, three closed questions providing tick box responses using the Lickert scale were used covering the international mindset of the interviewee, specific problems experienced and the support providers used.

Data from five of the interviews was rejected as being unsuitable for our purposes and the analysis presented below is therefore based on data collected from 75 firms. Analysis of the qualitative data from the 2500 pages of interview transcript, 150 pages of summary text and 75 sets of tick boxes was undertaken using a dedicated software package, N6. This software uses word or phrase recognition and the text was coded down to three levels using four key categories:

- Motivation: What are the motivations and drivers for international activity?
- Process: What form does this activity take and how does it impact on the firm?
- Problems: What are the key problems encountered?
- Solutions: Where do they go to find solutions to these problems?

Key findings

Below are the key findings from the quantitative study:

- Almost as many internationalised firms were involved in importing (61 per cent) as exporting (77 per cent).
- Just under half of all internationalised firms were involved in two or more forms of international activity, for example, exporters who also import.
- The two main reasons for not becoming involved in international activity were: i) lack of international opportunities in the particular sector and ii) 'benign' conditions in the domestic market.
- The most frequent mode of export was by specialist exporter or agent (35 per cent) followed by 'own sales office' (20 per cent) and 'direct sales' (13 per cent). If Internet, word of mouth and through current customers are added to the direct sales category this would then increase to 30 per cent. This changes the interpretation considerably and challenges the traditional view that intermediaries are the most appropriate route to international markets for SMEs when considering market entry.
- The majority of experienced and inexperienced internationalised businesses self-generated solutions to their problems (87 per cent). Amongst exporters, networks of suppliers were used by 23 per cent of firms interviewed and 31 per cent said they used business support organisations, mainly BusinessLink and the Department for Trade and Industry (including Trade Partners UK). Just 5 per cent of importers had used business support organisations.

Company classification

Based upon the immediate results from the qualitative study, the interviewed companies could be classified in five bands:

1. **The Curious**: Have considered international activity, but have not yet taken action. Little awareness of available support.
2. **The Frustrated**: Have previously been, or are occasionally involved in, international activity, but are no longer actively pursuing this, often due to negative experiences. Little awareness of available support.
3. **The Tentative**: Have limited experience of international activity, have developed some skills but have some major problems looking for solutions. Some experience of available support.
4. **The Enthusiastic**: Have considerable experience of international activity and are keen to grow this side of their business but are experiencing barriers to that growth. Have developed a range of skills but suspect that these need to be developed. Largely aware of available support with some experience, often positive.
5. **The Successful**: Have extensive experience of international activity with some major successes. Very high skills and knowledge development, very aware of available support with a high degree of usage. Often aware of skills and knowledge gaps and very keen to improve effectiveness in international activity.

Key findings from the qualitative study included the following:

- Planning (the way in which the firm plans its involvement in foreign markets), manning (the way the firm organises or develops its resources to service foreign markets) and scanning (the way in which the firm informs itself about those markets) are the areas of skills and knowledge required by all firms active in international markets.
- The configuration of these skills, and the support designed to improve them, varies according to experience, sector and size.
- All firms benefit from strategic planning and management development.
- All firms benefit from the development of international skills (foreign languages and/or intercultural awareness). It is the development of these skills within successful firms that facilitates the transfer of business acumen from domestic to international markets.
- Firms new to international activity (the Curious and the Frustrated) are very receptive to, and appreciative of, current support provision.
- Successful firms have specific skills and knowledge needs which are not all met by current provision.
- We identify an intermediate set of firms (the Tentative) whose international activity is static, who have lost the initial enthusiasm for international activity and who need tailored support which is not currently available.
- Demand transformation: There is a need to distinguish between what companies want and what they need. They want information, money and solutions to precise, small problems. They need to learn to plan, to broaden their management mindset and build better manning and scanning skills.

- Skills and knowledge development for international trade takes place via the processes of exporting, importing, inward investment and international research arrangements.
- Best practice in firms often emanates from patterns of trading involving one or more of these elements (a multi-modal approach).

Skills and knowledge

The method adopted for this study was to observe and record the behaviour of companies from a wide range of sectors and of varying size, age and international experience. We did not seek to squeeze these companies into a preconceived analytical framework but have attempted, in our analysis, to identify the variables in their composition, culture and context which have played a significant part in their progress, or otherwise. It was not our aim to locate the companies or their personnel on a scale of educational achievement, though we are able to make some general estimates of the relationship between performance and the educational qualification of key personnel.

Our analysis therefore focuses on the skills and knowledge required by companies, in normal circumstances, to sustain successful performance in a competitive international trading environment. Some of these skills (general management) may apply equally to the domestic trading environment. Others (foreign language skills) may be specific to the international environment. Very importantly, and this is something we need to research further, we will discuss the nature of the transition from domestic trading to international trading from a skills and knowledge perspective, as it emerged from our study. Do all companies make this transition successfully, or is there something about the make-up of some that helps them do it better?

Skills

In order to simplify the complexity of the issues surrounding skills and knowledge development, we conclude our analysis with an identification of skills and knowledge needs across the five categories of firm interviewed. We referred to the Cambridge Advanced Learner's Dictionary to define a skill as 'an ability to do an activity or job well, especially because you have practised it'.

Planning The Planning skill set poses serious challenges to the typical small and medium enterprise. Most companies came into existence not as a deliberate, rational response to a set of market conditions but in response to an opportunity or a passion. To ask such an organisation to adopt a strategic planning approach to foreign markets is therefore asking it to do something foreign. All of its personal and commercial history may even militate against the suggestion. The firm has built its persona around the value of being pragmatic, problem- and sales-oriented and commercially astute. That is, at this point, strategy is driven by sales rather than the other way round. Indulging in abstract concepts and calculations about markets and competences seems to managers to be the antithesis of business success. Even if they could see the case for it, it is usually not something they would see themselves as capable of. Most, when questioned, said that their reason for starting exporting was to respond to an opportunity. When these companies approach business support agencies it is not usually to ask for advice, but to ask for support or information to help them achieve something specific they have already resolved to do. In our study we found evidence of a transformation process at work. Good advice will not simply give them what they want. It will alert them to what they need and help them find a way to obtain it.

We can therefore distinguish between what companies want and what they need. They want information, money and solutions to precise, small problems. They need to learn to plan, to broaden their management mindset and build better manning and scanning skills.

Manning Most of the companies we interviewed have limited resources with which they can develop their international trade ambitions. Some, however, often as a result of sound strategic planning, develop a clear idea of how they need to develop their material and human resources to make their international activities more profitable. This often involves investing in skills which are not critical to domestic business success, such as foreign language skills.

We found a close correlation between valuing foreign language use and sustained success in international trade. Successful companies value relationships and market intelligence and these are best cultivated and exploited by use of the language of their client and market. We also discovered a complex appreciation of foreign language use by successful companies. Good managers will see occasions on which they individually, or a member of their personnel, will profitably exhibit the ability to speak or write the foreign language.

We can say much the same about other skills needed to enact international trade well. The international company has to equip itself with the skills to dispatch the goods, satisfy customs and excise requirements and ensure customer satisfaction in a more complex transaction than most which apply in a domestic environment. It is however important to note the key role played by the owner-manager in this context. He or she has to provide the leadership and informed decision making in this challenging environment. There is a strong body of literature that suggests that owner-managers with a strong international orientation tend to be more successful in the long term as they appreciate the need for new skills more quickly. The skills they possess are therefore the critical ones and they need to be in place before any of the others can be developed or effectively deployed. In this respect, manning follows on from planning, which, as a process, needs to identify skills shortages and devise a plan to redress them.

Scanning Much export support has traditionally leapt straight to the process of scanning, bypassing the first two stages. Information about opportunities in a foreign market can be sufficient to create an exporting opportunity which a company will seek to exploit.

In a more competitive and strategic environment where the company first needs to assess its readiness and ability to export effectively and in a sustained manner, information about the foreign markets needs to be aligned in a more structured way with the company's plans. Information is not just about one-off opportunities, it is about market conditions, national regulations and competition. The successful companies we interviewed used the Internet, trade fairs and exhibitions, personal relationships and networks and visits to the foreign market regularly and effectively to improve their decision making and adjust their business strategy. Managers we observed who were successful at international trade tended to be people able to carry out these tasks with similar confidence and ease to what they show in the domestic market. Some, but not all of these managers may have had had previous experience of international trade. Others did not but simply felt comfortable in different environments and with foreign clients. The ability to read signals, solve problems, interpret data and understand clients in other cultures can be developed alongside or, in some cases, independently of foreign language skills and some are more predisposed to it than others.

Here once again, the process of scanning needs to be seen, not just as an activity in itself, but as a part of a strategic approach towards international trade. The issue is not the obtaining of information, but the decision as to what information to look for and where to look for it. Answers to these questions should emerge from a strategic business plan. This does not preclude the possibility of a fortuitous order coming through the letterbox and proving to be the start of a successful exporting venture. The strategic plan will ask of the company and the owner-manager questions that will help him or her devise the tools and skills to take advantage of such an opportunity, to develop it and to apply it to other markets. In this way, the firm continues to behave opportunistically or entrepreneurially, but within a more strategic framework so that international activity becomes targeted rather than ad hoc.

Knowledge

Whilst the concept of skills currently carries a great deal of significance in economic and educational strategy in the UK at the moment, it is probably correct to say that the concept of knowledge has even greater import within the context of global economic and corporate competitiveness. As a concept, it is less easily grasped than is the notion of a skill. It takes many more forms and is less easy to quantify and to isolate in its manifestations in daily life. This quality has made of it something of a holy grail in contemporary management theory. As Holden (2002) points out, 'It can be shared, in principle, universally. [Alternatively] . . . it can be forgotten and not used.' The operating assumption for many theorists and corporate leaders is that much of the knowledge that makes a critical contribution to the modern organisation is tacit, that is, we do not necessarily know we are using it in our daily decision making. It is therefore particularly difficult to analyse and exploit as it is sometimes conscious and sometimes unconscious. According to the Cambridge Advanced Learner's Dictionary, knowledge is 'understanding of or information about a subject which has been obtained by experience or study, and which is either in a person's mind or possessed by people generally'.

Planning As already acknowledged, the process of strategic planning is a rather vague, abstract concept. It involves the assembling of data from the past and observations about current trends in an attempt to prepare the company for the future. It is no surprise that these predictions often turn out to be wrong, no matter how good the data were or the intellectual ability of the planners.

Nonetheless, planning has a number of benefits. The process of planning:

- increases the familiarity of the planner with the business and the market
- forces the planner to consider and reflect on a variety of possible scenarios
- puts the planner into a position of informed readiness to confront emerging realities.

These are all very valuable experiences for anybody who has to deal with the international environment, where political events, natural catastrophes or mergers and acquisitions can change the competitive position of their company overnight in a foreign market. Clearly, planning is a demanding process and it is no surprise that, where declared in our study, all the individuals responsible for exporting in successful companies were educated to at least CCE A level standard, with a good number having at least a degree. Conversely, the Tentative companies, which we found generally to have stagnated in their international operations, had a poor record here. The majority of individuals were educated just to GCSE level or equivalent.

Manning Once a business strategy has been defined, the resources and skills of the company have to be aligned with it and the target markets. This process requires a sound knowledge of both the company and its markets. When these markets are overseas, the data on them are inevitably distant and complex. The owner-manager needs to ensure the quality of the data and its application to the company's operations. Our research found that whilst the Curious and the Successful companies were attentive to this issue, once again the Tentative companies lacked commitment to it. Eighty per cent of Curious companies and 72 per cent of Successful companies possessed foreign language skills but only 23 per cent of Tentative companies did.

The flow of knowledge about clients and the market to the company that is facilitated by foreign language skills and other examples of commitment to and experience of the foreign market becomes a critical tool in the company's attempts to sustain and improve its performance there. This knowledge is present in the individuals who work in and for the company (including distributors) and a key management task is to help facilitate the flow of this information through the management process.

Scanning Knowledge about foreign markets usually resides primarily in the owner-manager (or the sales manager) who goes there and liaises with clients. The quality of the data obtained will depend on the quality of the relationships he or she can build with the market. Here, as earlier, we can identify skills which help obtain that data. Equally important, however, is the flow of information from the owner-manager to other stakeholders. This process has to be managed if the data are to have meaning beyond the owner-manager. On a mundane level, sending personnel to overseas markets can be expensive but savings and benefits can be obtained if information about travel, customs or expectations are passed on. On a more critical level, what might appear on the surface to be unimportant information to the owner-manager about a particular client can become invaluable information in the hands of the finance director or the production manager. Once again, obtaining data is only half the task. Knowing what to do with it is equally important.

Skills and knowledge needs

In the discussion above we have attempted to examine some of the key issues surrounding skills and knowledge development through an examination of the key role these play in building the ability to compete effectively in international markets. In order to summarise these complex issues, in Boxes 8.1–8.3 we identify the skills and knowledge needs of the firms interviewed across the five categories.

BOX 8.1 SKILLS AND KNOWLEDGE NEEDS: THE CURIOUS AND THE FRUSTRATED

Inactivity in international markets is largely due to the lack of perceived international market opportunities (no pull factor) and generally benign domestic conditions (no push factor)

Key questions facing these two groups:

Planning: Do we really want to grow the business through international activity?

Manning: If so, do we have the skills and resources to achieve this objective? If not how do we fill the skills and resource gaps?

Scanning: How do we find out if there is a potential international market for our products?

Skills and knowledge needs

Planning

How to build a business plan
How to map courses of action and learn basic processes
How to anticipate the consequences of the decision to go international
How to identify the actual costs associated with new market development
How to evaluate company responses to export opportunities

Manning

How to assess strengths and weaknesses of resources
How to obtain extra resources, where necessary
How to approach support agencies
How to manage doing business in a foreign language
How to modify products to meet market needs better
How to process orders
How to plan market visits and trade fair strategies

Scanning

How to find out about potential market opportunities
How to assess competitive position in selected markets
How to identify where and when problems with foreign languages occur
How to identify potential partners
How to triangulate market intelligence sources
How to find out about market regulations that affect market development
How to find the type of information and/or contacts to comply effectively
How to identify and approach support agencies

BOX 8.2 SKILLS AND KNOWLEDGE NEEDS: THE TENTATIVE AND THE ENTHUSIASTIC

The Tentative: Little ability to self-analyse. Have discovered that international trading is complex and challenging and have lost their initial enthusiasm. Perceive problems to be largely external to the firm and largely expect support agencies to solve them on their behalf.

The Enthusiastic: Understand complexity of the international trading environment and perceive the critical challenge to be (in)ability to compete effectively – that is, they understand that the key problems are internal rather than external. Much more receptive to support agencies than the Tentative.

Key questions facing these groups:

Planning: Are we committed to international activity? Do we need to revisit our business objectives? Are we being strategic enough in the way we deal with our international markets and customers? How can we develop more established guidelines and procedures?

Manning: How do we identify our skills gaps? How do we acquire and/or develop dedicated resources? How do we find and assess appropriate support?

Scanning: How can learn to understand the differences between markets and how to manage those differences? How do we evaluate market opportunities?

Skills and knowledge needs

Planning

How to develop more established guidelines and procedures
How to identify processes by which to evaluate current international activity

Manning

How to affirm market operations and negotiate changes, if necessary
How to identify the appropriate type of market presence
How to undertake an audit of skills and resources
How to move towards a geocentric HR strategy
How to understand the differences between markets and how to manage them

Scanning

How to service the needs of current international customers
How to identify new market opportunities
How to develop a framework for new market development
How to find and assess the most appropriate type of support

BOX 8.3 SKILLS AND KNOWLEDGE NEEDS: THE SUCCESSFUL

Have a number of strengths: internal – high level skills development; external – strong products and well-established markets. Understand that the key to success is their ability to manage an increasingly complex and challenging international business environment.

Key questions facing this group:

Planning: How do we control the new market development process? How do we influence key stakeholders? How do we manage/influence support?

Manning: How do we acquire dedicated resources for key markets? How do we develop specific higher-level skills?

Scanning: How do we service customer needs at distance? How do we ensure appropriate local presence?

Skills and knowledge needs

Planning

How to control the new market development process
How to influence key stakeholders
How to develop a strategic approach to establishing a local presence effectively
How to manage/influence support

Manning

How to identify and develop specific skills
How to build a tighter international team
How to acquire dedicated resources for key markets
How to assess support in the new market development process

Scanning

How to develop client relationship management systems, particularly the management of client relationships at distance
How to use cultural differences to benefit the business

Support infrastructures for the improvement of company performance

Having identified these needs, we now return to the process by which they can be cultivated or improved. Given the limited resources, human and material, of most small companies, the role of government agencies is central to this question. What does this support look like in the United Kingdom and does it match company needs?

There is a wealth of evidence within the academic literature and government statistics that demonstrate that exporting is the predominant mode by which SMEs engage with

Table 8.1 Percentage of providers in East of England and England offering each type of service

Service	East of England (%)	England (%)
Advice	42.3	74.2
Consultancy	38.4	35.5
Finance	19.2	51.6
Information	50.0	74.2
Networking	30.7	29.0
Training	34.6	12.9
Other	76.9	61.3

Note: Percentages add to more than 100 as multiple responses allowed.

international markets and trading. Since the mid-1990s, there has been a great deal of debate around the exporting activities of small and medium-sized enterprises (SMEs), in both a regional and a national context. A brief review of the academic and practitioner literature highlights a number of perceived benefits to businesses from exporting. These include exposure to differing ways of doing business (Barclays Bank 1996), additional demand for the product or service of the business (Julien *et al.* 1997) and opportunities for modifications of existing products and new product development. The successful development of export markets by SMEs has also been recognised by government as critical to enhancing the competitiveness of these businesses and hence to the strengthening of regional and national economies. It is these public benefits – principally the generation of a larger number of more secure jobs – that provides the basis for the substantial expenditure of government funds in the support of private businesses. In the United Kingdom, for example, policies have drawn upon research by Girma, Greenaway and Kneller (2001) that provides evidence of causal link between exporting and improved business performance.

In mapping provision across the English regions, Sear *et al.* (2001a) note a plethora of information-type services to exporting companies (see Table 8.1), though the figure for the East of England is significantly lower (50.0 per cent) than the national norm (74.2 per cent). There is also a lack of financial provision nationally (51.6 per cent), which is even lower in the East (19.2 per cent). There is therefore evidence from this study that there are significant differences in support provision across the English regions, which the authors attribute not only to differences in the socio-economic characteristics of the regions but also to differences in entitlement to European monies to underpin business and export support services and differences in regional strategies. The East of England emerges as a region with a relatively balanced provision of support services across the exporting process (see Table 8.2).

The majority of these services are configured around the needs of small and medium-sized companies exporting for the first time or seeking to break into a new overseas market having had some success with their first venture. Market research, translating services and market visits predominate as subsidised activities. A review of the efficacy of these services (Wilson 1999) led to the introduction across the United Kingdom of a more structured and sustained support package whereby companies are assisted in the development of an

Table 8.2 Percentage of providers in each region catering for each stage of the exporting process

Activity	East %	England %
DMC	50.0	25.8
RM	57.6	54.8
ELP	53.0	45.2
Selling	42.3	71.0
OF	69.2	64.5
S&D	65.3	41.9
Strategy	23.0	12.9
Financing	3.8	58.1

Note: DMC – Developing motivation and confidence; RM – Researching the market; ELP – Establishing a local presence; OF – Order fulfilment; S&D – Shipping and delivery.

export plan, its implementation and the first stages of managing international business. *Passport to Export Success* has been a successful offering with companies mainly because of the sustained and programmed support and its aim to nurture companies through the formative, planning stages before leaving them to fend for themselves, though even on completion of the programme owner-managers are able to call on the International Trade Advisers for occasional support.

The provision of such support has placed skills demands on International Trade Advisers, who hitherto had been primarily a conduit for the fulfilment of requests for market and technical data, and problem solvers. Most consultancy activities (see Table 8.1) have traditionally been offered by private enterprises. In complementing information-type services with more structured support in recent years, UK Trade and Investment has therefore taken a significant step in the provision of strategic advice (see Table 8.2) and support to companies and appears to have met a real market demand. More sustained, strategic involvement with companies has yielded better exporting results and higher satisfaction rates with the service providers. UK Trade and Investment responded to this development in a number of ways. Firstly, and in response to broader changes in macro-economic strategy in the UK, they focused more sharply on industrial sectors and clusters as motors of growth (Keeble and Wilkinson 2000). Specialist advisers were appointed in each region to service sectors such as life sciences, ICT and energy, in the first instance, and then agriculture and education and training later. In this way, companies could access expert technical advice more readily and clusters and networks could be promoted. Secondly, further review of current services and market positioning was commissioned to assess whether funds could be more effectively targeted at specific markets. A study carried out by PriceWaterhouse Coopers proposed some significant shifts in strategy, not least of which was an increased focus on 'middle-market' companies as a source of significant growth potential in international markets.

What emerges strongly from this review of research and service provision is the need for strategic and soft management skills and knowledge which enable owner-managers to critique their own organisation, re-engineer it and build the competencies needed to succeed in competitive environments. Similar issues were explored in the study *The Management Skills Gap in Technology SMEs: Real or Perceived* (YTKO 2003). This study investigated whether a market gap in the existence and availability of these capabilities exists. The study comprised a representative telephone survey of some 400 technology-based SME owner-managers across the region, a series of in-depth interviews and focus groups, and further analysis of existing secondary data and intelligence. The findings of the study supported the hypothesis that the restrictions on growth are mostly connected with the inability of the SMEs' own management to adopt and utilise management capacity within their companies, rather than an inherent lack of management advice and support available to SMEs. This disconnect between perceptions and reality, however, is complex and is related fundamentally to the nature of how enterprises are formed, operate and develop.

The study provides a model for understanding the dynamics and psychology of how SMEs develop and acquire the management capabilities required to grow firms over time. By highlighting the key constraints, the reasons behind these constraints, and how they have been overcome within more successful firms, it shows examples of best practice from which SME owner-managers can usefully learn. Rather than a shortage of available management talent, support and training, the study indicates that, as a consequence of the lack of complete understanding of SMEs' development and of company life cycles, skills are wrongly targeted or are inappropriate to the growth requirements of SMEs.

The report goes on to recommend a repositioning of management support and advice to attempt to respond appropriately to the ubiquitous and well-documented reluctance of British SMEs to buy in training and management development:

- The importance of close informal networks in the management development of SMEs means that not only are depth and breadth of management development opportunities limited, but there is little desire to search outside the immediate community. Management support providers must therefore seek ways to become part of these personal networks and offer more tailored and informal support.
- Management support organisations need to work harder on instilling trust in their professional advice. This requires working within the comfort zone of individual companies' knowledge networks, where recipients are familiar and confident in the support provided.
- The clear value of management learning through training and education means that greater effort is required not just on raising awareness but in effective marketing and selling of quality management support services to SMEs.
- Trusted mentors have a clear impact on the management development and growth of an enterprise, yet most of these successful case studies are a result of chance. Effort should be made in providing SMEs with greater opportunity to access mentors.

Trust building is a key element of support to companies. Schein (2002) talks of a development of effective consulting through building 'levels of mutual acceptance'. This involves a shift away from support to small companies based on classical training and information-giving processes towards a less structured, responsive and mutually helping one. That this process might be similar for both smaller and larger companies may surprise some, yet the findings of the two aforementioned reports make it clear that smaller companies also need customised, strategically oriented advice delivered in a manner appropriate to their individual operating and learning circumstances.

In this context, consulting activities can have multiple rewards also for the service-providing agencies. Tunwall and Busbin (1991) highlight the true valuation and appreciation of this support by small and medium-sized enterprises, which only turn to outside advice if they are in real need. Consulting and training projects within SMEs place the adviser in a central and visible position within these organisations, resulting in the possibility of developing knowledge networks and creating hubs for sharing concepts and experience on the one hand and allowing for deepening of sector knowledge and valuable market relations on the other. Also the long-term impact and the educational effect of the individual adviser's work can be considerably increased by a consulting rather than solely information-based approach developing out of a deep process understanding of the specific customer needs and the joint framing of implementable solutions. Further to this a possible shift from a staff identity to more of a consultant identity may also result in beneficial impacts on the self-esteem of the individual adviser regarding continuous training and education as well as the variety and flexibility of services offered.

Conclusions

On the basis of empirical research, we proposed that the Planning, Manning, Scanning model emerges as a viable means of distinguishing between successful and less successful internationalised firms. We furthermore find that successful companies become and remain so because they enhance these skills through a multi-modal approach to international business. Sourcing goods and knowledge internationally is in many sectors an essential adjunct of the exporting process. An understanding of how the sector within which the company is operating is developing on a global scale and the impact this is having on products and markets is becoming increasingly critical to sustained success in international markets. This understanding is cultivated not just by access to information but by participating in networks of learning facilitated by support agencies.

Consultants and agencies seeking to offer the most appropriate forms of support for companies aspiring to this level of success should take account of these findings. It is no longer enough to provide information about foreign markets and expect exporters to succeed. The integration of planning, manning and scanning skills with greater knowledge of the range of opportunities and threats emerging from the globalisation of supply chains represents a leading challenge which is largely unmet at the small and medium enterprise level. This provision will entail the adoption of a deeper process of engagement with SMEs to facilitate sustained learning and networking and is best delivered through a consulting process rather than the classical information- and training-based processes.

Questions emerging from this chapter

1. Success in foreign markets depends almost entirely on economic conditions and currency movements. Discuss.

2. In what way can companies control and improve their chances of succeeding when first considering going international?
3. How can a domestic manager become an international manager?
4. What kind of information about foreign markets does an SME need?
5. What kind of support does a company need when preparing to enter foreign markets?
6. Does the Planning, Manning, Scanning model cover all the issues a SME needs to master over time to be effective in distant markets?

Bibliography

Andersen, O. (1993), 'On the internationalization process of firms: a critical analysis', *Journal of International Business Studies*, Vol. 26, Issue 2, pp.209–31.

Ashkanasy, N.M., Trevor-Roberts, E. and Earnshaw, L. (2002), 'The Anglo cluster: legacy of the British Empire', *Journal of World Business*, Vol. 37, pp.28–39.

Atherton, A. (2003), *Examining Cluster Formation from the 'Bottom-Up': An Analysis of Four Cases in the North of England*, Durham, University of Durham.

Atherton, A. and Sear, L. (1998), 'Facing new (or no) frontiers? An examination of the new market development process in small businesses', 28th EFMD European Small Business Seminar, Vienna, 16–18 September.

Atherton, A. and Sear, L. (2001), *Working Within the Global Economy: Insights into the Internationalisation Process in the North-East of England*, Durham, University of Durham.

Barclays Bank (1996), *Realising Your Export Potential*, Coventry, Barclays Bank.

Barney, J. (1991), 'Firm resources and sustained competitive advantage', *Journal of Management*, Vol. 17, No. 1, 99–120.

Bell, J., Crick, D. and Young, S. (2004), 'Small firm internationalization and business strategy. An exploratory study of "knowledge-intensive" and "traditional" manufacturing firms in the UK', *International Small Business Journal*, Vol. 22, Issue 1, 21–52.

Bradshaw, R., Burridge, M. and Ötzel, H. (2002), 'The types and use made of market information: an analysis of UK exporters', 47th ICSB World Conference, Puerto Rico, 16–19 June.

British Trade International (2000), *Audit of Export Services. Analysis Template: Organisational Matrix*, London, BTI.

Cavusgil, S. Tamer (1980), 'On the internationalisation of firms', *Europe Research*, Vol. 8.

Cavusgil, S.T. and Naor, J. (1987), 'Firm and management characteristics as discriminators of export marketing activity', *Journal of Business Research*, Vol. 15, Issue 3, pp.221–235.

Centre for Enterprise Management & Leadership Development in the East Midlands (2002), 'Is supply meeting demand?', Leicester, The Centre.

Chalmers, R.A. (2002), 'Facing the global challenge: a New Zealand manufacturer develops strategic relationship', 47th ICSB World Conference, Puerto Rico, 16–19 June.

Coviello, N.E. and McAuley, A. (1999), 'Internationalisation and the smaller firm: a review of contemporary empirical research', *Management International Review*, Vol. 39, Issue 3, pp.223–256.

Crick, D. and Chaudhry, S. (2002), *Technological Entrepreneurship in the Electronics Industry: Collaborating with Partners in Developing Economies as a means for 'Deinternationalised' U.K. SMEs to Compete in Overseas Markets*, Birmingham, University of Central England.

Doole, I. and Hair, N. (1997), *Benchmarking Survey*, Sheffield, Sheffield Business School.

Douglas Westwood Associates (2002), *Export to Thrive – An Export Strategy for the Supply Chain Serving the Southern Gas Basin*, Great Yarmouth, East of England Energy Group.

East of England Development Agency (2001a), *East of England 2010 – Prosperity and Opportunity for All, the Regional Economic Strategy*, Cambridge, EEDA.

East of England Development Agency (2001b), *Evaluation of the Skills Development Fund*, York, York Consulting Limited.

East of England International Trade Forum (2004), *International Business Strategy*, EEITF.

Fillis, I. (2001), 'Small firm internationalisation: an investigative survey and future research directions', *Management Decision*, Vol. 39, Issue 9, pp.767–783.

Fletcher, D. (1998), *Growing Business and the Internationalisation Process*, Nottingham, Nottingham Business School, BDO Centre for Growing Business Available from: http://www.nbs.ntu.ac.uk/DEPTS/CGB/ research/papers/gbip.htm

Foundation for SME Development (2002), *Functional Abilities and Knowledge – Assessment of Development Needs*, Durham, University of Durham.

Gemser, G., Brand, J., Mascow, D.F.F.R. and Sorge, A.M. (2002), 'Internationalization patterns of SMEs: Exploring the role of international strategic alliances for old and new economy firms', 47th ICSB World Conference, Puerto Rico, 16–19 June.

Gibb, A.A. (1997), 'Small firms training and competitiveness: building upon the small business as a learning organisation', *International Small Business Journal*, Vol. 15, Issue 3, pp.13–29.

Girma, F., Greenaway, D. and Kneller, R. (2001), *Exporting and Business Performance*, Nottingham, Leverhulme Centre for Research on Globalisation and Economic Policy.

Grankema, H.G.J., Snuif, H.R. and Zwart, P.S. (2000), 'The internationalization process of small and medium sized enterprises' an evaluation of stage theory', *Journal of Small Business Management*, Vol. 38, No. 4, 15–27.

Grant, R.M. (1991), 'The resource-based theory of competitive advantage: implications for strategy formulation', *California Management Review*, Vol. 33 (Spring), 114–135.

Greenaway, D. and Kneller, R. (2003), *Participation in Export Markets and Productivity in UK Manufacturing*, Report to Trade Partners UK, Nottingham, University of Nottingham.

Haahti, A., Hall, G. and Dockels, R. (1998), *The Internationalization of SMEs – The Interstratos Project*, London, Routledge.

Holden, N. (2002), *Cross-Cultural Management: A Knowledge Management Perspective*, Financial Times Prentice Hall, London.

Holzmüller, H. and Stöttinger, B. (1996), 'Structural modelling of success factors in exporting: cross-validation and further development of an export performance model', *Journal of International Marketing*, Vol. 4, Issue 2, pp.29–55.

Ibeh, K. (2000), 'Internationalisation and the small firm', in Carter, S. and Jones-Evans, D. (eds), *Enterprise and Small Business Principles: Practice and Policy*, London, Pearson Education.

Interactive Business Partnership (2003), *Trade Partners – Your Passport to Export Success*, Evaluation Report to Trade Partners UK.

Javidan, M. and House, R.J. (2001), 'Cultural acumen for the global manager: lessons from project GLOBE', *Organizational Dynamics*, Vol. 29, Issue 4, pp.289–305.

Javidan, M. and House, R.J. (2002), 'Leadership and cultures around the world: findings from GLOBE – An introduction to the special issue', *Journal of World Business*, Vol. 37, pp.1–2.

Jeannet, J.-P. (2000), *Managing with a Global Mindset*, London, Pearson Education.

Johanson, J. and Vahlne, J.E. (1977), 'The internationalization process of the firm: a model of knowledge development and increasing foreign market commitments', *Journal of International Business Studies*, Vol. 8, Issue 1.

Johnson, S., Sear, L. and Jenkins, A. (2000), 'Small business policy, support and governance', Chapter 4 in Jones-Evans, D. and Carter, S. (eds), *Enterprise and Small Business: Principles, Practice and Policy*, Harlow, Financial Times.

Julien, P.A., Joyal, A., Deshaies, L. and Ramangalahy, C. (1997), 'A typology of strategic behaviour among small and medium-sized exporting businesses: a case study', *International Small Business Journal*, Vol. 15, Issue 2, pp.33–50.

Kalantaridis, C., Mughan, T. and Lloyd-Reason, L. (2001), 'Competing effectively in international markets: mapping internationalisation in the Eastern Region', Proceedings of the 25th Institute for Small Business Affairs (ISBA), National Small Firms Policy and Research Conference, University of Brighton, November.

Keeble, D. and Wilkinson, F. (2000), *High Technology Clusters, Networking and Collective Learning in Europe*, Aldershot: Ashgate.

Kessler, A. and Hienerth, C. (2002), 'Entrepreneurial SMEs in economies of transition: the building of strategic configurations', Paper presented at the 47th ICSB World Conference, Puerto Rico, 16–19 June.

Knight, G. (2000), 'Entrepreneurship and marketing strategy: the SME under globalization', *Journal of International Marketing*, Vol. 8, Issue 2, 12–32.

Lamb, P.W. and Liesch, P.W. (2002a), 'The internationalization process of the smaller firm: re-framing the relationships between market commitment, knowledge and involvement', *Management International Review*, Vol. 42, Issue 1, pp.7–26.

Lamb, P.W. and Liesch, P.W. (2002b), 'Creating dynamic strategic relationship by intensifying international involvement of small business', 47th ICSB World Conference, Puerto Rico, 16–19 June.

Lloyd-Reason, L. (1995), *The Business Support Services Environment in Eastern Europe*, Final Report to the European Commission, Brussels.

Lloyd-Reason, L. (2000), *Internationalisation and the SME*, Research Report to Business Link, Central and Southern Cambridgeshire.

Lloyd-Reason, L. (2001), *Accession, Internationalisation and the SME in Central and Eastern Europe*, Final Report to the Open Society Foundation, Prague.

Lloyd-Reason, L. and Mughan, T. (2002), 'Strategies for internationalisation within SMEs: the key role of the owner-manager', *Journal of Small Business and Enterprise Development*, Vol. 9, Issue 2, 120–129.

Lopez, J.A. (2002), *The Empirical Relationship between Average Asset Correlation, Firm Probability of Default and Asset Size*, paper presented at BIS Workshop 'Basel II: An Economic Assessment', May.

Melin, L. (1992), 'Internationalization as a strategy process', *Strategic Management Journal*, Vol. 13, 99–118.
Mahmood, M. (2002), 'The sources of support and training for export oriented manufacturing SMEs in Australia', 47th ICSB World Conference, Puerto Rico, 16–19 June.
Manolova, T.S., Brush, C.G., Edelman, L.F. and Greene, P.G. (2002), 'The internationalization of small firms – personal factors revisited', *International Small Business Journal*, Vol. 20, Issue.1, pp.9–29.
Maureen O'Sullivan Associates (1999), *Consultation with Export Development Counsellors in England* (Report).
McAuley, A. (1998), 'Research into the internationalisation process: advice to an alien', *Journal of Research in Marketing and Entrepreneurship*, Stirling Scotland: University of Stirling.
McGrath, R.G. and MacMillan, I. (2000), *The Entrepreneurial Mindset – Strategies for Continuously Creating Opportunity in an Age of Uncertainty*, Boston MA, Harvard Business School Press.
Morgan, R.E. and Katsikeas, C.S. (1995), *Determinants of Export Intention*, paper presented at the Marketing Education Group Conference, July.
Mughan, T. (1988), 'Why British firms must break through the language barrier', *The Times*, 17 September.
Mughan, T. (1992), 'Is languages for export enough?' *International Business Communication*, Volume 2, Issue 3.
Mughan, T. (1993a), 'Culture as an asset', in Preston, J. (ed.), *International Business – Text and Cases*, London: Pitman.
Mughan, T. (1993b), 'Culture and management crossing the linguistic Rubicon', *Language and Intercultural Training*, Vol. 13, No. 1.
Mughan, T. (1995a), 'Cross-cultural communication training', *Business and Education*, Issue 7.
Mughan, T. (1995b), *Going International: The Human Dimension*, Research Report, Cambridge, Anglia Polytechnic University and CambsTEC.
Mughan, T. (1998), 'The international SME', *Training Officer*, Volume 34, Number 5.
Navigator (2003), *Strategic Development*, Report to Trade Partners UK.
Network Research (2003), Brand Awareness, Report prepared for COI Communications and Trade Partners UK (ref 256281).
Newbould, G.D., Buckley, P. and Thurwell, J. (1978), *Going International: The Experience of Smaller Companies Overseas*, London, Associated Business Press.
Nordstrom, K.A. (1991), *The Internationalization Process of The Firm in a New Perspective*, Stockholm, Institute of International Business.
One North East (2000), *Review of Business Development Infrastructure* (Final Report), EDAW & The Foundation of SME Development.
Orser, B., Riding, A. and Townsend, J. (2002), 'Supporting exporting: a means of growth for women-owned Canadian SMEs', Paper presented at the 47th ICSB World Conference, Puerto Rico, 16–19 June.
Penrose, E.T. (1959), *The Theory of the Growth of the Firm*, Oxford, Basil Blackwell.
Perren, L. and Grant, P. (2001), *Management and Leadership in UK SMEs – Witness Testimonies from the World of Entrepreneurs and SME Managers*, London, The Council for Excellence in Management and Leadership.
Pichler, H. (2002), 'Toward an SME-specific policy framework: challenges from a global, European and systemic perspective', 47th ICSB World Conference, Puerto Rico, 16–19 June.
PragMedic (2003), *Fulfilling Eastern Promise, Internationalisation Support for Knowledge Based Industry Sectors*, Final Report to Trade Partners UK.
PricewaterhouseCoopers (2002), *Customer Needs*, Review for Trade Partners UK, London.
Schein, E. (2002), 'Consulting: what should it mean?' in Clark, T. and Fincham, R. (eds), *Critical Consulting: New Perspectives on the Management Advice Industry*, Oxford, Blackwell Business.
Sear, L. (2000), 'Adviser knowledge and business needs and requirements: complementary or worlds apart?', 25th ISBA National Small Firms Conference: *Competing Perspectives of Small Businesses and Entrepreneurship*, University of Durham, 13–15 November 2002.
Sear, L., Dodd, M. and Atherton, A. (2000), *A National Audit of Export Services for Small and Medium Sized Enterprises (SMEs) – Regional Report for the East*, Durham, Foundation of SME Development, University of Durham.
Sear, L., Dodd, M. and Atherton, A., Doole, I. and Williams, H. (2001a), *A National Audit of Export Services for SMEs*, Report to TPUK, Sheffield Business School and The Foundation for SME Development, University of Durham.
Sear, L., Dodd, M. and Doole, I. (2001b), 'An audit of export services in England: developing business focus support', The Small Business and Enterprise Development Conference, University of Leicester, 14–16 November.
Smith, B., Wilson, H., Blanchard, A. and Bruce, L. (2003), *Business Planning Support for Healthcare Companies*, Final Report to Trade Partners UK East of England.
Smith, H.L., Clark, G. and Tracey, P. (2000), *UK SMEs, Technology, Competitiveness and Development*, Working Paper (RASTEI) 00-07, Oxford, School of Geography & the Environment, University of Oxford.
Spence, M.M. (2002), *Evaluation of Export Promotion Programmes: UK Overseas Trade Missions and Export Performance*, Ottawa, University of Ottawa.

TLDempster (Management Services) Ltd. (1998), *Export Culture in the UK Oil and Gas Industry*, Report to British Trade International, London.
TLDempster (Management Services) Ltd. (2002), *South West Regional Office Trade Development Study: Key Service Sectors*, Report to Trade Partners UK, London.
Trade Partners UK (2000), *Sector Partnership Report: Promotion and Development of Export Trade*, London, Trade Partners UK.
Trade Partners UK (2002), *Annual Review*, London, Trade Partners UK.
Tunwall, C.A. and Busbin, J.W. (1991), 'Consulting effectiveness in smaller companies: guidelines for the consultant and user', *Journal of Organizational Change Management*, Vol. 4, No. 4, 16–23.
Uhlaner, L., Thurik, R. and Hutjes, J. (2002), 'Post-materialism: a cultural factor influencing entrepreneurial activity across nations', 47th ICSB World Conference, Puerto Rico, 16–19 June.
University of Durham (1995–97), 'Staying in control in the global market', *Small Business Foresight Bulletin, Issue 2, 1995*, Available from: http://www.dur.ac.uk?~dbr 0www/bulletin/bull_95/b2_95.html
Vernon, R. (1996), 'International investment and international trade in the product cycle', *The Quarterly Journal of Economics*, Vol. 80, 190–207.
Wernerfeld, B. (1984), 'A resource-based view of the firm', *Strategic Management Journal*, Vol. 5, Issue 2, 171–180.
Wernerfeld, B. (1995), 'The resource-based view of the firm: ten years after', *Strategic Management Journal*, Vol. 16, 171–174.
Wilson, R. (1999), *The Review of Export Promotion*, London, Department of Trade and Industry/ Foreign and Commonwealth Office.
Wilson, R. (2003), *The Foreign Markets, Business Performance and Trading Experiences of IoD Exporters in 2001–2002*, Policy Paper, London, Institute of Directors.
Wood, P. (2002), 'The rise of consultancy and the prospect for regions', in Clark, T. and Fincham, R. (eds), *Critical Consulting: New Perspectives on the Management Advice Industry*, Oxford, Blackwell Business.
YTKO (2003), *The Management Skills Gap in Technology SMEs: Real or Perceived? Report to East of England Deveolpment Agency*, Cambridge, YTKO.
Zinger, T. (2002), 'The balanced scorecard and small business: A stages of development perspective', 47th ICSB World Conference, Puerto Rico, 16–19 June.

9 Competitive intelligence and the global SME

Jonathan Calof and Paul Dishman

Introduction

Making better decisions is at the heart of business intelligence. Think of intelligence as a decision support system that focuses the entire organization on scanning its current and future environment. Business intelligence has emerged as a tool for small and large businesses alike. Used properly, it has the potential greatly to assist companies in formulating and implementing better international business decisions. The objective of this chapter is to describe what competitive intelligence is and how it can be best used by small businesses. It is built on an article written in *SCIP Online* (Calof, 2003) and a working paper laying out the theory of competitive intelligence (Calof and Dishman, 2002). One small note, the word business intelligence (BI) and competitive intelligence (CI) will be used interchangeably throughout, as to this chapter's authors they fundamentally mean the same thing.

The chapter starts with a general discussion of what intelligence is and then describes the role of intelligence in small businesses; it ends with advice on what small businesses can do to implement intelligence systems better. Perhaps the biggest challenge to small business arising from this chapter is that they must recognize that if they are competing against large multinational firms then there is a good chance that their competition is already engaged in intelligence activities. As a result, intelligence is becoming perhaps a necessary activity for all companies whether large or small. This chapter addresses three questions:

1. What is competitive/business intelligence?
2. Do small businesses do intelligence?
3. Should small businesses conduct intelligence operations?

An introduction to intelligence – what is it?

Intelligence – the word brings up images of spies, cloak and dagger. A review of a competitive intelligence book is headlined 'get out your trench-coat'. But this view of competitive intelligence is incorrect. CI is one of the fastest growing disciplines in business. A Futures Group survey found that 76 per cent of the firms surveyed report that they need better intelligence. In fact, when asked to rate their CI's effectiveness, the average rating was 6.4 out of 10 (Harkelroad, 1997). John E. Pepper, Chairman of Procter and Gamble, stated,

> I can't imagine a more appropriate time to be talking about competitive intelligence than right now, for I can't imagine a time in history when the competencies, the skills, and the knowledge of the men and women in competitive intelligence . . . are more needed and more relevant to a company being able to design a winning strategy and act on it (Pepper, 1999).

It is estimated that approximately 20 per cent of Fortune 500 companies have formal competitive intelligence support functions. This discipline developing within corporations is indicated by the membership growth of the international Society of Competitive Intelligence Professionals that has averaged 36 per cent per year since 1990 (Weber, 2001). Within the competitive intelligence popular literature (contained within *Competitive Intelligence Review*, *Competitive Intelligence Magazine*, and proceedings from Society of Competitive Intelligence Professionals annual conferences), CI is seen as an important element in the strategic decision-making framework of companies.

What is competitive intelligence? Here are a few definitions:

> Actionable recommendations arising from a systematic process involving planning, gathering, analyzing, and disseminating information on the external environment for opportunities, or developments that have the potential to affect a company's or countries competitive situation (Calof and Skinner 1998).

> Information which tells us how competitive the firm is. It's understanding the competitive arena, being able to predict competitors' moves, customers' moves, government moves and so forth (Gilad 1996).

> Timely and fact-based data on which management may rely in decision making and strategy development. It is done through industry analysis, which means understanding the players in an industry; competitive analysis, which means understanding the strengths and weaknesses of competitors; and bechmarking, the analysis of individual business processes of competitors (SCIP literature).

Differences in definitions of intelligence tend to focus on the process. Some authors write about competitor intelligence (defined loosely as an application of the process on competitors), while others talk about the overall environment (as in the definitions listed above). Despite differences in focus, all definitions point to a systematic program for gathering and analyzing information about key stakeholders such as customers, competitors, legislation and suppliers to find new opportunities and stay competitive. Experts in the field refer to a multistage process called the competitive intelligence wheel (Figure 9.1)

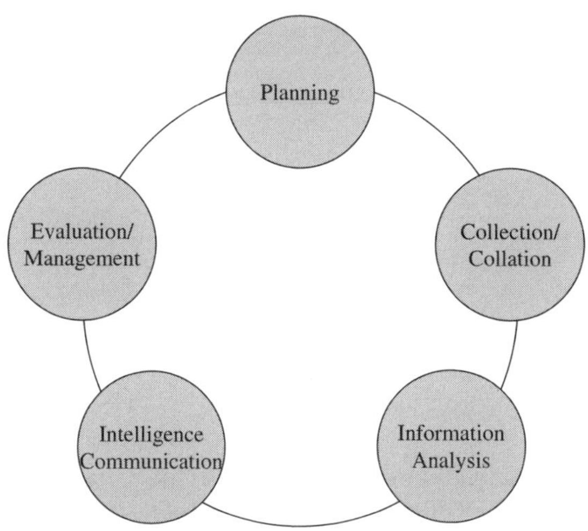

Figure 9.1 The CI wheel

consisting of defining intelligence need, planning the intelligence project, data collection, analysis and then dissemination. As you read through the variety of authors on intelligence, you will notice slight differences in their drawing of the 'wheel'.

Most companies consider themselves adept at competitor intelligence, but what of competitive intelligence? To what extent do they truly understand customers, suppliers and legislators both in the domestic market and in foreign markets? How adept are they at forecasting environmental change and integrating this within the decision-making process? Japanese companies are renowned for gathering biographies prior to negotiations with suppliers and customers. This gives them an edge in the negotiation process.

How good are most firms at even competitor intelligence? Lorry Hathaway, President of Best Foods said it best:

> This does not mean we did not have any competitive data. We had a fair amount of competitive data around. It was bits and pieces of information that were interesting but were isolated, they certainly weren't cohesive and they were coming from various areas of the company, nobody was pulling them together, and they tended to be marketing and sales activities that our competitors had but there was nothing about integrating them and trying to understand most importantly the why – why our competitors were doing this thing, how it related to their strategy and more importantly, how does it relate to us. We were not spending any time even thinking about that so that was the issue. The final overall point on that was that we tended when we got competitive information to react to it and the key seems to me to be proactive to try to do something before the fact rather than when they do something we react to them. (SCIP 1995)

Lorry Hathaway draws out several important CI principles:

1. It is proactive; the intent is to predict what is going to happen, not determine what did happen.
2. The process involves analyzing the information, not just finding it and using 'best judgment'. Best Foods uses side-by-side profit and loss statements and war games exercises to predict competitors' moves. These techniques are needed to understand the 'why' issue. No one picks up intelligence, they develop it through analysis.
3. It integrates information already existing in the organization; it is not spying.
4. It involves a clear focus.
5. Companies which think they are doing competitor intelligence well, need to look at it more carefully.

The academic perspective on competitive intelligence

From an academic perspective, portions of competitive intelligence can be seen within a variety of literature streams including decision making, environmental scanning and strategy planning. There have been many proposed models of strategic frameworks. In his article *An Integrated Framework for Strategy-making Making Processes*, Hart (1992) articulates five different models of strategic decision making, taken from a summary of the literature. Perhaps the model that predominates could be termed the command and rational mode. Under these approaches the senior management of the organization conducts a systematic analysis of its environment, assesses internal capabilities, management preferences and organization within the context of specific goals, evaluates a series of alternatives, and develops appropriate strategies and implementation plans (Ansoff, 1965; Andrews, 1971; Porter, 1980; Beamish and Woodcock, 1999; Hart, 1992). To implement the classic strategic decision-making model requires a well-developed formal strategic planning system (Lorange and Vancil, 1977). In looking at this planning system itself, authors have focused on the processes involved in assisting the decision maker make appropriate decisions. Information and decision making processes must be designed that are consistent with the structure and strategy of the organization (Galbraith and Kazanjian, 1986).

This formal planning system component of the strategy paradigm has then been linked with organizational design literature and environmental scanning literature as a basis for gathering and processing the information, and the information processing theory paradigm. In fact, the importance of environmental scanning has often been linked to firm performance (Daft, Sormunen and Parks, 1988). Perhaps the marriage of environmental scanning and information processing for effective strategic decision making was best summarized by Belich and Dubinsky (1999).

The ability to develop adequate organizational mechanisms for information acquisition, dissemination and effective utilization may be precursors to identifying and adapting effectively to major market shifts. Indeed, failure to enter markets successfully can frequently be traced back to executives who did not establish adequate information process within their organizations (Moorman, 1995; Pearce *et al.*, 1982).

Information processing theory, similar to the classic rational model of decision making, describes several processes that occur within an organization including: gathering, communicating, and organizing information (Egelhoff, 1982; Glazer, 1991); interpreting and synthesizing information (Daft and Macintosh, 1981); and giving meaning to the information (Moorman, 1995). As will be discussed later, this maps directly on to the competitive intelligence framework developed for this chapter.

Environmental scanning and information processing activities have been found to be moderated by the level of environmental uncertainty (Daft and Macintosh, 1981). Daft *et al.* (1988), posited that as uncertainty increases, information processing activities increase (Culnan, 1983; Daft *et al.*, 1988). Environmental uncertainty therefore leads to increasing information processing activities within firms (Tushman, 1977; Daft *et al.*, 1988). Further, as environmental, technological and product diversity increases, greater levels of information processing arise to deal with the uncertainty (Egelhoff, 1982). Another moderating variable for information processing is complexity. Complex tasks usually involve more people and diverse contingencies, thus requiring a greater amount of information processing to reduce uncertainty. Research suggests that there is a strong link between complex or varied tasks and information processing (Hage and Aiken, 1969). Regardless of the complexity and uncertainty in any environment, information processing (a firm's ability to adapt to existing market conditions) is largely dependent on its ability to process relevant market information effectively (Egelhoff, 1982).

In summary, the rational model of strategic decision making suggests the need for environmental scanning in order to align the organization's strategy with its environment. This in turn requires the design of appropriate information processing infrastructures. Competitive intelligence is a process involving the gathering, analyzing and communicating of environmental information to senior management to assist in strategic decision making. As such, it is the basis of the strategic decision-making process.

The concept of intelligence as a process has long been proposed as an effort to increase the firm's competitiveness and its strategic planning process (Guyton, 1962;

Pearce, 1976; Montgomery and Weinberg, 1979; Porter, 1980). In 1966 William Fair proposed the formation of a corporate 'Central Intelligence Agency' within the firm whose function it would be to 'collect, screen, collate, organize, record, retrieve and disseminate information'. Since that time, this proposition has grown to become an emerging business construct with delineated job functions directly responsible for intelligence collection, analysis and dissemination (Kahaner, 1996).

Competitive Intelligence (CI) is synonymous with Business Intelligence, but it is believed that CI implies the true purpose of intelligence, that is to gain strategic advantage (Porter, 1980). Therefore, Competitive Intelligence includes competitor intelligence as well as intelligence collected on customers, suppliers, technologies, environments or potential business relationships (Guyton, 1962; Fair, 1966; Grabowski, 1987; Gilad, 1989). A broad examination of the literature shows that intelligence is not only about monitoring competition but the entire business environment. Mere environmental scanning does not capture all of the multiple functions within the intelligence process. Gilad (1996) talks about the objective of intelligence as 'being able to predict competitors' moves, customers' moves, government moves and so forth'. CI consists of both internal and external research efforts (Hambrick, 1982; Prescott, 1987; Prescott and Smith, 1987). CI projects and results can be strategic (Aguilar, 1967; Montgomery and Weinberg, 1979; Porter, 1980; Gilad, 1989), tactical (Prescott and Smith, 1987; Keep *et al.*, 1994), or operational (Moriarity and Spekman, 1984; Stone and Good, 1994). In the broadest sense, intelligence (including the collection, analysis and dissemination of knowledge) is the process of reducing managerial decision uncertainty.

Although part of the nature of competitive intelligence can be found in the environmental scanning literature, subsequent studies prove that intelligence is more than just collecting information – it is a systematic process involving planning, data collection, collation and preparation for analysis, analysis, communication and process management. In fact, one study has shown that no more than 25 per cent of a typical intelligence project is spent in collecting information (Calof and Miller, 1997).

There have been numerous studies that have examined CI within the business environment. Various components of the intelligence definition appear to fall under several academic disciplines. CI theory and processes applied to predicting future moves of customers, regulators, competitors and so on are in environmental scanning, market(ing) intelligence, and market signaling. CI that focuses on using internal sources of management for decision-making purposes is now being covered in the area of knowledge management, market orientation and competitive technical intelligence (CTI). Finally, many of the techniques used in intelligence analysis come from the strategy field. Thus, components of the intelligence paradigm have been investigated in many academic fields. However, no holistic view of intelligence has been examined nor has the process of intelligence been examined empirically.

The existence of CI (or its forerunners) as a business activity has previously been examined by studies involving CEOs and executives (Daft *et al.*, 1988; Gelb *et al.*, 1991; Maltz and Kohli, 1996), planning and other managers (Fahey and King, 1977; Zinkhan and Gelb, 1985; Ghoshal and Westney, 1991), and CI managers and practitioners (Prescott and Smith, 1987; Cartwright *et al.*, 1995). The current study utilized primarily a sample of CEOs and executives as in previous studies (Keegan, 1974; Montgomery and Weinberg, 1979; Gelb *et al.*, 1991; Maltz and Kohli, 1996). Again, from previous studies there appear to be clear and distinct stages in the CI process. Key areas that appear to emerge in the literature are:

1. **Planning and focus** – CI is not about collecting all possible information or researching everything related to a subject, but focusing on those issues of highest importance to senior management (Aguilar, 1967; Montgomery and Weinberg, 1979; Porter, 1980; Gilad, 1989). This phase is required to set required resources for the CI project or process as well as to establish the purpose and result of the findings. It is during this phase that the assessment is made of the intelligence required for the managerial decision which is under uncertainty.
2. **Collection** – It is during this phase that information is collected from a variety of sources for examination during the CI process. Collection comes from a variety of different sources and acquisition methods including environmental scanning (Aguilar, 1967; Keegan, 1974; Fahey *et al.*, 1982; Hambrick, 1982; Lenz and Engledow, 1986; Preble *et al.*, 1986; Daft *et al.*, 1988). Other subjects related to the collection stage are the information source (Guyton, 1962; Fair, 1966; Porter and Millar, 1985; Young, 1989) and information usage (Murray, 1972; Grabowski, 1987; Menon and Varadarajan, 1992; Garvin, 1993; Maltz and Kohli, 1996).
3. **Analysis** – Many practitioners believe that this is where 'true' intelligence is created, that is, converting information into 'actionable intelligence' on which strategic and tactical decision may be made (Calof and Miller, 1997; Herring, 1998). Much work has been done in the areas of competitive analysis (Brock, 1984; Smith *et al.*, 1989; Smith *et al.*, 1992; Keep *et al.*, 1994; Chen, 1996), strategic analysis (Ansoff, 1979; Boulton *et al.*, 1982; Barney, 1986), environmental analysis (Lenz and Engledow, 1986a, 1986b), and competitive theory (Porter, 1980; Narver and Slater, 1990; Slater and Narver, 1994).
4. **Communication** – The results of the CI process or project need to be communicated to those with the authority and responsibility to act on the findings. The transfer of strategic information was theoretically proposed by Crawford and Sobel in 1982. Corollaries to this include the impact of environment on strategic planning (Boulton *et al.*, 1982; Hambrick, 1982; Gilad, 1989), study of marketing knowledge within the firm (Menon and Varadarajan, 1992; Moorman, 1995; Maltz and Kohli, 1996; Saxby *et al.*, 2002) and knowledge dissemination (Huber, 1990; Garvin, 1993; Kahaner, 1996; Hurley *et al.*, 1998).
5. **Process/structure** – CI requires appropriate policies and procedures, and a formal (or informal) infrastructure so that employees may contribute effectively to the CI system as well as gain the benefits from the CI process. There is much support for a formal structure and a systematic approach to CI (Porter, 1980; Gilad and Gilad, 1985a, 1985b; Ghoshal and Kim, 1986). However, many firms' CI efforts are short-term projects and do not have ongoing CI processes in place, but still conduct CI activities (Prescott and Smith, 1987).
6. **Organizational Awareness/Culture** – For a firm to utilize its CI efforts successfully, there needs to be an appropriate organizational awareness of CI and a culture of competitiveness. Wall in 1974 proposed that a firm must have an internal sense of competitiveness in order to gain the maximum effectiveness of an intelligence department. There has been support for this awareness/culture construct in the area of market orientation (Ghoshal and Kim, 1986; Kohli and Jaworski, 1990; Narver and

Table 9.1 Key intelligence needs

Decision to be made	Intelligence needed
Do I sign a joint venture with company X?	Profile of the company
Is the UK a good market for me?	Five forces of the market
Should I do business with company Y?	Psychological profile of Y
Should I develop this new technology?	Patent assessment of ____
Whom should I hire for the position?	Core capabilities assessment

Slater, 1990; Gelb *et al.*, 1991; Ghoshal and Westney, 1991; Slater and Narver, 1994, 1995, 2000). The heightened awareness of a firm's competitive environment (which the existence of CI within a firm may create) is one of the bases for organizational learning theory (Garvin, 1993; Sinkula, 1994; Slater and Narver, 1995). Imbedded in the organizational awareness/culture construct is also the application of ethical standards and behavior (Beltramini, 1986; Cohen and Czepiec, 1988; Schultz *et al.*, 1994).

The Focus of intelligence

If the objective of intelligence is to help companies make better decisions, then exactly what decisions should intelligence focus on? Much of the literature talks about intelligence for competitor assessment, the key question being that I need intelligence to help determine what the competition is up to and what should I do about it? However, intelligence is broader than this. The objective of the intelligence process is to develop the intelligence required to make any decision that the firm feels is important. The starting point for the intelligence process is therefore to identify what decision makers need to make better decision. Table 9.1 gives a few examples from intelligence sessions held with small businesses (see Calof, Fox and Nguyen, 2002). In each of these cases described in this table, the company focused intelligence development in areas that were designed to support critical decisions, and was clearly able to articulate the decision-making needs and the area of the competitive environment that needed to be focused on to make these decisions. Jan Herring (1999) refers to these as Key Intelligence Topics or KITS. In his writings, he refers to three categories of KITS:

- **Strategic decisions and actions**, including the development of strategic plans and strategies.
- **Early-warning topics**, including competitor initiatives, technological surprise and governmental actions.
- **Descriptions of the key players** in the specific marketplace, including competitors, customers, suppliers, regulators, and potential partners.

Competitive intelligence and small business – an international perspective

Much research has focused on the use of intelligence by larger businesses. Even within the popular press the concept of competitive intelligence for smaller businesses has been downplayed. When asked by a reporter from *Business Week* if intelligence was truly needed by smaller businesses, the response from Calof was as follows:

> If you are a large company and you read the market wrong, what are the risks? Coca Cola came out with the new coke – a dismal failure; Microsoft was late to market with a web browser but now holds most of the market share [Netscape's market share was at 7 per cent after Internet Explorer 6 was released]. How is it that these companies were able to survive despite such poor intelligence – deep pockets comes to mind . . . If you're Coca-Cola, and you read the market wrong, you can buy your way out of the problem. If you're a small business, and you read the market wrong, you're dead (*Business Week* 16 June 2000).

Competitive intelligence may be more important for small business than it is for larger ones. Organized properly, good competitive intelligence can level the playing field between small and large businesses. More importantly, small businesses are the cornerstone of most economies around the world. Ensuring their viability and success is of paramount importance for a thriving domestic economy. For example, in Canada less than 1 per cent of all businesses are large (0.3 per cent to be exact) and most employment arises from small business. As for the United States, Donald A Manzullo, US House of Representatives, estimated that 25 million small businesses in the United States employ over half the US workforce. From a CI growth perspective, over the past decade in the United States, 75 per cent of all new jobs and 50 per cent of all new technologies have come from small businesses. It is not that CI is not important for larger businesses – everyone needs to conduct CI to thrive and identify opportunities. But smaller companies cannot absorb market mistakes in the same way that large firms can. Besides, today's large business did start out as a small business (Microsoft was once a two-person operation). Smaller businesses must take advantage of CI to grow and become a large business. Reality 1: CI is very important for small businesses.

But to what extent do smaller businesses conduct competitive intelligence activities? Several years ago, the Canadian Institute of Competitive Intelligence conducted a survey on the intelligence practices of Canadian firms:

> After analyzing the results of over 1000 respondents, it was concluded that there were few differences between the intelligence practices of smaller versus larger firms with the exception of larger firms conducting more formal analysis and making greater use of their employees.

The study looked at 40 different aspects of CI including:

- The culture of information sharing
- The type of analytical techniques used
- The formal structure for intelligence
- Counterintelligence procedures
- Collection systems.

These questions were then grouped into 13 different areas of competitive intelligence (for example CI awareness or CI focus – see Tables 9.2 and 9.3). Follow-up interviews were carried out with several companies. Based on the responses and the subsequent scoring of the study, company practices were divided into four categories, ranging from low or non-existent CI practices to world-class CI practices. The results:

> While the chance of having world class CI practices was higher in larger firms, there were more small firms with top level competitive intelligence practices.

Table 9.2 Results by company size (number of employees) (i)

	Total	CI Awareness	CI Focus	CI Target	Collection	Analysis 1	Analysis 2
Max. Pts	83 (100%)	6	6	10	9	8	6
Very Small (1–9) (265)	29.8	3.3	2.6	4.3	4.3	0.8	2.5
Small (10–24) (197)	32.3	3.9	2.9	4.9	4.6	1	2.4
Medium (25–99) (157)	32.6	3.9	3.1	5.0	4.5	1	2.4
Large (100–499) (74)	35.2	4.1	3.1	5.4	5.1	1.7	2.8
Very Large (>500) (32)	41	4.1	3.8	6.6	5.3	2.7	3.6

Note: Maximum points in the Total column is the sum of the maximum points rows in Tables 9.2 and 9.3.

Table 9.3 Results by company size (number of employees) (ii)

	Technology Assessment	Communication	Counter-CI	CI Culture	Employee Role	Technology Tools	KM Readiness
Max. Pts	6	3	6	6	8	6	3
Very Small (1–9) (265)	1.2	1.2	2.5	2.9	2.8	0.6	0.7
Small (10–24) (197)	1.3	1.1	2.5	3.0	3.0	0.9	0.9
Medium (25–99) (157)	1.3	1.3	2.7	3.2	2.9	0.7	0.7
Large (100–499) (74)	1.2	1.2	2.6	3.5	2.5	1.2	0.8
Very Large (>500) (32)	1.4	1.5	2.9	4.2	2.7	1.4	0.8

In fact, of the 85 top scores, only 9 came from large businesses – the rest came from small and medium-sized businesses, including 26 that came from businesses with ten or fewer employees.

Building a CI culture

From the study reported above, it was clear that larger firms have the resources required to run large sophisticated intelligence programs but that smaller firms could also run intelligence applications at a world-class level. Small businesses generally have fewer intelligence objectives, could not conduct as varied intelligence analysis techniques and obviously could not have a formal intelligence unit with full time employees – they rarely have marketing departments, finance departments and so on. It is just a few people pitching in and helping out.

In other words, the resource limitation required a more scaled-down intelligence operation. But, small businesses could still coordinate collection, focus on top management concerns, train employees in intelligence, consider the counterintelligence implications of their information, share information, conduct some analytical techniques and in general be aware of the role of and need for CI.

> The key for small business is to recognize that CI for them is more about developing an appropriate culture for intelligence and a focus for intelligence activities (Canadian Institute of Competitive Intelligence, 1999).

So how does a small business create a process for intelligence?

- Assign CI to someone in the organization.
- Ensure that this person gets appropriate training.
- Gather everyone and discuss what the key intelligence plan should be.
- Get all employees focused on reporting the information needed for the plan – whether they find it on the net, hear it on the phone, or see it at an event – and make sure they know what is important.

Emerging small business intelligence trends – international

Recognizing the importance of competitive intelligence to smaller businesses, several governments around the world have begun to offer training in intelligence to small firms. Within Canada, this training has led to an international trade show intelligence initiative where small businesses are trained and then work together to collect information at trade shows, sharing portions of their intelligence plans with each other, government officers and association executives (Calof and Fox, 2003). Also, small businesses are being offered project intelligence courses – this involves training in competitive intelligence and mentoring on a specific project (Calof *et al.*, 2002).

Competitive intelligence (CI) may be more important for small businesses than it is for larger ones. Everyone needs to conduct CI to thrive and identify opportunities, but smaller companies cannot absorb market mistakes in the same way that large firms can. Organized properly, good competitive intelligence can level the playing field between small and large businesses. Smaller businesses must take advantage of CI to grow.

Summary

This chapter has focused on three areas:

1. A description of competitive/business intelligence. The discussion has focused on understanding that intelligence is a process designed to support critical decision making by systematically and continually analyzing the external environment. Examples from both the popular press and academic journals were provided to help better develop the overall concept. Intelligence is a systematic process involving planning, collection (involving the entire organization), analysis, communication and management. This system should be focused on providing the intelligence (output of this process) required to help management make better decisions.
2. Intelligence activities within small businesses. The chapter discusses the results of a survey that examined intelligence practices in Canada. Several examples were found of world-class intelligence practices in smaller businesses. As well, there are now significant training efforts in Canada and in other countries designed to build intelligence awareness within smaller companies.
3. The case for small businesses doing intelligence. Why should small businesses do business/competitive intelligence? Perhaps the most compelling argument is that small businesses can ill afford not to understand their environment. They do not have the resources to withstand the failure associated with developing the wrong product or choosing the wrong market due to failure to understand the dynamics of the environment. The second reason may be that the rapid growth in intelligence activities within larger companies suggests that if a small business has one of these types of companies as a direct competitor then it is operating at a competitive disadvantage.

The importance of intelligence for small businesses and in turn the importance of small businesses for most economies in this world probably explain why governments around the world have been working on programs and policies designed to support and enhance small business intelligence capabilities.

Questions emerging from the chapter:

1. What are small businesses intelligence needs?
2. How can a small business develop intelligence capability?
3. What role can government play in helping companies develop intelligence capability?
4. What are the barriers in developing intelligence capability?
5. Why is intelligence important to small business?
6. What is the difference between intelligence and market research?

Bibliography

Aaker, D. (1983), Organizing a strategic information scanning system, *California Management Review*, **25**(2), 76–83.

Aguilar, F.J. (1967), *Scanning the Business Environment*, Macmillan, New York, NY.

Albagli, A., Dawson, P. and Hasnain, S. (1996), Competitive science and technology intelligence, *International Journal of Technology Management*, **12**, 320–329.

Andrews, K. (1971), *The Concept of Strategy*, Irwin, Homewood, IL.

Ansoff, I. (1965), *Corporate Strategy*, McGraw-Hill, New York.

Ansoff, I. (1979), Managing strategic surprise by response to weak signals, *California Management Review*, **18**(2), 21–33.

Barney, J.B. (1986), Types of competition and the theory of strategy: toward an integrative framework, *Academy of Management Review*, **11**, 791–800.

Beamish, P. and Woodcock, C.P. (1999), *Strategic Management, Text, Readings, and Canadian Cases*, 5th Edition, McGraw-Hill, New York.

Belich, T. and Dubinsky, A. (1999), Information processing among exporters: an empirical examination of small firms, *Journal of Marketing Theory and Practice*, **7**(4), 45–58.

Beltramini, R.F. (1986), Ethics and the use of competitive information acquisition strategies, *Journal of Business Ethics*, **5**, 307–311.

Benjamin, W.A. (1979), Management of business information, *Industrial Marketing Management*, **8**, 51–56.

Boulton, W., Franklin, S. and Rue, L. (1982), Strategic planning: determining the impact of environmental characteristics and uncertainty, *Academy of Management Journal*, **25**, 500–509.

Brock, J.J. (1984), Competitor analysis: some practical approaches, *Industrial Marketing Management*, **13**, 225–231.

Brockhoff, K. (1991), Competitor technology intelligence in German companies, *Industrial Marketing Management*, **20**, 91–98.

Calof, J. and Fox, B. (2003), Trade show intelligence: intensive, exhaustive and fun, *Competitive Intelligence Magazine*, **6**(5), 17–21.

Calof, J., Fox, B. and Nguyen, D. (2002) Making intelligence grow: a mentoring approach, *Competitive Intelligence Magazine*, **5**(3).

Calof, J. and Miller, J. (1997), The status of CI across the globe, *12th Annual Conference of the Society of Competitive Intelligence Professionals*, 213–223.

Calof, J. and Skinner, B. (1998), Competitive intelligence for government officers: a brave new world, *Optimum*, **28**(2), 38–42.

Calof, J.L. (2003), The myths and realities of small business and CI, *SCIP.online*, Issue 41, 29 October.

Calof, J.L. and Dishman, P. (2002), 'The intelligence process: front-end to strategic planning', School of Management Working Paper, University of Ottawa, Ottawa, Ontario.

Canadian Institute of Competitive Intelligence (1999), Survey of Canadian R&D companies, NRC/CISTI, February 1.

Cartwright, D.L, Boughton, P.D. and Miller, S.W. (1995), Competitive intelligence systems: relationships to strategic orientation and perceived usefulness, *Journal of Managerial Issues*, **7**(4), 420–434.

Chen, M.J. (1996), Competitor analysis and inter-firm rivalry: towards a theoretical integration, *Academy of Management Review*, **21**(1), 100–134.

Chonko, L.B., Tanner, J.F. and Smith, E.R. (1991), Selling and sales management in action: the sales force's role in international marketing research and marketing information systems, *Journal of Personal Selling and Sales Management*, **11**(1), 69–70.

Cleland, D. and King, W. (1975), Competitive business intelligence systems, *Business Horizons*, **19**(6), 9–28.

Cohen, W. and Czepiec, H. (1988), The role of ethics in gathering corporate intelligence, *Journal of Business Ethics*, **7**, 199–203.

Crawford, V. and Sobel, J. (1982), Strategic information transmission, *Econometrica*, **50**, 1431–1451.

Culnan, M.J. (1983), Environmental scanning: the effects of task complexity and source accessibility on information gathering behavior, *Decision Sciences*, **14**(April), 194–206.

Daft, R. and Macintosh, N.B. (1981), A tentative exploration into the amount and equivocality of information processing in organizational work units, *Administrative Science Quarterly*, **26**(June), 207–224.

Daft, R., Sormunen, J. and Parks, D. (1988), Chief executive scanning, environmental characteristics, and company performance: an evaluative study, *Strategic Management Journal*, **9**, 123–139.

Egelhoff, W.G. (1982), Strategy and structure in multinational corporations: an information processing approach, *Administrative Science Quarterly*, **27**, 435–458.

Fahey, L. and King, W. (1977), Environmental scanning for corporate planning, *Business Horizons*, **20**(4), 61–71.

Fahey, L., King, W. and Narayanan, V.K. (1982), Environmental scanning and forecasting in strategic planning: the state of the art, *Long Range Planning*, **14**, 32–39.

Fair, W.R. (1966), The corporate CIA: a prediction of things to come, *Management Science*, **12**(10), B489–503.

Galbraith, J. and Kazanjian, R. (1986), *Strategy Implementation*, West Publishing.

Garvin, D.A. (1993), Building a learning organization, *Harvard Business Review*, **71**(4), 78–91.

Gelb, B.D., Saxton, M.J., Zinkhan, G.M. and Albers, N.D. (1991), Competitive intelligence: insights from executives, *Business Horizons*, **34**(1), 43–47.

Gilad, B. (1989), The role of organized competitive intelligence in corporate strategy, *Columbia Journal of World Business*, **24**(4), 29–36.

Gilad, B. (1996), *Business Blindspots*, 2nd ed., Infonortics, Tetbury, England.

Gilad, B. and Gilad, T. (1985a), Strategic planning: improving the input, *Managerial Planning*, **33**(6), 10–14.

Gilad, B. and Gilad, T. (1985b), A systems approach to business intelligence, *Business Horizons*, **28**(5), 65–70.
Glazer, R. (1991), Marketing in an information-intensive environment: strategic implications of knowledge as an asset, *Journal of Marketing*, **55**(October), 1–19.
Ghoshal, S. and Kim, S.K. (1986), Building effective competitive intelligence systems for competitive advantage, *Sloan Management Review*, **28**(1), 49–58.
Ghoshal, S. and Westney, D.E. (1991), Organizing competitor analysis systems, *Strategic Management Journal*, **12**(1), 1–15.
Grabowski, D.P. (1987), Building an effective competitive intelligence system, *Journal of Business and Industrial Marketing*, **2**(1), 39–44.
Guyton, W.J. (1962), A guide to gathering marketing intelligence, *Industrial Marketing*, March, 84–88.
Hage, J. and Aiken, M. (1969), Routine technology, social structure, and organizational goals, *Administrative Science Quarterly*, **14**, 366–379.
Hambrick, D.C. (1982), Environmental scanning and organizational strategy, *Sloan Management Review*, **3**, 159–174.
Harkelroad, D. (1997), Ostriches and eagles, *Competitive Intelligence Review*, **9**(1).
Hart, S.L. (1992), An integrated framework for strategy-making processes, *Academy of Management Review*, **18**(2), 327–352.
Herring, J. (1998), What is intelligence analysis? *Competitive Intelligence Magazine*, **1**(2), 13–16.
Herring, J. (1999), Key intelligence topics, *Competitive Intelligence Review*, **10**(2), 10–14.
Huber, G. (1990), A theory of the effects of advanced information technologies on organizational design, intelligence, and decision-making, *Academy of Management Review*, **15**(1), 47–71.
Hurley, R.E., Thomas, G. and Hult, M. (1998), Innovation, market orientation, and organizational learning: an integration and empirical examination, *Journal of Marketing*, **63**(3), 42–55.
Kahaner, L. (1996), *Competitive Intelligence*, Simon and Schuster, New York.
Keegan, W.J. (1968), Global intelligence: a framework for action, *Columbia Journal of World Business*, **3**, 35–41.
Keegan, W.J. (1974), Multinational scanning: a study of the information sources utilized by headquarters executives in multinational companies, *Administrative Science Quarterly*, **19**, 411–421.
Keep, W.W., Omura, G.S. and Calantone, R.J. (1994), What managers should know about their competitors' patented technologies, *Industrial Marketing Management*, **23**(3), 257–264.
Kohli, A.K. and Jaworski, B.J. (1990), Market orientation: the construct, research propositions, and managerial implications, *Journal of Marketing*, **54**(2), 1–18.
Lenz, R.T. and Engledow, J.L. (1986a), Environmental analysis units and strategic decision-making: a field study of selected leading-edge corporations, *Strategic Management Journal*, **7**(1), 69–89.
Lenz, R.T. and Engledow, J.L. (1986b), Environmental analysis: the applicability of current theory, *Strategic Management Journal*, **7**(4), 329–346.
Lorgange, P. and Vancil, R. (1977), *Strategic Planning Systems*, Prentice-Hall, Englewood Cliffs, NJ.
Maltz, E. and Kohli, A. (1996), Marketing intelligence dissemination across functional boundaries, *Journal of Marketing Research*, **33**(1), 47–61.
Menon, A. and Varadarajan, P.R. (1992), A model of marketing knowledge use within firms, *Journal of Marketing*, **56**(4), 53–71.
Montgomery, D.B. and Weinberg, C.B. (1979), Toward strategic intelligence systems, *Journal of Marketing*, **43**, 41–52.
Moorman, C. (1995), Organizational market information processes: cultural antecedents and new product outcomes, *Journal of Marketing Research*, **21**, 137–147.
Moriarity, R.T. and Spekman, R.E. (1984), An empirical investigation of the information sources used during the industrial buying process, *Journal of Marketing Research*, **21**, 137–147.
Murray, A. (1972), Intelligence systems of the MNCs, *Columbia Journal of World Business*, **7**, 63–71.
Narver, J.C. and Slater, S.F. (1990), The effect of a market orientation on business profitability, *Journal of Marketing*, **54**(4), 20–35.
Pepper, J.E. (1999), Competitive intelligence at Proctor and Gamble, *Competitive Intelligence Review*, **10**(4), 4.
Pearce, F.T. (1976), Business intelligence systems: the need, development and integration, *Industrial Marketing Management*, **5**(2–3), 115–123.
Pearce, J.A., Chapman, B.L. and David, F.R. (1982), Environmental scanning for small and growing firms, *Journal of Small Business Management*, **20**(3), 27–34.
Pinkerton, J. (1969), How to develop a marketing intelligence system (five articles), *Industrial Marketing*, **5**(4–8), various.
Porter, M.E. (1980), *Competitive Strategy: Techniques of Analyzing Industries and Competitors*, The Free Press, New York, NY.
Porter, M.E. and Millar, V. (1985), How information gives you competitive advantage, *Harvard Business Review*, **63**, 149–160.

Preble, J.F., Rau, P.A. and Reichel, A. (1986), The environmental scanning practices of US multinationals in the late 1980s, *International Management Review*, **28**, 4–14.
Prescott, J.E. (1995), The evolution of competitive intelligence, *International Review of Strategic Management*, **6**, 71–90.
Prescott, J.E. and Smith, D.C. (1987), A project-based approach to competitive analysis, *Strategic Management Journal*, **8**(5), 411–423.
Rothschild, W.E. (1979), Competitor analysis: the missing link in strategy, *Management Review*, **68**(7), 22–28.
Saxby, C.L., Parker, K.R., Nitse, P.S. and Dishman, P.L. (2002), Environmental scanning and organizational culture, *Marketing Intelligence and Planning*, **20**(1), 28–34.
Schultz, N.O., Collins, A.B. and McCulloch, M. (1994), The ethics of business intelligence, *Journal of Business Ethics*, **13**(4), 305–314.
Sinkula, J.M. (1994), Market information processing and organizational learning, *Journal of Marketing*, **58**, 35–45.
Slater, S.F. and Narver, J.C. (1994), Does competitive environment moderate the market orientation-performance relationship? *Journal of Marketing*, **58**, 46–55.
Slater, S.F. and Narver, J.C. (1995), Marketing orientation and the learning organization, *Journal of Marketing*, **59**(3), 63–74.
Slater, S.F. and Narver, J.C. (2000), Intelligence generation and superior customer value, *Journal of the Academy of Marketing Science*, **28**(1), 120–127.
Smith, K.G., Grimm, C.M., Chen, M.J. and Gannon, M.J. (1989), Predictors of competitive strategic actions: theory and preliminary evidence, *Journal of Business Research*, **18**, 245–258.
Society of Competitive Intelligence Professionals (1995), *Understanding the Competition: the CEO's Perspective* (video), SCIP, Alexandria, VA.
Stone, R.W. and Good, D.J. (1994), Information support for sales managers, *Industrial Marketing Management*, **23**(4), 281–285.
Tushman, M. (1977), Special boundary roles in the innovation process, *Administrative Science Quarterly*, **22**, 587–605.
Wall, J.L. (1974), What is competition doing? You need to know, *Harvard Business Review*, **52**(6), 22–42.
Walle, A.H. (1999), From marketing research to competitive intelligence: useful generalization or loss of focus? *Management Decision*, **37**(6), 519–525.
Weber, B. (2001), Report to the Membership. *15th Annual SCIP Conference*, Seattle, WA, 9 March.
Young, M.A. (1989), Sources of competitive data for the management strategist, *Strategic Management Journal*, **10**(3), 285–293.
Zinkhan, G.M. and Gelb, B.D. (1985), Competitive intelligence practices of industrial marketers, *Industrial Marketing Management*, **14**(4), 269–275.

10 The choreography of internationalisation: innovative forms of learning and activities of small and medium-sized enterprises in international markets

Jay Mitra

Introduction

The successful internationalisation of small and medium-sized firms (SMEs) is a function of their learning process and environments. Based on this hypothesis, this chapter examines a range of theoretical models and some empirical evidence to identify the modes, forms and methods of learning adopted by SMEs as they enter and grow in an international business environment.

Learning for internationalisation operates at various levels. Individual entrepreneurs bring to bear their own knowledge and experience, growing firms accumulate knowledge and skills with which to interact with international partners, and the environment in which firms operate also opens up opportunities for learning. Various forms of learning (such as 'imitating' by 'doing', or 'interacting' by 'clustering') enable identification of opportunities for innovation and their realisation. In the international environment firms take different routes to enter and operate in unfamiliar territory. How they reduce uncertainties in such territory is the basis of new product, service and business development, together with changes to organisational forms necessary for sustaining these developments.

Using the metaphor of the theatre, this chapter explores different forms of learning at multiple levels of individual, organisational and pan-organisational effort. Consideration of each of these levels of learning yields five sets of propositions. Taken together, these propositions offer a framework for analysing how firms internationalise and why they adopt different strategies for engaging in the international market. The chapter identifies complex forms of learning associated with SME internationalisation strategies and actions, and ends with generating ideas for new communities of creation and innovation across borders.

Learning to be entrepreneurial in international environments – the scope and purpose of focused research on small firm internationalisation

Systematic investigation of the literature on small firm internationalisation suggests that there are a variety of theoretical models that encapsulate the behaviour of firms in the international environment. These models, and their relevance in today's environment and by reference to practice, are referred to later. While much can be gleaned from the existing canon of knowledge and information, there appears to be little in the form of a distinctive approach to the study of entrepreneurship in the international context. This apparent deficit is seen in:

1. the dearth of systematic comparative work on new venture creation and entrepreneurship in different countries and regions;
2. the absence of a historical perspective on the evolution of entrepreneurship and its place in society in different nations and environments (classical works on innovation and technological revolutions restrict their Eurocentric canvas to the industrial revolution and to subsequent developments in Europe and the USA); and
3. the limited amount of work in the field of entrepreneurship on the flows of knowledge, ideas, technologies, capital and organisational forms, across the geographical boundaries of nation states, that help to create new business opportunities for both or many regions affected by such flows.

There is insufficient space in this chapter to do justice to the issues emanating from a brief consideration of the deficit in our knowledge of international entrepreneurship. Each of the deficit areas demands separate attention and each has its distinctive discourse. However, an attempt is made here to identify some of the critical elements of the internationalisation process affecting new business creation that, taken together, could contribute to a theory of international entrepreneurship based on ideas of learning, connectivity and flows of knowledge. Some of these elements have been drawn from existing literature, especially from those silent spaces in between paragraphs of observation and analysis, and others have been taken from new empirical work. Additionally, reference has been made to international case studies to reflect the significance of the main argument in this chapter, namely that sketches of international entrepreneurship are best understood when drawn on an international canvas.

This chapter takes the form of key propositions that enable the reader to examine how:

1. people in small firms are motivated to make international connections;
2. the organisation of the small firm evolves through the internationalisation process; and
3. people and organisations in certain spaces connect with their counterparts in other spaces to create flows of knowledge, ideas and new constructs of entrepreneurship.

Three forms of connectivity – people, organisations and spaces – emerge from the investigation carried out for this chapter. Underpinning these forms is the learning process that enables new ideas to be realised into new products, new services and new ways of doing business. This chapter addresses the learning and connectivity issues with specific reference to small firms in an international environment and by reference to different data sets and international case studies.

The three forms referred to above are separate units of analysis; traditional epistemological approaches would prefer to keep such analysis from being 'sullied' by methodologies that mix these units of analysis or combine, for example a positivist approach to the study of organisations with a constructivist model for the study of the environment in which these organisations evolve. In this chapter we make reference to mixed methodologies, and use a variety of data generated from multiple forms of analysis to try to understand the evolutionary process of international entrepreneurship.

It is the metaphor of the theatre, and especially the modern stage with its panoply of technologies and cultural influences, that provides this author with some clues to examine the subject of international entrepreneurship, its processes and the use of mixed methods of articulation of key themes and issues. It is, therefore, to this metaphor of the theatre to which we now turn to begin the exploration.

Metaphors of learning and diversity in international entrepreneurship

Consider Ong King Sen – the youngest of six children born to Chinese immigrants in Singapore, whose discovery of the world of theatre came through his primary school drama club and local British expatriate productions, but most viscerally, from Chinese street opera. Fast forward to 2004 to the Institute of Contemporary Arts in London, where Sen brought his multifaceted show, 'Insomnia', which took a contextual look at Singapore and south-east Asia, focusing heavily on young artists working in alternative media such as the Internet and digital arts, and delving deep into such controversies as the 'pink dollar', an examination of Singapore's pragmatic capitalism in recognising the spending power of gay culture despite its illegal status there.

Ong King Sen studied law in Singapore, and discovered Theatre-Works, a troupe founded by lawyers who had returned from London set on creating a distinctively Singaporean theatre. Sen combined Chinese opera and pop music to direct 'Beauty World' for this troupe – a 'Singlish nostalgia musical'. Underpinning this multifaceted and international approach to his work is Sen's knowledge of his father's family and how they had been scattered across south-east Asia, coupled with his formal theatre studies at New York University, where he came across the experiments of Philip Glass, Meredith Monk and Robert Wilson – artists who had borrowed heavily from Asia without losing their individual signature. Sen's post-modern deconstruction of Shakespeare's 'Lear', sponsored by the Japan Foundation and developed by his 'Flying Circus Project', mixed Peking Opera, Noh theatre, Thai Court Dancing and a handful of Asian musical styles, with performers working in their own native language and stage technique. Sen refers to his 'product' not as Singaporean art but as 'Singaporean hybridity' (Smith, 2004).

Ong King Sen's approach to theatre is reflected in the work of numerous other international artists in dance, music and the digital arts. Technology fuses with culture, with disparate sources of cultural inspiration, with individual techniques and languages, and with flows of knowledge, ideas and resources, to create fluid, creative forms of art. The popularity of such art reflects multiple levels of different influences, and a response to the demands of the viewer, the ordinary consumer of art and not simply the aficionado.

Ong King Sen's work and his art are metaphors of entrepreneurship in the international arena. Theatre, being one of the collective forms of art, allows this metaphor to unravel itself at many levels. At the level of people there are the individual producers, directors, the protagonist actor and the wider grouping of supporting cast, and the crew of stage staff. At the level of the organisation there are the theatre group/company and the theatre itself. At the level of art, and especially the art of Peter Brook, Shobhana Jeysasingh and Ong King Sen, there is the 'absorptive capacity' of learning creators combining and valorising multiple experiences and influences from both within and outside their physical environments. The use of modern technologies in enabling the revelation of universal realities of life in art, suggests another layer of meaning, which is the use of relevant tools and techniques to help with the convergence of ideas, influences, methods and organisation.

Table 10.1 The mirror of international theatre and entrepreneurial activity

The theatre of Ong King Sen – strands of fusion	**Features of entrepreneurial endeavour of the internationalising small firm**
The theatre producer – background and personal influences; source of inspiration	The individual entrepreneur/owner-manager, locus of control
Education, travel, international influences, motivations for growth of ideas and forms	The knowledge base – local and international, motivations for growth of business in terms of products, services and markets
Involvement of diverse actors all retaining their own languages and techniques; fusing cultural nuances while retaining diversity	Involvement of disparate range of skills especially in terms of networks of people from different environments, but also employees – relating to and valorising cultural nuances, while retaining diversity
Emergence of new forms of productions for international audiences; creation of hybrid forms of theatre	Innovation process – development of new products and services incorporating new ideas, technologies and resources; development of new organisational forms representing international interests
Diffusion of ideas – different, innovative productions of classic works; development of new works	Diffusion of ideas, products and services – developing existing products and services for new markets
Generation of communities of artists working together in global theatre	Collective forms of business activity across borders; generation of learning communities of entrepreneurs working in a global environment
Sustaining and enriching local environment of activity (as in Singapore for Ong King Sen)	Sustaining and enriching local hub of economic activity as in a region or a regional cluster of firms
Enriched individual and collective aesthetics and learning; generation of new works and new organisations, the art of enterprise in theatre – the theatre of entrepreneurship	Enriched individual and collective learning; generation of new products, services; exploration of new markets, creation of new organisations – the business of entrepreneurship in an international context

Each aspect of Ong King Sen's work and its foundations are symbolic of the different strands and dynamics of creative endeavour of nimble small firms internationalising their products and services across borders. Elaborating in prosaic form, these strands mirror the essential components of internationalisation, especially those which serve to generate value and meaning for small firms. The metaphorical strand that has the most immediate appeal to the modern economic environment for international business activity is that which is concerned with the trading of ideas, knowledge and resources. Table 10.1 is a demonstration of the mirror effect generated by a consideration of Ong King Sen's work, with the second column reflecting the strands of individual and organisational co-ordinates that inform the international business agenda of small firms.

The basic proposition (P1) here is that small firms exploring international markets evolve as members of different communities of international interest, working together to:

1. create new forms of economic activity that meet their own economic needs together with those of their counterparts;
2. generating distinctive forms of economic activity that transcend their separate needs;
3. retain their own involvement in hubs of local activity which are enriched by the experience of their exploration and the creation of new forms of economic activity; and
4. generate innovative growth and promote entrepreneurship through individual and collective learning, and in an international context.

Testing this proposition requires critical investigation using different units of analysis. This is because inputs, processes, influences, innovations, outputs and outcomes, are all realised at the level of the individual, the organisation, the region and the global market place. Researchers using traditional epistemological paradigms may encounter some difficulty in exploring such a proposition, and it may require isolation of the various elements to investigate issues using different units of analysis. For the purpose of this chapter, what is proposed is a review of selected literature and some empirical data to explore the relationship between learning, entrepreneurship and internationalisation in the context of innovative small firm growth. This relationship between learning, entrepreneurship and internationalisation takes place at the level of the individual, the firm and networks of communities in a region and across international borders.

The examination of the relationships referred to above spawns other propositions, which when examined together could help to develop a framework for the better study of international entrepreneurship.

Internationalisation, learning, the individual entrepreneur and the firm

If opportunity identification is the key to entrepreneurial endeavour, then the scanning of markets looking for new opportunities and marshalling resources to exploit those opportunities can be considered to be a strong motivational factor at the individual level (Oviatt and McDougall, 1994; Zacharakis, 1997). Similarly, certain pull-push factors such as external forces drive the entrepreneur to search for opportunities in foreign markets, if only to survive (Westhead *et al.*, 1998). A population ecology approach (Ibrahim, 2004) attempts to link entrepreneurial traits with the entrepreneur's decision to internationalise, but this raises issues of relevant and measurable empirical evidence.

The belief that entrepreneurs are opportunity driven and are, therefore, 'built for internationalisation' is tempered by the reality of barriers to entry brought about by financial market imperfections, differences in languages and culture, differences in legal systems, lack of intellectual property rights protection, and the risk factor of high levels of investment in uncertain conditions. A consideration of these external factors suggests that organisational factors probably have to be reckoned with more than entrepreneurial traits. If the survival of the firm is a motivating factor then that is different from the nature of existence of the individual entrepreneur. Moreover, if, as is commonly believed, the entrepreneur/owner-manager is the face, arms and limbs of the small firm, then separate analysis of the individuals is almost irrelevant. The separate analysis of traits simply distinguishes entrepreneurs from non-entrepreneurs, and suggests that all members of the

Table 10.2 The locus of decision-making processes in SMEs

	Size of SME	Manager (%)	Managers (%)	Personnel (%)
A	Micro (1–10)	100	0	0
B	Small (11–49)	88.68	11.32	0
C	Medium (50–250)	14.95	85.02	0
D	Large (251+)	0	100	0

Source: Mitra and Matlay (2004)

Table 10.3 Internationalisation tendencies

	Size of SME	NII	Direct	Indirect
A	Micro (1–10)	86.2	2.38	11.42
B	Small (11–49)	84.25	3.5	12.25
C	Medium (50–250)	56.59	14.73	28.68
D	Large (251+)	51.61	48.39	0

Source: Mitra and Matlay (2004)

homogeneous first group pursue opportunities at local and international levels in an identical manner. This latter suggestion is reinforced by overwhelming emphases on performance rather than the way in which objectives are realised.

Much has been argued in the name of the individual entrepreneur or the owner-manager, and the locus of control that resides in him or her. This applies equally to several decision-making processes, including the decision to internationalise. Table 10.2 indicates that the locus of decision-making processes for all types of decisions is essentially in the hands of the owner-manager. It is only when firms acquire 'medium' sized status that other managers are delegated with some of those tasks. The smaller the firm, the greater the possibility of such decisions being made at the level of the owner-manager. The evidence referred to in this table would also suggest that the decision to enter international markets is mostly confined to the owner-manager, and the chances of the small firm entering the international market are severely constrained by size factors.

That small firms tend not to be international players is almost a tautology when we note that the internationalisation process is a function of size (see Table 10.3). If small firms do not represent a significant proportion of the community of international players, two questions can be posed:

1. Is the study of small firm internationalisation relevant? and
2. Does internationalisation make any difference to those small firms that do?

The first question is easily answered. The study of the internationalisation process of small firms is important because it is the Schumpeterian (Mark 1) small firms that are the standard bearers of innovation and it is their ability to innovate constantly that is critical to the prosperity of most economies (Acs *et al.*, 1997). Secondly, the fact that most small firms do not internationalise does not mean they cannot do so. If barriers to entry are removed, and various trajectories of small firm entry into the international market are considered, then small firms could find effective ways of playing a larger role in the global market place. Thirdly, there is growing evidence of small firms playing critical roles in networks and clusters of small and large firms in specific and related industries operating in different regions across the world. Their 'secondary' or linked status often hides the significance of the role just as much as the numbers do not reveal the nature and scope of their operations. Finally, there is also increasing evidence of small, innovative firms emerging as key players in high-technology-based producer services in networks of global cities (Sassen, 2002).

As regards the second question, Acs *et al.* (1997) argue that smaller firms that do expand abroad are more profitable than those that do not (profit to sales ratio of 7.9 per cent in 1990 compared to 4.2 per cent). Secondly, and with reference to the points made in the previous paragraph, the specific role of small, innovative firms in industrial clusters or in urban agglomerations linked to international counterparts, is indicative of the fact that those firms that participate in such environments are more likely to gain from such exposure than those that do not do so.

What small firms gain by entering international markets is dependent on whether the costs are outweighed by the benefits derived from international business activity. These include the costs of entry barriers and protection of property rights; of building up organisational support infrastructures; of efficient operations in foreign markets; and of transactional elements, including those of contracts, spending and monitoring, and rents payable to intermediaries. The economic argument offers learning opportunities for the small business owner-manager especially when he or she is considering direct forms of entry as against using intermediaries. The owner-manager will be motivated to enter and operate in the international market as long as there is net gain from the activity.

The motivational–learning axis of small firm internationalisation can also be understood when we examine empirical data showing us the different types of motivation for small firm owner-managers and the specific factors affecting their involvement. The study examined the motivations and underlying heuristics that guide the internationalisation decision making process in SME. Figure 10.1 shows the motives for internationalisation of small firms in the UK which had entered the market for at least three years. Whatever the personal orientation or characteristics of the entrepreneur, the motivational issues referred to in this figure suggest that it is the circumstances of the business that push or pull small firms to internationalise. Chance does feature to some extent, in that enquiries from foreign agents and personal contacts can open up opportunities when they are not expected. But how do the owner-managers translate their motivations into the realisation of opportunities? How do we know whether the motivations can influence entrepreneurial outcomes? To answer such questions we need to examine factors affecting the internationalisation process. Such factors are both internal and external to the firm, indicating the level of control owner-managers can have over how these factors affect firm behaviour. Table 10.4 identifies these factors from the same data source that was used by Mitra and Matlay (2004) to examine motivations.

What the data in Table 10.4 show is the particular importance of the knowledge and skills base in the firm that is required to convert the motivation to internationalise to genuinely realisable opportunities. Of note, however, is the motivation for firms providing

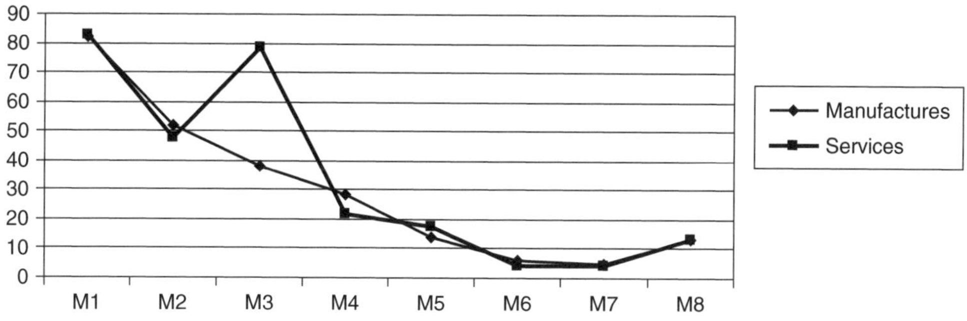

Note:
M1 = greater strategic opportunities in foreign markets
M2 = inquiries from foreign agents/firms
M3 = stagnating/declining domestic markets
M4 = product/service saturation in domestic market
M5 = internationalisation drive of known competitors
M6 = personal/professional contacts abroad
M7 = competitive pressures from large firms
M8 = other

Source: Adapted from Mitra and Matlay (2004)

Figure 10.1 Motives and factors affecting small business internationalisation

Table 10.4 Internal and external factors affecting the internationalisation process of small and medium-sized firms

Internal Factors			**External Factors**		
Type of Factors	**Manufacturing n = 2157**	**Services n = 3683**	**Type of Factors**	**Manufacturing n = 2157**	**Services n = 3683**
Owner-manager knowledge/competencies	78.26	73.2	Global networks & contacts	48.27	48.87
Skills & human resources	67.13	66.41	Specific global & marketing information	44.14	45.72
Internal financial resources	53.87	55.99	Global distribution channels	41.49	42.87
Other	11.68	16.43	Economic conditions	36.72	31.25
			Availability of external agents	28.38	22.18

services to seek international opportunities, namely the decline in local markets, which is almost as high as the availability of strategic opportunities (Figure 10.1). What the data also tend to suggest is that this learning process can be incremental in so far as it is based on the experience of existing firms. This incremental approach does not take into consideration the opportunities realised by so-called 'born global' firms, and to that extent our understanding of the learning process is limited to a particular category of experience. In view of this limitation we can only suggest that studies purporting to explain the internationalisation process of small firms through an examination of existing firms' motivations can lead us to a second group of propositions (P2).

As far as existing firms are concerned:

1. Internationalisation occurs on an incremental basis.
2. They can be motivated by a range of factors of which knowledge of opportunities and markets tends to be the dominant one.
3. While manufacturing and service firms show similar patterns, there is a significant difference in some motivational factors. This in turn suggests different modes of learning for service and manufacturing firms.
4. The existence of a strong knowledge and skills base correlates positively to internationalisation.

In taking the propositions made so far for the purpose of exploring the subject of internationalisation, new questions emerge. These questions are concerned with modes of entry. As there are variations in these modes according to the circumstances of individual firms, they open up different pathways of learning for owner-managers and their employees.

Different models of internationalisation and the learning process

The stage or incremental process of internationalisation resulting from organisational learning is referred to by some authors (Coviello and McAuley, 1999) as being shaped over time. Owner-managers gain experience and knowledge of foreign markets in much the same way as the respondents to the survey carried out by Mitra and Matlay (2004) suggest. Specific models, such as the Uppsala model (Johanson and Vahlne, 1977) and the innovation model (Cavusgil, 1980) elaborate on the incremental or stage processes and tend to maintain an internal perspective, specific to the firm and managerial-related issues. Experiential knowledge of the international market and of business in general lead to resource commitments (Oviatt and McDougall, 1997; Camino and Carorla, 1998) and changes in the firm's 'global horizon' (Ahroni, 1966).These process models have also considered internal and external factors influencing managerial decisions and the role of tacit managerial knowledge (Johanson and Vahlne, 1977) or experience (Cavusgil, 1980) as the key determinants of internationalisation.

The life cycle (industry or product) theory of internationalisation is similar in concept to the stage process because the firm follows the various stages of the product or industry life cycle (Roboch and Simmonds, 1989). Essentially firms generate 'firm-specific assets' first and then use 'firm-addressable' assets available in the external environment to generate new business opportunities (Mitra, 2000), and to acquire, accumulate and assimilate new market-based, entrepreneurial and technological knowledge (Autio and Sapienza, 2000; Zahra *et al.*, 2000).

The resource-based view of the firm suggests that the firm uses internal resources and explores international opportunities to build up existing, limited resources (Penrose, 1980; Almeida and Kogut, 1999; and Ibrahim *et al.*, 2001). It also reflects the gradual evolution of the firm's capacity and capability for internationalisation.

Figure 10.2 provides a snapshot of the incremental process of internationalisation of the firm as it progresses through different stages of development. As the diagram shows, the gradual process of development is evolutionary and the learning processes that inform the development and help to identify new opportunities in the international arena, also evolve, as the firm seeks variation, selection, retention and new modes of survival. Each stage of its evolution is marked by different forms of learning appropriate to that stage, and it is through a combination of these forms that the firm gradually becomes an international player. The movement through each stage is also characterised by the accumulation of experiential knowledge. It is this critical mass of knowledge that acts as a foundation for the firm's ability to interact with others in the international arena, increase its capacity of production, and emerge as a global player.

A variation of the process stage model is the theory related to foreign direct investments (FDIs). Firms will consider FDI only when they have a sufficient stock of knowledge and learning which outweighs any disadvantage that may accrue as a result of entering unknown territory. Largely a prerogative of larger firms, the theoretical contributions are dependent on economic considerations of levels of investment, transaction cost, locational factors and competitive advantage (Dunning, 1988; Zacharakis, 1997). The notion of competitive advantage that a foreign direct investor may enjoy over a local firm, is based on the idea that competition creates imperfect markets, and that competitive advantage is a function of product differentiation, product innovation and technological superiority (Ibrahim, 1990).

It is unclear whether the larger firm with significantly more resources has more advantage even over the highly innovative smaller firm as far as FDIs are concerned. Setting up, transaction and management costs may be stacked up too high for the smaller firm, and it is only in situations where the latter can piggyback on the larger intermediary firm with an existing presence in another country, that it can realise particular gains. However, Manalova (2003) has suggested that SMEs are likely to undertake FDI under particular circumstances. Such circumstances include, inter alia, those where there are lower economies of scale achieved through worldwide production volume, lower levels of technological intensity of a globally integrated industry, the higher level of technological intensity of a globally fragmented industry, lower levels of capital cost intensity, higher growth rates of an industry, higher degrees of standardisation of market demand in a globally fragmented industry, and higher degrees of localisation of market demand in a globally integrated industry.

The gradual, incremental process has, however, been challenged by Oviatt and McDougall (1994) and Schrader *et al.* (2000), who argue that the process theory is too limited and does not take into account the entrepreneurial motives for internationalisation. Entrepreneurial small firms seek rapid growth and are not fazed by 'quantum leaps' into different and unexplored markets because they act fast when they see a good prospect. In some cases, the search for resources is combined with the exploration of new opportunities, and the learning process is symbiotically tied in to this exploration. Figure 10.3, showing the rapid progress of a firm in Hong Kong, tends to support this argument.

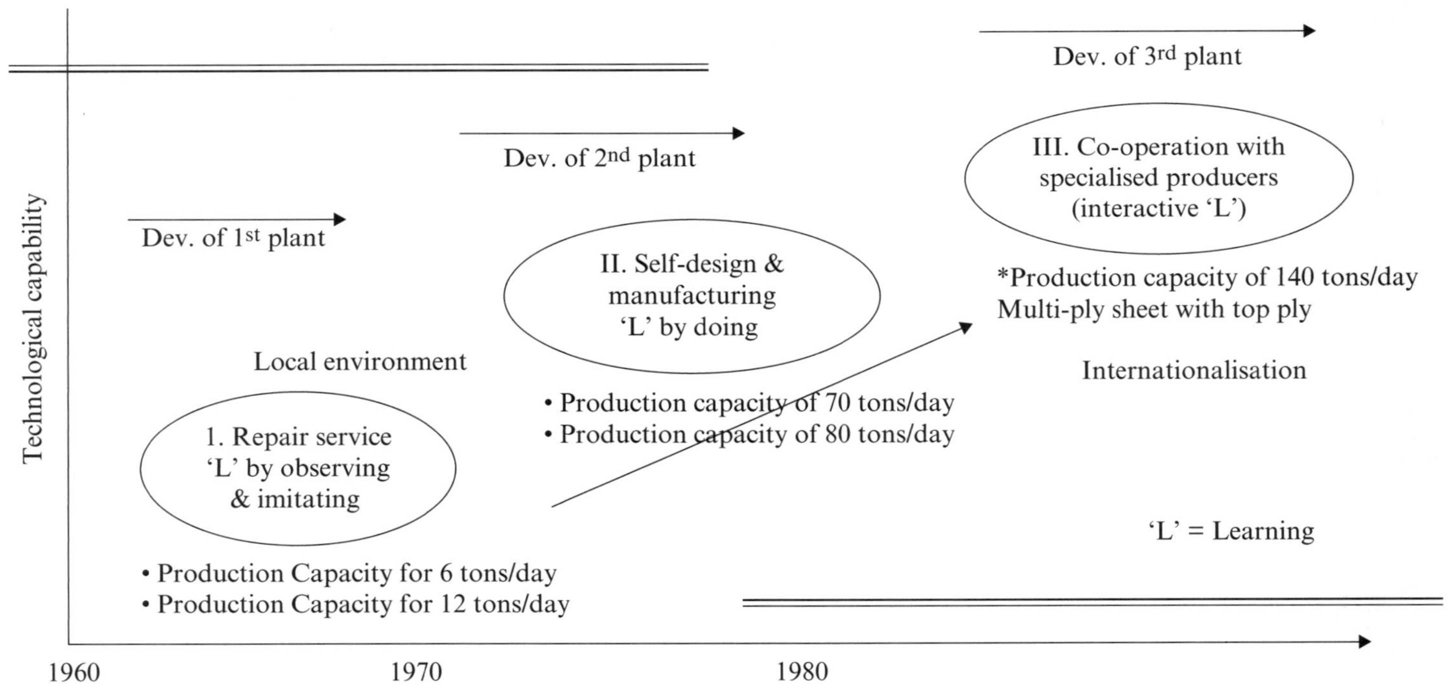

Source: Adapted from Kim (1977), cited in Mitra (2001)

Figure 10.2 Technological learning for capital goods of Shinpoong Paper

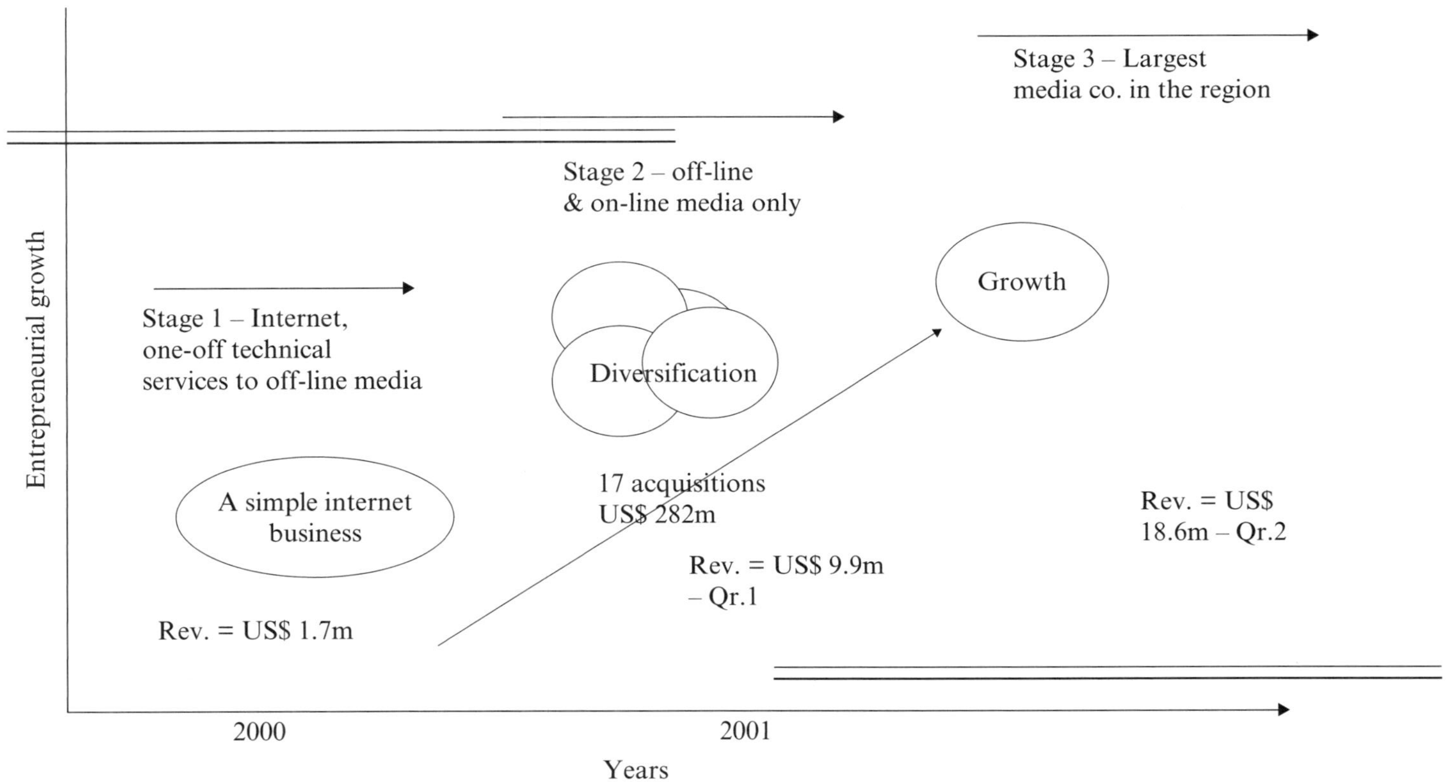

Source: Adapted from Thompson Date Stream, Financial Times (date unknown), cited in Mitra (2001)

Figure 10.3 The evolution of an innovative firm – tom.com

The accelerated pace of internationalisation may have something to do with the nature of the firm and the industry in question. High-technology firms, including information and communications technology (ICT) firms, source technologies and skills from diverse international sources, and the organisation of the sourcing process takes various forms, from diversification through joint ventures through to FDIs, networks and strategic alliances, depending on the specific business proposition with which it is concerned. What is significant is the pace at which these variations to or transformations of the routine can take place.

A great deal of recent debate, mostly of the political kind, has taken place around the idea of outsourcing. The internationalisation of firms, large and small, has tended to focus around manufacturing industries. Large and small firm internationalisation has subsumed outsourcing of goods which are produced abroad, assembled in a second country, and shipped back to the original buyer of outsourced goods. However, the globalisation agenda has witnessed a major change in the trajectory of outsourcing, as it finds a range of services, especially those which were previously considered non-traded services, being produced abroad and then sent back via the Internet or telephone wires. There is a suggestion that knowledge-based and white-collar economic activity is moving its production base from the 'advanced' West to developing countries such as China, India and Russia. In reality, however, just as in manufacturing, businesses have reorganised industrial production into intricate layers of designers, subcontractors, assemblers and logistics specialists, but have continued to manufacture close to where the goods are consumed; in the same way, the service industry has started using cheap and abundant telecommunications, bandwidth, and excellent skills sets to hand over work to specialist suppliers but provide the actual services close to where they are required. Innovative SMEs are more likely to gain from this evolution in the service industry both at 'home' and 'abroad', with distinctive opportunities opening up where it was not economically feasible for that to occur or where high-value niche services are required (Bhagwati *et al.*, 2004; Edwards, 2004).

The review of some of the different models of internationalisation leads to the third set of propositions (P3) in this chapter:

1. Firms use different methods for internationalisation depending on the nature of industries in which they operate.
2. The differences in the methods offer variable forms of learning, from linear models to more accelerated forms of speedy, interactive learning.
3. The nature, scope and type of learning process that entrepreneurs use in different locations and industries, distinguish different types of entrepreneurs rather than any fixed model of the entrepreneur using his or her traits to identify and seize opportunities for economic gain.
4. The internationalisation process is a function of the innovative firm's connections to its industry, its location, its use of specific technologies, and the use of a range of different organisational forms.
5. Firms in manufacturing and service industries tend to follow similar routes to internationalisation, with similar effects on the opportunity index of small firms.

Spatial aspects, collective learning, the Internet and the internationalisation process

One of the critical questions that the various models referred to above have not answered is whether the learning process is simply an organisational phenomenon, occurring either within individual firms or between different firms. There is no indication whether spatial aspects of the firms' activities have any significance or not. Do firms engage randomly in international business activity, using their particular resources irrespective of their location? Do they establish international links without any consideration of the location factors of their buyers, partners or suppliers? In a technologically connected global business environment, geographic proximity has tended to diminish in importance (Cairncross, 1997), especially as it offers a paradox for scholars, making investigation and analysis more difficult. This is further complicated by the fact that the traditional unit of analysis (either the entrepreneur or the firm), is not well served by spatial considerations. Finally, spatial analysis tends to regard firm size issues as being less important than innovative organisational outcomes resulting from different levels of interactions among various players for multiple objectives.

There are a number of reasons why the ostensible neglect of the spatial aspect of firm size related to the internationalisation process need to be dealt with critically. Firstly, as Teece (1992) argues, the discussion of the link between 'firm size and innovation remains inconclusive since the boundaries of the firm can no longer be assessed independent of the co-operative relationships which particular innovating firms may have formed' (p. 381). Moreover, firm boundaries are difficult to delineate, especially where there are complex alliances in place as in Japan. Here legal contracts become less important than alliances and networks of relationships.

Secondly, global industrial competence has dispersed widely over a century of industrial production as a result of increased competition, the liberalisation of trading and investment regimes and the growth of venture capital. The resulting geographical and organisational dispersion of industrial competence is coupled with the generic nature of new technologies such as microelectronics and biotechnology. The organisational co-ordination necessary for such dispersed activity is not necessarily provided by the price mechanism, which tends to ignore the uncertainty attached to the inability of firms to predict future actions, preferences and states of technological imperfection. Strategic alliances and inter-firm networks across national boundaries provide for more effective co-ordination upstream, downstream, laterally and horizontally. This means that owner-managers of firms need to manage externalities evinced in the relationships and alliances with other firms.

Thirdly, the new literature of economics and business studies has demonstrated the value of geographic proximity and of the processes occurring in localised clusters, especially the influence on the structure of firms and industries (Porter, 1990, 1994, 1998; Ohmae, 1995; Enright, 1998). The processes of knowledge creation and diffusion are also well served by the clustering of firms in geographically constrained areas and the geographic embeddedness of tacit knowledge and interactive learning processes. That these dynamics have positive implications for the competitiveness of multinationals, especially in terms of diffusion of knowledge within such firms and between them and other, smaller firms when they operate in geographic clusters, has been well noted by Dunning (1997, 1998) and Cantwell *et al.* (1998). The competitive advantage of firms in geographic clusters is derived from the concentration of specialised skills and knowledge, institutions, rivals, related businesses and customers (Porter, 1998), and the interaction between those firms. 'However, firms based in localised clusters often participate, . . . in international competition, and the question thus arises as to the extent to which locally-based processes can provide these firms with the necessary sources of knowledge and expertise needed to compete successfully in international markets' (Nachum and Keeble, 1999, p. 2).

The economic advantages found in localised clusters also appear to exist in the interaction between broader spatial configurations, in particular, global networks, and in the synergies between firms in different spatial scales. Amin and Thrift (1992) have emphasised the need to consider local clusters as the outgrowth of a world economy which is rapidly internationalising, leading to the development of 'neo-Marshallian nodes in global networks' (p. 571). Storper (1997) and Scott (1998) have suggested that these clusters are shaped and configured by the growing integration and globalisation of markets, innovation and production. This form of international integration does not disrespect differences in cultural values and attitudes across countries, thus indicating that there are multiple and diverse levels of spatial influences on and learning by firms. All of these levels and the ways in which they are managed affect the competitiveness of firms. Firms are not only managing 'externalities' in the local environment but internal and external resources in the global environment.

What successful firms in geographical clusters, and especially those that are linked globally, tend to find is that the concentration of specific assets such as skills, knowledge, institutions, suppliers, customers and collective learning is as much a function of local supply as it is of international sourcing. In examining the media cluster in Soho, London, Nachum and Keeble (1999, 2000) found that:

1. in relation to labour supply, the availability of high-quality and low-cost skills eliminates any dependency on external division of labour, and that this availability attracts more firms and resources to the area. Furthermore the non-routinised and non-standard work of media production requiring close interaction encourages use of local labour;
2. scale economies in distribution and technological advances allow for the growth in spatial linkages with customers, especially for post-production firms. But this does not hold for non-standard production processes involving small-scale designers and photographers who serve local markets almost exclusively;
3. while film production firms enjoying horizontal investment patterns typical of larger multinational firms, tend to collaborate across countries with suppliers and clients, this does not apply to those firms with vertical investment patterns, such as post-production firms or advertising agencies;
4. global links have become as important for accessing intangible resources such as knowledge and learning, and larger firms tend to demonstrate a greater need than smaller firms because of their wider geographic scope; and
5. the particular mix of local and global dynamics reduces the significance of interaction at the national level. The orientation of these clusters with their specialised characteristics is towards the global economy. Thus both the firms and the regions in which they are located operate as linked communities of interest across borders, where the learning and business development processes are occurring both at the level of the region and across spatial concentrations, depending on the type of industry, the levels of investment and size relative to the functions that they carry out. This is what links London more closely to Munich and New York than Birmingham in the UK, and Bangalore with Silicon Valley. The urban focus of these linkages is well documented

> by Sassen (2002), who recognises the anchoring of multiple cross-border dynamics in a network of places, prominent among which are cities, particularly global cities.

One of the outcomes of networking among firms in global communities of varying interest is the distributed innovation process. If firms operate across borders directly or indirectly, and especially as part of a cluster of firms with mixed forms of organisation, then collective forms of learning enable firms to manage the external relationships, albeit at various levels for different types of firms. In this scenario the locus of control for innovation and internationalisation has shifted in part from the owner-manager to outside the boundaries of the firm. This poses a difficult problem for the typical owner-manager, who is 'naturally' tuned into control structures that lend themselves to hierarchical governance systems that follow the growth of firms.

In isolation, growth through internationalisation opens up opportunities for control of intellectual property rights, and the development of appropriate management systems to reduce transaction costs emanating from co-ordination. This in itself is a challenge for owner-managers of growing firms, who find it hard to relinquish control to managers. That he or she may even need to consider other forms of management to enable him or her to take advantage of the benefits from the creativity, diversity and compatibility of partners, complicates the learning process. There is a need for the socialisation of knowledge which can be afforded in 'communities of creation' (Sawhney and Prandelli, 2004), which requires its members to work with a social epistemology of knowledge.

In interactive, geographical clusters, firms forge different relationships in time and space to benefit from innovative outcomes of the socialisation process. The dependency on multiple levels of skills, knowledge and financial resources across geographical space, coupled with the uncertainty surrounding the pace of change in product development or the extension of the value chain for both products and services, call for a greater degree of reliance on the socialisation process and the corollaries of sharing and trust building.

> Any process of knowledge socialisation and collective learning is based on relationships of meaning building and sharing. Such relationships cannot be enacted in the absence of a context of co-participation. It is important to create a 'cognitive minimum common denominator' for all the individuals and the groups participating in knowledge creation. This context promotes the development of shared values, reciprocity and mutual trust (Sawhney and Prandelli, 2004).

as part of a development of appropriate governance mechanisms for innovative firms.

The influence of international entrepreneurship on geographical space and the realisation of entrepreneurial opportunities across space leading to new forms of economic organisation, allow for the fourth set of propositions (P4) in this chapter:

1. SMEs are able to derive specific competitive advantages through internationalisation by being part of different communities of interest represented by both similar and different firms in the same or different industries.
2. SME internationalisation occurs through participation in different communities of interest in geographical concentrations of firms, suppliers, customers and institutions, or geographical clusters.
3. Firms in geographical clusters attract the interest of global competitors and multinationals, which provide the business case for being part of the cluster.

4. Operating in geographical clusters with an array of firms with complementary or different technologies, skills and other resources, and their international links, allows for the creation of different types of organisational forms based on principles of networking.
5. Forms and methods of learning need to adjust with the evolution of new forms of business activity, increasing levels of co-operation, and the availability of learning resources outside traditional, geographic or institutional spaces.

The Internet and the new theatre of international entrepreneurship

The complex social structure of trust and collective learning acquires a new dimension of complexity with the emergence of the Internet, e-business and e-learning, and other variations of the 'e' word (not forgetting the 'm' word in mobile commerce!) The growth in the use of computers and the Internet has resulted in the mushrooming of a wide range of communities to serve customer needs for communication, information and entertainment. This has for some time resulted in the cult of hyperbole as numerous forays into 'journalese' have argued for the extraordinary possibilities of the Internet. The bursting of the dot.com bubble may have calmed down the hype, as various authors have been critical of the strategies adopted by the Internet pioneers. Porter (2001) argued that nearly every precept of good strategy was violated. Christenson and Tedlow (2000) suggested that doing business on the Internet represented only a fourth major disruption in retailing, and some have argued that e-commerce is simply an extension of direct marketing.

For the smaller firm, the ability to gather information, promote the business and identify and service customers in new markets can, it is argued (Quelch and Klein, 1996), be carried out relatively cheaply. The barriers to internationalisation are reduced because of:

1. the diminished importance of economies of scale;
2. increased price standardisation;
3. reduced marketing costs;
4. greater levels of contact between buyers and sellers;
5. avoidance or changes in intermediary relationships;
6. reduced amount of time for information flows;
7. lowering of transaction costs; and
8. opening up of time zones for continuous business activity (asynchronous time).

How a small firm or an entrepreneur can take advantage of the removal of the barriers to internationalisation by taking advantage of the Internet, depends on critical management issues of product and market characteristics and organisational design. The scope of the business activity is affected by the availability of the Internet technology but this does not mean that it can or should be adopted easily. Firms in different contexts will experience different benefits from e-business. These differences subsist despite the fact that Internet firms are inherently global – the web site opens up opportunities across the world. Thus different firms have adopted a variety of approaches to internationalisation using the Internet. High-cost multi-country entries marked the strategy of Boo.com, the luxury clothing retailer. On the other hand Amazon.com finds that it is limited by the high cost of shipping overseas from its base in the USA. They, together with others, have pursued strategies of acquisition and joint ventures with firms in other countries (eBay with NEC

Table 10.5 Comparison of key constructs of internationalisation

Key Constructs	**Traditional Firm**	**E-business Firm**
Speed	Incremental	Rapid
Scope	Unidirectional	Multidirectional
Sequence	Distinct	Indistinct

Source: Zha and Du (2000)

in Japan, and Yahoo with Alibaba in China and others in the UK, France, Germany and Korea).

The Internet has allowed for the rapid emergence of many small firms in the global market place. These firms have leapfrogged their traditional counterparts and are virtually 'born global' as they have ignored national boundaries in operating in global markets almost immediately after their inception. They operate in 'market space' (as opposed to a market place), where they transcend both time and space. Zhao and Du (2000) identify three key constructs of internationalisation in differentiating between traditional and Internet-based firms, as Table 10.5 shows.

While the Internet's common platform across countries tempts the user to think immediately of global reach, the non-homogeneous international environment of legal and regulatory structures (better organised in India and relatively poor in China), the state of communications infrastructure (relatively poor in India and stronger in China), and cultural, language and related differences, can cause disruption in the market place for e-business. The key to success in e-business is the ability to personalise the Internet experience and to identify the products and services that most lend themselves to the Internet market space.

Craig, Douglas and Flaherty (2000) refer to three categories of products in the Internet environment – physical products, transaction-related products and virtual products (see Table 10.6). With the first category, while information search can be conducted online, the purchase or delivery of the product has to be done physically (as with Amazon.com). 'Transaction-related products' such as rental cars or travel tickets, have their search done online but their actual consumption takes place in a particular, physical environment. Real digital products are 'virtual products' such as music, software, internet video and e-news, and physical locations do not restrict their search, delivery or consumption. Key differences in terms of reaching different global markets (depending on communications infrastructure), product standardisation, and information as the key element in the product offering, are central to the strategies adopted by firms to sell on the Internet.

The complexity of Internet product typologies and destination-specific differences in the global market place, suggest that firm size may be a crucial factor in realising competitive business advantage. In a typical international market place, lack of access to information, and the inability to supply small batches of products or services, target market niches and carry out international visits, may all hinder small firms using the Internet relative to larger organisations. E-business is supposed to either overcome or reduce these difficulties as stated earlier. Fundamentally, the Internet enables small firms to bypass many of the constraints of the market place networks found in traditional or

Table 10.6 Internet product typology

Key Dimensions	**Physical Products**	**Transaction-Related Products**	**Virtual Products**
Ease of reaching a global segment	Difficult	Moderate	Easy
Degree of product standardisation	Varies	Moderate	Customised
Role of information	Complements	Enhances	Equivalent
Role of infrastructure	Infrastructure constrained	Conforms to infrastructure	Unconstrained

Source: Craig *et al.* (2000)

even cluster-type environments by allowing for direct connections between customers, suppliers, competitors and business partners. Working collectively and using their associations, SMEs and entrepreneurs can further overcome the disadvantages, as Poon and Jevons (1997) have suggested. These include:

1. confederations or small groups of SMEs sharing resources through contractual agreements – virtual service agencies to provide, for example, reciprocal home page links between contracted members;
2. conjugate collectives or closed group agreements between suppliers and customers – making available market intelligence on the group's intranet to improve supplier–buyer relationships;
3. agglomerate collectives – where trade associations provide market intelligence with a mutual agreement between international trade associations to market members' products and services;
4. organic collectives – where products and services are advertised or other services provided at low cost for charity members or community groups.

The advantages that small firms can derive from the Internet are complemented by the possibilities for product and service innovation. The Internet facilitates each element in the organisation, including design, service and support, customer relations, logistics and links to other products (Hollensen, 2001). For example, data can be gathered from an existing product and integrated directly into the design, modification or development of a new product. New product features can be built directly into the product from the Internet. Troubleshooting and correction can be carried out by the service manager directly through the Internet, and customer feedback can be facilitated and taken directly into account for future innovation.

The Internet's role in disintermediation, or the removal of the middleman, has been seen to be its main advantage. But as stated earlier, the Internet has also generated growing communities of interest leading to what Carr (2000) calls 'hypermediation', a situation in which content providers, affiliate sites, search engines, portals, Internet service providers, software makers and others are positioned to capture most e-commerce profits. Interestingly, however, their individual search for the holy grail of profits is also a function of their interaction as they share technologies, information and, in the case of Linux or the Sun Microsystems' Jini project, open source models, based on the simple notion that it is difficult for a single company to house all the expertise it needs to succeed, especially when it intends to build infrastructure on which other businesses depend.

The learning outcomes from the use of the Internet, or e-learning, rest on the understanding of how knowledge is created. Unlike traditional goods and services, where knowledge is embodied in the product or the service, digitisation detaches information from tangible objects by allowing information to be transported freely and instantaneously (Sawhney and Prandelli, 2004). This is evident in the growth of Internet trade from backroom services to business process outsourcing. Ideas can be separated from their physical expression (goods and services), thus dislocating the trajectories of traditional learning. Much learning, and the economic rent that is derived from learning in business activities, are a function of the security provided by intellectual property rights of goods and services which embody information and ideas. However, when information flows freely, then a new community of learning needs to emerge to protect the rights to ideas.

For the owner-manager of small firms, it is not enough to be simply a competitor; it is also necessary to consider being an 'adaptive innovator' or a 'good evolver'. This is because the competitive advantage that may be derived by any one firm may only be temporary. Secondly, understanding and appreciating the complex factors involved in creating communities of practice and interest in different geographical regions or in cyberspace, call for higher levels of interaction among knowledge creators and users, which can involve both the producer of goods and services as well as the customer both within areas of geographical proximity and outside defined spaces.

The above analysis leads to the fifth and final set of proposition (P5) in this chapter. This final set, which is concerned with e-business issues, includes the following:

1. SMEs are best able to derive advantages from e-business activity in the international arena by concentrating on their own size-related advantages of niche markets and flexibility, and by exploiting the benefits of Internet-based activity in reducing transaction costs.
2. Small firm entrepreneurship in the Internet-based international environment is best facilitated by firms taking advantage of the types of products and services that best lend themselves to a virtual market place, where information search, delivery and consumption of goods and services are not affected by place or geography (for example, recorded music).
3. Larger firm entrepreneurship can best be generated where such firms take advantage of both the use of physical resources offered by large firm infrastructure and the virtual benefits of the Internet (for example, sale of books and physical products).
4. Organisation and management of Internet-based activity are crucial to the realisation of entrepreneurial advantage.
5. SMEs establish niche capabilities and expertise but are linked across the globe and the e-value chain of the same industry or across related clusters of industries.
6. Collective relationships are easily afforded by the Internet but their effective use is best sustained by understanding the different sets of relationships (of people,

organisations and geographical environments) and the learning outcomes that are made possible by the Internet.

Conclusion

This chapter has focused on the evolution of the learning process associated with SME internationalisation and innovation. The metaphor of the theatre was used to lead the discussion of forms of international activities of SME, and the different levels of learning that inform the internationalisation process. Learning takes place at the level of the individual entrepreneur (the protagonist) who brings his or her own knowledge base and motivations to bear on the decision to internationalise. Learning also occurs at the level of the firm (the theatre company or the troupe of actors), especially the existing firm, as it graduates to international working standards, using its experience, its influences and its collective skills and knowledge base to generate international business activity. It has also been noted that in some cases the learning process is more immediate, as with 'born global' firms, which tend to occupy high-technology sectors. Their learning in more uncertain environments suggests that the entrepreneur(s) have a higher starting threshold of knowledge with which to take advantage of new forms of learning. Finally, the spatial aspects of learning and small firm internationalisation are best examined in the context of networks and geographical clusters where learning is part of the process of managing distributed innovation in communities of creation. The Internet affords e-learning through e-business activity where the shared and open source of information and ideas becomes part of the immediate exchange of ideas and information in communities of creation.

Communities of creation are the theatres of internationalisation for small firms. They are not simply another community of interest or a community of practice. The creation of their community where diverse interests are connected, sometimes without the explicit motivation to do so, is a product of the innovation process itself. The entrepreneurs in these communities are able to innovate both personally and collectively, just as Ong King Sen's Lear is able to rail against his daughters against the backdrop of Noh theatre or Thai court dancing. The community of creation brings together the basic tenets of the internationalisation process by considering the role of the individual entrepreneur, the organisational forms that are generated and that interact with each other, and the environment or the stage in which these entrepreneurs and organisations best manage the innovation process inherent in successful internationalisation activities.

Questions emerging from this chapter

The research questions that follow are drawn from some of the discussion on concepts and issues in this chapter, namely the international production process, collective learning, new skills development, cluster-based internationalisation and Internet-based internationalisation. These questions are aimed at testing some of these issues and they have been formulated to help generate empirical data which could throw more light on the subject and on the topics of discussion.

1. To what extent do large and small firms benefit from niche-based organisation in their use of the Internet for international business activity? Do smaller firms benefit more from virtual market places than larger ones?

2. To what extent do internationalisation and the particular location of firms lead to a new hierarchy of firms in the global value chain?
3. What form does collective learning take and how is collective learning enabled through internationalisation? How do individual firms reap benefits from collective forms of learning?
4. Do small firms make opportunistic adjustments to the adoption and use of skills (managerial and technical) when they enter international markets or do they graduate to a more organised or planned environment for skills development?
5. Are small firms similarly affected by changes in the production processes as large firms? Does this affect manufacturing and service industries differently?
6. Can firms operating in clearly defined clusters benefit from the 'cluster differential' in exploring international market opportunities?

Bibliography

Acs, Z., Morck, R., Myles Shaver, J. and Yeung, B. (1997), 'The internationalisation of small and medium sized enterprises: A policy perspective', *Small Business Economics*, **9** (1), 21–31; also in Oxley, J.E. and Yeung, B. (eds) (1998) *Structural Change, Industrial Location and Competitiveness*, Globalisation of the World Economy Series, Cheltenham, UK and Northampton, MA, USA: Edward Elgar.

Almeida, P. and Kogut, B. (1999), 'Localisation of knowledge and the mobility of engineers in regional networks', *Management Science*, **45**, July, 905–17.

Amin, A. and Thrift, N. (1992), 'Neo-Marshallian nodes in global networks', *International Journal of Urban and Regional Research*, **16** (4), 571–587.

Autio, E. and Sapienza, H. (2000), 'Comparing process and born global perspectives in the international growth of technology based new firms', *Frontiers of Entrepreneurship Research*, Centre for Entrepreneurial Studies, Babson College, MA, pp. 413–424.

Bhagwati, J, Panagariya, A. and Srinivasan, T. (2004), 'The muddles over outsourcing', *The Journal of Economic Perspectives*, **18** (4), 93–114.

Cairncross, F. (1997), *The Death of Distance: How the Communication Revolution will Change our Lives*, Boston MA, Harvard Business School Press.

Camino, D. and Cazrola, L. (1998), 'Foreign market entry decisions by small and medium sized enterprises: an evolutionary approach', *International Journal of Management*, **15** (1), 123–9.

Cantwell, R. and Iammarino, S. (1999), *Multinational Corporations and the Location of Technological Innovation in the UK Regions*, Working Paper, no.262, Reading, Reading University Department of Economics.

Carr, N. (2000), 'Hypermediation: commerce as clickstream', *Harvard Business Review*, **78** (1), 46–47.

Cavusgil, S.T. (1980), 'On the internationalisation process of firms', *European Research*, **8** (6), 273–281.

Christensen, C. and Tedlow, R. (2000), 'Patterns of disruption in retailing', *Harvard Business Review*, **78** (1), 42–45.

Cantwell, J., Iammarino, S. and Noonan, C. (2001), 'Sticky place in slippery places – the location of innovation by MNCs in the European regions' in Pain, N. (ed.), *Inward Investment, Technological Change and Growth: The Impact of Multinational Corporations in the UK Economy*, London, Palgrave Macmillan in association with the National Institute of Economic and Social Research, pp. 210–39.

Coviello, N. and McAuley, A. (1999), 'Internationalisation and the smaller firm: A review of contemporary empirical research', *Management International Review*, **13** (3) 223–56.

Craig, C.S., Douglas, S.P. and Flaherty, T.B. (2000), 'Information access and internationalisation – the internet and consumer behaviour in international markets', *Proceedings of the eCommerce and Global Business Forum*, 17–19 May, Santa Cruz, CA, Accenture Institute for Strategic Change, pp. 30–31.

Dunning, J. (1988), 'The eclectic paradigm of international production: A restatement and some possible extensions', *Journal of International Business Studies*, **19** (1), 1–31.

Dunning, J.H. (1997), *Trade, Location of Economic Activity and MNE: A Search for an Eclectic Approach*, International Allocation of Economic Activity: Proceedings of a Nobel Symposium held at Stockholm, London and Basingstoke, Macmillan, pp. 395–418.

Edwards, B. (2004), 'A world of work', *The Economist*, 13 November.

Enright, M.J. (1998), 'Regional clusters and firm strategy', in Chandler, A.D., Hagstrom, P. and Solvell, O. (eds), *The Dynamic Firm*, Oxford, Oxford University Press.

Hollensen, S. (2001), *Global Marketing: a Market-Responsive Approach*, 2nd edn, Harlow, Prentice Hall.

Ibrahim, A. Bakr (1990), *Entrepreneurship and Small Business Management: Text, Readings and Cases*, Dubuque, IA: Kendall Hunt Publishing Company.

Ibrahim, A.B. (2004), 'Internationalisation: motive and process', in Dana, L.-P. *Handbook of Research on International Entrepreneurship*, Cheltenham, UK and Northampton, MA, USA: Edward Elgar, pp. 129–136.
Ibrahim, A. Bakr and Goodwin, J.R. (1986), 'Perceived causes of success in small business', *American Journal of Small Business*, **12**, 11–25.
Johanson, J. and Vahlne, J.-E. (1977), 'The internationalisation process of the firm: A model of knowledge development and increasing foreign commitments', *Journal of International Business Studies*, **8** (3), 23–32.
Kim, L. (1977), *Imitation to Innovation: The Dynamics of Korea's Technological Learning*, Boston MA, HBSC Press.
Manalova, T. (2003), 'Small multinationals in global competition: An industry perspective', in Etmad, H. and Wright, R. (eds), *Globalisation and Entrepreneurship: Policy and Strategic Perspectives*, The McGill International Entrepreneurship Series, Cheltenham, UK and Northampton, MA, USA: Edward Elgar.
McDougall, P. and Oviatt, B. (2000), 'International entrepreneurship: The intersection of two research paths', *Academy of Management Journal*, **43** (5), 902–906.
Mitra, J. (2000), 'Making Connections: Innovation and collective learning in small businesses', *Education and Training*, **42** (4/5), 228–237.
Mitra, J. (2001), 'The management of innovation: from the firm to the region', presentation at the 2nd international forum on *Management of Innovation*, Beijing, 13–14 September.
Mitra, J. and Matlay, H. (2004), 'The internationalisation efforts of growth oriented entrepreneurs: Lessons from Britain', in Etmad, H. (ed.), *International Entrepreneurship: The Globalisation of SMEs: Orientation, Environment and Strategy*, Cheltenham, UK and Northampton, MA, USA: Edward Elgar.
Nachum, L. and Keeble, D. (1999), *Neo-Marshallian Nodes, Global and Firm Competitiveness: The Media Cluster of Central London*, WP 138, ESRC Centre for Business Research, Cambridge, University of Cambridge.
Nachum, L. and Keeble D. (2000), *Foreign and Indigenous Firms in the Media Cluster of Central London*, WP 14, ESRC Centre for Business Research, Cambridge, University of Cambridge.
O'Farrell, P.N. and Hitichins, P.N.W. (1988), 'Alternative theories of small firm growth: a critical review, *Environment and Planning*, **20** (10), 365–83.
Ohmae, K. (1995), *The End of Nation States: The Rise of Regional Economies*, London, Harper Collins.
Oviatt, B. and McDougall, P.P. (1994), 'Toward a theory of international new ventures', *Journal of International Business Studies*, **25** (1), 45–64.
Oviatt, B. and McDougall, P.P. (1997), 'Challenges for internationalisation process theory', *Management International Review*, **37** (2), 85–99.
Penrose, E. (1980), *The Growth of the Firm*, Oxford, Basil Blackwell Publishers.
Poon, S. and Jevons, C. (1997), 'Internet-enabled international marketing: A small business network perspective', *Journal of Marketing Management*, **13** (1–3), 29–42.
Porter, M. (1990), *The Competitive Advantage of Nations*, London and Basingstoke, Macmillan.
Porter, M. (1994), 'The role of location in competition', *Journal of the Economics of Business*, **1** (1), 35–39.
Porter, M. (1998), 'Clusters and the new economics of competition', *Harvard Business Review*, November/December, 77–90.
Porter, M. (2001), 'Strategy and the Internet', *Harvard Business Review*, **79** (3), 62–78.
Quelch, J.A. and Klein, L.R. (1996), 'The internet and international marketing', *Sloan Management Review*, **37** (3), 60–75.
Schrader, R., Oviatt, B. and McDougall, P.P. (2000), 'How new ventures exploit trade-offs among international risk factors: lessons for accelerated internationalisation of the 21st century', *Academy of Management Journal*, **43** (6), 1227–47.
Sassen, S. (2002), 'Locating cities on global circuits', in Sassen, S. (ed.), *Global Networks, Linked Cities*, London, Routledge.
Sawhney, M. and Prandelli, E. (2004), 'Communities of creation: managing distributed innovation in turbulent times', in Starkey, K., Tempest, S. and McKinlay, A. (eds), *How Organisations Learn: Managing the Search for Knowledge*, London, Thompson Learning.
Schrader, R., Oviatt, B. and McDougall, P. (2000), 'How new ventures exploit trade-offs among international risk factors: Lessons for accelerated internationalisation of the 21st century', *Academy of Management Journal*, **43** (6), 1227–1247.
Scott, A. (1998), *Regions and the World Economy: The Coming Shape of Global Production, Competition and Political Order*, Oxford, Oxford University Press.
Smith, K. (2005), 'Interview: Sleepless in Singapore', *Financial Times*, 24 February.
Storper, M. (1997), *The Regional World*, New York, The Guildfor Press.
Teece, D. (1992), 'Competition, cooperation and innovation: Organisational arrangements for regimes of rapid technological progress', *Journal of Economic Behaviour and Organisation*, **18**, 1–25.
Westhead, P., Wright, M. and Ucbasaran, D. (1998), 'The internationalisation of new and small firms', *Frontiers of Entrepreneurship Research*, 464.

Zacharakis, A. (1997), 'Entrepreneurial entry into foreign markets: A transaction cost perspective', *Entrepreneurship Theory and Practice*, **21** (3), 23–39.
Zahra, S., Ireland, D. and Hitt, M. (2000), 'International expansion by new venture firms: International diversity, mode of market entry, technological learning, and firm performance', *Academy of Management Journal*, **43**, 925–950.
Zhao, J.H. and Du, J. (2000), 'Electronic commerce and international business: a new test of internationalisation theory', *Proceedings of the eCommerce and Global Business Forum*, 17–19 May, Santa Cruz, CA, Accenture Institute for Strategic Change.

PART IV

SMEs IN THE GLOBAL ECONOMY: POLICY PERSPECTIVES

11 Foresights, futures and scenarios for the global SME

Stuart Smith

Introduction

This chapter aims to show how 'futures thinking' can benefit the development and support of international SMEs or those SMEs wishing to engage with international trading. It aims to do this by introducing the reader to future thinking methodologies and also by presenting a range of visions of plausible SME 'internationalisation' futures.

The material contained herein is a synthesis of data, anecdote, personal experience and theory. The main objective of the chapter is not to provide empirical evidence for the alternative future scenarios presented, rather to stimulate thinking. As we shall see, the main purpose of 'futures thinking' is to do just that. This chapter should be of particular interest to support agencies engaged in developing the global SME and to those running and working in global SMEs.

The global economic building block

The world has always been a global market, but over recent decades we have seen an increasing pace of change and global connectivity, which results in the phenomenon popularly labelled as 'globalisation'. There is much academic discussion about whether globalisation is a real phenomenon or only an analytical artefact ('a myth'). Although the term is widespread, many argue that the characteristics of the phenomenon have already been seen at other moments in history. Some may also conclude that those features that make people believe we are in the process of globalisation, including the increase in international trade and the greater role of multinational corporations, are not as deeply established as they may first appear.

As we see elsewhere in this book, the contribution of the SME to globalisation and economic development in many countries is significant and arguably understated by a global (business) media dominated by stories about the giants of the corporate world (for example, see Chapters 2 and 4). In a world where we regularly witness protests against corporate power, and the omnipresence of some large global corporations gives them turnovers in excess of many countries, then it is easy to forget that the SME remains the building block of economies around the world.

There are several different definitions of SMEs and the EU recently published guidance on definitions:

> The category of micro, small and medium-sized enterprises consists of enterprises which employ fewer than 250 persons and which have either an annual turnover not exceeding 50 million euro, or an annual balance sheet total not exceeding 43 million euro (European Commission, 2003).

Whatever the definition, the SME is increasingly becoming the economic force within many countries. In the UK, small and medium-sized enterprises account for more than half of the employment (58.5 per cent) and turnover (51.3 per cent). Small enterprises alone (0 to 49 employees) accounted for 46.8 per cent of employment and 37.0 per cent of turnover (www.sbs.gov.uk).

The Small Business Service (SBS) also estimates that 4.3 million business enterprises in the UK existed at the start of 2004. This compares with an estimated 4.0 million business enterprises in the UK at the start of 2003. Almost all of these enterprises (99.3 per cent) were small (0 to 49 employees). Only 26 000 (0.6 per cent) were medium-sized (50 to 249 employees) and 6000 (0.1 per cent) were large (250 or more employees). At the start of 2004, UK enterprises employed an estimated 22.0 million people, and had an estimated combined annual turnover of £2400 billion.

This data indicate that it is of national economic importance that governments and support agencies across the globe understand what the future might hold for global SMEs. For example, how will the global drivers that shape the world affect the development and operation of the SME (UK Ministry of Defence, Joint Doctrines and Concept Centre, 2000)? Do any of these drivers impact upon the global SME disproportionately (either negatively or positively) and if so what are the strategies or policy interventions which need to be in place to offset these? What are the emerging trends in society, business and technology that will provide the opportunities for the next generation of entrepreneurs?

Why futures thinking is of growing importance

At the time of writing this chapter, the most recognised technology brand on the planet is Google. This company is seven years old and is already arguably more powerful than that other giant of the technology age, Microsoft. Deloitte and Touche named Google the fastest growing company of all time, noting that its five year revenue growth exceeded 400 000 per cent (Batelle, 2005).

In its seven years of life, Google has grown from virtually nothing to being the most dominant force on the internet, and now in the wider media and entertainment industry. Google is an extreme example of how quickly the landscape can change in the densely connected and dynamic 21st century world. The business world that has emerged provides huge potential for the SME as well as many risks. Traditional ways of thinking about small business enterprise development are being revised every day.

Sense making in all of this can be a problem. This is where 'futures' thinking can help. For example, many SMEs operate on three to five year business plans which spell out their vision to achieving some end goal (usually growth and more profit). They are encouraged in the development of these plans by support agencies, banks and investors which, quite rightly, want to see some kind of surety for their investment. The problem with these plans, as we have seen, is that they are developed in a context which is increasingly dynamic, complex and unpredictable.

Some of the better plans may have utilised basic strategy development techniques such as SWOT or PESTEL analysis. However, these will nearly always have been done by an internal management team who will be unlikely to consider (honestly) the world external to them. This issue of honestly considering risks, drivers and ideas is highlighted through a parable known as the Abilene Paradox (Harvey, 1974). This was written by Jerry B. Harvey and is used to good effect by Van Der Heijden *et al.* (2002) when describing the limitations on organisational thinking.

Essentially, the paradox is about a man suggesting a family trip to the distant Texas town of Abilene on a hot, dry Sunday afternoon. Whilst all inwardly harbouring reservations about the trip the family all outwardly agree to go. Predictably, the trip is terrible. It is hot and uncomfortable, and the meal they eat when they get to Abilene is also terrible. On completion of the trip the family argue about whose idea it was to go and how they only went along with the idea because they thought that it was what the other members of the group wanted. Harvey argues that the Abilene Paradox is similar to many organisational paradoxes in that choices are validated even though all the individuals concerned have reservations – they just aren't voiced. Individuals avoid conflict because conflict carries risk. In an organisation the risk could be losing face, or losing your job if you upset your seniors. In a typical SME the closeness of the working group can make this problem even more acute.

It is here that applying futures or foresight techniques can improve an organisation's (or individual's) strategic thinking and ability to deal with future challenges. If the management utilise some of the futures techniques detailed here, alongside the more traditional techniques, they would not only begin to develop more rounded business plans, but also find mechanisms to discover the issues and confront the risks that are either hidden because we don't yet know about them or are unspoken because it is too uncomfortable to consider them. These issues are particularly acute when looking to engage with or develop international activities, where the trading environment is highly complex and uncertain (see Chapter 6).

Not enough time

Most global SMEs do not get bogged down in planning for the future. They usually have too much to do in the present to think about that. Very few allocate time for this on an annual basis or even allocate a few hours each month to talk about what is happening in the marketplace. Most small business owners or operators are good at internal focus. Knowing what is happening inside their own companies is one of the strengths that allows them to compete effectively and often outmanoeuvre their larger cousins. However, if a business wants to grow it needs to 'see' the future, its future. This is not point prediction, but rather exploring, mapping and scanning the horizon. It is about developing outstanding 'market intelligence' and the internal capacity to respond to change and uncertainty. This is where bigger enterprises, with large research budgets and market analysts, can often gain back the advantage.

One of the most common barriers to developing a robust strategy of thinking about the future is a perceived 'lack of time'. Many SMEs will consider themselves too busy delivering to customers and keeping going from one month to the next to be thinking about the future. What this chapter will demonstrate is that thinking about the future need not be a time-consuming idea nor should it be regarded as a 'luxury'. In the words of the futurist Alvin Toffler (1970): 'You've got to think about big things while you're doing small things, so that all the small things go in the right direction'. Futures thinking can be done on a large or small scale. One marketing firm we work with has three employees (including the owner) and as a result of attending a futures workshop (see below) the owner decided to take a personal subscription out to *New Scientist* magazine. This cost him very little but has hugely broadened his thinking, so much so that his firm is now developing a niche for itself as an expert in sustainable development and environmental technology which has involved developing markets outside of the UK. This was a 'trend' which he identified and became interested in directly as result of that subscription.

Whether you are sole trader, a larger SME or a support agency your futures thinking activity should always be proportional. But there should be *some* future thinking activity.

What is futures thinking?

Having argued that to survive and adapt to the increasingly dynamic and complex global trading environment of the 21st century, SMEs and their supporters need to engage in 'futures' thinking, we now examine what exactly that entails and how common techniques can be adapted for the global SME.

Perhaps the easiest way of describing futures thinking is to point out what it isn't. Futures thinking is not about predicting the future. What futurologists do, and what futures thinking is really about, is looking out at possible future scenarios and using these to inform the present. The UK Cabinet Office (2002) provides a more formal definition of horizon scanning and foresight: 'The systematic examination of potential threats, opportunities and likely future developments which are at the margins of current thinking and planning'. The organisational purpose of futures and horizon scanning is to:

- improve resilience and capability to anticipate and prepare for new risks and opportunities
- challenge and extend thinking on future science and environmental challenges
- engage staff from across the organisation and encourage high-quality external contributions
- generate innovation and creativity by extending the boundaries of perception.

There are several futures thinking techniques which are commonly used. How they are deployed depends very much on context, and methods can be applied to everything from strategy development, marketing and branding through to organisational development and change management. All the techniques described here are of use and can be adapted for the global SME.

Toffler (1970) once said that the difference between classical education and 'future' education was that the former involved learning and then stopped learning, while the latter involved learning, unlearning and relearning. Indeed, several studies highlight that entrepreneurs often see things outside of the traditional educated worldview, which then allows them to act and exploit opportunities before others.

Traditional business education (including that provided by support agencies) is often an extension of traditional learning, and it can be extremely useful in educating SMEs in the basic hygiene factors they need to understand to operate their businesses. However, it also reinforces 'a more of the same' mindset, which can lead to reinforcing stereotypes or preconceptions of what makes a good business. Incorporating some of the futures thinking techniques described here can significantly add value to that education and increase the ability to see the wider picture.

Some future thinking techniques for the SME

Trend analyses

Trend analyses (quantitative and qualitative) are probably the most common methods of forecasting or futures thinking. Some of these methods are fairly primitive, while others utilise complex statistical analyses, neural networks or agent-based modelling approaches.

Quantitative analyses are based on data. They are, therefore, often applied to areas where there are solid and preferably long historical data collections. They play an important role in areas such as demographics, economics and technology, but they can be applied to most areas and subjects. In most SMEs future sales forecasts or workloads are based upon historical trends, as are analyses of market conditions and trends. Quantitative trend analyses are often criticised for their lack of creativity and consideration of future developments (there is a tendency to project from the past to the future in a straight line and not to consider less predictable possibilities; see the Abilene Paradox earlier). Nevertheless, quantitative analysis is an essential part of futures thinking. It is also the most likely format that the average SME will use in its business planning.

Quantitative analyses also perform an important function by showing what will not be the future. If, for example, an extrapolation of a defined trend shows a logical inconsistency, this could force a market, societal or structural change. Many environmental scenarios focusing on finite natural resource constraints use this approach.

The principal problem with quantitative analyses is a tendency for people to accept them unquestioningly as a kind of truth about the future – rather than simply a starting point for discussion. They work best for projecting forward in a relatively stable system. But an increasing number of dynamic and unpredictable forces may influence the field and therefore affect the forecast. As shown elsewhere, the increasingly dynamic and complex nature of the global economy makes it just such a system. Using this tool risks overlooking aspects which are less easy to quantify, but may nevertheless be significant for the subject.

Qualitative trend analysis, on the other hand, is something that most of us do all the time in our daily lives. As single individuals or organisations, we constantly assimilate and filter a great many signals from the external world around us. Qualitative trend analyses are typically concerned with social (value-based or moral), institutional, commercial and political themes.

The future does not suddenly arrive without warning on any given day – traces of the future already exist. Those traces, however, are unequally distributed among people, organisations and countries. The 'art' in qualitative trend analyses is to spot these trends, their consequences and how they may affect the system being investigated. 'Trend spotting' is big business. For example, many global consumer brands are not particularly interested in what they will be selling in 30 years time. However, they are very interested in the next five years' trends. Many of these global brands employ teams of 'trendspotters' to scour the globe for new and emerging ideas. These could come from youth culture, science and technology, design or the media. The corporations aim to tap into an emerging trend as it develops into a mass market proposition.

Megatrends are major, broad developments which can change society in all areas such as politics, economics, technology, values and social relations. Schwartz (2004) refers to megatrends as 'inevitable surprises'. Megatrends are relevant to all areas of futures work. A basic futures toolbox, therefore, will always include an understanding of megatrends. These can be formed in several ways, for example, in 2006 The Scottish Executive, as part of its futures work, published a set of megatrends known as GLIMPSES. This work identifies the following trends:

- Globalism
- Life choice
- Individualism
- Media and technology
- Politics and government
- Shape of society
- Employment
- Sustainability.

This is one set of megatrends, and there are several publicly available studies which detail others. Most studies have a fair degree of agreement on what the major trends are. Hence, these are of critical importance when carrying out futures work. If an SME interested in international trading understands the direction of these trends and how they may play out in its market then it has a chance of identifying opportunities which it can address through the provision of a product or service.

Weak signal monitoring and horizon scanning

A common mistake made by SMEs and business support and government agencies is the inability to recognise and act upon subtle (or micro) changes in markets that lead to macro changes. Futurists often refer to these subtle changes as 'weak signals' or the 'Devox' (Deviant Voice) (Matthews and Wacker, 2003).

Even to the experienced owner or manager, these weak signals can often be dismissed as anomalies or outliers. To the entrepreneur they could be seen as noteworthy data points. They could represent potential opportunities or threats and may require immediate action. Many entrepreneurs are practised in the art of weak signal monitoring. At its most simple this is the ability to scan the horizon and detect the tiny shoots of a new trend or technology that could fundamentally change or create a business. In sustaining global reach as a smaller enterprise, such a skill is highly critical (Gibb, 1997).

In a standard probabilistic trend analysis, outliers are usually discarded and the mean average is of most interest. In weak signal monitoring, it is the outliers that are examined in more depth. Often, the more irreverent and upsetting a new idea is to the status quo, the more chance it has of reaching a level of macro importance. In the current dynamic global market place, for example, it is argued that the time taken for an idea to appear at the fringe and then become 'mainstream' is shrinking rapidly. Five years ago, we would work with small businesses saying 'watch China'. They would nod sagely but you got the sense that many did not really believe it. Talk to these same businesses now and they feel the impact of the Chinese economy first hand.

Identifying and monitoring weak signals should be an ongoing, systematic process in any organisation interested in sustained growth and international trading. If you hear about a new thing in a popular magazine or on mainstream television, you are probably too late to capitalise or react to it.

The UK government recommends that 'horizon scanning and futures' are carried out in order to improve organisations' ability to deal with risk and uncertainty (UK Cabinet

Office, 2002) and most large departments have begun to implement horizon scanning programmes. In many cases these programmes provide outputs that SMEs can tap into.

Weak signals often grow by joining forces with other weak signals. Or in other words, weak signals often need reinforcement from other ideas floating outside the established boundaries before they can be seen or heard. It is interesting that since the terrorist attacks on 11 September 2001, many UK government departments (including the Small Business Service) have begun horizon scanning activities in an attempt to detect weak signals.

Scenario planning

Until 1970, futures work and planning were based mainly on traditional extrapolative methods, that is, extrapolating from the past into the future. The onset of significant social changes, the growing speed of these changes and the greater uncertainty that comes with them, meant that new futures techniques needed to be developed. Scenario planning became one of these techniques. First used by the RAND Corporation but popularised by Royal Dutch Shell and other multinational companies, scenario planning is one of the most frequently used futures methods.

Scenarios can be defined as 'internal coherent descriptions of alternative images of the future'. Scenario thinking is an art and not a science (Schwartz, 1998). There are two key elements of the scenario method. Firstly, scenarios are not predictions of the future. The aim is not to foresee the future, but to show how different interpretations of the driving forces of change can lead to different possible futures. Secondly, scenarios are aimed at making better decisions in the present about issues that have long-term consequences for the future.

A variety of different scenarios are usually prepared in order to emphasise the possibility of different alternative futures. By setting up several scenarios, a 'possibility space' is created. It is somewhere within this 'possibility space' that the future is likely to unfold. Scenario methods are best suited for a changing environment, for example, a society experiencing rapid change or shifts in values. Given the now common assumption that the future is uncertain and unpredictable, scenario methods are applied to an increasing number of areas. The scenario method creates visions of different futures; at the end of this chapter we have used a scenario approach to detail alternate visions for global SME futures.

Wild cards

Scenarios work within an agreed space of probability. Wild card exercises, though, lie on the edge of, or even outside, this space. Wild cards are events which, while they have a low probability of occurring, would have a big impact if they did. Increasing uncertainty about the world has encouraged the use of wild cards in futures work. They are an attempt to adapt to an increasing pace of change.

It is interesting to observe that wild cards are more likely to be man-made nowadays – acts of terrorism, technological disaster and so on – rather than acts of god. We live in an age and society increasingly obsessed with 'risk'. The 'risk society' suggests the growing importance of wild cards as we try to anticipate what misfortune could befall us next. Recent events in the UK confirm the significance of wild cards or unpredictable risks such as BSE, foot and mouth disease, terrorist attacks and avian flu. The book *Massive Change*, by Mau and Leonard (2004) reflects upon this and how most people in society now exist oblivious to the design and engineering infrastructure that surrounds them and makes their day-to-day lives possible. Recent events in reacting to Hurricane Katrina in New Orleans or the Boxing Day 2004 tsunami have highlighted how susceptible our modern society is if our designs or engineering fail. Examining this through wild cards can be an extremely useful exercise.

Delphi survey

The Delphi method was developed by the RAND Corporation in the 1950s. It is a method for gathering information or beliefs from a panel of experts about the timing, probability, importance, implications, trends and events relating to the subject under consideration. Delphi surveys are an anonymous process and are carried out over several rounds. The main result of the Delphi Survey is typically a consensus forecast, although other results must not be ignored as there may be diverse views. If a forecast appears highly contentious, the survey may have to be followed up by scenarios. On the other hand, if all the experts agree about certain trends, it would be more productive to focus on other uncertainties.

Futures workshops

The final method we examine here is futures workshops. They are a very open process. Jungk (Jungk and Mullert, 1987) is credited with inventing the concept when he conducted workshops in Vienna at the end of the 1950s. Futures workshops were first intended to mobilise citizens who did not normally express themselves during debates. 'The silent majority' would be given the opportunity to formulate their own desires and visions for the future. Futures workshops have since been used in political parties, grass root movements and training institutions. This method can engage a wider range of people in envisioning 'future states' than other methods. The workshops are founded on participation, which is an important ingredient of futures work. Workshops try to deal with the preferred future – in contrast to the many methods focusing on the probable futures. The approach finds a close cousin in the 'Planning for Real™'[1] approach currently being used extensively in community regeneration projects across the UK.

In the workshops the participants are encouraged to:

- think the unthinkable
- meet the irrational with an open mind
- be receptive to all possible interests and information
- risk errors and fiascos.

Established ways of thinking must be challenged in the workshop. Thereafter, the purpose of the subsequent work is to match the hopes with reality, thereby creating an awareness about what can be done and how. We have used this approach successfully as a business planning tool for SMEs and in a community regeneration context (see Appendix 11.1).

SME 2015: global SME futures

Having examined why and how futures thinking can be applied to understanding events and trends which will impact on the development of international trade by the SME, and also having examined futures methodologies, this chapter now explores a series of possible futures which present different barriers and opportunities for the SME competing in the global economy. We hesitate to call these scenarios as they have not been developed in that way. Rather they describe plausible future trajectories for the global SME. They have been developed using existing megatrend studies, available quantitative data and the 'art' of an experienced futurist.

Future trajectory 1: the rise of business ecosystems

In 2005 business ecosystems are developing within a range of industries and across very different market economies as both small and large businesses recognise and leverage their interdependency. By 2015 the idea of business ecosystems will have totally replaced traditional notions of how markets and business work. The term 'ecosystem' is an appropriate metaphor as it moves thinking away from the mechanistic or 'winner takes all' competitive terminology that dominated business thinking in the 20th century and acknowledges that whilst many firms continue to compete, many also cooperate. In a business ecosystem they compete *and* cooperate. The organic metaphor also indicates that in 2015 the need for business to be environmentally sustainable is also critical.

Business ecosystems are an evolutionary step beyond thinking about business networks. Ecosystems consist of many networks and suggest a level of complexity, interdependency, self-organisation and coherence which transcends simple market mapping (see Chapter 6). The ecosystem view also examines resource flows through the system. These resources could be capital, energy, labour or knowledge.

The western industrial economy of the 19th and 20th centuries depended on the movement of physical goods and services. Mass production addressed the problems of scarcity and the high costs of mobilising raw materials, fabricating and assembling goods, and delivering them to their destinations. In contrast, in the economy of 2015 (that is, post-industrial and post-knowledge) many offerings such as software, entertainment and business services are non-physical and knowledge-based whereas the value of 'physical' items (such as cars, pharmaceuticals and so on) depends on the knowledge embedded in their design, production or brand. Increasingly, this knowledge comes from the SME sector as large corporations nurture and develop these ecosystems. Large corporations will have a growing stake in the health of the smaller companies supplying them. Those small businesses in return will be invested in the success of large corporations.

As industries become ecosystems rather than 'supply chains' we are likely to see more technology sharing. The ubiquitous broadband communication networks in many urban cities allow SMEs to embrace the same advanced systems that their larger cousins have long enjoyed, at a fraction of the cost. Larger organisations begin to place significant investment (both in terms of financial resource and training) in the smaller businesses in their ecosystem. This began with the reseller programmes of the big software corporations such as Microsoft and Oracle but is now the norm throughout many industries.

Because SMEs in the ecosystems often lack the heavy commitment to past ways of doing things, they become quicker and more innovative. This means that the small businesses supplying larger companies are likely to be in the places where innovation finds a home first. However, the ecosystem's larger companies will still be the market makers. Unfortunately, there will still be plenty of SMEs that will resist change – probably to their own detriment.

To succeed in this world, firms will need to understand the dynamics of both large and small business and of something new – the ecosystem they share. Likewise, to those engaged in development and delivery of small business support, the emergence of business ecosystems means that they will have to think in these terms. Ecosystems are not traditional industry segments and anyone who spends more than five minutes looking at Standard Industrial Classification (SIC) Code handbooks will quickly realise that the barriers between traditional sectors have long since broken down.

Trajectory 2: born global
By 2015 all SMEs will be 'born global'. Whether they choose to exploit these global opportunities will be down to those involved in the business. However, the ability to trade and compete at a global level will be present from business start-up and inception.

In the early decades of the 21st century we have seen a rapid rise in 'virtual business'. This is as true for the SME as it is for the global corporation. 'Virtual' in this context does not necessarily mean that the physical presence disappears; rather it implies that just like their larger cousins, adopting technology and exploiting transport connectivity mean that the SME can trade in the global market place from day one. Cross-border markets that were once the domain of only the largest corporations will be open to a business of any size. For example, the forthcoming changes to the EU Services Directive suggest that it will create a genuine single market across the EU which could result in an almost seismic upheaval in the market for business services across Europe.[2]

The U.S. Small Business Administration itself reports that 97 per cent of U.S. exporters qualify as small businesses. However, the influence of globalisation will be felt on more than sales. Suppliers to small businesses will increasingly be located in other countries. Small businesses are already outsourcing software development, preparation of tax returns and the manufacture of goods. It is likely that all of these will increase and that new areas will open up.

The internet has displaced expensive libraries and information publishing services as the dominant sources of business intelligence. It lets small businesses quickly research their markets, find critical information, and stay on top of the latest trends. Moreover, the advent of free Web 2.0 productivity tools and ubiquitous wireless broadband means that technology is lowering the barriers to entry. By 2015 many home-based businesses will have better communication capabilities than the largest corporations had in 2005. Email, voice mail, mobile phones, conference calling and video calling through VOIP (the voice-over internet protocol) are readily available to the smallest business and sole trader.

In 2005 the average laptop contains similar processing power to that which existed in the whole of NASA during the 1960s moon expeditions. Computers now cost less than the chairs and desks we use to furnish our offices.[3] By 2015 the exponential acceleration in computing power means that all industrial sectors will be deeply transformed by this power. As small businesses experience the advantages of rapid technological advancement, they become more likely to be customers for the 'next new thing'. They may not be the first buyers, but the clever small business will be close on the heels of early adopters. The sellers of the latest technology will be looking for ways to take their products and services to the small business market more rapidly than ever before.

Not every business in the future will want to go global. But as the line between what is local and what is global blurs, going global will be the norm rather than the exception.

The cultural (and perhaps legislative) barriers which exist now will still be there in some form and will still need to be overcome. However, the technical and physical barriers to global trade will have been entirely removed by technology.

In terms of direct business areas to benefit from this global trade, there could be a huge increase in translation services, import/export specialists, and other services to help smaller enterprises find partners and do business across borders. English will continue to be the lingua franca of business around the globe. However, the ability to communicate in the languages of the markets into which firms sell will be a sought-after competitive edge.

More experienced companies, especially those large global players who court the SME, will have to make further investment to recognise the special needs of the global small business. The same will apply to governments and support agencies, as they will have to alter their thinking and culture to be in step with these businesses.

Trajectory 3: freelance economy

Self-employment, contracting and consulting have changed the nature of work and are likely to continue to do so. As the book *Free Agent Nation* (Pink, 2002) suggests, the U.S. and the wider western economy is becoming a nation of people freelancing their skills and talents. There is no reason why this trend should not be repeated across all emerging market economies. 'Consulting' has become a real business for millions of former corporate employees who have been displaced by corporate restructuring and have no desire to enter such a world.

As large corporations (and increasingly government departments) want to be leaner and more efficient, rather than recruit, they will continue to outsource functions, which will provide further opportunities for SMEs. As the same organisations continue to restructure, they will also continue to replace employees with contract workers. Once again this provides further opportunities for freelancers and SMEs. We know that very often these freelancers will be the same people who used to be on the payroll. When the person doing the work is not on payroll it is easier to change the workforce to meet changing needs.

By 2015 the 'networked' firm will be commonplace. These freelance collectives will trade together under a coherent brand. The brand provides them with a larger, recognisable market identity without having to indulge in much of the corporate 'hassle' that often goes with working for large organisations. The large brand, however, reassures clients and provides access to opportunities that single freelancers could not meet on their own.

It is not just freelance consultants that are experiencing a boom by 2015 – we will have seen the return of the small retailer. Despite suffering at the hands of large multiples and planning policies which favoured larger out-of-town malls, many entrepreneurial small retailers have adopted technology and used the internet to allow them to reach new and wider markets. Niche retailers in many market segments, for example, use the global reach of the internet to boost their sales and to cross-subsidise their presence on the high street.

Auction websites have turned over 50 000 Britons into part-time entrepreneurs. According to *The Financial Times*, the Centre for Economics and Business Research (CEBR) estimates that more than £4 billion of 'eBay-nomics' is likely is to be made in the UK in 2006, equivalent to 1.3 per cent of total retail sales (*The Financial Times*, 15th August 2005). Because of the difficulties in recording internet trading, CEBR claims that government statisticians will find the exact amount difficult to track. In the world of eBay, small niche traders can thrive with access to massive national – and often global – markets, while consumers are able to realise the value in the goods that they own but no longer need or want.

Every change creates new market niches. As larger companies rely on contract workers and outside consultants, small businesses develop and change to fill those needs. For example, the old style 'temping or recruitment' industry has already begun to morph into something new, with larger agencies picking up the training and development needs of the workers on their books. Likewise, we can already see niche businesses emerging around ebay, Google and Skype – just as we saw with Microsoft, IBM and others before.

Trajectory 4: the sustainable SME

By 2015 we will see a major explosion in the numbers of 'social enterprises' as a subset of the global SMEs. There are number of competing definitions of a social enterprise, which create problems in identifying their number and type. In the UK, the Department of Trade and Industry defines social enterprise as: 'A . . . business with primarily social objectives whose surpluses are principally reinvested for that purpose in the business or in the community, rather than being driven by the need to maximise profit for shareholders and owners' (UK Department of Trade and Industry, 2004). Social enterprises have the potential to tackle a wide range of social and environmental issues and operate in all parts of the economy. By using business solutions to achieve public good, social enterprises have a distinct and valuable role to play in a helping create a strong, sustainable and socially inclusive economy.

In 2005 there were around 15 000 social enterprises in the UK. This means that they account for around 1.2 per cent of all enterprises in the UK. The turnover (income) derived from this part of the business population is substantial at approximately £18 billion, which represent 1 per cent of the turnover of all UK businesses which have employees. A small number of social enterprises have a very large turnover; almost one in five turn over more than £1 million per annum. Social enterprises employ nearly half a million people (475 000), of whom two-thirds are employed full time. A further 300 000 people work for social enterprises on a volunteer basis, contributing an average of two hours each per week (a total of 580 000 hours volunteered per week). The typical social enterprise employs 10 people. Almost half (49 per cent) employ fewer than 10 people, 38 per cent employ between 10 and 49, 11 per cent have 50–249 employees and 2 per cent employ more than 250.

The rise in ethical issues across the globe (especially relating to business under the guise of responsible entrepreneurship or socially responsible business) (Grayson and Hodges, 2004) and a growing global eco-consciousness will mean that by 2015 this SME sub-group will have grown significantly. However, it will not just be a societal trend which will be driving this. As western economies face mounting environmental pressures from climate change, waste and energy, social enterprise will increasingly become the solution to fix various problems that traditional free market forces cannot address. Governments will consider social enterprise as another tool in their armoury towards encouraging a more sustainable approach to business.

By 2015, the social enterprise sector (in line with its growing contribution to national economies) will provide a growing range of sophisticated services. Public services which were once delivered by local government will now be 'outsourced' to community-led social enterprises. Likewise, many people will be buying their energy from local micro-generators and having their waste recycled by social enterprises.

Conclusions

None of the possible futures outlined above will come true. At least not in the way extrapolated here. The future reality for the global SME will probably combine several aspects of all those possibilities along with something that we have not yet thought of (or considered) within this chapter. The key issue raised by the chapter is that these are *not* predictions. However, by reading through the plausible futures described above most people are now reflecting on how they relate to their own position. Hence, futures thinking has been encouraged.

The opportunities provided by technological advances, the current business-friendly cultural climate and the lowering of barriers to entry in all markets, provide a fertile ground for the SME to develop international activities and trading. However, with all upsides come downsides, as we have seen: whilst the global market provides huge opportunities, it is a market of increasing complexity and dynamism (see Chapter 6). It is a place where a cutting-edge business can find itself obsolete overnight; it is a place where the notions of time and distance are being rethought. To survive and prosper, SMEs must possess a set of key strengths. They must be able to make changes, reinvent themselves on a regular basis and do so positively. Change usually has negative connotations in most organisations (Senge *et al.*, 1999) but in the coming decades those that embrace change are more likely to succeed than those that resist. One of the key tactics in making change positive is to anticipate the change and its implications before it happens. This is where futures thinking can help in terms of bringing the future forward, which Herrmann in Chapter 6 notes will be a key entrepreneurial ability for the global SME.

As a final thought, between 1965 and 1975, R. Buckminster Fuller conducted five two-year 'advanced design science' intensives and pulled together all of the participants' research and analysis into several volumes of what he called the *World Resources Inventory* (Buckminster Fuller and McHale, 1965). In Phase 1, Buckminster Fuller noted that:

> There are very few men today who are disciplined to comprehend the totally integrating significance of the 99 per cent invisible activity which is coalescing to reshape our future. There are approximately no warnings being given to society regarding the great changes ahead. There is only ominous apprehension that man may be about to annihilate himself. To the few who are disciplined to deal with the invisibly integrating trends it is increasingly readable in the trends that man is about to become almost 100 percent successful as an occupant of the universe:

Whether you agree with this statement or not, the disciplined few will be those that find the time to look to the future and appreciate the 'invisible activity'.

Questions emerging from the chapter

Five key questions emerge from the consideration of foresighting and futures for the 'global' SME. These are:

1. What are the key global drivers of change which will impact upon how SMEs do business?
2. Will the broad adoption of advanced technology mean that all SMEs are 'born global'?
3. How does being born global sit with environmental sustainability? Are they mutually exclusive?

4. What elements of the four future trajectories will provide opportunities for SMEs to develop international activities and trading?
5. How can futures thinking be reconciled with day-to-day operations?

Notes

1. See www.communityplanning.net/methods/method100.htm
2. See http://europa.eu.int/comm/internal_market/services/index_en.htm.
3. As an illustration of this, at the time of writing (September 2005), Dell Computing is advertising a 1.6GHz, 256 MB RAM laptop on its website for £299 (ex VAT). A check on an office furniture supplier indicates that a corner workstation desk (without chair) will cost £235 (ex VAT).

Bibliography

Batelle, J. (2005), 'All the World's a Platform', *The Guardian*, 29 September.

Buckminster Fuller, B. and McHale, J. (1965), *World Design Science Decade, 1965–1975, Phase 1 (1965) Document III – Comprehensive Thinking; Phase 1 (1965) Document IV – The Ten Year Program*, Southern Illinois University, Carbondale.

European Commission (2003), *The New SME Definition: User Guide and Model Declaration*, Enterprise and Industry Publications, Luxembourg.

Grayson, D. and Hodges, A. (2004), *Corporate Social Opportunity*, Greenleaf Publishing, Sheffield.

Harvey, J.B. (1974), *The Abilene Paradox: The Management of Agreement*, Organisational Dynamics, San Francisco.

Jungk, R. and Mullert, N. (1987), *Future Workshops: How to Create Desirable Futures*, Institute for Social Inventions, London.

Margolis, J. (2001), *A Brief History of Tomorrow: The Future, Past and Present*, Bloomsbury, London.

Matthews, R. and Wacker, W. (2003), *The Deviant's Advantage – How Fringe Ideas Create Mass Market*, Random House Business Books, New York.

Mau, B. and Leonard, J. and The Institute Without Boundaries (2004), *Massive Change*, Phaidon Press, Boston.

McHale, J. (1965), *World Design Science Decade 1965–1975: Phase 1 1963 – Document 1 – Inventory of World Resources and Human Trends and Needs*, Southern Illinois University Press, Carbondale.

Pink, D.H. (2002), *Free Agent Nation: The Future of Working for Yourself*, Warner Books, Clayton, Victoria, Australia.

Ringland, G. (1998), *Scenario Planning: Managing for the Future*, John Wiley and Sons Ltd, Chichester, West Sussex.

Schwartz, P. (1998), *The Art of the Long View*, John Wiley and Sons Ltd, Chichester, West Sussex.

Schwartz, P. (2004), *Inevitable Surprises: A Survival Guide for the 21st Century*, Gotham Books, New York.

Senge, P., Roberts, C., Ross, R., Smith, B., Roth, G. and Kleiner, A. (1999), *The Dance of Change*, Currency, New York.

Svendsen, S., Granzau Andersen, L., Jensen, T., Steen Olsen, S. and Larsen, G. (2000), *Fremtidens Fagbevæ-gelse (The Trade Union of the Future)*, The Danish Confederation of Trade Unions, Copenhagen.

Toffler, A. (1970), *Futureshock*, Random House Publishing, New York.

UK Cabinet Office (2002), *Risk: Improving Government's Capability to Handle Risk and Uncertainty*, Strategy Unit Report, Cabinet Office, London.

UK Department of Trade and Industry (2004), *Social Enterprise: A Strategy for Success*, HMSO, London.

UK Ministry of Defence Joint Doctrines and Concept Centre (2001), *Strategic Trends*, Ministry of Defence, London, www.mod.uk/DefenceInternet/AboutDefence/CorporatePublications/DoctrineOperationsandDiplomacyPublications/DCDC/GlobalStrategicTrends 20072036.htm

UK Small Business Service (2005), *A Survey of Social Enterprises Across the UK*, IFF Research Ltd, Small Business Service, Sheffield.

Van der Heijden, K. (1996), *Scenarios: The Art of Strategic Conversation*, John Wiley and Sons Ltd, Chichester, West Sussex.

Van der Heijden, K., Bradfield, R. and Burt, G. (2002), *The Sixth Sense: Accelerating Organisational Learning with Scenarios*, John Wiley and Sons Ltd, Chichester, West Sussex.

Appendix 11.1: Future case studies

Case Study 1 – The Big Ideas Lab, SME Futures Project

The Big Ideas Lab is part of a much wider complex known as the Business Innovation Centre (BIC). Built on a derelict shipbuilding site in Sunderland (North East England) in the early 1990s, the centre consists of a series of incubator units coupled with business advice infrastructure. The BIC set up the Big Ideas Lab in 2004 on the premise that it was not so much advice for the established or growing SME that was missing, but the initial innovation and ideas generation required to start a new business.

The Big Ideas Lab focuses on teaching innovation, creativity, product and service design skills to adults, children and businesses. As part of this, we introduced a one day 'SME Futures' workshop to the curriculum. The purpose of this was to encourage SMEs attending to think about the future and secondly to demonstrate that futures thinking can aid idea generation and creativity by challenging current worldviews and perceptions.

In the initial round, a total of 21 SMEs from several different sectors took part in four futures workshop sessions. The only objective that was set at the beginning of each session was that all participants would leave having learnt something new and would also have some aspect of their current worldview challenged.

During the day the participants were introduced to the key concepts of futures thinking and then were taken on a quick tour through major trends and drivers affecting their world along with possible future scenarios for these.

Case Study 2 – community futures

Many communities across the UK (and the wider world) are undergoing substantial change as a result of the rapid disruptions in the economic system. For example, the coalfield communities of County Durham in the UK have experienced serious and rapid decline, primarily as a result of the loss of the main industry in the area – deep coal mining. This has led to large amounts of government monies being invested into these areas to help them readjust and regenerate for the 21st century.

We have worked on several of these projects utilising futures workshops techniques to enable communities to create visions of how they want their settlements to develop.

12 SMEs in the global economy: policy perspectives

Leigh Sear and Lester Lloyd-Reason

Summary

The previous chapters and contributions have critically assessed and reviewed a number of different aspects of how SMEs engage, develop and embed global activities and trading in developing a small and medium enterprise (SME). The chapters have not only explored the type of activities and paths to international trading which are pursued by SMEs (Part I), but also how these activities and paths are managed (Part II). In comparison to other commentaries on SMEs in the global economy, the book has also critically explored the skills, knowledge and learning associated with managing global operations (Part III).

Within these contributions, a consistent theme has emerged in terms of the complexities and realities faced by SMEs in developing global activities and markets. Various chapters have identified that the trading environment for SMEs interested in developing global markets has shifted considerably over the last ten years, creating a set of new barriers, challenges and opportunities for the global SME. Through different learning styles, SMEs have developed a set of responses to overcome these challenges and opportunities, such as the rise of new ways of trading globally and the introduction of new forms of IT, often through learning by doing and learning by copying (Gibb 2000).

As a result, however, a policy mismatch has emerged between the needs of SMEs trading globally and the responses of business support agencies and professionals. In the majority of developed market economies, central government agencies and other support agencies have developed a set of responses and interventions based on traditional thinking and evidence that assumes amongst other things that exporting is internationalisation, businesses need assistance with spotting opportunities to trade globally (that is, trade promotion), as opposed to the skills required to manage global activities (that is, trade development) and that businesses develop global activities through a series of sequential stages or phases.

The contributions in this book have explicitly challenged these assumptions and in so doing have identified their own set of challenges to policy and practice in terms of effectively supporting SMEs to trade globally. This final chapter presents a synthesis of the key challenges to emerge from the previous 11 chapters, drawing together the various strands of understanding and learning related to:

- who is doing it, how, and the processes developed to engage with global activities and markets (Part I)
- leadership and management of global activities, particularly in terms of business structures, organisations and function (Part II)
- learning, skills and knowledge required to translate strategies and plans into operational efficiencies (Part III).

The key challenge or theme that arises from this synthesis and critical reflection on current understanding is how to develop a set of policy frameworks and initiatives that are flexible enough to respond to the complexities and uncertainties faced by the global SMEs in such a fast-changing trading environment. As a contribution to creating a more demand-led and focused policy agenda, this chapter sets out five key sets of policy implications and actions. These relate to:

1. Consideration that internationalisation is more than exporting
2. Developing an international entrepreneurial environment
3. Fostering and supporting networks and relationships
4. Creating a better evidence base on the global SME
5. Developing skills and knowledge to manage globally.

Internationalisation is more than exporting

A consistent theme within the book is that SMEs develop global markets through a number of processes, only one of which is exporting. Chapter 2 identifies that importing, joint ventures, strategic alliances and international production and outsourcing are used by SMEs to develop global reach. For example, in the majority of UK regions, levels of importing now exceed levels of exporting by SMEs, with overseas sourcing of products being an integral part of modern-day supply chain management. Evidence presented in Chapters 2, 3 and 4 demonstrate that in reality the situation is far more complex and that exporting is only one type of international activity. For example, a small engineering company based in the South East of England has two manufacturing plants in China and Sweden, outsources the majority of its materials from Romania, and exports to more than 20 countries. Despite huge regulatory barriers, it has recently purchased the Romanian company in order to safeguard its supply of raw materials. This example is neither extreme nor atypical, as demonstrated by the previous chapters (for example, see the case studies underpinning Chapter 5). These contributions highlight that SMEs draw upon a variety of activities to engage and trade globally.

For many people reading this chapter, the above is plain common sense and common business practice. However, there is a gap between these trading realities and an understanding of what constitutes internationalisation amongst the academic and policy community. A review of studies which have audited and mapped provision focused on supporting SMEs to develop new markets and internationalise will identify a set of assumptions that exporting and internationalisation for all practicable purposes mean one and the same thing (Observatory of European SMEs 2003; Sear and Hamilton 2003). Within the majority of developed market economies, for example, there is a relative lack of support to assist SMEs to develop and manage importing strategies effectively. International trade strategies and action plans from business support agencies focus largely on encouraging exporting within SMEs at different stages of development (for example, new exporters, growing exporters, established exporters), reflecting the impact of internationalisation stage models which discuss primarily exporting activity and a linear progression from non-exporter to committed exporter and active exporter.

In part, this focus on exporting is not surprising given the wider policy priorities attached to supporting exporting and internationalisation of SMEs as a route to enhancing levels of regional or national productivity and economic growth (Observatory of European SMEs 2003). It would be more difficult for regional or national governments to develop a coherent policy case for encouraging importing activity, particularly given the balance of payment deficits of many developed market economies.

Internationalisation is not exporting and there is a need for policy and programmes of support to recognise this difference and respond accordingly. At a policy level, this will involve developing a policy case for supporting international activities of SMEs, particularly the contribution of these different activities to regional and national economic development and growth. There is a role here for research in terms of how SMEs use different activities to develop global markets, and this evidence can be used by policy makers to develop a case for supporting SMEs as part of improving the productivity of the business community through encouraging and embedding international activities.

This strategic framework will provide a structure within which interventions can be developed and delivered which assist SMEs to engage with different types of international activity, including exporting, and reflect the reality of the global trading environment for SMEs. Such a shift in provision will not necessarily involve a radical overhaul of provision. For example, outward trade missions to markets could be extended to include an inward element which encourages businesses within particular target sectors to visit SMEs, or existing training provision could be extended so that it assists businesses to identify which strategies are appropriate to address specific needs related to competing globally. This would assist the business in identifying the barriers and opportunities associated with developing different paths to trading globally, the outcomes from which could be used to underpin some form of action plan.

Developing an international entrepreneurial environment

A number of studies (see, for an overview, OECD 2004) have highlighted the often unwitting contributions made by governments in inhibiting SME global trading through inappropriate rules and regulations, with a cumulative effect of slowing down business responsiveness, diverting resources away from productive investment, hampering entry into markets and reducing innovation. In the report of the Second OECD SME Ministerial Conference held in Istanbul in June 2004, it was recorded that 'the success and growth of international SMEs will be enhanced by a more internationalised infrastructure geared to the smooth growth of firms across borders. This applies to the infrastructure for financial markets, advisory services, information access, telecommunications, intellectual property rights, dispute resolution processes, etc.' (OECD 2004).

In their analysis in Chapter 2, Griffiths *et al.* clearly identify the need for an international infrastructure geared to the trading realities faced by the SME wishing to trade globally or to extend its global operations. Currently, there are a number of aspects of the international entrepreneurial environment which hinder the development of global activities by SMEs vis-à-vis larger businesses. These relate to:

- the ever-increasing volume of and change in regulations and legislation, particularly relating to issues such as product packaging
- irregularities and inconsistencies between national and supranational (for example, EU) technical and legal standards
- restrictive import and export tariffs, particularly between trading blocs (as recently highlighted by the EU–China clothes dispute (Smith 2005)
- fluctuations in prices and currencies.

At the same time, however, a number of developments related to the growth in the use of information communication technologies such as broadband and electronic trading, and low-cost air travel, have provided opportunities for SMEs to trade globally. Despite such developments, reliable access remains an issue which merely increases the cost of doing business for the SME (see Chapters 7 and 11). Indeed, Herrmann in Chapter 6 identifies that smaller businesses face far higher transaction costs in doing global business, as they lack the resources of larger businesses which are deployed to monitor (and in some cases shape) developments in policies, regulations, currencies and so on. It is estimated that compliance costs for firms employing less than 20 people are approximately 35 per cent higher than for larger businesses. Some estimates show that for small firms the cost of compliance is between 4 and 6 per cent of turnover.

There is clearly a role for national government agencies to respond to a number of specific issues as follows:

- Reviewing the impact of the new and modified legislation and regulations, particularly on the ability of SMEs to trade effectively in global markets.
- Generating innovation and new product development opportunities which can be accessed by SMEs. For example, in the US, the Small Business and Innovation Research Program provides a framework in which SMEs can access Government R&D monies (Audretsch 2003).
- Providing reliable, low-cost access to ICT, particularly in less accessible areas where distance to market is an issue.
- Supporting access to low-cost and flexible air and freight services. If SMEs cannot readily access low-cost air travel or communications services, they will effectively be restricted from participating in the global market. This will in turn have flow-on consequences for the productivity of the business but also the local and regional economy.

Although such a response by national governments would clearly be very welcome, any significant impact on the international trading environment for SMEs can only emerge through a global response rather than piecemeal actions. A key global policy stance for increasing SME internationalisation and contribution to global trading will involve the development of a more conducive international entrepreneurial business environment, with the policy focus on a 'framework' rather than specific policy instruments, and providing a level playing field on which SMEs can compete with larger organisations. At the Istanbul Ministerial meeting, the OECD clearly set out the policy agenda when they said that 'Governments need to collaborate more to set up monitoring systems to identify these impediments, understand their longer term impact and establish mechanisms for addressing them, at bilateral and multilateral levels' (OECD 2004, p. 19).

Fostering and supporting networks and relationships

A key theme to emerge from Parts II and III of the book is the increasing importance of networks and relationship management to developing global activities and markets successfully. Chapters 5 and 7 highlight that internationalisation processes are increasingly driven and made possible by the social and business networks of the entrepreneur or business owner-manager and that SME internationalisation is a pattern that emerges and is shaped by an array of formal and informal relationships. These relationships involve a variety of different stakeholders ranging from customers and suppliers, to banks and financiers, to government agencies and business support professionals. These networks are not only a source of business and resource, but also advice, knowledge and learning (Gibb 1997).

To manage these networks effectively on a global scale, the SME will use a variety of methods including face-to-face contact, email, videoconferencing and weblogs. However, there is evidence to suggest that this is not recognised in policy initiatives and programmes of support, which often fail to take account of larger geographical regions, with a predominant focus on sub-regional and regional programmes and the impact of technology on how businesses communicate and manage relationships. For example, a large inward investor to a region in the EU, such as Nissan in the North East of England, will often use small businesses as suppliers from a wide geographical area (for example, Northern Europe) and manage supply chains across different national boundaries using email and intranet systems. This has implications in terms of how businesses in specific regions respond and compete and how agencies embed SMEs into global networks through specific interventions.

This creates the need for two sets of response and intervention from government business support agencies. Firstly, there is a need to assist SMEs in gaining awareness and exposure to competitor regions and the opportunities to facilitate and develop partnerships around specific needs and requirements across national boundaries. Whilst there are a number of programmes designed to achieve transnational partnerships, uptake by SMEs is relatively low. This reflects the administrative burden associated with applying to such projects, which in turn suggests a need to develop application processes which are appropriate to the way in which SMEs use support in developing global activities and markets.

At a more qualitative level, there is a need for programme interventions to focus on the development of relationships as a key critical entrepreneurial skill. Studies such as Sear and Hamilton (2003) and Observatory of European SMEs (2003) identify a lack of programmes explicitly focused on developing the networking capabilities and relational abilities of the entrepreneur, in order to promote SME internationalisation. It is not only a question of establishing formal networks, but providing the conditions for entrepreneurs to expand their own network of relationships and assist in the development of skills to underpin relationship management. Such skills are needed to be able to manage a diverse and complex set of stakeholder needs and relationships within a global context; this is particularly important given different cultures.

Creating a better evidence base on the global SME

A number of chapters, in particular Chapters 4 and 11, identify a role for policy in encouraging and supporting the collection and review of evidence that can be used by the policy community to inform policies targeted at supporting SMEs to trade globally. For example, there is a lack of available evidence related to the extent to which SMEs engage in different types of international activities, particularly if it does not include exporting. In addition, there is an issue with the comparability of the evidence base across national boundaries, particularly in terms of definitions of smallness and enterprise, classifications of the nature of business activity and approaches to segmenting the global SME. As a result, researchers and policy makers have to rely on a set of proxies which either tend to reinforce traditional approaches to understanding internationalisation or are based on a set of myths, misconceptions or outdated assumptions.

However, there are a number of challenges to improving the extent and depth of the evidence base. Firstly, the majority of government-commissioned research is seeking insights to issues which are driven by short-term political priorities and considerations, which can change rapidly (Girma, Greenaway and Kneller 2001). This manifests itself in commissioning research projects which have to be completed within short timescales and provide evidence which can be used as part of the policy process. Invariably, this results in commissioning quantitative surveys of the business community, exploring attitudes and extent of engagement, based on existing concepts. In comparison, there is a lack of policy-commissioned research which uses different types of evidence such as more qualitative, longitudinal-based evidence which understands how SMEs develop global activities and the processes which are developed to manage these activities. Whilst collecting similar types of data and insight, national governments use different definitions of smallness, sectoral classifications and market segmentation frameworks (Sear and Hamilton 2003). This results in a set of problems and difficulties for researchers and policy makers in undertaking comparative analysis and identifying good practices, even though there are a number of commonalities in the challenges faced by SMEs in trading globally within different economies.

There is a need, therefore, for systematic collection and review of quantitative and qualitative data and insights on the levels and types of business involved in global trading within and across countries. Such evidence would assist and support collaboration of researchers across national boundaries in investigating the activities, needs and requirements of global SMEs. In so doing, this would strengthen the depth and coherence of the evidence base and provide insights which could be used by policy makers in developing demand-led forms of support.

In addition, there is a need for better understanding of the assumptions, beliefs and values underpinning different communities of interest and practice surrounding the global SME. In the introductory chapter, we discussed the rationale for the book as addressing the current gap between research and practice, which has resulted in a set of inappropriate policy mechanisms and interventions targeted at addressing the needs of the global SME within the current and future trading environment. In this way, Figure 12.1 represents an attempt to address this gap between research and practice by placing the SME at the heart of the policy and research agenda. As Herrmann identifies in Chapter 6, the tendency for policy workshops to be around key areas of 'need to know' which do not include SMEs will not generate greater understanding of how businesses develop global activities. Similarly, the tendency for academics to divorce the worlds of practice and policy has supported the development of the myths and misconceptions such as 'internationalisation is exporting and exporting is internationalisation'. Therefore, there is a need to develop mechanisms which encourage learning and experience exchange across the boundaries of different communities of practice. For example, as outlined in Figure 12.1, to understand how businesses internationalise, it may be useful for academics and policy makers to 'live' and experience the life world of the global SME and develop understanding from the 'inside' rather than the 'outside'. This could be achieved through secondment of staff to SMEs or the use of business panels or councils. Other strategies could include:

- The development of 'how to' tools and intensive training and development programmes on internationalisation by academic institutions which assist SMEs to manage the process of trading globally.

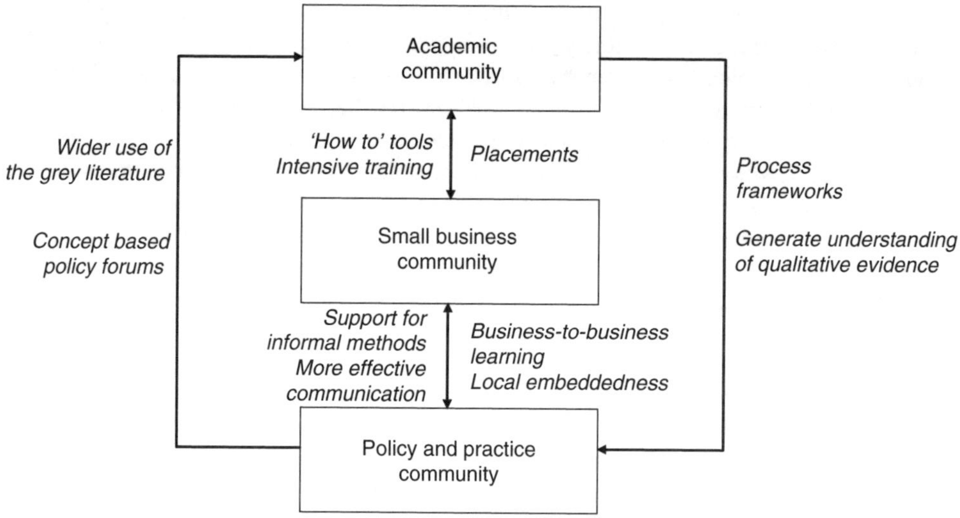

Figure 12.1 Bridging the research-practice gap – engagement strategies

- The generation of process frameworks by researchers which identify activities undertaken by SMEs in developing international activities and markets, barriers encountered and responses required.
- The use of concept-based policy forums by policy makers and support agencies to identify latest thinking and examples of good practice.
- The greater use of different types of available evidence by policy makers and support agencies in the design, development and delivery of support programmes.

Developing skills and knowledge to manage globally

In the first few years of the 20th century, there has been an increasing recognition amongst government departments and business support agencies involved in supporting the internationalisation of SMEs that there is a need to balance the development of trade opportunities with the development of skills to take advantage of these opportunities (Sear and Hamilton 2003). This shift in policies away from trade promotion to trade development has not been consistent across different types of SME involved in global trade. For example, someone curious or with limited experience of managing international activities will need a different set of skills and knowledge in comparison to a business with more experience of trading globally. However, available provision for SMEs interested in developing international activities is still rooted in providing awareness of market opportunities, market conditions and developing business and action plans. Provision rarely assists such businesses to 'learn by doing' (Gibb 1997).

However, Mughan and Lloyd-Reason and Calof and Dishman, in Chapters 8 and 9, highlight that a package of international skills is important when developing global activities, particularly in newer economies. Language abilities and skills are only one part of this package. It needs to be complemented by understanding of 'know-how' (for example, how business relationships work and the nature of trading conditions) and 'know-who' (for example, the support infrastructure). This acquisition of 'know-how' and 'know-who' is important for newer and less experienced businesses as they need to acquire such knowledge and learning quickly to retain competitive positioning, particularly given the complexities and uncertainties in trading globally (see Chapter 6).

In the majority of developed market economies, there is a gap in provision between assisting those businesses with no or limited experience of managing international activities and more experienced or 'expert' businesses. In part, this gap reflects our state of current understanding of how SMEs trade globally. Some insights are five to ten years behind global developments, so SMEs are learning by doing as opposed to being supported to develop such learning.

This implies that there is a need for policy makers and researchers to develop more sophisticated techniques to identify different markets segments, such as experience of managing international activities, and a set of tools which can be used to develop responses to address the skills development needs of different segments. These tools can also be used to identify where government intervention is required vis-à-vis the private sector. A number of such frameworks are provided within this book (see, for example, Chapter 8). The skills required may vary by segment; competitive intelligence will be a key skill for those businesses with no or limited experience in that it will assist them in understanding and managing the global trading realities. In comparison, more experienced businesses may need access to specific language skills. Here, there may be a role for government agencies in signposting businesses to embassies and/or education institutes in specific markets. In turn, this places a need for business support professionals within government and support agencies to continually update their knowledge and skills of how SMEs trade globally and address key areas of 'need to know'.

This book provides a critical starting point to developing such an evidence base and increasing understanding of different communities of practice between academics, policy makers and small businesses.

Bibliography

Audretsch, D.B. (2003), 'Standing on the Shoulders of Midgets: The U.S. Small Business Innovation Research Program (SBIR)', *Small Business Economics*, **20** (2), 129–35.

Gibb, A.A. (1997), 'Small Firm's Training and Competitiveness: Building upon the Small Business as a Learning Organisation', *International Small Business Journal*, **15** (3), 13–29.

Gibb, A.A. (2000), 'Corporate Restructuring and Entrepreneurship: What Can Large Organisations Learn from Small?' *Enterprise and Innovation Management Studies*, **1** (1), 19–35.

Girma, S., Greenaway, D. and Kneller, R. (2001), *Exporting and Business Performance: A Report for Trade Partners UK*, Leverhulme Centre for Research on Globalisation and Economic Policy, University of Nottingham, Nottingham.

Observatory of European SMEs (2003), *Internationalisation of SMEs*, KMPG Special Services and EIM Business and Policy Research, European Commission, Luxembourg.

OECD (2004), *Facilitating SMEs, Access to International Markets*, 2nd OECD Conference of Ministers Responsible for SMEs, 3–5 June, Istanbul, Turkey.

Sear, L. and Hamilton, R.T. (2003), 'Matching Supply with Demand: Reflecting on Support for Business Internationalisation in England', in Dana, L.P. (ed.) *Handbook of Research on International Entrepreneurship*, Edward Elgar, Cheltenham UK and Northampton, MA, USA.

Smith, J. (2005), 'Mandelson moves to end "bra wars" dispute', *The Scotsman*, 29 August.

Index